Quick Cobbler *Jy 2 '12*

THE SATURDAY EVENING POST
ALL★AMERICAN
COOKBOOK

"Freedom from Want" *painted for* THE SATURDAY EVENING POST, *by Norman Rockwell, March 6, 1943.*

THE SATURDAY EVENING POST
ALL★AMERICAN COOKBOOK

500 All-American Recipes by
Charlotte Turgeon
Food Editor and Author

With a Light-Hearted History
of Eating in America by
Frederic A. Birmingham
Managing Editor of
The Saturday Evening Post

THOMAS NELSON INC. & CURTIS PUBLISHING COMPANY

Charlotte Turgeon and Frederic A. Birmingham
wish to express their gratitude
to the personnel of the following institutions
which assisted with research:
The Smithsonian Institution, Washington, D.C.
The Library of Congress, Washington, D.C.
The Worcester Antiquarian Society, Worcester, Mass.

The Staff for this Book:
Jack Merritt, Director of Production
Jean White, Copy Editor
James Beaudry
Astrid Henkels
Dwight E. Lamb, Art Editor
Bonnie Duart
Jinny Sauer
Book design by DesignCenter, Inc.

Jointly published by Thomas Nelson Inc., Nashville, Tennessee,
and The Curtis Publishing Company, Indianapolis, Indiana,
and simultaneously in Don Mills, Ontario, by
Thomas Nelson & Sons (Canada) Limited.

DINING TABLE
OF CONTENTS

INTRODUCTION: OUR BRAVE NEW WORLD OF FOOD

We may live without poetry, music and art:
We may live without conscience and live
*   without heart;*
We may live without friends, we may live
*   without books,*
But civilized man cannot live without cooks.

*   —Owen Meredith*

The glory and strength of America have always derived, in awesome simplicity, from just two things. The idea of a democracy where men may live in freedom. And second, the natural resources of a continent virtually unknown to the rest of the world until the seventeenth century, a land where untold treasures lay waiting, not in the gold explorers sought so greedily, but in the vast storehouse of nature in a continent so huge it took another century for the world to realize its amplitude.

Only today are people realizing that food—not metal, not guns, not oil—is the answer to peace and well-being in the world, no matter how slowly that realization is dawning. Kansas wheat carries more clout than Arabian oil. Nutrition and the health-giving properties of proper diet are saving nations and increasing the life span of mankind. Food, and the lands which produce and control it, is the true treasure of the future.

This book, written on the occasion of our country's two-hundredth birthday, is a salute to every person who has played a part in the nation's culinary heritage, starting with the arrival of the Jamestown colonists in the early seventeenth century and coming down to the present time.

It is a salute to those who first braved the rigors and hardships that faced the early settlers in Virginia and a little later in Massachusetts when they arrived on these shores. Seeking spiritual, physical and political freedom, they dared to cross the treacherous seas, bringing with them what little they could carry in household goods, seeds, plants, animals and food to carry them over the first perilous months. They came to a land of untold bounty, and the irony is that so little were these men and women accustomed to fending for themselves in the growing of food or the baking of meat and bread that many died of starvation or diseases caused by malnutrition right in the midst of plenty.

Yet, our American food is magnificent. We say that not because that is our subject of the moment. There are worthy books on lesser subjects. For example, flower cookery—the essences of rose-hip tea, marigold celery, nasturtium soup (which President Ike Eisenhower favored, by the way), eggs in tulips, and turkey chowder with chrysanthemums—is not to be sneezed at, unless perchance a sprig of goldenrod has worked its way into one's petal basket. Some gourmets will even go on for hours over the Lilliputian charms of chocolate-covered ants, which have quite a vogue in a certain New York shop, possibly visited upon occasion by a few affluent gourmet anteaters from the Bronx zoo. But our subject—All American Cooking—pulls out all the stops! It is a grand hymn of praise and thanksgiving, from sea to shining sea.

Think of it, from beginning to end, from that very

Cover painting, THE SATURDAY EVENING POST, *December 20, 1924.*

first Thanksgiving by the Pilgrims in 1621, which is when America really enjoyed its first decent meal, until today—think of the riches in our national larder. Read on, if you are able to do so without catching a case of runaway taste buds and galloping salivary glands.

Picture the foods of this great land: Not only have we our own specialties, but we are the inheritors of the entire culinary history of the earth, as the peoples of every land brought us their secrets and we worked them into our own recipes.

When Columbus first put mailed foot on the strand of Santo Domingo in 1492, 80 percent of our present plant foods were unknown to Europeans! Corn, potatoes, squash, tapioca, cocoa, pineapples, avocados, tomatoes, different members of the capsicum family (wild pepper), vanilla beans—they had never been heard of before!

Captain John Smith, the doughty warrior of the Virginia colony, first in our land in 1607, wrote ecstatically of the fresh bounty of the new world:

" . . . Of beasts the chief are deer, nothing differing from ours . . . Their partridges are little bigger than our quails. Wild turkies are as big as our tame. . . . In winter there are great plenty of swans, cranes, gray and white . . . herons, geese, brants, duck, widgeon, dotterel, oxies, parrots, and pigeons . . . Of fish we were best acquainted with sturgeon, grampus, porpoise, seals, stingrays . . . brets, mullets, white salmon, trout, soles, plaice, herrings, coneyfish, rockfish, eels, lampreys, catfish, shads, perch of three sorts, crabs, shrimps, crayfishes, oysters, cockles and mussels . . .

"Virginia doth afford many excellent vegetables, and living creatures . . . The wood that is most common is oak and walnut . . . The acorns of one kind, whose bark is more white than the other and somewhat sweetish, being boiled, at last afford a sweet oil, that they keep in gourds to anoint their heads and joints. The fruit they eat made in bread or otherwise. There is also some black walnut tree . . . Of walnuts there are two or three kinds . . . By the dwellings of the savages are some great mulberry trees . . . In some parts were found some chestnuts, whose wild fruit equal the best in France . . . Plums there are of three sorts. The red and white are like our hedge plums, but the other, which they call putchamins [persimmons], grow as high as a palmetto . . . If it be not ripe, it will draw a man's mouth awry, with much torment; but when it is ripe, it is as delicious as an apricot. They have cherries . . . Of vines great abundance . . . but these bear few grapes. Except by the river and savage habitations, where they are not overshadowed from the sun, they are covered with fruit . . . They have a small fruit growing on little trees, husked like a chestnut, but the fruit most like a very small acorn . . . "

From such a start, how could we fail? At first, of course, American dishes were chiefly those brought over from the old country, but soon adapted to the foods found and grown in our own soil. What this

If, after exercise, we feed sparingly, the digestion will be easy and good, the body lightsome, the temper cheerful, and all the animal functions performed agreeably.

Benjamin Franklin

book on cookery is about is how generation after generation of American cooks—starting with Ben Franklin, Thomas Jefferson and George Washington, all of whom were voracious trenchermen, tempered with refined tastes—adopted and then adapted the traditional dishes of Europe to the miraculous plenty of their brave new world.

America has been happily unhampered by centuries of rigid traditionalism in its cooking, and rockbound food lore, which might have stood in the way of change—this country more than any other has been open and receptive to new knowledge in nutrition, diet, and scientific food preparation which has contributed to our good health without decreasing our wealth of enjoyment at the dining table.

In the eighteenth and nineteenth centuries, as different nationals arrived on these shores in search of wealth, work and a place to live, they brought many of their native foodstuffs and recipes, some of which have become a part of the mainstream of American cooking.

So, we salute these people and all the ingenious housewives, chefs and cooks who have handed on new ideas and constantly improving methods of cooking. We salute also the farmers, the herdsmen, the researchers and the technicians, the transportation people and the storekeepers who make it possible for America to set with ease the most bounteous table of any country on this earth. We salute also the brave vintners who have struggled to bring us a wine we can be proud of. The salute takes the form of a presentation of recipes that seem to us to be the rightful descendants of recipes that were handed on to us by our antecedents.

Challenge any French Cordon Bleu chef to suicidal despair, any Germanic culinary fuehrer to despair in a bierstube with the incredible variety of purely American dishes, then overlap them with the rich counterpane of world cuisine! Nothing in any country anywhere is even comparable.

Take as a brief rundown the luscious viands so conspicuously American that they constitute a language of their own—the mangoes, loquats, calamondins, guavas, lychee fruit, avocados, and papayas that make so many Florida specialties. Brunswick stew, egg break (no flour), hush puppies, grits and buttermilk biscuits that are staples in Georgia, not to overlook pecan pie, Hoppin' John, hog jowl, sweet-potato pudding, cracklings and crackling bread. Huge Idaho potatoes, big as footballs, baked to a fare-thee-well as a side dish to venison and elk steaks of that rugged terrain. Braised possum from Arkansas. Black walnut pie from the Ozarks. Sample the Bayou catfish bits, seafood and okra gumbos topped with a mound of rice, turtle soup, duck gumbo, shrimp creole, jambalaya, garlic grits and country "dirty rice" from Louisiana, where the French took over from Indian cooks (already experts with the bay leaf and the filé) in 1718; the Spanish in 1762; and the Americans in 1803 with the Louisiana Purchase, and then season with the expertise of African slaves and Acadian wanderers from faraway Canada. On to Ohio, Indiana and Vermont in the early spring, and pour pure maple syrup on fresh snow, and just forget about old man

Escoffier and his French pastries. In Pennsylvania, the German immigrants provided the great rifles which became the "Kentucky rifles" of history (dubbed "widow makers" by the British soldiery of the Revolution) and the Conestogas, the covered wagons that rolled out to conquer the West. The Pennsylvania Dutch also savored the countryside with the heavenly aromas of "fastnacht," shoofly pie, apfel kuchen, and kartoffelkloesse. Just a few hills away, the regional dishes of Philadelphia graced the Colonial table—pepper relish, snapper soup, and what the Indians had called "Pomhaus," which is not very much improved by being called "Philadelphia Scrapple," although it is a culinary tradition approaching the religious.

Oh, just think of Rhode Island's New England Boiled Dinner, Boston's black bread and oyster stew with cream in it, New York's shad roe and oyster stew with tomatoes in it! Tennessee's pork chop casserole, with green beans and "shellies" on the side. The wild turkeys and sweet potato biscuits of old Virginny, four-pound silver salmon, tiny Olympia oysters, and blackberries in the Northwest Washington, the luscious geoduck, a giant clam weighing six pounds or more, if you can fight him to a finish in Puget Sound. Seattle's Alaska salmon. The hard and soft-shelled crabs of Maryland's and Virginia's shores. Colorado trout, buffalo and deer. In Kentucky, hickory-smoked old hams, beaten biscuit, corn breads, burgoo and green beans cooked with meat. Wild duck and pheasant from Minnesota. Fish fries and possum stews in North Carolina. And Americans on the move. Ham-n-eggs and pancakes invented by outdoorsmen

with only one pot to cook in. Sourdough bread and Red Flannel Stew from Alaska and California gold hunters. Texas barbecues dating back to chuck wagon days. And the foods we have inherited from other cultures!—Mexico's own tortilla, guacamole salad, enchiladas, frijoles, chili con carne, tamales, sopaipillas ... *gracias, amigos* ... from Texas, New Mexico and California cooks.

And, ah Hawaii! Have you eaten there? Shades of a new science of American cookery, a very way of life in itself. Elements from Polynesian, Chinese, Japanese, Korean, Spanish, Portuguese, Malayan and Philippine recipes suddenly with a Western accent: Flavors of worlds apart—coconut milk from the Polynesians, marinades of soy sauce, sugar wine, garlic, ginger and scallions from the Orient and the sweet-sour artistry of the Filipinos—all in one Hawaiian kitchen.

So, we originally found so many new foods here in America, we integrated others in our cultural melting pot, and then, we also invented a few beauties of our own. (We shall cover our inventiveness very adequately in a chapter on wines and beverages, in the quaffing of which Americans have always been potent, and on the vintner's art in which we are becoming increasingly sophisticated.) But, consider these little culinary inventions, just by the way. Chow mein and chop suey, invented in San Francisco. The hot dog in New York. The hamburger is our very own, notwithstanding Germany's claims to the contrary. We invented Waldorf salad, peanut butter, and the potato chip. The latter was a product of almost apologetic pique,

> *The Creator, who made man*
> *such that he must eat to live,*
> *causes him to eat by means of*
> *appetite, and for a reward gives*
> *him pleasure in eating.*
>
> *Brillat Savarin*

on the part of two natural non-affinities—a dyspeptic diner and a trigger-tempered chef. Seems a patron at a famous resort hotel in Saratoga Springs kept sending his fried potatoes back to the kitchen again and again to have them more crisply prepared. The outraged chef finally crisped them to nothing but a crisp—and the potato chip was born!

Boston invented the Parker House Roll. Lobster Newburg was named for an American chef. Eggs Benedict is not an ancient religious nicety but a confection for Diamond Jim Brady's delight. And, finally, there is no steak like an American steak. We raise the best beef, cook it the best, and eat the most of it in many forms. You'll know that as gospel truth if you've ever been so foolhardy as to order a steak— any kind—east or west of the shores of this massive country of ours.

First, know that in this book of some five hundred recipes, not only have traditional secrets been tracked from their original sources, but they have all been modified, tested and refined until they represent the ideal in modern cuisine, in terms both of taste and contemporary scientific dietary knowledge. Age does not in itself ordain perfection, as in some fine antique carpentry. On the contrary, it was frequently found to be something of a disadvantage. It took a bit of a while for Americans to lend refinement and artistry to the food at their fingertips. What they did with it was sometimes horrendous. Witness this comment from the *Boston Medical and Surgical Journal*, in 1835, describing how New England farmers ate:

"In the morning at breakfast they deluge their stomach with a quart of hot water, impregnated with tea, or so slightly with coffee that it is mere colored water; and they swallow, almost without chewing, hot bread, half baked, toast soaked in butter, cheese of the fattest kind, slices of salt or hung beef, ham, etc., all of which is nearly insoluble. At dinner they have boiled pastes under the name of puddings and their sauces, even for roast beef, are melted butter; their turnips and potatoes swim in hog's lard, butter, or fat; under the name of pie or pumpkin, their pastry is nothing but a greasy paste, never sufficiently baked."

Such monstrous fare was soon brought under civilized control, of course, mainly induced by urban people who traveled to Europe and the Orient and learned new ways of making their own foods more delicious. Our own book is a grateful record of that kind of endeavor, the raw materials, as you find them in our recipes, have now become culinary achievements.

Fairly recently, due to overindustrialization in the food industry as a whole, and a demand on the part of the public for foods which make for "easy" eating, we begin to see danger signals on the food horizon which cannot be ignored. Too extensive use of over-refined flour and sugar and of foods that contain additives to replace natural flavors, vitamins and minerals has created real problems. The grocery shelves are filled with beautiful, appetizing products well able to stand the test of time, but not of proper nutrition.

*Taking food and drink is a
great enjoyment for healthy
people, and those who do not
enjoy eating seldom have
much capacity for enjoyment
or usefulness of any sort.*

Charles W. Eliot

Fortunately, there is an ever-growing number of Americans, including doctors and nutritionists, who have recognized the danger signals and are urging the production of more high-vitamin and mineral-content foods with an emphasis on unrefined sugar. Like all theories, this can be carried too far and there is a well-deserved place of honor for delicious foods based on highly refined flour and sugar. We trust we have offered a judicious mixture in this book.

The greatest culinary chauvinist America has ever known was Mark Twain. While in Europe he had nightly visions of a "mighty porterhouse steak an inch and a half thick, hot and sputtering from the griddle; dusted with fragrant pepper; enriched with little melting bits of butter of the most unimpeachable freshness and genuineness; the precious juices of the meat trickling out and joining the gravy, archipelagoed with mushrooms; a township or two of tender, yellowish fat gracing an outlying district of this ample county of beefsteak; the long white bone which divides the sirloin from the tenderloin still in its place," and wrote that the only good food in the world is American food. We make no such claim but we do say that based on the American theory that food should be delicious as well as nutritious, well seasoned while not exotic, well prepared but not complicated, Americans can hold their heads up high and do honor to their forebears.

Among our forebears was a gentleman named Thomas Jefferson who was recognized as one of the greatest epicures in all history. Having resided in Paris as our first ambassador to France, Jefferson learned to enjoy the subtleties of Parisian haute cuisine, and he went to great lengths to satisfy these tastes in later years. He sent his private valet, James Hastings, to a cooking school in Paris so as to grace the table at Monticello with European delicacies. Jefferson himself learned personally to make ice cream while he was in Europe and was one of the first Americans to serve the delicacy at a state banquet.

There is, in fact, a very exclusive little society which consists of his descendants and the trustees of his estate, Monticello (possibly the most beautiful residence in America, which Jefferson himself designed), which yearly gathers together on April 13 to toast the great man in the fine champagne and Madeira he prized so highly, to tell stories of his rare tastes, and to eat a different dinner each year featuring some of his favorite dishes. Jefferson credited his long years of health to eating as many vegetables as possible and drinking wine instead of whisky. One of the most charming wonders of his home at Monticello is the little dumbwaiter secreted in the interior of the fireplace structure in the dining room which he invented to bring up his wines, properly chilled, to the kingly banquets he so enjoyed.

But why must we talk when we should be eating? Let us to the kitchen first, then to table. And there in the company of loved ones, family or friends, or preferably both, learn the eternal truth spoken by the greatest philosopher among all the sages of dining, Jean-Anthelme Brillat-Savarin:
"The discovery of a new dish does more for the happiness of mankind than the discovery of a star."

Cover painting, THE SATURDAY EVENING POST, *November 27, 1920*

PILGRIM'S PROGRESS: A MEATING OF THE MINDS

It all started when the Pilgrims celebrated our first Thanksgiving. They had every reason to do so, reasons we do well to recall today in their honor.

The New World, seen through the myopic eyes of the kings of England, France, Spain and Portugal, was a place where plain men died to make royalty richer. But the Pilgrims had left England, tarried in Leyden, Holland, and now were about to sail again from England for America in 1620 for a finer thing than gold—for religious tolerance and freedom. King James had no more concept of such Roundhead fantasy than his primping hairdresser, but after much haggling the Pilgrims did in fact obtain a royal patent to settle in Virginia.

Virginia was not the place we know now. It started at the James River and ran with grandiloquent inaccuracy as far north as the Hudson River. It was near the Hudson, in fact, that the Pilgrims planned to settle "in Virginia." Their own ship's log tells the story. They settled for the nearest landing place, Cape Cod, for a couple of reasons. One, the Gulf Stream had pushed them there, a power beyond all seventeenth-century nautical reckoning, as Giovanni Verrazano had long ago discovered in 1524 when he thought he was actually heading straight for Florida. Second, as the *Mayflower*'s log recorded, they steered for the nearest landing place because *"we could not now take time for further search or consideration; our victuals having been much spent, especially our beere."*

The little 180-ton ship, a cork on the enormous swells of the North Atlantic, had not left Plymouth, England without considerable fanfare and a wave of sympathy from the English. It tells something of the importance attached to such voyages in that seventeenth century—not unlike those of our own astronauts celebrated in their takeoffs on TV—that rare Ben Jonson, the great Elizabethan playwright, had penned lines on the week previous referring to the departure. Immortal John Dryden was at the dock to bid them bon voyage, in lines not quite as immortal. Even peerless Will Shakespeare, if you will examine closely the stanzas of *The Tempest* (the only play he ever wrote, by the way, with an original plot line) was inspired by the misfortunes of supply ships sent to succor Virginia settlements to pen lines referring to the *still-vex'd Bermoothes.* (Not many Bermudians know today that they were once the inspiration of the Bard of Avon.)

The Pilgrims knew exactly what they were up against. Of the nearly 14,000 colonists who had arrived in Jamestown between 1607 and 1622, only 911 were left after the Indians got through cutting them down and occasionally eating them. Another settlement in Maine, attempted at the mouth of the Kennebec River a few years after the original Jamestown settlement, had resulted in a complete wipe-out—a lost cause never reattempted. But the Pilgrims were men of rocklike determination. One Pilgrim described their main occupation as "survival." Their nobility is enough to move one to wonder and almost to tears—"*. . . It is not with us as with other men, whom small things can discourage, or small discontentments cause to wish themselves at home again.*"

"Small discontentments"! A cockleshell of a ship,

*A rich soup; a small turbot; a
saddle of venison; an
apricot tart: this is a dinner
fit for a king.*

Brillat Savarin

Cover painting, THE SATURDAY EVENING POST, *November 25, 1899*

named after the blossom of the hawthorn, setting out for a savage lashing by the winter seas for sixty-seven full days. The little bark fought contrary gales, and in William Bradford's fine phrase, "many fierce storms in which the ship was shrewdly shaken." Shattered, her upper works strained and leaky, one of her main beams amidship strained and cracked, she was ready to go down. She rolled, pitched, yawed, bucked and leaped, crashed and shipped tons of water. One hundred two people lived in one low-ceilinged cabin, twenty-five feet by fifteen at its largest—each in a space like a grave—and there for over two months had to pursue life's necessities. Miraculously, only one failed. Young William Butten died and his body was committed to the deep. But a sign arose for hope: a child was born to Elizabeth Hopkins, wife of Stephen, and given the marvelously poetic name of Oceanus. In his birth cry a new world had begun indeed.

But they had nothing aboard to build this world with. Since this book is about food, be it noted that they had very little of that but smoked herring, dried ox tongues, sacks of vegetables, pickled eggs, and barrels of dried fish, beef and pork. Spices, salt, and conserves. Tea and salt were unknown. They drank beer and wine, gin and brandy, rather than risk the water. Since these people were thinkers rather than doers, their supplies with which to conquer a continent were pitiful. They brought no cattle, no horses or oxen, just a few pigs and goats and chickens. Some sheep and rabbits and poultry to eat on the voyage, if the poor things lived out the days of the sea's batter-

ing. Strangely, some pets: two dogs (one mastiff and one spaniel), a few cats and birds. Food for all was cooked in a firebox, an iron tray with sand in it where a live fire was kept burning. Clanking around them were their household utensils: kettles and pans and pots and candlesticks and tubs and buckets and crockery and mugs. They brought spades, scythes, mattocks, hammers, chisels, ropes, nails, fishhooks, saws and rakes. Guns, muskets, swords, cutlasses, daggers, even a drum and a trumpet for the gallant charge. Some few pieces of furniture. And four small cannon.

But they weren't very good at using such things. These Pilgrims were better at reading books, and these they had in plenty. Bibles and prayer books for all, books for the children, for they believed in education. The doughty Captain Miles Standish, a tough little redheaded fighting cock of a soldier, carried with him Caesar's *Commentaries,* Bariffe's *Artillery,* and probably the most useless object on board the entire craft, a history of Turkey.

Finally, on November 9, 1620, land! They were equipped to conquer this country morally, but not physically. They were looking at Cape Cod, a seemingly hospitable land where the dark conifers rolled down like a great green wave to the very edge of the bay. There were white-tailed deer and black bear in there; quail and wild ducks and ruffed grouse, wild turkey, small game, fruit and nuts. But the Pilgrims had no knowledge of this and fewer ideas on what to do about providing food for themselves. Mammoth whales played around the tiny *Mayflower,* but

*The popular idea of health
. . . the English country
gentleman galloping after a fox
—the unspeakable in full pursuit
of the uneatable*

Oscar Wilde

Leviathan was not to be caught by midgets such as these just yet. Even the codfish, the state emblem of Massachusetts-to-be, were out of season and wouldn't take to the hook. Farther south, the explorers of Chesapeake Bay had found so many fish they claimed gleefully they could walk across the water on them. Here there were only clams and mussels for the Pilgrims to munch—and the salt made them sick.

Here is how their leader, William Bradford, saw their prospects:

"But here I cannot but stay and make a pause, and stand half amazed at this poor people's present condition; and so I think will the reader, too, when he well considers the same. Being thus passed the vast ocean, and a sea of troubles before in their preparation (as may be remembered by that which went before), they had now no friends to welcome them nor inns to entertain or refresh their weatherbeaten bodies; no houses nor much less towns to repair to, to seek for succour . . . and for the season it was winter, and they that know the winters of that country know them to be sharp and violent, and subject to cruel and fierce storms, dangerous to travel to known places, much more to search an unknown coast. Besides, what could they see but a hideous and desolate wilderness, full of wild beasts and wild men—and what multitudes there might be of them they knew not. Neither could they, as it were, go up to the top of Pisgah to view from this wilderness a more goodly country to feed their hopes; for

which way soever they turned their eyes (save upward to the heavens) they could have little solace or content in respect of any outward objects. For summer being done, all things stand upon them with a weatherbeaten face, and the whole country, full of woods and thickets, represented a wild and savage hue."

As they looked more closely at this land of the weatherbeaten face, and the chill November wind whistled through the shrouds, the Pilgrims, staunch as they were, must have been appalled. Bradford continues:

"But that which was most sad and lamentable was that in two or three months' time half of their company died, especially in January and February, being the depth of winter, and wanting houses and other comforts; being infected with the scurvy and other diseases which this long voyage and their inaccommodate condition had brought upon them. So as there died sometimes two or three of a day in the aforesaid time, that of one hundred and odd persons, scarce fifty remained. And of these, in the time of most distress, there were but six or seven sound persons who to their great commendations, be it spoken, spared no pains night or day, but with abundance of toil and hazard of their own health fetched them wood, made them fires, dressed them meat, made their beds, washed their loathsome clothes, clothed and unclothed them. In a word, did all the homely and necessary offices for them which dainty

and queasy stomachs cannot endure to hear named; and all this willingly and cheerfully, without any grudging in the least, showing herein their true love unto their friends and brethren; a rare example and worthy to be remembered. Two of these seven were Mr. William Brewster, their reverend elder, and Myles Standish, their captain and military commander, unto whom myself and many others were much beholden in our low and sick conditions. And yet the Lord so upheld these persons as in this general calamity they were not at all infected either with sickness or lameness. And what I have said of these I may say of many others who died in this general visitation, and others yet living; that while they had health, yea, or any strength continuing, they were not wanting to any that had need of them. And I doubt not but their recompense is with the Lord. . . ."

And this is what it did to them. In less than one year, by April 1621, one-half of the human freight of the *Mayflower* was dead—drowned, killed by Indians, disease, cold, malnutrition, and perhaps some by sheer terror. Little Oceanus was gone. This first winter of the new world saw almost the entire destruction of the wives of the Pilgrims. Fourteen out of eighteen died. Twenty-four entire households were obliterated. As one historian puts it, with chilling accuracy: "Fifty-four persons, twenty-one of them under sixteen, were left to start the process that created the United States of America."

But they stuck it out. When the *Mayflower* returned to England on April 15, 1621, not one of the original Pilgrims was aboard. "Small things . . and small discontentments" indeed! They had come to stay: and they stayed.

There is some chance that even willpower like theirs might not have prevailed were it not for two fortunate happenings.

One was that the Pilgrims encountered an unusually mild winter. As it was, they spent most of their time tending to the sick and burying their dead on the headland overlooking the sea. But almanacs of the day, crude as they were, and the Pilgrims' own accounts of subsequent lustier winters indicate that the stiff kind of New England blast which surely would have wiped them out entirely did not strike that year of 1620-21.

Their other good fortune lay in encountering Indians—but just three Indians, no more—who may well have been responsible for the saving of this entire nation. The winter went badly as far as illness was concerned—scurvy and "consumption" (actually acute pulmonary tuberculosis) were wasting those who lived on land. Those who tried living on the *Mayflower*, hoping that the familiarity of the old ship might make matters better, fared even worse in the damp cold. Men turned on their wives for urging them into coming. The crew members of the *Mayflower* cursed the Pilgrims they had brought, and who had brought them.

The Pilgrims eked out the winter on their food, but . . . just. In those days, only "gentlemen" in

*That old English saying: After
dinner sit a while, and after
supper walk a mile.*

Thomas Cogan

England were handy enough with their muskets to shoot game on their estates. Anyone else was a poacher. Being neither noblemen nor poachers, the Pilgrims at first couldn't hit the broad side of the widest deer in Massachusetts with their clumsy fowling pieces. They simply lived in a state of semi-famine. They had no bread, because the seeds they had brought with them would not grow in this inhospitable soil. They were forced to live out of the sea on clams and fish, with an occasional feast of some ground nuts found in the forest. As Governor Bradford wryly put it, "the best dish they could present to their friends was a lobster or a piece of fish without bread or anything else except a cup of fair spring water."

They even had to feed new immigrants—a half dozen newcomers arrived from Maine, and another group from along the Massachusetts coast.

What saved the Pilgrims is told in every schoolboy's book, but it belongs here in our story of food. The terrible winter which had struck down half their number began to break up somewhat and birds began to peep in the forests and flowers to spring from the earth. The Pilgrims knew the time was at hand to try cultivation, which might be their last if it did not succeed.

At this point, on a "warm, fair day," as their records tell us, a solitary Indian strolled into their camp and astonished everyone by gravely saying "Welcome." This was, of course, Samoset, an Indian chief who had picked up the word from the Englishmen he had met on Monhegan Island, where Miles Standish was wont to watch the whales sport in the blue Atlantic (and where you still can). The fact was that Samoset was one of the few Indians who had survived a great pestilence in the neighborhood of Plymouth or there might have been some unwelcoming parties to wipe out the Pilgrims as they stepped ashore.

Samoset was a native of Pemaquid, where Bristol, Maine now stands, and he told the Pilgrims a bit about the history of where they lived. Among other things, he mentioned that in 1614, British slave traders had kidnapped twenty-seven Indians and sold them into the slavery of various Spanish galleys. This was displeasing to the Plymouth Indians, he hinted, and could have been a reason for annihilating the new settlers, had the Indians survived the pestilence.

The Pilgrims got along well with Samoset, however, and in a few days he returned with his friend Massasoit, chief of the Wampanoags, and twenty braves. These chaps gave the Pilgrims a sample of their songs and dances, but what is far more important, introduced an Indian named Squanto to the Pilgrims. There is a statue today of Massasoit in Plymouth, but perhaps it should be of Squanto, for he was the veritable lifesaver of the colony.

There was no reason that he should have been. He had been kidnapped years before by an English captain, taken to London, where he lived as a curiosity and a slave. But ultimately returning to American waters as part of a ship's company, he jumped ship and regained his freedom. He then became a first-rate interpreter between Chief Massasoit, his well-armed Indians and the enfeebled Pilgrims. What is far more

important, Squanto seems to have developed some kind of affection for the English, which is difficult to understand after the treatment he had received at European hands. But one telling thing had happened— when Squanto was returned to America by a Captain Dermer's ship and disembarked at Patuxent, where his tribe had lived before, they were all dead of the plague. Dermer was killed on Martha's Vineyard in 1620, so Squanto threw in his lot with Massasoit. He evidently felt the need of some relatives.

So now Squanto elected to be with the Pilgrims. He taught them where the best fish were and how to catch them. He taught them how to plant corn and fertilize it—Indians did their plowing with a stick, but corn doesn't have to be planted very deep and it flourished. Squanto taught them where the forest game lurked, and in due time the Pilgrims learned how to shoot for their larder.

Squanto was really no great shakes as a provider. None of the Indians were. In fact, they customarily went out on raiding parties to steal food from other tribes as winter came on, and sometimes when such foraging trips were unsuccessful, they ate some of the more unpopular members of the party to keep their spirits up and their appetites down. But the Eastern Indians could farm three crops—corn, beans, and squash—after a fashion. These were originally foods from Mexico, which had worked their way up to the northern tribes over the centuries of cultural infusion. Some murky memory of this must have remained in the minds of the New England Indians since Squanto told the Pilgrims that a dead Indian's spirit went south "where the beans come from."

He had a few tricks. He planted his beans after the corn had begun to grow, so that the bean vines grew up the stalks of corn. He fertilized his crops with chopped-up fish, mixed into the soil, without knowing that phosphorus was thus renewing its strength.

The green spring now began to have some promise for them, as Squanto stayed on with the Pilgrims. He had his family, now, and they had their teacher in the arts of survival in America. The cod they had missed the November before were running aplenty here in the summer. The peas the Pilgrims planted blossomed, but parched in the sun and were not worth the eating. But the corn, or maize, turned out to be then—as it is today—America's most important crop. It saved their lives.

Later, ships were to bring cattle, three cows and a bull, in 1624. And pigs were to become the chief meat dish of the first Americans. The pig is a splendid fellow to bring up, because he doesn't need any bringing up. To begin with, he is a form of condensed corn, and the Pilgrims soon had plenty of that. It takes a lot of grain to feed a pig, and a lot of land to raise a lot of grain. But such a problem bothered only the English. In America there were millions of acres where a pig could roam and forage on nuts. And a million ways to prepare him when he was fat enough to butcher. No other animal grows as fast as a pig—foraging over hill and dale, he increases his weight one hundred fiftyfold in the first eight months of his life. And preserved pig tastes better than any other kind of preserved meat. Tasty smoked hams and bacon,

*Better is a dinner of herbs
where love is, than a stalled ox
and hatred therewith.*

Proverbs, xv, 17.

and other parts of a pig carcass were always there with the meat immersed in a crock of brine until needed. The bacon pieces found a way into clam chowder and a dozen other mixed dishes as prime flavoring. Most colonists preferred the salted meat to the fresh, which possibly might be tainted.

The wild turkey is so much the hero of the Pilgrim's story that perhaps a small tribute to the fowl is in order. Only a few weeks ago we came across three wild turkeys in the woods of Pennsylvania: walking with regal calm and grace, kings of all they survey, until the fatal shot rings out. This time, happily, they went their way unhurried and unharmed, only a few feet from an automobile, which they disregarded with turkified disdain.

The meat of animals was probably the very first thing enjoyed by primitive man. Charred bones in prehistoric caves, as well as his canine teeth, indicate that man is very much a carnivorous animal. Meat had religious significance as well: Roman priests burned the entrails of cattle as sacrifices to their gods, the poet Horace was convinced that liver was a potent aphrodisiac, and in certain African tribes young wives avoid eating pork for fear that their offspring will resemble pigs, as well as act like them. The Pilgrims, troubled by no such scruples, had merely to make the most of the plenty around them. Fowl as a delicacy followed soon after and became the utmost in speciality. King Edward I of England graced his coronation in 1274 by serving 22,600 chickens. A queen of France, eager to please courtiers who were difficult to please, once offered a mere fifty guests 300 roast

peacocks, 33 pheasants, 90 cranes, 21 swans, 66 guinea fowl, 30 capons, 90 pullets and 99 quail. Roman emperors considered nightingale tongues a special delicacy. But for good all-around food, the succulence of an American turkey is hard to beat.

The whole American continent was feathered with turkeys when the Spanish conquistadores first arrived in the sixteenth century and took numbers back to Spain, where they were believed to be some kind of peacock. They called them *toca* which is what peacocks are called in India, and so the word *toca* came in time to be the "turkey." Oddly enough, because the bird seems to say its own name, the Indians in America were meanwhile calling their feathered friend the "furkee." The turkey, in fact, has some legitimate claims to being our national bird, bald eagle or no. Thomas Jefferson wrote the Declaration with a pen made from a turkey feather, and Ben Franklin tried very hard to have his confreres at the Constitutional Convention make the turkey our national bird rather than the marauding bald eagle (he described the latter as "a Bird of poor moral character, like those among men who live by sharpening and robbing"). He failed, but don't ever think that the turkey lacks fighting power. You may attempt to emulate Tom Jefferson with a turkey feather pen, but do not—repeat, *do not*—attempt to pull one out of a Tom Turkey's plumage. A turkey can kick like a mule, as you will very swiftly learn.

Today the wild turkey, once in danger of extinction, is now on the increase. This large, beautiful bronze native bird can be shot in limited quantity in certain states—Indiana, Ohio, Pennsylvania and New York all have a short turkey-hunting season. The wild turkey, being extremely wary and fast-moving, is a challenge to the hunter, but if you do bag one, you will find that it is totally unlike the domesticated turkey of which it is the ancestor. While the flesh is not really gamy, due to the turkey's mild diet of nuts, berries, leaves and grasses, it is definitely wild.

The autumn following their first harvest, when the corn and the beans and the pumpkins were in, William Bradford could write contentedly:

"They began now to gather in the small harvest they had, and to fit up their houses and dwellings against winter, being all well recovered in health and strength and had all things in good plenty. For as some were thus employed in affairs abroad, others were exercised in fishing, about cod and bass and other fish, of which they took good store, of which every family had their portion. All the summer there was no want; and now began to come in store of fowl, as winter approached, of which this place did abound when they came first (but afterward decreased by degrees). And besides waterfowl, there was great store of wild turkeys, besides venison, etc."

And as Edward Winslow did indeed write to a friend in England: "Our harvest being gotten in, our Governor sent four men on fowling, that we might after a more special manner rejoice together, after we had gathered the fruit of our labors. The four in one day killed as much fowl as, with a little beside, served

the Company almost a week. At which time, among other recreations, we exercised our arms, many of the Indians coming among us, and amongst the rest their greatest king, Massasoit with some ninety men, whom for three days we . . . feasted. And they went out and killed five deer, which they brought to the plantation and bestowed on our Governor and upon the Captain and others."

Freedom from want. And Thanksgiving for that freedom. That is why Norman Rockwell's marvelous painting is virtually on the very first page, the place of honor in this modest book. The Pilgrims' Thanksgiving was a modest one, by any standards we can think of. But as Carlos Bulosan wrote so eloquently in *The Saturday Evening Post*, as a lyric accompaniment to the Rockwell masterpiece:

"We know there were men who came and stayed to build America. We know they came because there is something in America that they needed, and which needed them.

"But we are not really free unless we use what we produce. So long as the fruit of our labor is denied us, so long will want manifest itself in a world of slaves. It is only when we have plenty to eat—plenty of everything—that we begin to understand what freedom means. To us, freedom is not an intangible thing. When we have enough to eat, then we are healthy enough to enjoy what we eat. Then we are not merely living but also becoming a creative part of life. It is only then that we become a growing part of democracy."

Cover painting, THE SATURDAY EVENING POST, *December 1, 1923.*

Sunday Roast Beef with Yorkshire Pudding

A time-honored custom in America has been Sunday dinner after church at home or at grandmother's house and the favorite meat has been roast beef. Perhaps in recent years there hasn't been as much church or as much roast beef as formerly but it's a custom worth preserving.

The best beef for serving 6 to 8 people is a 6- to 8-pound rib roast, or a 5- to 7-pound rolled and boned rib, a 5- to 7-pound standing rump or a 4- to 6-pound rolled rump. The use of a meat thermometer is almost indispensable for making sure of the cooking time. It should be inserted into the thickest part of the meat away from the bone. Preheat the oven to 300 degrees F. Allow the meat to stand at room temperature for 2 hours before cooking. Place the meat on a rack in an open roasting pan, fat side up.

Timing:
For a standing rib allow per pound:
    18 to 20 minutes for rare beef (140 degrees F)
    22 to 25 minutes for medium (160 degrees F)
    26 to 30 minutes for well done (170 degrees F)
    For a rolled roast allow 8 to 10 minutes extra.
    Salt and pepper the roast ½ hour before the end of the cooking time. Time your roast so that it can rest 20 to 30 minutes before carving.

Thick Brown Gravy: Transfer the roast to a warm platter and keep warm. Pour off all but about ¼ cup of the fat into a small container so that the fat will rise to the top quickly. Place the roasting pan over moderate heat and stir in 4 tablespoons of flour, stirring and scraping the pan with a sturdy fork. Add 2 cups of cold liquid (water, stock, or canned bouillon). Stir until the gravy boils and thickens. Add any pan juices distilled from the fat. If the gravy needs coloring add some commercial gravy caramel. Season with salt and pepper and strain into a hot gravy boat.

Thin Brown Gravy: Pour off almost all of the fat from the pan. Add a half cup of water and scrape the pan with a fork to loosen the juices. Add water or beef bouillon and taste for seasoning.

Yorkshire Pudding

Instead of baking the pudding in the roasting pan, try this method. You can get started earlier and the pudding is less greasy.

3 tablespoons beef drippings
3 eggs
1 cup milk
1 cup bread flour
½ teaspoon salt

Preheat oven to 450 degrees F.
    Grease a soufflé or other deep medium-size baking dish with 2 tablespoons of the drippings and heat the dish while preparing the batter. Beat the eggs until well blended. Add the milk, flour and salt and beat for 30 seconds. Add 1 tablespoon of the drippings and pour into the baking dish. Bake 20 to 25 minutes. Serve in the baking dish.

New England Boiled Dinner

4- to 5-pound piece of corned beef
4 large carrots, scraped
1 large rutabaga, pared
3 white turnips, pared
12 small onions, peeled
6 medium potatoes, peeled
2 small parsnips, pared

Cook the corned beef as for Corned Beef and Cabbage without the carrots and onions. At the end of 2½ hours add the carrots and the rutabaga, cut in chunks. Fifteen minutes later add the turnips, onions, and potatoes, cut in half, and the parsnips, cut in similar-sized chunks. Boil until all the vegetables are tender. Theories differ about the presence of cabbage in New England Boiled Dinner. If you are on the affirmative side, quarter and core a small cabbage and cook it 12 to 15 minutes in a separate saucepan with some of the broth from the kettle.
    Serve the meat on a platter surrounded by the vegetables. Horseradish and mustard pickles are traditional accompaniments to a boiled dinner.

Chuck Wagon Pepper Steak

3 to 3½ pounds bottom round
   steak, cut 2 inches thick
2 teaspoons meat tenderizer
1/3 cup minced onion
1 large clove garlic, minced
2 teaspoons powdered thyme
1 teaspoon marjoram
1 bay leaf, crushed
1 cup wine vinegar
½ cup olive oil
3 tablespoons lemon juice
2 tablespoons cracked black pepper

Put the steak in a deep nonmetal bowl and sprinkle with the tenderizer, turning it once or twice.

Mix all the remaining ingredients except for the black pepper and pour over the meat. Marinate in a cool place, turning the meat occasionally, for 12 hours.

Take the meat out of the marinade and dry it with paper toweling. Pound the pepper into the meat with a wooden mallet or a rolling pin.

Grill the meat 6 inches away from hot coals, allowing 15 minutes per side. Paint with the marinade every 5 minutes. Serve with Skillet Potatoes (see Vegetables).

Pan Broiled Sirloin with Brandy Sauce

3 to 4 pounds sirloin steak
   cut 1½ inches thick
2 cloves garlic
1 teaspoon cracked black pepper
Butter
Salt
1 tablespoon lemon juice
3 tablespoons Worcestershire sauce
1 cup brandy

Wipe the meat with paper toweling and rub in the garlic, forced through a garlic press or very finely minced, and the black pepper. Fingers are the best tool for this process.

Heat 6 tablespoons of butter in a heavy skillet the size of the steak. Brown the steak on both sides over high heat. Reduce the heat and continue to cook, allowing 12 minutes on each side or a little less if you like steak really rare.

Remove the steaks to a hot platter and sprinkle well with salt. Add the lemon juice, Worcestershire and brandy and 2 tablespoons of butter to the pan juices. Swirl the pan around until the butter is melted and the sauce begins to bubble. Pour over the steak and serve immediately.

Court-Bouillon is a certain way of boiling any large Fiſh.

Entremets are the leſſer ſort of Diſhes that compoſe the Courſes.

Hors-d'Oeuvres are the choice little Diſhes or Plates, that are ſerv'd in between the Courſes at Banquets or feſtival-Entertainments.

Lardons are the little Bits of Bacon, Anchoves, Eels, &c. that we uſe to lard our Fleſh or Fiſh withal.

Bards of Bacon are Slices of the Fat of a Flitch of Bacon cut the broad way of the Flitch. How they are uſed will be found in the Receipts.

Blanc-manger ſignifies white Food; a ſort of Jelly ſo called.

Braiſe is a certain way of ſtewing moſt ſorts of Fiſh as well as Fleſh, which extreamly heightens the Taſtes of them, and is very much in Vogue. The ſeveral Ways of it may be ſeen in the Receipts.

Pressed Corned Beef

This simple dish is so delicious that it should not be considered a leftover.

4 cups chopped corned beef
1 tablespoon gelatin
¼ cup cold water
2 cups hot corned beef broth
1 teaspoon Worcestershire sauce
Horseradish Sauce (see Sauces)

Chop (do not grind) the corned beef rather coarsely. Soften the gelatin in the water. Taste the broth before measuring. If it is too salty, add water to the broth before measuring and heating. Flavor with Worcestershire sauce and add the gelatin, stirring a moment until it is completely dissolved. Cool the broth to lukewarm.

Pack the corned beef into a medium-sized loaf pan. Add enough broth to moisten it well. Put another pan on top of the meat and weight it down with a heavy object. Chill several hours. Unmold on a platter, garnish with parsley. This is delicious with Baked Potato and Broccoli Pudding (see Vegetables).

Chuck Wagon Soused Beef Stew

4 pounds chuck beef or venison
1 pound salt pork
8 onions, peeled and sliced
8 potatoes, peeled
1 pint corn liquor
½ teaspoon black pepper

Leave the red meat in one piece. Slice or dice the salt pork and sizzle it with the sliced onions in a heavy pot or kettle until the onions are soft. Add the meat, browning it on both sides. Add the potatoes, the "likker" and enough water to cover the meat by 1 inch. Add the pepper and let the whole thing simmer for 2 to 2½ hours or until the meat is tender. Serve right from the kettle.

Broiled Flank Steak

3 pounds flank steak, well trimmed

Marinade:
1 cup soy sauce
½ cup tomato catsup
½ cup brown sugar
1 large clove garlic, pressed
3 tablespoons red wine vinegar

Butter
Salt
Black pepper

Put the steak in an enameled dish. Combine the ingredients of the marinade and pour it over the steak. Marinate for 1 to 2 hours, turning occasionally.

Broil the meat over glowing charcoal, under a pre-heated broiler or in a slightly buttered very hot skillet. Cook no longer than 5 to 6 minutes on each side, painting every 2 minutes with a little of the marinade.

Transfer the steak to a wooden board or heated platter. Spread liberally with butter and sprinkle with salt and black pepper. Cut the meat on the diagonal in thin slices. Serve 2 slices or more to each person.

Steak with Béarnaise Sauce

A steak is an admitted luxury but it's cheaper to eat it at home than in a restaurant. Buy porterhouse, sirloin or T-bone steaks cut 1½ inches thick. Depending on the size of the appetites and of the budget, allow a pound of steak for two to three people.

If broiling, preheat the broiler for 10 minutes. Line a roasting pan with aluminum foil. Brush the grill with oil and preheat before putting on the steak. If pan-broiling, sprinkle a heavy frying pan with salt and heat before cooking. Steak is at its best broiled over hot glowing charcoal.

Make Béarnaise Sauce (see Sauces) before cooking the steaks.

Cook the steaks 10 to 12 minutes on each side for rare, 15 minutes for better done.

Serve the steak on a heated platter and serve the sauce in a separate bowl.

Filets Mignons on Croutons

Unless you have a very knowledgeable butcher it's better and cheaper to make your own filets mignons, which constitute one of the principal dishes Americans took from the French and made their own.

1 beef filet
10-ounce piece of fat salt pork,
  10 inches long
6 to 8 large mushroom caps
6 to 8 slices firm white bread
4 tablespoons butter
½ lemon
Salt and pepper

Maître d'Hôtel Sauce:
6 tablespoons butter
1 teaspoon chopped tarragon
1 teaspoon lemon juice
1 tablespoon chopped parsley
¼ teaspoon cracked black pepper

Cut the filets into 6 to 8 steaks of equal thickness. Trim them and shape them so that they are round. Ask your butcher to slice the long piece of salt pork into 8 very thin slices (or do it yourself with a sharp knife, making sure the pork is very cold for easy slicing). Cut the slices to be the width of the steaks' thickness and wrap them around, trimming them so that the edges just meet. Tie with kitchen twine. Bacon can be substituted although it does impart a smoky flavor to the steak. Keep in the refrigerator until ½ hour before cooking.

Mix the ingredients of the sauce until well blended. Shape into a 1½-inch roll and wrap in wax paper. Chill in the refrigerator.

Cut circles of bread a little larger than the steaks. Sauté the circles in butter until golden brown on both sides. These may be reheated later in the oven. In the same skillet sauté the mushrooms 4 minutes on each side over a moderate flame. Sprinkle with salt, pepper and lemon juice. Keep warm. Sprinkle a skillet with salt and heat it well. Sear the steaks 1 minute on each side. Reduce the heat slightly and pan-broil 2 to 3 minutes on each side. Remove the pork and twine. Place each steak on a crouton, top with a round of Maître d'Hôtel Sauce and cap with a mushroom. Garnish with watercress.

Open Fire Eye-of-the-Round of Beef

The eye-of-the-round is a compact triangular piece of beef which is ideal for outdoor cooking and a good cut for barbecuing. See Barbecue Sauce (see Sauces). This cut can also be oven roasted, in which case it should be covered with beef suet or salt pork.

3 to 3½ pounds eye-of-the-round
Salt and pepper

Build your charcoal fire in advance so that the coals are glowing hot. Roast the meat 10 minutes on each side, meaning 30 minutes. Sprinkle with salt and pepper just before carving.

Corned Beef and Cabbage

This was a favorite dish of President Cleveland who, according to legend, was jealous when the servants ate it and he had to eat more regal fare. It has always been considered an economical dish but, alas, that is no longer the case.

4-pound piece of corned beef brisket
1 large bay leaf
8 peppercorns
2 onions, each stuck with a clove
2 carrots
1 head cabbage

Wash the beef under cool water to remove the brine. Place in a kettle with enough water to cover the bay leaf and the peppercorns. Bring the water very slowly to a boil, removing the scum that will rise to the surface. Keep skimming for the first 15 minutes. Add the carrots and the onions and cook slowly for 3 hours. Cut the cabbage in wedges and cook for the last 15 minutes. If the broth seems too salty, dilute it with water.

Place the corned beef on a heated platter. Slice half of it and surround the meat with wedges of cabbage. Do not serve the onions and carrots. Moisten well with the broth. Reserve 2 cups of drained broth to make Pressed Corned Beef with the leftover meat.

Sauerbraten

This dish brought from Germany is an integral part of American cooking. Recipes vary in different parts of the country, but if it's Sauerbraten it's good.

3 pounds chuck beef
Salt and coarse black pepper
1 pint water
1 pint red wine vinegar
1 large onion, sliced
1 clove garlic
2 bay leaves
6 peppercorns
3 cloves
2 tablespoons flour
2 tablespoons oil
2 tablespoons butter
1 tablespoon brown sugar
6 gingersnaps

Wipe the beef with toweling and rub well with salt and pepper. Place in a deep nonmetal bowl. Bring the water, vinegar, onion, garlic, bay leaves, peppercorns and cloves just to a boil. Pour it over the beef. Cover and when cool, store in the refrigerator for 24 to 48 hours, turning the meat occasionally.

To cook: Remove the meat from the marinade. Wipe it dry and rub well with flour on all sides. Heat the oil and butter in a Dutch oven or other deep heavy pan. Brown the meat well, turning it without piercing it. When well browned add 2 cups of the marinade. Cover tightly and simmer very slowly for 2½ hours. Remove the meat to a warm platter. Add the sugar and crumbled gingersnaps to the liquid in the pan and boil hard for a few moments, stirring well. If a thicker gravy is desired add a teaspoon of cornstarch mixed with ¼ cup of water.

Beef or Buffalo Barbecue

One of the chief mainstays of all immigrants traveling west was the buffalo. Buffalo tongue was considered the greatest delicacy but every part of the animal had its use. So enormous were the amounts consumed—according to one account 10 pounds per day was a man's portion—that eventually the buffalo was in danger of becoming extinct. Now they are being protected, and although buffalo steak is not available at the corner grocery store, it does exist and may well become more plentiful. A good beef loin boneless steak is a good substitute. This can be cooked over glowing charcoal or in the oven.

4 to 5-pound buffalo or beef steak

Coating:
2 tablespoons dry mustard
2 tablespoons flour
1 teaspoon salt
½ teaspoon black pepper
¼ pound butter, softened

Sauce:
1 cup olive oil
¼ cup catsup
1 tablespoon brown sugar
1 tablespoon salt
4 tablespoons brandy
¼ cup Worcestershire sauce

Mix the dry ingredients into the butter until thoroughly blended. Rub well into the meat on all sides. Heat a heavy pan and sear the meat on all sides. Cook the meat 6 inches from the coals or roast in 400-degree oven, basting frequently with the sauce and turning every 15 minutes. Roast 45 to 60 minutes depending on degree of doneness desired and the thickness of the steak. Twelve minutes per pound will achieve medium-rare beef.

Braised Beef Tongue

Serve this hot one day and cold the next. It's delicious!

1 (4- to 5-pound) smoked beef tongue
2 cups dry white wine
1 onion stuck with 3 cloves
6 peppercorns
1 bay leaf
6 sprigs parsley
2 sprigs thyme or
 ¼ teaspoon powdered thyme
½ cup grated onion
½ cup grated carrots
¼ cup finely diced celery
4 tablespoons butter

Place the tongue in a deep kettle. Add the wine and enough cold water to cover. Add the onion with cloves, the peppercorns and the herbs tied in a bouquet. Cover and simmer 3 to 4 hours or until tender. Skim off any scum that rises to the surface. Remove from the kettle and cool enough to handle. Save the broth. Meanwhile sauté the prepared vegetables just to soften them. Place them in a casserole deep enough to accommodate the tongue. Slit the tough outer skin and remove it and the cords attached to the tongue. Place the tongue in the casserole. Add 1 teaspoon of Kitchen Bouquet or other gravy caramel to 3 cups of the tongue broth and pour it over the meat. Cover and braise one hour on the stove or in a 300-degree oven.

Serve hot with hot mustard and Deep Dish Sweet Potato Pie or cold with Horseradish Sauce and Cole Slaw (see Sauces, Vegetables).

Creamed Chipped Beef

Jerked beef, which was beef put in a salt brine and then hung to dry, was a staple for pioneers heading west as well as for homesteaders wherever they were. Today's version is chipped beef.

½ pound chipped beef
1 teaspoon scraped onion
6 tablespoons butter
6 tablespoons flour
3 cups milk
½ pint cream
¼ teaspoon freshly ground pepper

Tear the beef into shreds. Heat the butter and add the onion and beef, stirring until the beef is well coated with the butter and lightly fried. Sprinkle with flour and stir until the flour disappears. Add the milk and cream. Stir until thick and smooth. Season with black pepper and salt if necessary. Some chipped beef is saltier than others. Serve on toast or with Baked Potato (see Vegetables).

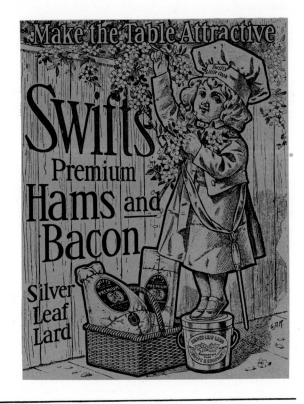

Roast Suckling Pig

Roast pig was very popular with our forefathers whether it was served with pomp and ceremony for a festive occasion or roasted on a spit near a covered wagon. As we became less hardy and more squeamish, the dish faded from fashion but now it has again become a favorite dish for spectacular occasions and deserves a place in this book.

1 suckling pig (10 to 12 pounds)
8 cups soft white bread crumbs
2 cups milk
2 large onions, grated
8 tablespoons butter
2 hard-cooked eggs
2 cups chopped celery
2 tablespoons chopped parsley
2 tablespoons poultry seasoning
2 teaspoons salt
¾ teaspoon black pepper
1 quart white wine or hard cider
Herb bouquet (2 bay leaves, 2
   sprigs thyme, several celery
   leaves)
1 small red apple
Cranberries
Parsley

Buy a piglet that has been well cleaned. Wash in cold water, making sure that all the orifices are clean. Pat dry. Lay on its back and prepare the stuffing.

Break up the bread with your fingers and soak it in the milk. Sauté the onions in the butter over low heat until soft. Remove from the heat and add the eggs, which have been peeled and chopped, the celery, parsley, seasonings and the bread, squeezed as dry as possible. Mix very thoroughly with two wooden spoons. Stuff the piglet and sew the sides together. Place the piglet in a kneeling position in a large open roasting pan with the hind legs trussed to the body with kitchen twine. Stretch the front legs out and tie them together. Put a child's wooden toy block or a ball of foil in the mouth to keep it open. Protect the ears and tails with small bits of buttered brown paper. Rub the flesh with butter, salt and pepper. Put the wine or cider and the herb bouquet tied with a string

in the pan. Roast 3½ to 4 hours, basting frequently with the pan juices. Transfer the roasted pig to a large serving platter. Put cranberries in the eye sockets and hang a wreath of cranberries around the neck. Put apple in mouth and garnish with parsley.

To carve: Run a sharp pointed knife along each side of the backbone and then carve in 2/3- to 1-inch slices at right angles.

Marinated Pork Loin Roast

This dish fit for the carriage trade or the covered wagon is simple to prepare and delicious to eat. When you buy the pork ask the butcher to prepare it for easy carving, which means separating the backbone from the ribs.

6 pounds center cut of pork loin
1 cup dry sherry
1 large clove of garlic, minced
6 tablespoons brown sugar
1 teaspoon dry mustard
2 tablespoons catsup
2 teaspoons soy sauce
A few drops of Tabasco
Salt and pepper

Wipe the loin with toweling and place in an enamel-lined dish. Combine the remaining ingredients and pour them over the roast. Let stand at room temperature, spooning the sauce over the roast frequently. Spear the roast with a spit for either indoor or outdoor cooking if you are equipped for this or place on a rack in an open pan in a 350-degree oven. Allow 30 minutes per pound, painting the meat frequently with the marinade as it cooks.

Serve with Mashed Rutabagas (see Vegetables) and seasonal greens.

Cover painting, THE SATURDAY EVENING POST, *December 2, 1911.*

Glazed Roast Pork

6- to 7-pound pork loin
Flour
Salt and pepper
Barbecue Sauce (see Sauces)

Rub the surface of the meat with flour, salt and pepper. Let stand at room temperature while preparing the sauce.

Preheat the oven to 350 degrees F. Roast 30 minutes. Paint the entire surface with some of the sauce and paint it every 20 to 25 minutes thereafter. Allow 30 minutes per pound for roasting. The remaining sauce may be used as a sauce for the meat.

Pork Chops in Cider

4 or 5 large sweet potatoes
Butter or margarine
1 large onion, peeled and diced
1 clove garlic, minced
1 tablespoon Worcestershire sauce
6 to 8 pork chops, ¾ inch thick
4 cooking apples
2 cups cider
Salt and pepper
Chopped parsley

Scrub the potatoes well and boil them in their jackets just until tender. Drain and cool.

Heat 6 tablespoons of butter and slowly sauté the onion and garlic without browning. Remove from the heat and add the Worcestershire. Sprinkle a large skillet with salt and heat it well. Brown the chops on both sides.

Peel and core the apples and cut them into 1/3-inch rings.

Preheat the oven to 350 degrees F. Peel and slice the potatoes and lay them in the bottom of a well-buttered baking-serving dish. Sprinkle with salt and pepper. Lay the pork chops on the potatoes and spread with the onion-butter mixture. Cover with the apple rings. Sprinkle with salt and pepper. Add the cider. Cover and bake 1¼ hours. Sprinkle with chopped parsley before serving.

Louisiana Pork Chops

6 to 8 thick loin pork chops
2 medium onions, sliced thin
2 green peppers, sliced thin
1 clove of garlic, minced
6 tomatoes, peeled
1 cup red Burgundy-type wine
6 sprigs parsley
1 bay leaf
1 sprig thyme
Celery leaves
Salt and black pepper

Trim the pork chops of excess fat and wipe them free of bone dust with paper toweling. Rub a wide shallow baking dish with some of the excess pork fat and lay the pork chops flat in the dish. Cover the chops with the onions, peppers and garlic. Halve the tomatoes and gently squeeze out the seeds. Cut the tomatoes in chunks and spread them over the other vegetables. Add the wine and the herbs tied in a little bouquet. Season well with salt and plenty of black pepper. Cover and bake 2 hours at 300 degrees F. Serve with wild rice or baked sweet potatoes.

Simple Barbecued Spareribs

6 to 8 pounds pork spareribs
Barbecue Sauce (see Sauces)

Preheat the oven to 350 degrees F. Lay the spareribs on 1 or 2 open roasting pans. Bake 1 hour. Meanwhile prepare the Barbecue Sauce. Brush the spareribs well with the sauce and continue baking for 30 minutes, basting frequently. Serve with Baked Sauerkraut (see Vegetables).

Homemade Bag Sausage

Bag sausage as opposed to link sausage can be made at home. The spices act as a kind of preservative and the sausage can be kept for a week or two in the refrigerator.

2 pounds fresh lean pork
¼ pound fat salt pork
1 teaspoon chopped fresh thyme or
  ½ teaspoon powdered thyme
2 teaspoons chopped fresh sage or
  1 teaspoon powdered sage
½ teaspoon celery seed
½ teaspoon marjoram
½ teaspoon allspice
½ teaspoon cracked black pepper
1½ teaspoons salt

Ask the butcher to grind the lean pork with the salt pork. Add the spices and mix thoroughly. Hands are the best tools. Make into patties. These may be precooked, cooled, packaged and frozen for later use or they may be rolled into pound rolls, wrapped well and used as desired. Fry the patties in a skillet allowing 8 to 10 minutes on each side, remembering that sausage should never be undercooked. Pour off the fat from the pan as it accumulates.

Sausage Pie

1½ to 2 pounds sausage meat
Popovers (see Breads)

Buy bag sausage or make your own (see Meats). Form the sausage into 12 to 16 small patties and brown them well on both sides. Remove to paper toweling to drain. Grease a large deep rectangular baking dish (10 by 13 inches) with the sausage fat. Arrange the patties in a row.

Preheat the oven to 425 degrees F. Make the popover mixture using sausage fat instead of butter. Pour over the sausages and bake 35 minutes. Serve immediately for brunch or lunch.

Fried Apples and Sausage

This is an early pioneer invention that never had the status of a definite recipe. However, it is easy to imagine how it was cooked, and this recipe is good for breakfast or as a companion to Virginia Spoon Bread (see Breads) or hominy grits.

12 to 16 link pork sausages
1 large onion, chopped fine
6 to 8 large tart cooking apples,
  cored and sliced
6 to 8 tablespoons brown sugar
2 tablespoons butter

Prick the sausages with a fork and brown well on both sides. Once the sausages are cooked remove them to paper toweling to drain.

Put 3 to 4 tablespoons of the sausage fat into a serving-cooking dish. Stir in the chopped onion and sauté until tender. Add the sliced apples. Cover and cook until the apples begin to steam. Uncover and sprinkle with sugar and dot with butter. Cook until almost dry. Put the sausages around the edge of the dish. Cover a moment to reheat and serve.

The Compleat Court-Cook. W. 301

Fire a Pint of *Champaign* or White Wine, and make it boil, then pour it into the Sauce-pan to your Weavers, as likewife the Veal-Gravy, and keep them fimmering in it over a flack Fire. Mean while make a Ragoo as follows. Cut fome flices of a *Weftphalia*-Ham, and beat them; then cut them in very fmall flices and lay them into a Sauce-pan, cover it and fet it over a Stove; when they begin to ftick to the Bottom of the Sauce-pan, moiften them with Gravy, put to them fome fmall Mufhrooms, and make them fimmer over a flack Fire: When the Gravy is pretty well wafted away, bind your Ragoo with a Cullis of Veal and Ham, and fet it over live Embers. When the Weavers are enough done, take them out of their Liquor and drain them, then lay them in a Difh, garnifh them with your flices of Ham, pour the Liquor of the Ragoo upon them, and ferve them for the firft Courfe.

Maryland Honey Spiced Country Ham

Maryland can boast of one of the most lavish cooking records in the country. In a state literally of milk and honey plus all manner of agricultural and natural abundance, where many large mansions staffed with countless servants in the eighteenth and nineteenth centuries made a business of producing extraordinary and historical meals, it is small wonder that so many fine recipes can trace their origin to that fair state.

10- to 12-pound country ham
2 bay leaves
1 onion, stuck with 2 cloves
1 bottle semidry white wine
Water
1½ cups brown sugar
½ cup golden honey
1 teaspoon cinnamon
½ teaspoon nutmeg
¼ teaspoon powdered cloves
2 cups cider
Glacéed red cherries (optional)

Place the ham in a deep kettle. Add the bay leaves, onion, wine and enough water. Cover and simmer gently for 3½ to 4 hours. If you are using a pre-cooked ham, simmer for 1 hour only. Drain overnight in a cool place. Place in an open roasting pan. Remove the rind and excess fat. Score the fat with a sharp knife in crisscross fashion. Make a paste of the sugar, honey and spices and spread it evenly over the surface. Put 2 cups of cider—preferably the hard variety—in the pan. Bake at 300 degrees for 1 hour, basting frequently with the pan liquid. Serve hot or cold. Decorate with the cherries if desired.

Sweet potatoes, green beans and applesauce are traditional companions, but almost any vegetable and fruit combination goes well with a tasty ham.

Wyoming Ham and Apple Pudding

Wyoming is proud of its apple crop and its hams. Here's a delicious and simple way of combining those prides.

4 tablespoons butter
1 medium onion, chopped fine
4 cups cubed cooked ham
3 cups apple cubes
2 tablespoons prepared mustard
¼ teaspoon nutmeg
½ cup brown sugar mixed with
    ½ cup soft bread crumbs

Heat 2 tablespoons of the butter in a small skillet. Sauté the onion until soft. Mix well in a bowl with the ham and apple cubes, the mustard and nutmeg. Place in a deep baking-serving dish. Top with sugar mixed with the soft bread crumbs. Dot with the remaining butter. Bake 30 minutes at 350 degrees F.

Baltimore Ham and Oysters

2- to 2½-pound precooked ham steak
2 pints oysters
Cheese Sauce (see Sauces)
Paprika
Chopped parsley

Preheat the oven to 300 degrees F. Wipe the ham steak free of bone dust and wrap it in buttered aluminum foil. Place in a roasting pan and bake 45 to 60 minutes.

Add ¼ cup of water to the undrained oysters, cover and simmer just until they begin to plump up. Drain the oysters, carefully reserving the liquor.

Make the cheese sauce, substituting oyster liquor for an equal amount of milk and substituting 1 cup of cream for 1 cup of milk.

Preheat the broiler. Place the ham on a heatproof platter. Cover with the oysters. Pour over the sauce and sprinkle with paprika. Slip under the broiler to brown it and sprinkle with chopped parsley. Serve immediately.

New England Ham with Mustard Sauce

This dish is homely fare typical of New England's simple ways.

2 center slices of ham,
  cut 1 inch thick
3 cups whole milk
3 tablespoons butter
Salt and pepper
3 tablespoons flour
1 heaping tablespoon strong mustard

Soak the ham slices in 2 cups of milk for several hours, turning once. Bake 45 minutes in a 350-degree oven. While the ham is baking, heat the butter in a saucepan. Stir in the flour and cook slowly for 2 to 3 minutes without scorching. Stirring constantly, add 1 cup of milk and the mustard and stir until thick. Set aside until the ham is done.

Place the ham on a warm platter and pour 1 cup of the milk from the pan into the prepared sauce and beat vigorously over heat until well blended. Taste for seasoning since the ham milk may tend to be salty. Serve with Individual Corn Soufflés (see Vegetables), which can be cooked in the same oven.

Tennessee Ham with Coffee and Cream

This makes a delicious breakfast or brunch dish or something different for a luncheon.

6 to 8 (½-inch) ham steaks
2 tablespoons strong coffee
1 cup cream,
  the heavier the better

Trim excess fat from the ham steaks. Heat some of the fat in a large skillet before browning the ham on both sides, allowing 3 to 5 minutes for each side. While the ham is still in the pan add the coffee and the cream and bring just to the boil. Serve on a heated platter.

Baked Ham with Bread Crumb Stuffing

There is nothing to compare with a well-cured country ham whether it be from Virginia, Maryland, Ohio, Pennsylvania, or Wisconsin. It makes most canned varieties seem pretty anemic. There are endless ways of preparing ham just because our forefathers found pigs easy to raise and transport and because the good cooks—mostly from the South—devised so many ways to prepare it. If the ham has been precooked start with Step No. 2.

10- to 12-pound ham
8 hard-cooked egg yolks
3 tablespoons butter, melted
4 tablespoons chopped onion
1 cup chopped parsley
3 cups soft white bread crumbs
½ teaspoon basil
Salt and pepper
Brown sugar

Step No. 1

Put the ham in a large kettle and cover with water. Simmer 3½ to 4 hours. Drain and refrigerate overnight.

Step No. 2

The next day, place the ham in an open roasting pan. Remove the rind and excess fat. Cut gashes 1 inch apart and 2 inches deep across the surface. Mash the egg yolks with butter. Mix thoroughly with the onion, parsley and bread crumbs made from day-old bread and season well with basil, salt and pepper. Using your fingers and a small spoon, fill the gashes. Spread with brown sugar and sprinkle with black pepper. Tie with kitchen twine to keep the gashes from spreading. Bake 1 hour at 300 degrees F. Serve with Green Beans and Herbs and Beaten Biscuits or Baking Powder Biscuits (see Vegetables, Breads).

Skillet Ham and Eggs

This is pretty much a universal American dish except in those spots where hardy rancheros prefer their eggs with beefsteak. Served on bone china or in a tin plate beside an open fire, it tastes good and gives a man courage to face the day. Depending on where you hail from, you can accompany this dish with hominy grits, fried potatoes, johnnycake or apple muffins.

Ham Steaks, cut ½ inch thick
Very fresh eggs,
   1 or 2 per person
Butter
Salt and pepper

Allow 3 servings to a pound of ham. Trim any excess fat from the ham and rub it in an electric frying pan or skillet. When the pan is moderately hot, fry the ham 3 to 4 minutes on each side. Remove the ham steak to individual warm plates. Add a little butter to the skillet and fry the appropriate number of eggs. Remove the egg with a spatula to the ham or alongside it according to preference. Sprinkle the eggs with a very little salt and some freshly ground black pepper. Don't try to make too many servings at once. This is a dish that has to be eaten immediately.

Skillet Bacon and Apples

This pioneer dish was probably first cooked over an open fire beside a covered wagon. A side of bacon was part of the family provisions and apples were to be found almost everywhere in the country. Served with johnnycake or flapjacks, this made a hearty meal at any time of day, but especially early in the morning.

6 to 8 large cooking apples
12 to 18 thick slices of bacon
Brown sugar
Pepper (optional)

Wash and core the apples but do not pare them. Cut into 8 wedges apiece. Sauté the bacon starting with a large cold skillet and cooking over moderate heat, turning the pieces occasionally. Cook until thoroughly done but not too dry. Place the bacon on toweling to drain and keep warm. Pour off all the fat and return 4 tablespoons of the fat to the skillet. Reheat and add the apple wedges. Sprinkle with brown sugar. Cover and cook about 5 minutes or just until tender but not mushy. Remove the cover and continue cooking until the apples are brown on both sides. Turn carefully with a wide spatula.

    Serve directly from the skillet on to the plates and garnish with the bacon.

"Not pork chops again!"

Jellied Veal Loaf

Jellied veal loaf seems to be of southern origin, as do so many of our national favorites. In small individual loaves, it makes a nice present to a convalescing friend and a change from the inevitable custard or wine jelly. Properly garnished it makes a delicious hot weather party dish.

2 pounds stew veal
1 cup dry white wine
1 small onion
1 bay leaf
Small bunch of celery leaves
1 teaspoon salt
1/8 teaspoon white pepper
1 small can pimiento
2 tablespoons gelatin
6 hard-cooked eggs
Garden lettuce
Mayonnaise
Rolled anchovies
Tomato wedges
Parsley

Place the veal in a pan with the white wine, onion, herbs and seasoning and enough water to cover by 1 inch. Boil gently for 45 to 60 minutes or until tender. Remove the meat and strain the broth. Place the broth in the refrigerator. Chop the meat but not too fine.

Shell the eggs and cut into even slices, preferably with an egg slicer. Rinse out a loaf pan in cold water. Cut the pimiento into strips or fanciful shapes and lay them in the bottom of the pan. Cover with a layer of chopped veal and then with a layer of egg slices. Repeat this process until everything is used up, adding any chopped pimiento trimmings to the final layer of chopped veal.

Skim off any fat that has risen to the top of the broth. Measure out 2 cups and taste for seasoning. It should be well seasoned. Heat the broth. Moisten the gelatin with a little cold water and add it to the broth. Stir over heat only until dissolved. Cool to lukewarm. Pour the broth carefully into the loaf pan. Chill for at least 4 hours.

Turn the loaf out on a serving platter. Surround with cups of fresh lettuce filled with mayonnaise and topped with an anchovy roll and tomato wedge. Garnish the top with a few parsley flowerets.

The cooling process may be hastened by stirring the broth over a bowl half full of ice.

Roast Veal

Good veal is not always easy to find, but like other good news on the American food scene, it is coming back in favor and more local farmers are raising it. Veal must be cooked carefully because it has a tendency to dry out. This is the simplest way to cook it.

4½- to 5-pound boneless leg,
  rolled and tied
½ pound salt pork, sliced thin
¾ teaspoon powdered thyme
¼ teaspoon white pepper
2 large garlic cloves
2 cups white wine

Preheat the oven to 300 degrees F. Rub the leg well with thyme and pepper and with the garlic forced through a garlic press. Place the roast on a rack in an open pan and cover with the salt pork slices. Add the white wine to the pan and place in the oven. Allow 40 minutes to the pound, approximately 2¾ to 3¼ hours. Baste twice during the first 30 minutes of cooking. Cover the whole pan with aluminum foil and continue cooking. Remove the foil for the last 45 minutes of roasting and baste every 15 minutes.

Veal Cutlets in Sour Cream, Jefferson Style

This is reminiscent of French cooking, which Jefferson admired so much and brought to this country.

6 to 8 veal cutlets
Margarine or butter
Salt, white pepper and flour
2 to 3 tablespoons minced onion
¾ cup white wine (not too dry)
1 pint commercial sour cream
½ cup grated Gruyère or
    Emmenthal cheese

Ask the butcher to cut 6 to 8 individual cutlets weighing 4 to 6 ounces each from the top of the leg. Have each one well pounded and for good measure pound each one again yourself between pieces of wax paper, using a wooden mallet or rolling pin. Season each with salt and pepper and dust with flour.

Using two skillets, heat a tablespoon of margarine or butter for each cutlet. Brown the veal gently on both sides. Cover and cook for 20 to 25 minutes or until the veal is tender. Transfer the meat to a shallow ovenproof serving dish.

Meanwhile heat 3 tablespoons of butter in a saucepan. Cook the onions in the butter until soft, over a low heat. Stir in 1 tablespoon of flour and stir until it disappears. Add the wine and let the mixture cook until the wine has almost evaporated. Stir in the sour cream and bring just to the boiling point. Season highly with salt and pepper. Spread over the cooked cutlets. Spread with the cheese and brown under the broiler. Serve with tiny new potatoes.

Luncheon Veal Benedict

This delicious dish takes more assembling than cooking. Take the crab meat out of the refrigerator for 30 minutes and spread it on a plate to bring it to room temperature. Save out 6 to 8 pieces of leg meat for garnish.

6 to 8 (3- to 4-ounce) veal scallopini
    (cutlets)
Flour
Salt and pepper
Hollandaise Sauce (see Sauces)
3 or 4 English muffins
4 tablespoons butter
½ pound crab meat
Chopped parsley

Ask the butcher to pound the small scallopini, sometimes called veal cutlets, or do it yourself. Dip them in flour seasoned with salt and pepper and let them stand while making the sauce.

Make either hollandaise recipe and remove from the heat.

Split the English muffins with a fork and toast lightly.

Heat the butter in a skillet and brown the veal over high heat on both sides.

Put the toasted muffins on individual warm plates. Cover with the veal, then with crab meat flakes, then with a spoonful of hollandaise. Sprinkle with chopped parsley and garnish with a piece of crab leg meat. Serve immediately.

Roast Leg of Lamb

Perhaps Roast Leg of Lamb is not an all-American favorite, but it deserves a place in this collection for those who do like it. Lamb fat should be trimmed off as much as possible with a small sharp knife before roasting. Preference varies from pinkish lamb to the well-done variety (170 to 180 degrees on a meat thermometer). Either way, lamb is delicious. A special lamb reserved for South Dakotans is one raised on gumbo grass. Nutmeg is the favorite spice for that lamb.

6- to 8-pound leg of lamb
Soft butter
Garlic (optional)
Rosemary, thyme or nutmeg
1 large onion (optional)

Gravy:
4 tablespoons of fat
¼ teaspoon sugar
4 tablespoons flour
2 cups chicken or beef
  bouillon or water

Preheat the oven to 325 degrees.

Trim as much fat as possible from the lamb and rub the surface with soft (preferably unsalted) butter. If garlic is appreciated, make 10 to 12 slits over the surface and insert slivers of garlic, pushing them below the surface. Rub a little powdered rosemary, thyme, or nutmeg into the leg and place on a rack in an open roasting pan. Do not salt, but spread thin slices of onion over the leg if you have not used garlic. Roast 20 to 35 minutes per pound depending on preference. Thirty minutes before the end of roasting, sprinkle well with salt and freshly ground black pepper.

To make the gravy, pour off all the fat except for about 4 tablespoonfuls. (If uncertain, pour off all the fat and measure that amount back into the pan.) Place over moderate heat and stir in the sugar and let it brown lightly. Mix in 4 tablespoons of flour and stir until brown. Add the cold liquid and stir vigorously until the gravy is smooth and thick. Strain into a warm gravy bowl.

Mixed Lamb Chop Grill

Mixed grill makes a wonderful breakfast, brunch or dinner dish. It does require some organization but it is a whole course in itself.

6 to 8 lamb chops, 1 inch thick
6 to 8 lamb kidneys
16 precooked sausage links
1 pound bacon
Flaming Bananas (see Desserts)
Broiled Tomatoes (see Vegetables)
6 to 8 slices of toast
Butter
Salt and pepper
Lemon wedges

1. Wipe the lamb chops free of bone dust and place them on a lightly greased rack.
2. Remove the film and fatty core of the kidneys. Halve them and place them on the same grill.
3. Thaw the sausages.
4. Precook the bacon in a skillet over moderate heat, turning each piece once. Fry until almost crisp but not quite. Drain on paper toweling.
5. Bake the bananas but do not use the rum.
6. Broil the tomatoes just before broiling the meat.
7. Lightly toast the bread.
8. Brush the chops and kidneys with butter and broil them and the sausages 6 minutes on each side.
9. Add the bacon for the last 6 minutes.
10. Melt 4 tablespoons of butter.
11. Place the toast on a large warm platter. Place a chop on each piece and surround with the rest of the elements. Put the broiled tomatoes around the edge and drape the bananas over the chops or serve separately. Pour the melted butter over it all and sprinkle well with salt and freshly ground black pepper. Serve with lemon wedges.

Mutton Chop Pie

This recipe is an adaptation of one of Martha Washington's favorites. Mutton chops are hard to come by but the lamb shoulder chops make a good substitute.

6 to 8 mutton chops or lamb
   shoulder chops, ¾ inch thick
6 to 8 medium to large potatoes
6 to 8 medium to small onions
2 cups chicken stock or water
Salt and pepper
3 tablespoons butter

Preheat the oven to 350 degrees.

Trim the chops of any excess fat and wipe them free of bone dust. Peel the potatoes and cut them in ¼-inch slices. Grease a shallow ovenproof serving dish with a little butter and spread a layer of potato in the bottom. Cover with a layer of onion slices. Sprinkle with salt and pepper and repeat the process until all the vegetables are in the pan. Add the liquid. It should come to just below the surface of the vegetables. Bring the liquid to the boiling point on top of the stove.

Meanwhile heat the butter in a skillet and quickly sear the chops on each side. Lay them on top of the vegetables, as they are seared. Season with salt and freshly ground black pepper and bake 45 minutes. Serve with apple sauce.

Shoulder Lamb Chops in Brown Sauce

Quick Brown Sauce (see Sauces)
6 to 8 shoulder lamb chops
   1 inch thick
3 tablespoons butter or margarine
Salt and pepper
Chopped parsley

Make the sauce and let it simmer. Preheat the oven to 350 degrees F. Wipe the lamb chops free of any possible bone dust. Brown them in hot butter on both sides and transfer them to a shallow baking-serving dish. Sprinkle with salt and pepper. Pour over the sauce and bake covered 40 minutes. Sprinkle with chopped parsley. Serve with Baked Potato or Old Fashioned Mashed Potatoes (see Vegetables).

Barbecued Oregonian Lamb Steaks

When many Southerners among others took refuge in Oregon in the mid-nineteenth century, they took a lot of their foods with them. That's why you see Hopping John being served along with Barbecued Lamb. The steaks are cut from the lamb leg about 1¼ inches thick.

6 to 8 lamb steaks
¼ cup red wine vinegar
½ cup salad oil
2 cloves garlic
2 teaspoons chopped tarragon
½ teaspoon rosemary
½ teaspoon salt
¼ teaspoon cracked black pepper

Wipe the lamb steaks free of bone dust with paper toweling. Place them in a shallow nonmetal dish and pour over the marinade made from the remaining ingredients. Marinate 2 to 3 hours, turning occasionally.

Start your fire in time so that the meat can be cooked over glowing coals. Count on 8 to 10 minutes per side. Lamb steaks should be dark brown on the outside but pink on the inside. Serve with Hopping John (see Rice), which should be timed to be ready when the steaks are served.

Crown Roast of Lamb

For many generations a crown roast of lamb has been a favorite for dinner parties. It is made by joining two loins into a circle and filling the center with either a meat stuffing or a vegetable as in this recipe. Allow 2 ribs to a serving when ordering. A 14- or 16-rib roast is the usual size.

1 crown roast of lamb
2 tablespoons butter
2 carrots, grated
1 large onion, grated
½ cup diced celery
1 bay leaf, crumbled
A pinch of thyme
Salt and freshly ground pepper

Preheat the oven to 325 degrees F. Cover each rib end with foil to keep it from charring. Heat the butter in the roasting pan and sauté the vegetables until soft. Add the herbs and make a flat mound of the mixture in the center of the pan. Place the roast on the vegetables. Sprinkle with salt and pepper and roast allowing 2 to 2¼ hours. The meat should register 170 or 180 degrees F, preferably the former, on the meat thermometer.

Transfer the roast to a warm round platter. Pour off all but 2 tablespoons of the fat from the pan and put the vegetables in a blender. Add 1 cup of cold water to the pan and scrape up the juices with a fork, stirring until the resulting gravy boils. Add this to the blender and spin just until blended. Season with salt and pepper and serve in a separate gravy dish. Remove the foil from the rib ends and replace with paper frills (bought or homemade) or with a pitted olive speared with a sprig of parsley. Fill the center with mashed potatoes, Saffron Rice (see Rice), Brussels Sprouts and Chestnuts (see Vegetables) or green peas. Garnish with a wreath of watercress or parsley.

Prairie Kidney Stew

When kidney stew was made on the prairie there wasn't any commercial sour cream but what's wrong with progress, especially that kind.

2 pounds baby beef kidneys
2 cups milk
1 teaspoon salt
Flour
¼ teaspoon pepper
4 tablespoons butter
4 tablespoons oil
1 large onion, chopped fine
2 cloves garlic, minced
1 bay leaf
2 teaspoons prepared French mustard
1 cup dry red wine
2 cups beef stock or bouillon
1 pint warmed sour cream
1 tablespoon chopped parsley

Remove the filament and core from the kidneys and place in a bowl with the milk for 1 hour. Discard the milk and pat the kidneys dry. Cut in bite-size cubes and place them in a bowl. Dredge with flour, salt and pepper, tossing them to be sure they are well coated.

Heat the oil in a skillet and brown the kidneys on all sides. Remove from the heat and transfer the kidneys to a deep casserole. Add the onion and garlic to the skillet and sauté until soft and tender. Do not brown. Add the mustard, wine and bouillon to the skillet and stir well to catch any juices adhering to the pan. Pour the contents of the skillet into the casserole. Add the bay leaf. Cover and simmer for 25 to 30 minutes either on top of the stove or in a 300-degree oven. Remove the cover and stir in the heated sour cream. Taste for seasoning. Sprinkle with chopped parsley and serve with potatoes.

Twice Baked Meat Loaf

This old-fashioned meat loaf can be prebaked a day in advance and easily rebaked at the appropriate time. It freezes well.

1 pound ground chuck beef
1 pound ground veal
1 pound lean sausage meat
1½ cups soft bread crumbs
½ cup grated onion
1 large clove garlic, pressed
2 teaspoons Dijon mustard
2 eggs, slightly beaten
1½ cups tomato juice
1 teaspoon marjoram
Flour
Salt
Pepper
Bacon fat
2 teaspoons tomato paste

Preheat the oven to 400 degrees F. Combine the meats, bread crumbs, onion, garlic, mustard, eggs, tomato juice, marjoram, 2 teaspoons of salt and ½ teaspoon of black pepper. Mix *thoroughly* with an electric mixer or with your hands. Shape into a long loaf or into 2 smaller loaves. Spread the bottom of either a French loaf tin or 2 regular bread loaf tins with 1/8 inch of bacon fat.

Combine ¼ cup of flour with a teaspoon of salt and a tablespoon of dry mustard. Dust the loaf or loaves with this mixture and place in the pan. Bake 20 minutes. Reduce the heat to 350 degrees. Bake 1 hour longer. Remove from the stove and immediately pour off all the juices into a bowl. Cool and chill so that the fat rises to the top. Cool and refrigerate the meat loaf.

Preheat the oven to 350 degrees F. When it is time for the second baking, heat 4 tablespoons of the fat and stir in 4 tablespoons of flour. When blended, add 3 cups of bouillon or water including the fat-free meat juices. Add the tomato paste and stir until the gravy boils. Pour the mixture over the loaf and bake 45 minutes. Turn onto a warm serving platter.

Plymouth Succotash

Succotash means corn and lima beans to most people, but the Pilgrims had a different idea. It could be a pot stew that included meat, poultry and vegetables and served a lot of people. Except for soaking the beans overnight, the system was to count back 4 hours from dinner time and start the cooking. This will feed 16 people.

1 quart dried lima beans
6 quarts hulled white corn*
6 to 8 pounds corned beef
1 pound streaky salt pork
4- to 6-pound roasting chicken
6 white turnips
10 medium to large potatoes

*Hulled corn which was boiled in lye and considered quite a delicacy is not available everywhere. Two No. 2 cans or their equivalent of white kernel corn make an acceptable substitute.

Soak the lima beans overnight. Change the water and cover with fresh water. Cook uncovered until soft and mash enough of the beans to absorb the water. Set aside.

Four hours before dinner, wash the beef and salt pork in water to remove excess brine and salt. Put in a large kettle of cold water and bring to a boil, removing the scum that floats to the surface. Two hours before serving put the corn and 4 cups of the meat liquor into the bean kettle. Put in a little piece of the salt pork. The beans and corn should be covered with liquid. Simmer slowly. Don't let them get too dry. Add more broth if necessary. About 1¼ hours before serving, put the chicken trussed as though for roasting in the meat kettle.

Forty-five minutes before serving add the turnips, pared and cut in thick slices, and the potatoes, peeled and quartered.

This is presented ritually with the beef and salt pork on one platter, the chicken on another, the turnips in one vegetable dish, the potatoes in another and the corn and beans, which should be mashed to the consistency of a very thick soup, in a tureen.

Meat

Cornish Pasties

These delicious morsels which hail first from England can be eaten hot or cold.

Unsweetened Pastry
¾ cup cold butter
6 tablespoons cold vegetable
   shortening
3 cups bread flour
½ teaspoon salt
1/3 cup ice water (more or less)

Meat Filling:
3 lamb kidneys
½ pound fat-free steak
2 medium-size potatoes
1 onion
1 carrot
1 clove garlic
2 tablespoons chopped parsley
¾ teaspoon salt
¼ teaspoon nutmeg
¼ teaspoon black pepper
1 egg, slightly beaten

Cut the fat into the flour with a pastry blender or 2 knives or an electric beater until the mixture is blended and forms lumps the size of peas. Rub the mixture between your fingers until you have a fine grained texture. Add just enough ice water to make it stick together and quickly knead it into a smooth and shiny ball. Speed is important. Cover and refrigerate for 60 minutes before rolling out.

Halve the kidneys and remove the film and fatty core. Dice the kidneys and steak very fine. Peel and chop the vegetables equally fine. Mix well in a bowl with parsley and spices.

Preheat oven to 375 degrees F. Roll out the Unsweetened Pastry to a thickness of 1/8 inch and cut into 3-inch rounds with a cookie cutter. Put a spoonful of the meat mixture in the center of the rounds. Paint the edges lightly with water. Cover with the remaining rounds, pinching the edges together very firmly. Prick well with a fork. Place on a baking sheet and paint with the egg. Bake 30 minutes. This makes 2 dozen pasties.

Sweetbreads and Oysters in Patty Shells

This is the type of dish that used to serve as a separate course for state dinners or as an entree for a gentlewoman's luncheon. It gives the modern cook a delicious dish that can be prepared in advance and served when convenient.

2 pairs of sweetbreads
Salt and pepper
1 teaspoon vinegar
1 pint oysters
2 slices boiled ham,
   ¾ inch thick
4 tablespoons butter
5 tablespoons flour
2 cups chicken stock
   (fresh or canned)
½ pint all-purpose cream
3 tablespoons sherry
1 teaspoon lemon juice
6 to 8 store-bought patty shells

Sweetbreads are very fragile and should be precooked the day they are bought. Soak the sweetbreads in cold water. If frozen, let them thaw in the water. Change the water several times as the blood comes out. At the end of an hour put the sweetbreads in a pan and cover with water. Add ½ teaspoon of salt and a teaspoon of vinegar. Bring to a boil and simmer gently 15 minutes. Drain and plunge again into cold water. Carefully remove the tubes and membranes. Cut the meat into bite-size pieces.

Drain the oysters saving the oyster liquor. Be sure there are no pieces of shell. Cube the ham. Place them and the sweetbread pieces in the top of a double boiler or chafing dish. (The addition of sliced water chestnuts is delicious, if not traditional.)

Heat the butter in a saucepan and stir in the flour. Cook for 2 to 3 minutes without browning. Add the chicken broth and oyster liquor and stir until smooth. Add the cream and the sherry. When well blended pour over the sweetbread mixture and cook over simmering water for 30 minutes. Season with salt, white pepper and lemon juice. Serve in a chafing dish with a side dish of warm patty shells.

Vermont Red Flannel Hash

4 beets (boiled or canned)
3 large cold boiled potatoes
1½ pounds lean ground chuck beef
8 tablespoons butter, margarine
  or bacon drippings
1 large onion, chopped
½ cup of cream or rich milk
6 to 8 eggs (optional)

Dice the beets and potatoes and mix well with the meat. Heat 4 tablespoons of the fat in a large heavy skillet. Fry the onion over low heat until soft and yellow. Add the meat mixture and stir well to incorporate the onion. Flatten the hash down smooth with the back of a large spoon. Turn up the heat to medium. Pour the cream over the surface and dot with the remaining butter. If you want a heavy crust do not stir the hash. Cook uncovered for 20 minutes and then cover for the remaining 20 minutes.

If hash isn't hash without eggs, make little nests in the surface of the hash with the back of the spoon. Break an egg into each hollow. Sprinkle each one with salt, pepper and a little paprika and cook for the final 15 to 20 minutes of covered cooking. Serve from the skillet.

Liver and Bacon

1½ to 2 pounds liver
6 to 8 slices bacon
¼ cup flour
½ teaspoon salt
1/8 teaspoon pepper
Butter
Buttered toast

Allow ¼ pound of liver per serving. If possible buy liver ½ inch thick. Thin pieces are apt to dry. Remove any filament or cords with a sharp knife. Mix the flour, salt and pepper and spread it on a plate.

Pan-fry or broil the bacon until crisp. Drain the bacon on paper toweling.

Dredge with flour and pan-fry the liver in some of the bacon fat, allowing 2 to 2½ minutes on each side,

depending on the thickness. The meat should be pink and moist though thoroughly cooked in the inside. Use 2 skillets or fry in shifts, keeping the liver in a warm place.

Broil the liver, allowing 2½ to 3 minutes on each side.

To serve: Present each serving on a piece of buttered toast. Sprinkle with salt and pepper, top with a dab of butter and a slice of bacon.

Boston Boiled Tripe

2 pounds fresh tripe
1 cup white wine
Water
6 peppercorns
1 bay leaf
2 sprigs thyme
1 onion stuck with 3 cloves
1 cup melted butter
1½ cups fine cracker crumbs
1 tablespoon chopped parsley
1 tablespoon chopped chives
1 tin anchovy fillets
4 sprigs parsley

Wash the tripe carefully under cool running water. Place it in a wide pan. Add wine and enough water to cover by 1 inch. Add the peppercorns, the herbs, tied in a bouquet, and the onion. Cover and simmer 3 hours or until tender. Cool in the broth overnight or for several hours. Cut the tripe into appropriate serving pieces with a kitchen scissors. Pat the pieces dry with toweling.

Preheat the broiler and grill. Dip each piece of tripe into melted butter and coat well with the crumbs. Place on the hot grill and broil 3 inches from the heat until golden brown. Turn with a spatula and brown the pieces on the other side. Transfer to a hot platter and sprinkle each piece with the remaining butter, reheated, and a mixture of chopped parsley and chives. Crisscross with anchovy fillets. Serve with Boiled Potatoes and Sautéed Eggplant (see Vegetables).

Roast Chicken

A 5-pound roaster will serve only 6 people well, so that a 6- to 8-pound capon is a better buy if you are feeding 8 people. Both are treated in exactly the same way. If the bird is the frozen variety, be sure to thaw it. Chicken should be at room temperature before it is roasted.

5-pound roaster or a
  6- to 8-pound capon

Giblets: Put the giblets, neck and wing tips in a saucepan or pressure cooker. Add a small onion, a few celery leaves, a small bay leaf and a little salt. Add 3½ cups of water and cook to make a broth. Simmer at least 1 hour, or 20 minutes in a pressure cooker.

Stuffing:
6 tablespoons butter
5 cups diced day-old white bread
1 cup chopped celery
1 teaspoon salt
¼ teaspoon white pepper
1 cup water chestnuts

Sauté the diced bread in the butter until lightly browned. This makes a drier dressing. Remove from the heat and add the other ingredients. Put the stuffing in the bird and sew up the cavities with needle and kitchen string or close the opening with small skewers and lacing. Fold the neck skin over and fasten with a skewer. Do not pack too much stuffing into the cavity. It swells in cooking. Unless you have bought a pretrussed frozen bird, bind the wings to the body with kitchen twine. Bind the drumsticks to the body, tying them to the tail. Preheat the oven to 300 degrees F.

To Roast: rub the skin with butter. Roast 30 minutes, basting every 10 minutes. Cover loosely with aluminum foil and roast without basting. Allow 30 to 35 minutes per pound. Remove the foil and put the liver in the pan for the last half hour of roasting. Sprinkle with salt and baste every 10 minutes. Transfer the chicken to a warm platter.

The Gravy: Pour off all but 6 tablespoons of fat. Stir in 6 tablespoons of flour and stir with a heavy fork until all the juices have been incorporated and the flour is light brown. Add 3 cups of giblet broth, supplementing it with water or chicken stock if you do not have enough broth. Stir until the gravy is smooth, using a small flat whisk. Add the chopped giblets if desired, and for extra goodness add ½ pint of all-purpose cream. Whisk until smooth. Pour into a warm gravy bowl.

"Eggs are up. Pork is up. Butter is up."

Chicken Fricassee

Chicken Fricassee used to be made with the tired old hen who could produce no more eggs and was condemned to be boiled for Sunday noon dinner. The sauce was thickened with flour and water, and more often than not it was boarding house fare at its best. Today's chicken fricassee is a far cry from its ancestor. Make it a day in advance and let it mellow.

2 frying chickens, each
　cut in 6 pieces
Flour
8 tablespoons butter
1 bay leaf
2 sprigs thyme or ¼ teaspoon
　powdered thyme
Celery leaves
1 onion, sliced
1 small carrot, sliced
2 chicken bouillon cubes
6 tablespoons flour
½ pint cream
2 egg yolks
1 teaspoon lemon juice
Salt and pepper

Dip the chicken pieces in a little flour. Heat the butter in a skillet and brown the pieces on all sides. As they are browned place them in a deep pan. Add the herbs and leaves tied in a little bouquet, the onion and the carrot. Add 1 quart of boiling water in which 2 chicken bouillon cubes have been dissolved. Cover and cook 45 minutes or until tender. Remove the chicken. Strain the broth. Boil down until it measures 3 cups. Heat the remaining 4 tablespoons of butter and stir in the flour. Cook a moment or two without browning. Add the broth and whisk until smooth and slightly thickened. Taste for seasoning. Add the chicken and let the fricassee stand overnight in a cool place. Reheat over boiling water. Combine the egg yolks and cream. Pour very gradually into the fricassee, stirring constantly until sauce thickens. Add the lemon juice and taste again for seasoning. Serve in a deep bowl, generously sprinkled with chopped parsley. Serve with mashed potatoes, rice or Spoon Bread (see Breads) and carrots.

Maryland Fried Chicken

There are countless recipes for frying chicken, Maryland style. This is a composite which is delectable if not slimming.

3 or 4 small broiling chickens,
　split and severed
1 quart milk
1½ cups flour
1 teaspoon salt
1/8 teaspoon white pepper
1/8 teaspoon cayenne
2 eggs
Cream Sauce (see Sauces)
Corn Fritters (see Vegetables)
6 to 8 strips bacon

Place the chicken halves in a shallow dish containing the milk and soak for 30 minutes or more. Combine the flour and seasoning and spread on a small platter. Beat the eggs with 4 tablespoons of water and put in a small bowl.

Heat 1½ inches of salad or vegetable oil in one very large or two medium-size skillets. The fat should register 350 degrees F.

Dip the chicken halves into the flour, coating each piece evenly, then into the beaten egg and then lightly into the flour again. When all the pieces are coated place them in the hot fat and fry them 10 minutes on each side. Scald 1 cup of the milk in which the chicken was soaking.

Preheat the oven to 300 degrees F. Put the chicken in a single layer in a preheated roasting pan and continue cooking for 30 minutes or until very tender and crisp. Make the cream sauce using 1 cup of the chicken milk and 1 cup of full-strength chicken stock or broth. Season well and keep warm. Prepare the corn fritters and fry rather small ones in the fat left from the chicken. Broil or fry the bacon separately and drain well.

Serve the chicken on a heated platter. Cover with the sauce. Garnish with the fritters and the bacon.

Squab on Croutons

Squab is a delicacy now as it was when it was favorite presidential fare in the early days of our country. The more common Cornish hen makes a convenient substitute.

6 to 8 squabs, dressed
Butter
½ cup chopped celery
½ cup grated carrot
½ cup grated onion
½ cup diced cooked ham
5 tablespoons Madeira wine
6 to 8 slices white bread,
   ½ inch thick
Salt, pepper and nutmeg

Remove the gizzards and liver from the squabs. Bind the legs and wings to the bodies of the birds with kitchen twine. Heat 3 tablespoons of butter in a large skillet. Brown the birds on all sides, turning them carefully. Try not to pierce the skin. At the same time, heat 2 tablespoons of butter in a smaller skillet and sauté the vegetables and ham, just until the vegetables are soft. Spread in a deep large casserole wide enough to accommodate the squab. Sprinkle with salt and pepper. Place the browned birds on the vegetable ham mixture. Sprinkle with 4 tablespoons of Madeira. Cover and bake 1 hour at 350 degrees F.

Using the large skillet in which the squabs were browned, sauté the gizzards and liver of the squab over low heat, adding more butter if necessary. As the innards become tender, crush them into the butter with a fork until you have a paste. Season with 2 tablespoons of Madeira, salt, pepper and a pinch of nutmeg. Set aside. Using the smaller skillet and more butter, fry large rounds of bread allowing 1 to a person. When browned on both sides, spread one side with the liver mixture. Keep warm.

To Serve: Place a squab on each prepared crouton. Serve garnished with parsley or watercress. Spin the vegetables and pan juices in a blender and spoon over the squab. Serve with Wild Grape Jelly (see Sauces).

Carolina Roast Chickens with Walnut Stuffing

The secret of a perfectly roasted small chicken is basting.

2 (4- to 4½-pound) chickens
Butter
½ cup diced celery
¼ cup minced onion
16 slices day-old bread
1 teaspoon poultry seasoning
1 tablespoon chopped parsley
1 cup boiling water
1 cup chopped walnuts
2 cups chicken giblet broth
Salt and pepper

Make a broth from the giblets. See Roast Chicken. Wash the chickens inside and out and dry them well. Heat 4 tablespoons of the butter in a small pan and gently cook the celery and onion for 3 to 4 minutes or until just tender. Remove the crusts from the bread and break it into small crumbs. If the bread is too moist, dry it in the oven for 10 to 15 minutes. Combine the bread, onion mixture, poultry seasoning, parsley and chopped walnuts in a bowl. Toss well and moisten slightly with the hot water. Season highly with salt and pepper.

Preheat the oven to 450 degrees F. Divide the stuffing between the two birds. Close the opening, sewing the edges together or using small skewers and lacing them with kitchen twine. Tie the wings and the legs close to the bodies. Place the birds on a small rack in an open pan. Smear with soft butter, preferably unsalted. Roast 15 minutes and reduce the temperature to 350 degrees F. Baste frequently while cooking for 1¾ to 2 hours, depending on the size of the chickens. Sprinkle with salt and pepper after 1 hour of roasting. Transfer the chicken to a warm platter while making the gravy, which in this case is unthickened. Pour off the excess fat from the pan. Stir in the broth. Scrape all the juices from the pan and strain them into a gravy bowl. For extra richness you can heat (but not boil) ½ pint of heavy cream with the gravy. Taste for seasoning.

Farmer's Chicken Pie

4- to 5-pound chicken, cut
  in pieces
1 onion
1 carrot
1 bay leaf
Celery leaves
1 teaspoon salt
4 tablespoons butter
6 tablespoons flour
¼ teaspoon white pepper
2 cups cooked peas
2 cups boiled tiny onions
2 cups boiled carrot slices
Baking Powder Biscuits (see Breads)

Place the chicken in a kettle or deep saucepan. Add 1½ quarts of water, the onion, carrot, bay leaf and celery tied in a bouquet, salt and pepper. Bring to a boil slowly, cover and simmer for 1 hour or until the chicken is tender. Strain and save the liquor. Discard the vegetables and herbs.

When the chicken is cool enough to handle, remove the skin and bones and put them back in the kettle with the liquor. Quickly boil down until the liquid measures about 3 cups. Strain and, if necessary, add water or milk to give the required amount. Heat the butter and stir in the flour, cooking it for 2 or 3 minutes without letting it brown. Stir in half the liquor and stir with a whisk until smooth and thick. Add the rest of the liquor and stir until blended. Cut the chicken into fairly large pieces and add the peas, the onions and the boiled carrots cut in inch-thick slices. Put the mixture into a large shallow baking-serving dish. Cool.

Preheat the oven to 425 degrees F. Make the Baking Powder Biscuits and cut them into 2½-inch rounds. Place them closely together over the surface of the chicken mixture. Brush with melted butter and bake for 20 minutes or until golden brown. Packaged baking powder biscuits may be substituted.

Pour the sauce over the chicken. Sprinkle with the cheese and cover with 6 to 8 very thin slices of lemon. Broil until golden brown.

Garnish the edge of the platter with orange slices and sprigs of parsley.

Florida Chicken

2 (3½-pound) chickens, quartered
Butter or margarine
Salt and pepper
1 orange
2 lemons
1 cup dry white wine
½ cup Madeira
1 pint cream
1 cup grated mild cheddar cheese
Parsley

Preheat the oven to 350 degrees F. Brown the chicken in the fat using a heavy skillet. When well browned on both sides, transfer to a covered oven dish. Sprinkle with salt and pepper, cover and bake for 45 minutes.

Put 4 more tablespoons of butter or margarine in the skillet. Add 1 tablespoon of grated orange rind, 2 teaspoons of grated lemon rind, 3 tablespoons of lemon juice, the white wine and Madeira and simmer very gently for 10 minutes with a cover on the skillet. Set aside. Slice the orange and 1 lemon very thin.

Transfer baked chicken to heatproof platter, and stir cream and juices from casserole into sauce. Preheat the broiler. Pour sauce over chicken. Top with cheese and slices of lemon. Broil until golden brown. Garnish with orange slices and parsley.

Chicken Hash

Chicken hash is supposed to have been a favorite of Andrew Jackson's and is still popular in Washington with those who believe in a hearty breakfast. Save leftover roast chicken or turkey and gravy for this dish.

3 or 4 cups finely cubed
  cooked chicken
Butter
Gravy
All-purpose cream
1/8 teaspoon nutmeg
6 to 8 slices bacon
Salt and pepper

Combine the chicken with all available gravy supplemented with cream. You need 1 cup in all. Add the nutmeg, parsley and salt and pepper to taste. Butter a serving skillet or other pan generously and heat the pan well. Add the chicken mixture and pat it smooth. Cook for 3 or 4 minutes over high heat. Reduce the heat and cover. Simmer 10 to 15 minutes or until thoroughly heated. Turn onto a warm platter.

Meanwhile fry the bacon, allowing 1 piece to a serving. Lay the bacon over the hash and serve.

Chicken Salad

2 or 3 cups cold cubed chicken
2 cups chopped celery
1 cup diced water chestnuts
1 tablespoon onion juice
½ cup French Dressing
1½ cups mayonnaise
1 can pimiento
1 can anchovies
2 tablespoons chopped parsley
Lettuce leaves

Combine the chicken, celery, water chestnuts and onion juice with plain French dressing. Let stand in the refrigerator for an hour or more. Fold in 1 cup of mayonnaise and shape the mixture on a serving platter.

Using a small spatula, "frost" the salad with the rest of the mayonnaise and decorate with alternate strips of pimiento and anchovies. Sprinkle with chopped parsley and surround with crisp leaves of garden lettuce. Serve with Muffins or Popovers (See Breads).

San Francisco Chicken Breasts

3 or 4 chicken breasts, boned and skinned
¾ cup dry bread crumbs
¾ cup grated Parmesan cheese
3 tablespoons finely chopped parsley
2 teaspoons salt
¼ teaspoon white pepper
12 tablespoons butter or margarine
1 clove garlic
2 lemons
Paprika

Preheat the oven to 350 degrees F. Split each chicken breast and pepper well.

Blend the bread crumbs, cheese, parsley, salt with a fork. Melt the butter and press the garlic into it. Simmer gently for 3 minutes. Dip each piece of chicken into the butter and then into the bread crumb mixture. Roll each piece up tightly and fasten it with a toothpick or small skewer. Place in a buttered baking-serving dish. Sprinkle the chicken liberally with lemon juice, the remaining butter and a dash of paprika.

Bake 1 hour, basting twice. Serve with Baked Rice and Water Chestnuts (see Rice) which can be baked in the same oven.

Cover painting, THE SATURDAY EVENING POST, *December 10, 1932.*

American Roast Turkey with Oyster Stuffing

12- to 14-pound turkey

Stuffing:
1 cup chopped celery
1 cup chopped onion
8 tablespoons butter
8 cups day-old soft bread crumbs
½ teaspoon powdered sage
½ teaspoon powdered thyme
½ teaspoon nutmeg
3 tablespoons chopped parsley
2 teaspoons salt
¼ teaspoon pepper
2 eggs, slightly beaten
1 pint oysters
1 teaspoon lemon juice

Gravy:
¾ cup fat
¾ cup flour
6 cups liquid
Parsley

If possible, buy a fresh turkey. If you are using the frozen variety thaw it completely before stuffing. Wipe the bird inside and out with a damp towel. Cut the neck off as close to the body as possible without cutting the skin. Cut off the wing tips. Rub a little salt and pepper into both the neck and body cavities. Keep the turkey in a cool place while preparing the stuffing.

Stuffing: Cook the chopped celery and onion in butter just until tender. Combine all the ingredients for the stuffing in a large bowl and toss well with a salad fork and spoon until thoroughly blended. The oysters should be left whole if very small, otherwise cut them in large pieces. Add any oyster liquor to the stuffing. Cool the stuffing before packing it loosely into the turkey cavities. Close both openings by sewing them up with kitchen thread or inserting small skewers and lacing the openings.

The Giblets: Place the wing tips, neck, heart and gizzard in 3 cups of water. Add ½ teaspoon salt, a small onion, a stalk of celery with leaves cut up, 1 small bay leaf and a small pinch of powdered thyme. Cover and simmer for 2 hours or cook in a pressure cooker for 15 to 20 minutes at 10-pound pressure.

To Truss: Cut 4 feet of kitchen twine and double it. Tie the midway point to the tail end of the turkey. Wind the twine around each wing and crisscross it across the body, drawing the wings to the sides of the bird. Bring the two pieces of twine forward to the leg tips and encircle each tip twice with the twine and draw the pieces together to bind the legs to the body. Cross the twine once more over the body, turn the bird over and tie. Remove string before serving.

Roasting: Place the turkey breast side up on a rack in a large roasting pan. Rub the entire surface with melted butter or margarine. Place the turkey in a 300-degree oven and allow 25 minutes per pound for a bird 12 pounds or less; 18 minutes per pound is sufficient for a larger bird. Baste the bird every 15 minutes for the first hour and every 30 minutes thereafter; *or,* after the first hour, cover the bird with aluminum foil or with a large piece of cheesecloth thoroughly saturated in melted butter and discontinue the basting process. There is nothing really as good as continued basting, however. Sprinkle with salt and pepper 1 hour before the end of cooking. Roast the liver for the last 45 minutes.

Gravy: Place the turkey and liver on a large platter. Pour off all the fat from the roasting pan. Measure and put back ¾ cup of the fat. Heat until it bubbles. Add the flour and stir hard, scraping the juices from the bottom of the pan. When well blended and browned, add 6 cups of liquid including the strained giblet broth. Stir until smooth and thickened. Strain into two heated gravy bowls, adding the chopped giblets to one only, since some like them and some, particularly children, don't.

To Serve: Surround the turkey with a garland of parsley and serve with pride.

Hot Turkey Salad

3 cups cooked rice
4 cups cooked turkey meat
1 cup mayonnaise
2 cups diced celery
1 cup slivered almonds or
  water chestnuts
¼ cup lemon juice
Cream Sauce (see Sauces)
1 medium onion, chopped
Salt and pepper
Potato chips

Preheat the oven to 350 degrees F. Combine all the ingredients. Season well. If you have turkey gravy or turkey broth on hand use it instead of some of the milk in the cream sauce. Place in a deep buttered oven-serving dish and top with crushed potato chips. Bake 30 to 40 minutes.

Roast Duck

2 (4½- to 5-pound) ducks
2 small onions, stuck with cloves
2 small apples
1 cup chopped celery
  and leaves
2 small bay leaves
Salt and pepper
1 cup cider

Thaw the ducks completely before roasting. Wipe them well inside and out with toweling. Sprinkle the interior with salt and pepper and fill each cavity with 1 onion, stuck with a clove; an apple, cored but not peeled; ½ cup chopped celery; and a small bay leaf.

Preheat the oven to 350 degrees F. Place the ducks on a small rack or 2 small trivets in a roasting pan. This makes it easier to remove the excess fat, which you do every 30 minutes, using a bulb baster. Roast the ducks 1½ hours unless you prefer duck very well done, in which case add 15 minutes. Serve with Sweet Apple Slices (see Relishes).

American Orange Duck

2 ducks
2 small oranges
1 (6-ounce) can frozen orange
  juice, thawed
½ cup brown sugar
2 tablespoons water
2 tablespoons Madeira
2 cups chicken broth
Salt and pepper
1 tablespoon cornstarch

Preheat the oven to 275 degrees F. Remove the innards from the body cavity. Wipe out the inside and sprinkle the interiors with salt and pepper. Put a small orange in each bird. Prick the birds in several places and place on a rack in an open roasting pan, breast side down. Roast for 30 minutes. Turn the ducks over and paint with the concentrated orange juice. Roast 3 hours longer, basting with the concentrate every half hour. Remove the ducks to a wire rack to cool and pour off the juices into a large measuring cup. Cool and chill.

Preheat the oven to 300 degrees F. Cut the ducks into quarters and place in the roasting pan. Combine the sugar, water and 2 tablespoons of the orange concentrate in a small saucepan. Cook until syrupy. Paint the quarters well and roast 1 hour.

Defat the gravy and mix with the Madeira, 2 more tablespoons of concentrate and the chicken broth. Bring to a boil. Thicken with the cornstarch dissolved in a little water. Bring to a boil and season with salt and pepper.

Put the duck on a warm platter and garnish with orange wedges and parsley.

Note: For extra flavor, put the innards in the chicken broth in a covered dish in the oven (no extra energy) along with the duck. Later, add water if necessary to make the required 2 cups of broth. Chop the innards and add them to the sauce.

Roast Wild Duck with Sauerkraut

Wild Duck is not as easy to come by as it was in times gone by, but for those who can have it, here is an old recipe in modern dress. Wild duck is apt to be a little strong in flavor, but here is an easy way to overcome that. The rule of thumb for duck is that you should allow 1 pound per person. For wild duck that may be a bit stingy.

2 or 3 wild ducks*, dressed
  and cleaned
½ cup diced celery
2 or 3 cooking apples
Salt
1½ to 2 pounds sauerkraut
Butter
2 cups dry white wine

Put ¼ cup diced celery and 1 apple, cored and sliced but not peeled, into the cavity of each duck. Sprinkle with ¼ teaspoon salt. Wrap in foil and freeze for 3 or 4 days. Remove the birds from the foil and thaw them before roasting. Discard the stuffing.

Preheat the oven to 375 degrees F. Place the ducks on a rack in an open roasting pan. Rub with a little butter and sprinkle with salt and freshly ground black pepper. Roast 50 minutes for rare duck, which is the way wild duck is supposed to be eaten, or 1 hour and 10 minutes for better done, if you prefer. Add 1 cup of wine to the pan and baste frequently during the roasting.

Meanwhile, cook homemade (see Vegetables) or storebought sauerkraut in a saucepan, to which 1 cup of white wine and enough water to cover by 1 inch have been added. Simmer as long as the duck cooks, adding more water if necessary.

Serve the ducks on a bed of well-drained sauerkraut and accompany with Steamed Potatoes (see Vegetables).

*If domestic ducks are used, stuff them as above but do not freeze or discard the stuffing. Sew up the cavity and roast, allowing 12 to 20 minutes per pound. Serve the same way.

Cold Duck Loaf

1 (4½-pound) duck
½ pound thick sliced bacon
1 large onion, finely chopped
6 tablespoons butter or margarine
½ pound chicken livers
6 juniper berries
2 cloves garlic, pressed or minced
¼ teaspoon allspice
¼ teaspoon mace
¼ teaspoon nutmeg
2 teaspoons salt
½ teaspoon black pepper
½ cup dry white wine
4 tablespoons brandy
4 tablespoons melted butter

Preheat the oven to 425 degrees F. Prick the skin of the duck in several places. Rub the interior and exterior with a little salt and pepper and place on a rack in an open roasting pan. Roast 1 hour. Cool the duck and cut off all the meat, free of skin, in small pieces. Set aside.

Simmer the bacon in boiling water for 2 minutes. Drain, pat dry and fry slowly until almost crisp. Drain on toweling.

Sauté the onion in the butter just until the onion is soft. Add the chicken livers and the duck liver and sauté briefly just until browned on all sides. Stir while browning.

Combine the remaining ingredients in a measuring cup.

Put a third of the meat and a third of the liquid mixture in the blender and spin until blended. Place the mixture in an earthenware terrine or Teflon-lined bread tin. Repeat the process twice and smooth the mixture evenly with a small spatula. Cover and chill until firm. Serve in the terrine or turn out on a platter and decorate with sprigs of parsley. Serve with crusty bread and a Green Salad (see Salads).

Roast Goose

12- to 14-pound goose

Stuffing:
5 cups soft bread crumbs
8 tablespoons butter, melted
½ cup grated onion
1 cup celery with leaves, chopped
1 cup diced tart peeled apple
1 teaspoon salt
½ teaspoon sage
¼ teaspoon nutmeg
¼ teaspoon thyme
¼ teaspoon black pepper
1 cup dry white wine

Wipe the bird inside and out, removing any yellow globules of fat. Place the fat in the top of a double boiler and let it cook over boiling water until all the liquid has been extracted. To save fuel, cook the giblets with ½ onion, a few celery leaves, a small bay leaf and a sprig of thyme in the bottom of the double boiler. Both operations take 1½ to 2 hours.

To Stuff: Break day-old bread into small crumbs in a bowl. Add the remaining ingredients and toss well. Chill in the refrigerator. Rub the inside of the bird with a little salt and put in the stuffing. Put most of the stuffing in the body cavity and the rest in the neck cavity. Sew the edges of the body opening together or use small skewers and lace them together. Fold the neck skin over the opening and fasten it with a small skewer. Tie the legs and wings to the body with kitchen twine. Tie the leg ends together. If the goose is not to be roasted until some time later, keep it wrapped in the refrigerator.

To Roast: Preheat the oven to 325 degrees F. Prick the bird around the legs and wings with a fork and place it on a rack in an open roasting pan. Rub the skin with salt and pepper. Allow 25 minutes to the pound. Remove the fat from the pan every 30 minutes with a bulb baster. Save it for future use.

The Gravy: Place the roasted goose on a heated platter and pour off all the fat from the pan except for ¼ cup. Sprinkle with 4 tablespoons of flour and stir well, scraping all the juices adhering to the pan with a fork. As soon as the flour is well mixed stir in the strained giblet broth and enough water or chicken broth to measure 2 cups. Stir until thick and smooth. Strain the gravy into a small saucepan. Add the giblets, chopped rather fine, reheat the gravy and serve in a small bowl or gravy boat.

The Liver: While the gravy is being prepared, broil or pan-broil the liver 2 to 3 minutes on each side. Spread with butter and sprinkle with salt, pepper and lemon juice. Cut into 4 pieces and serve only to those who appreciate it.

Venison Steak with Madiera

2 to 2½ pounds venison steak,
  cut 1½ inches thick
2 tablespoons flour
¼ teaspoon ginger
1/8 teaspoon thyme
1 teaspoon salt
¼ teaspoon cracked black pepper
2 tablespoons butter
2 tablespoons oil
¼ cup Madeira
½ cup currant jelly
Fresh parsley

Wipe the venison steak. Mix the flour, ginger, thyme, salt and pepper. Rub both sides of the steak with the mixture and then pound it with a potato masher to get the coating well into the meat.

Heat the butter and oil in a large skillet. Sear the steaks on both sides, turning frequently. Reduce the heat to moderately low or to 300 if you are using a temperature-controlled skillet. Cover and continue to turn the meat and cook for 15 to 18 minutes for medium rare or until done as desired. Transfer the meat to a heated platter. Add the wine and the currant jelly to the pan, stirring hard with a fork to break down the jelly and incorporate the pan juices. Pour over the steak and garnish with parsley.

German Hasenpfeffer

2 packages frozen rabbit or
   2 young rabbits or 1 hare,
   dressed and cut in pieces

Marinade:
2 cups red wine vinegar
2 cups water
½ cup salad oil
2 teaspoons salt
2 teaspoons sugar
2 teaspoons Dijon mustard
2 onions, sliced
2 cloves garlic, pressed
6 cloves
10 peppercorns
2 bay leaves

To Cook:
1 cup flour
3 tablespoons butter or margarine
3 tablespoons oil
2 cups light dry red wine

Sauce:
4 tablespoons butter or margarine
4 tablespoons flour
1 cup commercial sour cream
2 tablespoons chopped parsley

Thaw the frozen rabbit or wash and dry the young rabbit or hare pieces. Place in a large shallow non-metal bowl. Combine all the ingredients of the marinade and pour it over the meat. Marinate in a refrigerator 24 to 48 hours, turning the pieces from time to time. Remove from the marinade and dry the rabbit well. Reserve the marinade. Dip each piece lightly in flour. Heat half of the fat in a large skillet and brown the meat on both sides, transferring each piece as it is browned to a heavy pan or deep casserole. Add more fat as necessary to the skillet until all the pieces are browned. Add 1 cup of the strained marinade, the wine and 1 cup of water to the meat. Cover and simmer 45 to 60 minutes or until tender, or bake in a 325-degree oven. Transfer the rabbit pieces to a large warm platter and keep warm.

Strain the sauce into a measuring cup, adding whatever strained marinade is necessary to make 3 cups. Heat the butter and add the flour, cooking until quite brown. Stir constantly. Add the liquid and stir until smooth. Stir in the sour cream and reheat without boiling. Pour over the meat and sprinkle with chopped parsley.

Roast Rabbit with Mustard Cream

2 small rabbits, dressed and quartered
   or 2 packages frozen rabbit, thawed
6 tablespoons butter or margarine
1 jar Dijon mustard
Salt and pepper
½ pint heavy cream
Parsley

Preheat the oven to 375 degrees F. Brown the pieces of rabbit on both sides in a heavy skillet. As they are browned, transfer them to a roasting pan.

Using a small paintbrush smear each piece with a coating of mustard. Do not be afraid to paint generously. Sprinkle each piece with salt and pepper. Roast for 40 minutes.

Transfer the rabbit to a warm serving platter and garnish with sprigs of parsley.

Add the heavy cream to the pan juices and stir over direct heat until hot but not boiling. Spoon a little of the sauce over the rabbit and put the rest in a sauce bowl.

Advertisement for Universal Range, THE SATURDAY EVENING POST, *January 10, 1920*

Deer Roast

6-pound boned and rolled
leg of venison roast

Deer Marinade:
½ pint red wine vinegar
3 cups water
1 bay leaf
2 sprigs thyme or
¼ teaspoon powdered thyme
1 clove garlic, pressed
1 onion stuck with 2 cloves
1 celery stalk with leaves, cut
1 large carrot, cut in pieces
4 peppercorns
1 teaspoon salt
2 juniper berries, bruised
½ pound bacon
1 cup hard cider

Combine all the ingredients for the marinade in a deep nonmetal bowl. Put in the venison and turn it around several times. Cover and keep in a cool place for 2 or 3 days, turning occasionally. Remove from the marinade and dry well. Using a larding needle pull strips of thick cut bacon through the roast. Lacking a needle, make small cuts with a sharp knife all over the meat and insert pieces of bacon. Save a few strips for the top. Rub the surface with flour, salt and pepper. Place in a roasting pan. Cover with 2 or 3 strips of bacon. Strain half the marinade into the pan. Roast at 375 degrees F, allowing 15 minutes to the pound and basting frequently. Remove to a heated platter.

Add 1 cup of hard cider to the liquid in the pan. Bring to a boil and taste for seasoning. If too tart add a teaspoon of brown sugar. Serve with Deep Dish Sweet Potatoes (see Vegetables).

Ruffed Grouse or Pheasant

Ruffed grouse, sometimes called partridge in the North and sometimes called pheasant in the South, are best roasted. Two birds will feed 6 to 8 people sparingly. An extra is advised. Both birds have to be drawn and hung after killing for at least 48 hours. Some connoisseurs like them hung longer for a gamier flavor.

2 or 3 plump grouse or
pheasant, dressed and drawn
2 medium onions, chopped fine
½ cup celery, chopped fine
2 tart apples, peeled, cored
and chopped
4 tablespoons butter
1 tablespoon flour
1 teaspoon salt
1/8 teaspoon mace
1/8 teaspoon black pepper
1 pint cider
2 or 3 large thin slices
of salt pork

Wipe the birds inside and out and sprinkle the insides with a little salt. Cook the vegetables and apple in butter until just tender. Sprinkle with the flour and stir gently until the flour disappears. Add the seasoning and stir again. Cool the stuffing. Put some stuffing in each bird and close the opening either by sewing or with a piece of bread strategically placed. Cover each bird with a large thin piece of salt pork and tie it to the body. Place the birds on a rack in a roasting pan. Add the cider.

Roast in a 350-degree oven for 10 minutes. Baste well and cover with aluminum foil. Bake 40 minutes. Remove the foil for the last 10 minutes of cooking, basting frequently. Remove the salt pork before serving. Serve with Skillet Potatoes (see Vegetables).

Rabbit Fricassee

An ambushed rabbit saved many a pioneer from star-vation and deserves a place in this collection. Properly prepared, it is delicious and was popular with such connoisseurs as Thomas Jefferson. The modern fro-zen packaged rabbits are very satisfactory. A fresh dressed rabbit is cooked in the same way.

2 packages frozen rabbit, or 2 fresh
   rabbits, dressed and cut in pieces
1 cup flour
1 teaspoon salt
¼ teaspoon white pepper
½ cup bacon drippings
1 large onion, diced
1 cup dry white wine
3 or 4 cups chicken stock or
   bouillon
6 sprigs parsley
1 bay leaf
4 or 5 celery leaves
2 tablespoons butter
2 tablespoons flour

Thaw the frozen rabbit. Wipe the pieces with towel-ing and dip each piece into flour seasoned with salt and pepper. Heat half the bacon drippings in a skillet and brown the rabbit pieces on both sides, transfer-ring them as they are browned to a Dutch oven or heavy casserole. Add more drippings as needed. When all the pieces are browned, add the diced onion to the same skillet. Cook until soft and add the wine. Stir briskly with a fork and pour the contents of the pan over the rabbit. Add enough stock to cover the rabbit by ½ inch. Cover and cook gently on the stove or in a 300-degree oven for 1 hour or until tender. Transfer the pieces to a heated platter.

To thicken the sauce, mix the butter and flour with your fingertips until blended and drop the mix-ture into the sauce in small bits. Stir well. Taste for seasoning. Strain the sauce over the rabbit.

Broiled Quail

Quail, often called partridge in the South, require a lot of fat in cooking because they tend to be dry.

6 to 8 quail
Butter
Lemon juice
Salt and pepper
6 to 8 slices bacon
Wild Rice (see Rice)
½ cup sherry
1 cup chicken broth
1 cup heavy cream

Preheat the broiler. Split the quail down the back but do not sever. Place in a large buttered roasting pan. Dot each bird generously with butter, sprinkle with ½ teaspoon of lemon juice and a little salt and pepper. Cover with a strip of bacon and broil 30 to 35 min-utes or until tender, 6 inches away from the broiler. Turn every 10 minutes and baste with the pan juices.

At the same time prepare the wild rice. If the gib-lets are available sauté them in butter and add them coarsely chopped to the rice after it is cooked. Re-move the quail to a warm platter and keep warm. Reserve the bacon. Add the sherry and chicken broth to the pan. Stir over direct heat, scraping up the juices from the bottom of the pan. Stir until the liquid is reduced by half. Add the cream and reheat but do not boil. Season with salt and pepper. Pour the sauce over the quail and crumble the bacon over the sauce. Serve with the rice.

Small Game Birds
Woodcock, Partridges, Snipe, Quail

When the hunter comes back with his bag, suggest that he remove the breasts from his plucked catch. The rest will make a lovely soup. Allot the breast of 1 bird to each person.

Preheat the broiler and set the rack 6 inches be-low. Wrap each skinless breast in a slice of bacon and bind it with kitchen twine. Broil 10 to 20 minutes according to the size of the breasts. Prick with a fork to see if they are tender.

SOUP:
THE ALL-AMERICAN
MELTING POT

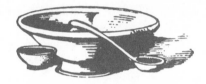

Most cookbooks start with soup, and then boil on right down through the rest of the meal. But on the theory that you will be reading this book and not eating it, we have started out with the culinary high note of our very first Thanksgiving and the fine entrees to follow as our nation developed and grew into a country of solid eaters.

But soup is a great starter, nonetheless, and so we hasten at this early point to stir the cauldron of thought and fancy it brings to mind. For example, if a man achieves his allotted threescore years and ten he is going to consume 76,650 meals of one sort or another, not counting snacks, cocktail tidbits, midnight forays to the icebox, hot dogs at ball games, which could well bring the figure up to a round 77,000. And many of these will include soups. So they might as well be a pleasure to schloop, aided by the God-given urgings of our appetite.

Some extraordinarily erudite studies have been made of man and his food. Thirty-five million years ago, it would appear, man decided to quit being an ape. The world was full of vegetation then, and from his vantage point in the trees, *Proconsul* man, getting a little tired of scuffling with the other apes over the leaves and nuts within reach on the branches he sat on, looked down on the huge prehistoric beasts of the time, munching on their greens, and in his dim mind a light dawned. Over the small brain, in a circle like in the cartoons, appeared the word "Meat." How in the world he ever managed to bring down these antediluvian monsters with hails of stones and a club or two, we can only imagine. But he did, and he chomp-

ed their flesh raw. He also ate some of his companions, when the hunting became a little too difficult, and it is quite possible that the first piece of delicious roast meat sizzled in the fire some 400,000 or 500,000 years ago when the Java or Peking man was chewing on a neighbor and carelessly dropped a piece of him into the campfire. When the French painter Gauguin lived for a time in the South Seas, he was assured by an old Samoan chief that human flesh, even that of the rather stringy missionaries, had the flavor of a nice, ripe banana. So our Peking man may well have been mighty pleased with such a pleasant new taste. A mere fifty thousand years ago, when the vegetarian planet suddenly became glaciated, man found himself rather hard put merely finding wandering beasts and neighbors to eat—they were in deep freeze, a lot of them—and he turned to eating such fruits and roots and grasses as he could find to supplement his diet. As the cold age warmed, and modern man emerged into the post-glacial period, he learned to plant his own cereals and grains, and mix them with his meats for variants in flavor.

The very first soup probably came to be when the very first pot was made out of hollowed stone, a bowl baked of clay, perhaps by accident, or metals melted and shaped to hold liquids. The word soup seems to have had a Teutonic origin. Prior to the Middle Ages, food was eaten with the hands, and, of course, no one was ever so hungry as to scoop up a handful of boiling liquid, no matter how temptingly flavored with roots, seeds, whatnot, and bits of flesh. That marvelously simple invention, the spoon, had not as yet

For
—meat—fish—eggs
—vegetable dishes
—salads—sauces—soups
—gravies—relishes—etc.
—Use it wherever you
use pepper and salt.

. . . . once you've tried the sample you'll want to buy it regularly. If your grocer doesn't have Gebhardt's Genuine Mexican Chili Powder and Gebhardt's Mexican foods in cans, ask him to stock them for you.

15c and 35c Bottles

been thought up, so it became the universal habit to dip bits of bread into steaming soupy concoctions, and thus convey the liquid, more or less drippingly, to the mouth. *Sop* or *sup* was the word coined to describe this slushing mode of eating. And so sop became *soup.* Englishmen ate soup at least once a day, as long ago as the thirteenth century. "Dried peas and bacon water" tasted good and was their idea of a feast. So were watercress, cabbage, cheese, and other basics mixed in with marjoram, sweet basil, sage, nutmeg, mace and cinnamon. Meat soups, fowl soups, fish soups, and anything an imaginative cook could dream up.

In those old days it was usually one pot, one family. In that one pot, soup was a staple of the family diet. When the cooking range was invented, a soup kettle was always simmering on the back of the stove and soup was the first course of the main meal. In elegant society terrapin, oyster or crab soup was the accepted preliminary to a sumptuous banquet, but in recent years, the first course is often eliminated and the canned-soup-for-luncheon has become an accepted fact of life. This is understandable because soup from scratch is time-consuming, but now, thanks to the invention of the blender, making good homemade soups is a matter of moments.

Americans have always had a nice tendency to an occasional serious *sup* as a changeover from the heavier roast or fry of our main meals. But 'tis always nice to buck it up with plenty of content as well.

You must know pretty well what you are about when you approach making a classic soup. Two great Americans, George Washington and Thomas Jefferson, laid down the lines of making a good soup or stew as carefully as they would have drawn up a declaration of independence or designed a cavalry charge. And still a third, although a bicentennial away, Ike Eisenhower, drew his culinary battle lines almost as clearly and in as much detail. Wrote Thomas Jefferson in his daughter's cookbook:

"Always observe to lay your meat in the bottom of the pan with a lump of butter. Cut the herbs and vegetables very fine and lay over the meat. Cover it close and set over a slow fire. This will draw the virtue out of the herbs and roots and give the soup a different flavor from what it would have from putting the water in at first. When the gravy produced from the meat is almost dried up, fill your pan with water. When your soup is done, take it up and when cool enough, skim off the grease quite clean. Put it on again to heat and then dish it up. When you make white soups, never put in the cream until you take it off the fire. Soup is better the second day in cool weather."

Here was Thomas Jefferson's Beef Soup:

1 shin bone or soup bone which still has lots of meat on it
3 tablespoons butter
4 onions
2 turnips
2 parsnips
2 celery stalks

> *The healthy stomach is nothing*
> *if not conservative. Few*
> *radicals have good digestions.*
>
> *Samuel Butler*

1 small cabbage
Any other vegetables in season
Another 3 tablespoons butter, melted
Salt and pepper to taste

Cut the meat from the bone in small pieces, and fry in 3 tablespoons butter. Stir until it is lightly browned.

Cover meat with water, adding bone, and let come to a boil. Skim any film from surface of liquid, and simmer slowly until meat is tender and falls apart, adding water if necessary.

Cut vegetables into small pieces, reserving cabbage until later, lightly heating them in the melted butter until well glazed. Cover with some of the broth from the soup, and cook slowly until thoroughly done. Season with salt and pepper to taste. Mix with meat and stock to serve. When the soup is almost finished, fry the cut-up cabbage, and place it in the pot last. Toward end of cooking add more salt and pepper if necessary. Soup is done when the cabbage is done. Serves 8 to 10.

But Dwight David Eisenhower really took over command as he approached the tactical problem of his very special vegetable soup:

"The best time to make vegetable soup is a day or so after you have had fried chicken and out of which you have saved the necks, ribs, backs, *uncooked*. (The chicken is *not* essential, but does add something.)

"Procure from the meat market a good beef soup bone—the bigger the better. It is a rather good idea to have it split down the middle so that all the marrow is exposed. I frequently buy, in addition, a couple of pounds of ordinary soup meat, either beef or mutton, or both.

"Put all this meat and the bone, early in the morning, in a big kettle. The best kind is heavy aluminum, but a good iron pot will do almost as well. Put in also the bony parts of the chicken you have saved. Cover it with water, something on the order of 5 quarts. Add a teaspoon of salt, a bit of black pepper, and, if you like, a touch of garlic (one small piece). If you don't like garlic put in an onion. Boil all this slowly all day long in the open kettle. Keep on boiling till the meat has literally dropped off the bone. If your stock boils down during the day, add enough water from time to time to keep the meat covered. When the whole thing has practically disintegrated, pour it out into another large kettle through a colander. Make sure that the marrow is out of the bones. I advise you to let this drain through the colander for quite a while as much juice will drain out of the meat. (Shake the colander well to help get out all the juice.)

"I usually save a few of the better pieces of meat to be diced and put into the soup after it is done. The rest of it can be given to your dogs or to your neighbor's dog. Put the kettle containing the stock you now have in a very cool place, outdoors in the wintertime or in the ice-

*Let onion atoms dwell within
the bowl, And, scarce suspected,
animate the whole.*

Sidney Smith

box; let it stand all night and the next day until you are ready to make your soup.

"You will find that a hard layer of fat has formed on top of the stock which can usually be lifted off since the whole kettle full of stock has jelled. Some people like a little bit of the fat left on and I know a few who like their soup very rich and do not remove more than about half of the fat.

"Put the stock back into your kettle and you are now ready to make your soup.

"In a separate pan, slowly boil in water about a third of a teacupful of barley. This should be cooked separately since it has a habit, in a soup kettle, of settling to the bottom and if your fire should happen to get too hot it is likely to burn. If you cannot get barley use rice, but it is a poor substitute.

"One of the secrets of making good vegetable soup is not to cook any of the vegetables too long. However, it is impossible to give you an exact measure of the vegetables you should put in because some people like their vegetable soup almost as thick as stew, others like it much thinner. When you use canned vegetables, put them in only a few minutes before taking the soup off the fire. If you use fresh ones, naturally they must be fully cooked in the soup.

"The things I like to put into my soup are about as follows: 1 quart canned tomatoes, ½ cup peas or cut green beans, 2 potatoes diced, 3 branches celery, 1 large sliced onion, 3 large carrots diced, 1 turnip diced, ½ cup canned corn, 1 handful raw cabbage chopped.

"Your vegetables should not all be dumped in at once. The potatoes, for example, will cook more quickly than the carrots. Your effort must be to have them all nicely cooked but not mushy, at about the same time.

"The fire must not be too hot but the soup should keep bubbling.

"When you figure the soup is about done, put in your barley which should now be fully cooked, add a tablespoonful of Kitchen Bouquet and taste for flavor. If necessary add salt and pepper and, if you have it, some onion salt, garlic salt, and celery salt.

"Cut up the few bits of meat you have saved and put about a small handful into the soup.

"While you are cooking the soup do not allow the liquid to boil down too much. Add a bit of water from time to time. If your stock was good and thick when you started, you can add more water than if it was thin when you started.

"As a final touch, in the springtime when nasturtiums are green and tender, you can take a few nasturtium stems, cut them up in small pieces, boil them separately as you did the barley, and add about one tablespoon of them to your soup."

From which it can be seen that in the matter of food preparation, soup probably provides the most stirring experience.

Cover painting, THE SATURDAY EVENING POST, *September 14, 1946.*

Montana Barley Soup

3- to 4-pound meaty soup bone
2 marrow bones
3 quarts cold water
¾ cup pearl barley
¾ cup split peas
1 large onion
2 cloves
2 stalks celery with leaves
3 carrots, scraped
6 sprigs parsley
1 bay leaf
3 tablespoons salt
¼ teaspoon white pepper

Put the bones in a large kettle and add the cold water. Bring very slowly to a boil. Simmer 1 hour, skimming off the scum that floats to the surface. Add the salt, pepper, barley, peas, and the onion, stuck with cloves. Cover and boil gently for 50 minutes. Again remove any scum from the surface.

Add the celery, carrots, parsley and bay leaf tied in a little bouquet. Continue to simmer for 2 hours. With a slotted spoon remove the bones, celery, onion, and herb bouquet. Scrape off any meat from the bones and put it back in the kettle. Cool the soup and chill overnight. Remove the fat that will coagulate on top, reheat and taste for seasoning.

Chicken Broth

4- or 5-pound chicken or fowl,
   cut up
4 tablespoons butter or margarine
1 veal knuckle
6 quarts cold water
5 teaspoons salt
2 carrots, scrubbed and cut in pieces
2 stalks celery with leaves
2 medium-sized onions, each stuck with 1 clove
8 peppercorns
1 bay leaf
2 sprigs thyme or ¼ teaspoon powdered thyme
4 sprigs parsley

Brown the chicken lightly in the butter and put the pieces into a large soup kettle. Add the veal knuckle, sawed in 3 pieces, and the water. Bring the water slowly to a boil, skimming off any scum that rises to the surface. When all the scum has disappeared add the remaining ingredients, tie the bay leaf, thyme and parsley into a small bouquet. Cover partially and cook gently for 3 hours. Turn off the heat and let the chicken cool in the broth.

Strain the soup through a fine strainer. Strain it again through a strainer lined with wet cheesecloth. Taste for seasoning. Cool and chill. Skim off all the fat that rises to the surface. *P.S. Feed the chicken to the cat.*

Breakfast Vegetable Soup

Many early farmers came into the kitchen after early-morning chores for a breakfast of vegetable soup made of anything and everything the garden had to offer. Even today it makes a nice breakfast variation, but it's good for any time of day.

1 large onion, chopped fine
2 carrots, grated
1 cup diced celery
1 green pepper, diced
1 white turnip, sliced thin
4 tablespoons butter
6 cups chicken or beef broth

Optional:
1 cup green beans
1 cup green peas
2 cups peeled and chopped tomatoes
1 cup lima beans
1 cup shredded cabbage
1 cup chopped zucchini

Prepare the onion, carrots, celery, green pepper and white turnip and cook gently in butter in a heavy kettle until tender. Add the broth. Cover and simmer for 30 minutes. Add any or all of the optional vegetables except the cabbage and zucchini and simmer 30 minutes longer. The cabbage and zucchini should be cooked only the last 15 minutes. Season well with salt and pepper. Serve with lots of buttered toast.

Portable Soup

This "soup," which appears in accounts of eighteenth- and nineteenth-century food, is a kind of old-fashioned bouillon cube but much better. It will keep indefinitely and is made without any salt. It can be the basis of soups, stews and gravies and has the nourishment to sustain a hungry traveler. Modern-day chefs use a meat glaze which is similar if not identical. A kitchen range or oil heater is ideal for this, since the long and slow cooking is a bit costly.

½ cup fat (lard, butter or margarine)
3 large onions, peeled and chopped
4 pounds beef shin
2 pounds or more veal bones
1 cup red wine
1 gallon water
2 cloves garlic, peeled
4 large carrots, sliced
4 stalks celery with leaves
   cut in pieces
8 peppercorns
3 cloves
6 sprigs parsley
1 bay leaf
2 sprigs (or ¼ teaspoon
   powdered) thyme

Heat the fat in a deep kettle and sauté the onions until soft. Put them on the side of the kettle a little off the heat while you sear the beef until brown on all sides, turning it with a large fork. Add the wine, veal bones and water, the prepared vegetables, peppercorns and the herbs tied in a bouquet. Place this over very low heat. Carefully and patiently skim off the scum that floats to the surface. When it is all cleared, add a cup of very cold water, to force more scum to the surface. Remove that. Cover and barely simmer for 6 to 7 hours.

Strain through a very fine sieve and then through a double thickness of cheesecloth. Save the meat and vegetables. They make a fine salad or the basis of a good hash. Chill the broth and remove every bit of fat that congeals at the surface. Boil the broth down until it has the consistency of syrup and measures 225 degrees F on a candy thermometer. Be careful not to let it burn. This can be stored in small steril-ized jars and covered with paraffin or it can be poured into a flat pan and allowed to jell. Cut into small squares and place them on a board in a warm room for 8 to 10 days, turning them frequently. They will dry out and become quite hard. These will keep for years in an airtight container. Allow about ½ teaspoon to a cup of water when making bouillon.

Vichyssoise
(Blender made)

Since this soup was invented in the United States, albeit by a French chef, Louis Diat, we can claim it for our own. It is certainly one of the most popular summer soups in the country wherever you go.

3 large leeks
4 green onions (scallions)
4 tablespoons butter
4 cups chicken broth
3 cups cubed potatoes
1½ teaspoons salt
¼ teaspoon white pepper
4 cups homogenized milk
1 cup heavy cream
Chopped chives

Cut off all the green from the leeks and green onions. Dice the white parts. Sauté them very gently in the butter in a deep saucepan until soft without letting them brown. Add the broth and potatoes. Cover and cook 30 minutes or until the potatoes are very soft. Place in a blender with the milk, doing this in two shifts. Reheat the soup for 10 minutes without letting it boil. Cool, add the cream and then chill thoroughly. Serve in individual soup cups with a generous garnish of chopped chives.

Bean Soup

2 cups black or pinto beans,
  cooked
1 ham or beef bone or
  chicken carcass
1 large onion
2 cloves
2 carrots
1 bay leaf
Several celery leaves
1 tablespoon cornstarch
Salt and pepper
2 to 3 tablespoons butter
Lemon
Chopped parsley

Soak the beans for several hours in cold water. Discard any imperfect beans. Drain and place in a large soup kettle with the bone or carcass and 5 quarts of water, the onion stuck with the cloves, the carrots, the bay leaf and celery leaves tied in a little bouquet. Cover and simmer for 3 to 4 hours. Remove the bones, the onions and the herb bouquet with a slotted spoon. Spin the beans, liquid and carrots in the blender in as many shifts as necessary. Add the cornstarch to the soup in the blender. Reheat the soup, stirring frequently. Taste for seasoning. Serve in individual soup plates with a little butter, a slice of lemon and a sprinkling of chopped parsley. If desired, 1 or 2 teaspoons of chili powder can be added to red pinto beans; in this case omit lemon.

Chilled Avocado Soup

2 large ripe avocados
3 cups chicken broth
1 tablespoon lemon juice
1 pint all-purpose cream
Salt and pepper
2 tablespoons chopped chives

Peel and seed the avocados. Cut in pieces and place in the blender. Add the broth and lemon juice and puree. Mix in a small tureen with the cream and season highly with salt and white pepper. Chill thoroughly before serving sprinkled with chopped chives.

West Virginia Chicken Corn Soup Parsley Butter Balls

West Virginia has always been a rugged state where food and the struggle to get it and the ability to offer it to kith, kin and stranger have been matters of prime importance. Soup for generations has been a staple of the diet and the progenitor of this recipe goes back to the early nineteenth century.

4- to 5-pound chicken,
  cut in pieces
1 large onion, peeled
  and sliced
1 large carrot, scraped
  and cut in chunks
1 bay leaf
6 sprigs parsley
Celery leaves
2 cups fresh corn kernels
Salt and pepper

Parsley Butter Balls

¼ pound butter
1 cup flour
1 tablespoon finely chopped
  parsley
¾ teaspoon salt
1/8 teaspoon white pepper
Ice water

Put the chicken in a kettle of water. Add the onion, carrot and the herbs and leaves tied in a small bouquet. Bring to a boil in a gallon of water and cook gently for 50 to 60 minutes or until the meat is falling from the bones. Meanwhile, cut the corn from 8 to 10 ears with a sharp knife and prepare the Parsley Butter Balls. Knead the butter until soft and pliable and work in the flour, parsley, salt and pepper. Add just enough ice water to make the mixture stick and quickly roll it into small balls. Keep in the refrigerator. Remove the chicken from the kettle and strain the stock. When cool enough to handle, bone and skin the chicken pieces and cut the meat into small pieces. Put the chicken and the corn into the stock and cook gently for a half hour. Add the butter balls and simmer very slowly for 10 minutes.

Cream of Corn Soup
(Blender made)

2 cups fresh cooked or canned corn
1 quart homogenized milk
1 medium onion, sliced
3 tablespoons butter
Salt and pepper
½ pint heavy cream
Popcorn
Parsley

Heat the milk with the onion for 5 minutes. Place in the blender with the corn. Puree and pour the soup into the top of a double boiler to reheat. Add the cream and season with salt and pepper. Serve hot in individual soup cups garnished with a little popcorn and chopped parsley.

Carolina Crab Bisque
(Blender made)

1 pound crab meat
2 tablespoons chopped onion
3 tablespoons butter
4 tablespoons flour
4 cups milk
½ cup sherry
1 teaspoon salt
¼ teaspoon nutmeg
¼ teaspoon good paprika
¼ teaspoon celery salt
1 pint all-purpose cream
Chopped parsley

Pick over the crab meat to be sure there are no shells. Take out 6 to 8 pieces of the leg meat for garnish.

Sauté the onion in butter in the top part of a double boiler over direct heat just until soft. Do not let the onion brown. Stir in the flour and when the flour disappears add the remaining ingredients except for the cream. Stir until smooth and slightly thickened. Blend with the crab meat in an electric blender. Cook over simmering water for 30 minutes to bring out the crab flavor. Add the cream and serve in individual soup cups with a piece of crab and a little chopped parsley for garnish.

Chicken Cream Soup
(Blender made)

1 leftover chicken carcass
1 pint all-purpose cream
1 medium-size onion
1 carrot
6 sprigs parsley
2 tablespoons blanched almonds
Salt and pepper
Chopped chives

Pick off any tidbits of chicken meat. Place the carcass, vegetables and parsley in a kettle and cover with water. Add 1 teaspoon of salt. Cover and simmer for 2 hours. Strain the broth. It should measure 1 quart. Blend the chicken meat, almonds and some of the chicken broth until smooth. Combine with the rest of the broth, and the cream. Season with salt and pepper to taste. Reheat and serve in small bouillon cups. Garnish with chopped chives.

Escarole Crab Soup

1 large head escarole
2 quarts chicken broth,
 canned or homemade
½ pound crab meat
Grated cheese
Salt and pepper

Wash the escarole in a large pan of water, cutting out the hard stems and any wilted leaves. Lift the escarole from the water into a deep kettle. Cover tightly and cook over moderate heat for 15 minutes or until tender. Lift the escarole out of the kettle into a wooden bowl and chop rather coarsely.

Heat the broth and the escarole together, adding a cupful of escarole broth. Cover and simmer very gently for 20 to 30 minutes. Just before serving add the crab meat. Season with salt and pepper.

Serve in soup plates with a side dish of grated Romano or Parmesan cheese.

Southern Chicken Gumbo

There are as many ways of cooking Chicken Gumbo as there were plantations in the sunny South. Some recipes call for shrimp, crab or ham in addition to chicken and oysters, but the essential element is the okra which provides a mucilaginous thickening that makes gumbo gumbo. The word, originally from the African Bantu language, has also been used to describe mud—but that is beside the point. The recipe given here is for a simplified version but one that is worthy of the name.

4-pound frying chicken
1 bay leaf
2 sprigs thyme
6 sprigs parsley
4 strips lean bacon
1 large onion, finely chopped
½ pod red pepper
1 pound small okra, sliced
1 pint small oysters
Salt
2 cups boiled rice

Have the fryer cut in quarters and place in a pan with the herbs tied in a bouquet. Cover with 10 cups of water and add a teaspoon of salt. Cook covered 45 minutes or until tender. Remove the chicken to a platter, and when cool enough to handle remove the skin and the meat from the bones. Put the skin and the bones back into the kettle and boil down until you have 2 quarts. Cut the bacon into small pieces and sauté them with the onion until the onion is soft. Add 1 quart of the strained chicken stock over the onion. Add the finely sliced red pepper and the okra. Simmer 30 minutes and add the rest of the strained stock and the oysters. Simmer just until the oysters' edges begin to curl. Stir in the boiled rice and season highly. Serve very hot.

Philadelphia Pepper Pot

"All hot!—All hot!—Pepper pot! Pepper pot!—Makes back strong—Makes live long—All hot!—Pepper pot!"

This is the song street vendors sang in Philadelphia all during the nineteenth century as they sold the historic soup attributed to George Washington's chef, who, confronted with starving troops and almost no rations at Valley Forge, invented this soup which retains its fame and popularity today. Allow a full day for this soup because the tripe requires lengthy cooking.

3 pounds fresh or pickled
　honeycomb tripe
1 meaty veal knuckle
6 large sprigs parsley
Several celery leaves
2 bay leaves
2 sprigs thyme
2 teaspoons salt
10 peppercorns
3 small onions
3 cloves
3 cups cubed raw potatoes
1 tablespoon cornstarch

Wash the tripe well and place it in a kettle. Cover with cold water, bring to a boil, cover and simmer, allowing 4 to 5 hours for fresh tripe and 3 hours for the pickled variety. Be sure that it is tender. Drain and cool.

Place the veal knuckle in a kettle of cold water. Bring to a boil very slowly, skimming off the scum that floats to the surface. After 15 minutes of this process add the salt. Add the parsley, celery leaves, bay leaf and thyme tied in a little bouquet. Cover and simmer for 2 hours. Remove the knuckle and add the onions. Continue to simmer for 45 minutes. Cut the tripe and the veal meat into bite-size pieces. Place them and the potatoes in the soup kettle and simmer until the potatoes are tender, or about 30 minutes. Thicken the soup with addition of the cornstarch dissolved in a little cold water. Bring to the boil again. Taste for seasoning and serve in a large tureen. If the soup seems too pale, add a little gravy caramel (Kitchen Bouquet or Gravy Master).

Virginia Peanut Soup
(Blender made)

The peanut grew as a kind of curiosity plant in Virginia and North Carolina until the time of the Civil War, when it was discovered to be so nutritious that it became commercially attractive and is now grown in great quantities. Although usually eaten as roasted peanuts or peanut butter or peanut brittle, it is also the basis of a popular soup. With a blender all the hard work is taken out of its preparation.

5 cups strong chicken broth
1 small onion, sliced
4 tablespoons peanut butter
8 tablespoons butter
3 tablespoons flour
¼ teaspoon celery salt
6 to 8 tablespoons scalded cream
Chopped parsley
Salt and pepper

Heat the chicken broth with the onion to the boiling point. Combine with the peanut butter, 5 tablespoons of the butter, the flour and celery salt and spin until well blended. Reheat in the top of a double boiler and cook over simmering water for 30 minutes. Taste for seasoning. Pour into warm soup cups and spoon a tablespoon of hot cream over the top. Garnish with a little chopped parsley.

New Orleans Onion Soup

This is a French dish that came early to New Orleans and quickly became an integral part of American cooking. Ideally it is made with homemade beef stock or poultry, but canned bouillon makes a very good substitute.

2 quarts beef or poultry stock
  (or a combination of both)
2 cups sliced onion
3 tablespoons butter
½ cup dry sherry
French bread
1 cup grated Gruyère or
  Emmenthal cheese
Salt and pepper

Heat the stock, which should be well seasoned. Sauté the onion in the butter until yellow and soft. Add the onions and butter to the stock. Add the sherry and simmer, covered, 30 minutes. Taste for seasoning.

Toast ½-inch rounds of French bread. Just before serving, preheat the broiler. Pour the soup into individual flameproof soup dishes. Top with a piece of toast and cover with the grated cheese. Broil until the cheese melts.

SOOPS.

To make Soop de Santé, the French Way.

PUT over twelve Pound of Beef, feafon'd moderately with Spices and Salt; boil it till your Broth is ftrong, ftrain it out to a good Knuckle of Veal blanch'd; then boil it up a fecond Time, putting your Pullet to it that you defign to ferve in the Middle of your Soop; let it boil till it comes to the ftrength of a Jelly; put to it in the boiling a bit of Bacon, that is not rufty, ftuck with fix Cloves. Your Broth being thus ready, at the fame Time make a Pan of good Gravy, thus. Take a Stew-pan or brafs Difh, place in the Bottom of it a Quarter of a Pound of Bacon, cut in flices, clean from Ruft, likewife the Bignefs of half an Egg of Butter; take five or fix Pounds of a Fillet of Veal, and cut it in flices, twice as thick as you do for *Scotch* Collops, and place it on your Bacon in your Stew-pan, covering all the Bottom over. If you have no Veal, ufe Buttock-Beef. Set it over a clear Fire, not very hot, and let it colour by degrees. Give it an Hour and a half to colour. When it begins to crack, put a little of the Fat of your boiling Broth to it; ftir it as little as poffible becaufe it makes it thick, and throw in three or four flic'd Onions, one Carot, two Turneps, a little Parfly, a fprig of Thyme, a little whole Pepper, and Cloves. All thefe Ingredients being fry'd together till you think it comes to a good Colour, if in Summer, a few Mufhrooms will give it a good Taft.

Maine Lobster Stew

Lobster stew, like many soups and chowders, is much better if it is given time to mellow.

Make it ahead of time, when you are planning a day's outing in the fresh air. Warm and serve, bolstered with a tossed salad, fruit and cheese, when you return with hearty appetites.

6 (1- to 1¼-pound) lobsters
8 tablespoons butter
2 quarts rich milk, scalded
1 pint cream
Salt and white pepper
Cayenne pepper

Put the lobsters in a kettle of fresh water. Cover and bring quickly to a boil. Reduce the heat and cook for about 15 minutes or until a feeler is easily detached from the body. Remove the lobsters from the kettle with heavy pincers and let them cool. Reserve the water. When the lobsters are cool enough to handle, crack the shells over the kettle to capture all the juices. Remove all the meat (not the tomalley, which can be used later as a sandwich or canapé spread). Don't forget to look for hidden nuggets in the tail and in the body. Put the shells in the kettle and boil quickly down to a quart.

Heat the butter in the top of a large double boiler and cook the lobster meat cut in small chunks until well coated, stirring frequently. Add the scalded milk and the strained lobster water. Season with salt and pepper to taste, cover and cook over simmering water for a half hour. Set aside to cool. Several hours or even a day later, reheat, adding the cream. Serve very hot with plenty of oyster crackers.

New England Fish Chowder

Fish chowder comes in various forms in different parts of the country. On the west coast there is a delicious version made with precooked abalone, then cooked in the New England manner but with the addition of white wine, which would have raised the eyebrows of the early New England housewife. In the South chowder is often made with river fish and seasoned highly. On the east coast chowder simply means salt pork, fish, onions, and milk with proper seasonings. For those living far from the ocean substitute ½ pint of bottled clam broth for the fish liquor and use 2 pounds of frozen fillets. Buy your fish from a reliable fish dealer who may give you some extra trimmings. Prepare chowder well in advance to give it time to ripen.

4 to 5 pounds haddock, cod or
   other white fish
3 tablespoons diced salt pork
1 large onion, diced
6 medium-size potatoes
1 quart milk, scalded
3 or 4 teaspoons salt
¼ teaspoon black pepper
4 tablespoons butter
Common crackers

Ask your fish dealer to fillet the fish and to give you the skin and bones. If he has a couple of extra heads or tails, take them. Put the trimmings in a quart of cold salted water. Bring them to a boil and simmer while you are preparing the rest of the chowder.

Heat the pork in a deep heavy pan over moderate heat, stirring frequently so that the pork bits will become brown on all sides. Remove them with a slotted spoon and reserve. Cook the onion in the pork fat until soft. Do not brown.

Peel and cut the potatoes into small chunks. Add them to the fat with enough boiling water to cover. Cover the pan and cook 10 minutes or until the potatoes are almost tender. Add the fish fillets cut in 1½-inch pieces and simmer 10 minutes longer. Add the strained fish liquor (2 or 3 cups) and the milk. Stir well, taste for seasoning, and set aside. Reheat in the top of a double boiler just before serving. Add the butter and pork chips and serve very hot with split, toasted and buttered common crackers.

Grand Central Oyster Stew

The first oyster stew wasn't made at the Grand Central but generations of businessmen have sat at the bar in the New York station and watched this dish being prepared on order. Here it is multiplied.

¼ pound butter
1 teaspoon Worcestershire sauce
Dash Tabasco
1 quart of oysters
1 quart milk
1 pint cream
Dash cayenne

Heat 6 tablespoons of butter in a chafing dish with strong heat or in a shallow pan on top of the stove. Add the Worcestershire and a very little Tabasco. Heat until the mixture bubbles. Add the oysters and cook gently for 4 or 5 minutes or just until the edges start to curl. Add any oyster liquor and the milk and cream. Bring just to the boiling point. Serve in hot soup plates. Add a bit of butter to each plate and dust with a little cayenne. Serve with old-fashioned oyster crackers.

Hot or Cold Boston Oyster Cream Soup
(Blender made)

1 quart oysters
1 pint water
2 teaspoons scraped onion
2 tablespoons butter
2 tablespoons flour
1/8 teaspoon celery salt
½ pint cream
Chopped parsley

Simmer the oysters and their liquor very gently with the water and the onion for 15 minutes. Place in a blender. Add the butter, flour and celery salt. Spin just until pureed. Reheat in a double boiler for 15 to 20 minutes, stirring occasionally. Add the cream just before serving and season to taste with salt and pepper. This is delicious served hot or chilled. Sprinkle with chopped parsley.

Clam Bisque

1 pint finely chopped Atlantic
  or Pacific clams
2 tablespoons finely minced celery
2 tablespoons finely minced onion
3 tablespoons butter
3 tablespoons flour
3 cups scalded milk
1 cup dry white wine
½ pint heavy cream
Salt and pepper
Chopped parsley

Freshly opened clams and their juices make this especially good, but the canned variety will do very well. Sauté the celery and onion in butter in the top of a large double boiler just over direct heat until soft. Add the flour and cook 2 to 3 minutes, stirring constantly. Add the milk and wine and cook until smooth, still stirring. Add the clams and their juice and cook over hot water for 20 to 30 minutes. Season to taste with salt and pepper. At this point, the soup can be pureed in a blender for extra smoothness. Just before serving, reheat, adding half the heavy cream. Whip the rest of the cream and season with a little salt. Serve in individual bouillon cups, with a dollop of whipped cream and a sprinkling of chopped parsley for garnish.

Scarboro Beach Clam Chowder

Split Pea Soup

This soup is universal in all but tropical climes since it is based on the dry pea, which is available the year round and almost the world round. But America has made it her own. It may be pureed and served in delicate soup cups or eaten unashamedly as a one-dish supper. Either way it is delicious. Make it a day in advance.

3 cups dried green split peas
1 ham bone with some meat on it
3 quarts boiling water
2 large carrots, cut in chunks
1 large onion
6 sprigs parsley
Several celery leaves
1 bay leaf
Salt
Freshly ground black pepper

Formerly dried peas had to be soaked overnight and carefully picked over. The modern packaged variety does not necessitate this process. Put the split peas and ham bone in a large kettle. Add the boiling water, the carrots, onions, celery and the herbs and leaves tied in a small bouquet. Bring to a boil. Cover and simmer for 3 to 4 hours. Remove the herbs, ham bone, carrots and onion and cool the soup. Chill overnight. The next day remove the fat on top of the soup. If you want an elegant soup, spin the soup in a blender and add a little heavy cream. If you prefer it hearty, leave it the way it is but add any ham left on the bone and supplement it with slices of Polish sausage or small frankfurters. Eat with dark bread and fresh butter.

Clam Chowder

Old-fashioned clam chowder is equally good made from Atlantic or Pacific clams. Whether you dig your own clams, buy them shucked or resort to the canned minced clams, you are still going to have the delicious soup that Americans have eaten for centuries.

2 dozen little necks or
  1 dozen quahogs or
  1 quart shucked clams or
  2 No. 1 cans of minced clams
3 tablespoons diced salt pork
1 large onion
2½ cups sliced potatoes
1 quart milk
½ pint cream
Salt and pepper

If you are using fresh clams in their shells, scrub them very well to remove the sand. Steam them in a cup of water in a tightly covered kettle for 8 minutes or until they are fully opened. Set aside until cool enough to handle. Open them over a bowl to catch the liquor. Strain the cooking broth through a clean dish towel to remove any sand. Chop the clams coarsely.

If you are using shucked clams, put them in a bowl with 2 cups of water and pick them over carefully to be sure there are no shells. Drain and chop the clams. Save the water.

If you are using canned clams use the entire contents of the cans.

Cook the diced salt pork in a deep heavy kettle over moderate heat until lightly browned. Stir frequently. Remove the pork with a slotted spoon and keep in reserve. Cook the minced onion in the pork fat until tender. Do not brown. Add the potatoes to the pan and cover with boiling water. Cook until the potatoes are tender. Add the milk, clams and clam liquor. Cover and simmer for 5 minutes. Add the cream and reheat but do not boil. Taste for seasoning, adding plenty of freshly ground black pepper. Add the pork bits. Serve with pilot biscuits or other common cracker.

Vermont Corn Chowder

The corn grows high in Vermont too, and this, along with all the maple products, is one of their contributions to American cooking.

½ cup salt pork, diced
1 large onion, diced
1 quart boiling water
3 cups corn kernels, cooked
   fresh or canned
5 medium-size potatoes,
   pared and cubed
1½ teaspoon salt
1 quart milk
Black pepper
Soda crackers

Cook the diced salt pork over moderate heat, stirring occasionally, so that pork pieces become brown but not too dry. Remove them from the pan with a slotted spoon. Sauté the onion in the pork fat just until tender but not brown. Add the water, corn, potatoes and salt, and cook uncovered until the potatoes are almost soft. Add the milk and simmer very gently for 10 to 15 minutes to let the flavor ripen. Taste for seasoning, adding a good bit of freshly ground pepper. Sprinkle the surface with the salt pork and serve with a large supply of soda crackers.

Old-Fashioned Potato Soup

Potato soup is the kind of thing you can prepare in a short time using staples that are usually on hand, even after a snowstorm or some other emergency prevents shopping trips. Powdered milk mixed with water will serve nicely as a substitute for whole milk and the parsley and onion can be the dehydrated flakes sold with spices.

6 to 8 white potatoes, peeled
   and sliced
3 medium-size onions, sliced
1½ teaspoons salt
6 cups milk, scalded
2 tablespoons chopped parsley
Black pepper

Put the potatoes and onion in a kettle with the salt and cover with cold water. Bring to the boiling point. Cover and cook gently for 20 minutes. Transfer to a blender and puree the vegetables or simply mash them to a pulp in the water. Add the milk and season to taste with salt and plenty of pepper. Garnish liberally with chopped parsley.

FISH:
TIPPING THE SCALES
IN OUR FLAVOR

Fish spend a lot of their time mulling over what other kinds of fish they propose to eat. We have something of the same problem, when you consider that there are about 350 varieties of edible fish finning their way through the world's waters. Although we are natural carnivores, fish make one of the most delightful dietary explorations one can imagine aside from our religious symbolism which in many homes makes the fish meal a weekly tradition.

In considering what one individual eats in a lifetime, we previously examined, in a moment of whimsy, how many meals a seventy-year-old man might be confronted with—the figure reached something like 76,650—but there is a great deal of serious truth in the matter. We do live to eat, and we are what we eat, and we might as well go about it in a knowing and enjoyable way.

For example, it has been estimated that the average seventy-year-old American who has had a job most of the time and money enough to feed himself in some decent fashion, will have consumed 1,500 times his own weight in food. Of beef, pork, sheep and fowl, he will have chewed and swallowed a quarter of a million pounds. He will have ingested 35,000 pounds of vegetables, grains and fruits, 4,000 to 6,000 eggs, 6,000 pounds of sugar, 1,000 pounds of cheese and dairy products other than milk. He will have gulped 33,000 quarts of liquids, such as milk, coffee and beer, and about 3,000 gallons of water. And chewed on about 3,000 pounds of fish, which is the subject of this chapter. Viewed as a machine fueled by the above nutrients, man comes out as a pretty low-class chemical mishmash. He has enough water inside his skin to fill a ten-gallon keg. Fat enough to manufacture seven bars of soap, barring perfume to make him olfactorily pleasant. Carbon for a few lead pencils. Magnesium for one dose of salts. Enough iron to make a small nail. Lime to whitewash a chicken coop, one coat only. Sulfur enough to rid at least one small dog of fleas. And phosphorus for 220 matches.

As fish are just full of phosphorus, think how they help us fulfill our role as perambulating matchboxes. Fish also have a good bit of iodine in them, which is a chemical helpful in preventing goiter (which explains why these ugly protuberances are more often found in inland areas than in coastal communities where fish are a natural part of diet by their proximity).

Early American accounts dating way back to the 1500's record the enormous abundance of fish and shellfish found along the eastern coast. Such abundance is what attracted the Vikings and hardy fishermen to this land long before the time of Christopher Columbus. One account claims that fish were so numerous in Plymouth Bay that a Pilgrim could walk across on their backs. The irony of this story, whether legendary or not, is that men starved to death in the midst of this nourishment because they didn't know how to catch it. By the early eighteenth century, however, fish had become an important item of the colonial diet.

Tales were told that they were so plentiful in certain water, off the Eastern Shore, for example, that it was difficult to navigate a boat through them and

Cover painting, THE SATURDAY EVENING POST, *August 20, 1955.*

that they fought to be caught. Captain John Smith, casting a line in early Jamestown, found "an abundance of fish, lying so thick with their heads above the water, as for want of nets (our barge driving amongst them) we attempted to catch them with a frying pan . . . neither better fish, more plentie; nor more varietie for small fish, had any of us ever seene in any place so swimming in the water."

He amused himself by nailing stingrays to the ground with his sword. "We tooke more in one hour than we could eate in a day," he wrote.

The Pilgrims soon learned how to fish. But then clams and lobsters were crawling all over the mudflats of those cold waters. Some of the lobsters were said to be big enough to feed four men. (One cannot resist at this point the priceless story of John Barrymore's lobster *bon mot*. The famous Shakespearean actor, a gourmet of Falstaffian appetites, had ordered a choice lobster, tucked his napkin under his chin, sampled the wine and found it good, when—to his chagrin—a lobster was delivered to him, superbly broiled and served, but bearing only one claw. Barrymore, like all the rest of us, was aware that the finest meat is to be found in the claw of the lobster. So he called for the maitre d', fixed a stern eye on him and demanded an explanation. The embarrassed captain of one of America's finest restaurants could only stammer out the excuse that lobsters being shipped alive from their native habitat sometimes managed to get rid of the wooden pegs thrust into their claws by fighting in their crates, not having much else to do with their time. Probably, that was how this lobster

lost his claw. The greatest Hamlet of all time glared at the poor restaurateur, and the voice that had stirred a thousand hearts rose to a bellow. "Take this wretched crustacean back to the kitchen," he intoned sepulchrally, "and bring me back the winner!")

Moving rapidly from Barrymore to our old friend, the Indian who had befriended the Pilgrims, Squanto did far better for them than the waiter had for John. At one point, showing off a bit, he caught an armful of "fat and sweet" eels with his bare hands. The Pilgrims loved eels, and from then on they learned how to catch them Squanto-wise.

They found out how to catch cod, later to be called "Cape Cod turkey" and to hang in effigy in the chief legislative hall of Massachusetts beneath a golden door, as the emblem of that state's wealth.

The North Atlantic was full of herring, and in due time it became known that George Washington himself preferred herring and corn cakes to anything else for breakfast. There was salmon on the East Coast in those early days, unspoiled as yet by pollution and dams, and free to swim up the rivers for their seasonal spawning, as they still do from our own Pacific Ocean waters. The early Americans learned from the Indians how to salt and cure salmon for winter use.

Besides the eels, there were oysters and clams. The settlers of Virginia and Maryland were gifted with the finest oyster beds in the world. Some say there would even be shooting wars over the rights to exploit those beds. But in the beginning there was plenty for all. Oyster roasts, oysters and nothing else, were considered great occasions in early America—the bivalves

*The discovery of a new dish
does more for the happiness
of mankind than the discovery
of a star.*

Brillat Savarin

being consumed raw, steamed, stewed, broiled, devil-ed, scalloped, pickled, and rendered into pies, omelets and fritters. Some of those oysters, according to contemporary accounts, measured over six inches across, each a meal in itself.

There is some thought given today to the dangers of eating any oysters, from any source, in the raw state, so wretchedly have we treated this marvelous bounty of our country with unthinking pollution close to their beds. But be that as it may, and the threat of hepatitis is no meager one, the oyster has had its day in American gastronomy as the very signal creature of the gourmand. Diamond Jim Brady thought nothing of polishing off a few dozen before eating a gigantic meal composed of nine or ten other courses. But even he would have quailed, if you will forgive the pun, over the experience related—we cannot resist telling here in all its full bivalve glory—by our eminent Jean-Anthelme Brillat-Savarin.

"In 1798 I was at Versailles as an emissary of the Directory, and had frequent dealings with the Sieur Laporte, who was secretary to the tribunal of the department; he was a great amateur of oysters, and used to complain of never having eaten his fill of them.

"I made up my mind to procure him full satisfaction at last, and to that end invited him to dinner.

"He came; I kept him company to the end of the third dozen, after which I let him go on alone. He went as far as thirty-two dozen, taking more than an hour over the business, for the servant was a little slow in opening them.

"Meanwhile I was inactive, and as that is an intolerable condition to be in at table, I stopped my guest when he was still in full career. 'My friend,' I said, 'it is not your fate to eat your fill of oysters today; let us dine.'

"We dined; and he acquitted himself with the vigor and address of a man who had been fasting."

That, dear friends, is probably the world's greatest tribute to the succulence of the oyster.

Of course there were trout in every stream and lake (one French traveler reported his catch "as big as one's thigh"), sunfish, perch, pike, pickerel, and, in southern waters, catfish bigger than hunting dogs. Striped bass and bluefish in eastern waters. The 5,000 lakes of Michigan fed many a trapper on his way to broaden the boundaries of the nation—yellow perch, crappie, bluegill, smallmouthed bass, and later on the little smelt, which was brought from Maine as an appetizing bite for the salmon, and introduced to the Great Lakes water. The Hudson River was famous for its shad and—believe it or not—its sturgeon. In the nineteenth century, some of the finest caviar to be found anywhere came from up around Newburgh, New York, where they caught the sturgeon, monster explorers from the Atlantic, swimming up the broad river which is salty at its mouth and halfway up to Albany. (Good news, by the way: New York is making progress, even though slow, in cleaning up the Hudson, and sturgeon are to be seen today, frolicking in the shadow of the tremendous bridge spanning the river at Tarrytown. For that matter, one misty evening musing on a Hudson dockside in Albany, we saw a seal, an adventurer a far cry from his home in northern ocean waters.) The trout of New England's lakes, their flesh firm and tasty in the cold waters, are among the nation's best.

Flounder and whitefish and drum abound in southern waters. And never pass by Florida's marvelous shrimp, where each mother *macruran caridea* takes an annual trip to the dry Tortugas, descends to the depth of 120 feet and deposits a half million babies, after which she blithely returns to Florida, her job of propagation well done.

One cannot think of fish, of course, without thinking of New Orleans. It was there that the great British novelist William Makepeace Thackeray immortalized a classic fish dish with his "Ballad of Bouillabaisse":

"This Bouillabaisse a noble dish is—
A sort of soup, or broth or brew,
Or hotchpotch of all sorts of fishes . . . "

Hotchpotch indeed. One New Orleans recipe called for eels, striped bass, haddock, whiting, red snapper, sole, flounder, halibut, lobsters, mussels, and clams as the fish ingredients of a bouillabaisse. Of course, bouillabaisse was originally a French dish, supposedly deriving its name from instructions shouted by a French chef to some muddlehead on how to prepare a wonderful fish stew. His words were reported to have been: *"Quand ça commence à bouiller, BAISSE!"* "When it starts to boil, STOP!" Whatever the truth of that little tale, Thackeray made no bones about his gustatory delights in our American version: "In New Orleans you can eat a bouillabaisse the like of which you have never eaten in Marseilles or Paris."

Lake Michigan's great coho deserves a sterling mention in any book of American fish cookery. Once a native of the Pacific Northwest, the coho was introduced in Michigan in 1966, and is a protected sport fish—commercial catchers keep away. Good thing, too. If you're lucky, you can catch a coho up to thirty pounds: delicious.

California's marvelous fisheries bring us largely ocean fare—albacore and bluefin tuna, mackerel, sole, squid, sardine, and salmon. Tuna accounts for about 50 percent of the catch. And speaking of catch, don't let us catch you passing through San Francisco without eating at one of its fantastic wharfside restaurants. It's half the fun of being on the West Coast.

A continent away, Florida's 4 million acres of water (of which 2,750,000 acres are actually inland) supply more than that maternal shrimp we were so enamored of; in fact, it has some 700 species of shellfish and fish to boast about. The largemouthed black bass is the state's foremost freshwater species, paddling along with others like bream, speckled perch, sunfish, and catfish. But the biggies are out there in the salt water, and there's no place better to see them than down at Key West, where the Ernest Hemingways of today try their best to catch them bigger and bigger—bluefish, pompano, flounder, mackerel, mullet, trout, redfish, snapper, grouper, snook, sailfish, tarpon, shad, weakfish, bonefish, marlin, swordfish and shark.

Really try some of these fish recipes: we promise you'll be hooked. As the French never really did say, one man's meat is another man's *poisson.*

Cover painting, THE SATURDAY EVENING POST, *May 19, 1951.*

Alabama Deep-Fried Catfish

The American catfish has a number of species and abounds in inland waters, particularly in the South. It seems to have withstood the ravages of man better than most fish, but because it is seldom seen in coastal markets it is not as universally appreciated as it should be. Catfish can be poached, panfried or sautéed, but frying them in deep fat seems to give them the true Southern sweet flavor.

6 to 8 (1-pound) catfish, dressed
Salt
Flour
2 or 3 eggs
1 tablespoon water
Cornmeal
Tartar sauce or
  catsup
Lemon wedges

Ask the fish dealer to remove the skins from the fish. If this is not possible make a little slit just below the head and strip the skin off with a pair of pliers. Cut off the heads.

Sprinkle each fish with salt. Spread the flour on a plate. Beat the egg with the water until blended and put in a soup plate. Spread the cornmeal on a plate.

Dip each fish lightly into flour, then into the egg mixture and then into the cornmeal. Let the fish stand in the refrigerator until just before serving. Deep-fry at 370 degrees F for 5 minutes, frying no more than 4 at a time. Drain on paper toweling and serve with tartar sauce or catsup or lemon wedges.

Baked Stuffed Bass

Bass comes in all sizes and under a variety of names depending on where in the country you are fishing or buying the fish. This is a good and easy way to serve fish to 6 or 8 people. Other fish such as haddock or bluefish can be prepared in the same way.

4½- to 5-pound bass, dressed
Butter or margarine
½ cup chopped celery
1 tablespoon grated onion
1 tablespoon finely chopped green pepper
1 tablespoon chopped parsley
1 cup soft bread crumbs
¼ teaspoon powdered thyme
¼ teaspoon basil
1 teaspoon lemon juice
Salt and pepper
Lemon wedges and parsley

If the scales have not been removed from the fish, scrape the skin against the scales with the dull side of a knife to remove them. Wash the fish inside and out and pat it dry with toweling. Line a baking sheet with foil and spread it lightly with butter. Sprinkle the interior of the fish with salt and pepper.

Melt 2 tablespoons of butter in a small skillet and sauté the vegetables for 2 to 3 minutes without letting them brown. Remove from the heat and stir in the bread crumbs, herbs, lemon juice, salt and pepper, allowing about ½ teaspoon of salt and 1/8 teaspoon of pepper. Season more highly if desired.

Preheat the oven to 400 degrees F. Stuff the fish and sew or skewer the edges together. Place the fish on the foil. Smear the top with soft butter and sprinkle with salt and pepper. Bake 45 to 50 minutes, allowing 10 minutes per pound. Use 2 spatulas to transfer the fish to a heated platter. Remove the thread or skewers. Garnish with lemon wedges and parsley. Serve with a small bowl of hot melted butter sprinkled with a little paprika.

Carolina Fish Muddle

It didn't matter a long time ago and it doesn't matter now how many or what kinds of fish fillets you use for this dish, just as long as you have ¼ to 1/3 pound per person

2 to 2½ pounds fish fillets
6 to 8 large potatoes, peeled
  and sliced
½ pound lean salt pork
Butter
Pepper

Butter a deep oven-serving Pyrex or earthenware casserole. Put in a layer of fish fillets. Dot with a little butter and sprinkle with pepper. Add a layer of potatoes. Dot with butter and pepper. Repeat the process using all the fish and potatoes and ending with a layer of potatoes. Cut the salt pork in ¼-inch slices. Wash them well and lay them on the potatoes. Fill the casserole with water. Cover and bake in a 300-degree oven for 45 minutes. Remove the cover and bake 15 minutes longer. Taste for seasoning before serving. Serve in soup plates.

Gulf Red Snapper with Shrimp Hollandaise

Many good fish come out of the Gulf—redfish, sheepshead, pompano, etc, but one of the best is red snapper, of which Northerners are justifiably jealous. Glorified in New Orleans where the French touch has been evident for over 250 years, this easily prepared dish typified the delectable offerings of that city.

4- or 5-pound red snapper, cleaned
Hollandaise Sauce (see Sauces)
1 teaspoon lemon juice
½ pound cooked shrimp
Chopped parsley

Leave the head on the fish or not, as you choose. Lay it in a fish poacher or wrap it in cheesecloth with extending long ends so that the fish can be easily removed from the water. Cover with water, allowing 1 teaspoon salt to a quart of water. Bring the water to a boil, reduce the heat and just simmer the fish, allowing 7 or 8 minutes per pound.

Meanwhile make a tart hollandaise, adding 1 teaspoon of lemon juice to the usual amount. Save out several whole shrimp for garnish and break the rest into pieces into the sauce. Keep warm.

Transfer the fish to a warm platter, draining it as well as possible. Remove the cheesecloth and wipe up from the platter any excess liquid with clean toweling. Put a little sauce over the center of the fish and sprinkle with reserved shrimp and chopped parsley. Surround with boiled potatoes, also sprinkled with parsley. Serve the rest of the sauce in a bowl.

Broiled Swordfish

Although there is no certain evidence that swordfish was eaten in colonial times (if it wasn't it's probably because it was too difficult to catch), it is now a favorite on the American table. The secret of good swordfish, like that of most fish, is its freshness.

2 to 2½ pounds swordfish steaks
  cut 1½ to 2 inches thick
Salad oil
Butter or margarine
Salt and pepper
Fresh herbs
Lemon

Preheat the broiler and the broiling pan for 10 minutes. Oil the grill well and lay the fish on it. Smear quickly with butter and sprinkle with salt and pepper. Broil about 2 inches from the flame for 12 to 15 minutes depending on the thickness. Baste frequently with the pan juices or with more butter because the fish is naturally dry.

While the fish is broiling, mix ¼ pound of butter with 3 tablespoons of one kind or a mixture of herbs (parsley, tarragon, chives, dill, basil, chervil), a little lemon juice, salt and black pepper to taste. Transfer the fish to a hot platter. Dot with the herb butter. Garnish with lemon wedges.

California Salmon Steaks with Avocado Butter

6 to 8 salmon steaks, 1 inch thick

Marinade:
½ cup peanut oil
½ cup olive oil
4 tablespoons lemon juice
1 clove garlic, sliced
1 small onion, sliced
½ cup chopped parsley
1 tablespoon Worcestershire sauce
1 tablespoon soy sauce
½ teaspoon black pepper

Avocado Butter:
1 large ripe avocado
¼ pound soft butter
1 small clove garlic, pressed
2 teaspoons lemon juice
1 tablespoon Worcestershire sauce
Salt and pepper

Place the salmon steaks in a shallow, nonmetal dish.

Combine the ingredients for the marinade and spoon them over the steaks. Marinate at least 4 hours in the refrigerator, turning the steaks occasionally. Fifteen minutes before cooking, place the steaks on a rack to drain.

Make the avocado butter. Peel and seed the avocado and mash it with a silver fork with the butter and seasonings until well blended. This can be prepared in advance and stored in a covered jar in the refrigerator.

Broil the steaks over glowing charcoal, allowing 5 minutes to each side or broil in an aluminum-foil-lined baking pan 6 inches from a preheated broiler.

Place the steaks on a heated platter. Spread with the avocado butter and serve immediately.

Down East Hake

This hearty dish is probably the invention of some unknown fisherman's wife many generations ago. It is made with hake, which for a long time was considered a rejected relative of the cod. Hake is an excellent fish often mistaken for cod or haddock. If you can't buy corned hake, lay fresh or thawed hake or other deep-sea fillets in a large shallow dish (nonmetal). Cover liberally with kosher salt (large crystal) and let stand in the refrigerator overnight.

1½ to 2 pounds corned hake
1 pound fat salt pork
12 to 16 new potatoes
2 large red or white onions
Black pepper

Wash the salt from the fish and place it in a large shallow pan. Cover with cold water.

Dice the pork into ¼-inch cubes. Sauté them very slowly in a large skillet so that they brown evenly but remain rather moist. Stir occasionally. This should take about 45 minutes. Remove the pork bits with a slotted spoon and keep both the pork bits and the fat warm. Scrub the potatoes but do not peel them. Steam them according to directions (see Vegetables).

Peel and chop the onions.

Fifteen minutes before serving bring the fish to the boiling point and barely simmer for 10 to 12 minutes or until the fish flakes easily when a fork is inserted.

To serve: Remove the fish from the water with slotted spatulas to a heated platter. Surround with the potatoes. Serve side dishes of chopped onion, pork bits and the warm fat. Each person helps himself to the fish and potatoes, which are slightly mashed on top of the fish, then topped with a generous sprinkling of the onions, pork and a spoonful of the pork fat. All that is needed is a good twist of the pepper mill.

Broiled Finnan Haddie

Finnan haddie is smoked haddock, a fish dish that originated in Finnan, Scotland but a natural for America where haddock is so plentiful. It is sometimes sold whole but more often in fillets and can be treated like salt cod. It is particularly good cooked in the following manner. Choose thick fillets.

2 to 2½ pounds finnan haddie
Butter
Black pepper
Cream (optional)

Place the fish in a shallow baking dish and cover with boiling water. Simmer very gently until the fish plumps up a little and flakes when pierced with a fork.

Preheat the broiler. Drain off the water. Transfer the fish to a baking-serving dish. Dot it generously with butter and grind a generous amount of black pepper over the top. Brown lightly under the broiler and serve with steamed or boiled potatoes. Cream poured over potatoes and fish is optional but delicious.

Grilled Bluefish with Anchovy

4- to 5-pound fresh bluefish
Salad oil
½ cup butter
2 teaspoons anchovy paste
Lemon
Parsley

Wash the bluefish inside and out and pat dry with paper toweling. Leave the head on or not as you choose.

Brush one side of the fish with oil and place it over smoldering hot charcoals or on an aluminum-lined baking pan 6 inches away from a preheated broiler.

Broil 8 to 10 minutes depending on the thickness of the fish. Brush the upper side with oil and turn the fish over. Broil another 8 to 10 minutes.

Meanwhile blend the butter with the anchovy paste until it is of spreading consistency. Place the fish on a hot platter and spread with the anchovy butter. Garnish with lemon wedges and sprigs of parsley. Serve with tiny new potatoes boiled in their jackets. (See Vegetables.)

Baked Halibut Steak

Halibut is one of the choicest fish that swim in American waters. It can be broiled, poached, fried and served in countless ways, but this is one of the easiest and best.

1½-inch halibut steak (2 to 2½ pounds)
4 tablespoons butter or margarine
2 tablespoons chopped chives
1 tablespoon chopped parsley
1 tablespoon chopped tarragon
½ lemon
Salt
Black pepper
Parsley
Lemon wedges

Preheat the oven to 400 degrees F. Line a baking pan with 2 sheets of aluminum foil. Butter the top sheet and sprinkle it with salt and pepper. Lay the steak on the foil. Smear with the rest of the butter and sprinkle with the chopped herbs, the juice of ½ lemon, salt and pepper. Cover with another sheet of foil and fold in the edges to seal the fish completely. Bake 20 to 25 minutes, allowing 10 minutes per pound. For the last 5 minutes, remove the top sheet of foil and turn on the broiler to lightly brown the fish. Transfer the fish, foil and all, to a heated platter. Slip the fish off the foil and surround it with boiled new potatoes. Sprinkle with fresh chopped parsley and garnish with lemon wedges.

Salmon Mousse
(Blender made)

When this dish was but a small part of an elegant dinner party in the nineteenth century, it was made with mortar and pestle and plenty of hard work. Using a blender makes it another story. In our simpler gastronomical era salmon mousse makes a fine luncheon dish for company or, served in individual molds, a delightful beginning to a formal dinner party.

1¾ pounds thin salmon steaks
3 egg whites
1 pint heavy cream
1 cup mayonnaise
1 teaspoon scraped onion
2 teaspoons lemon juice
¼ teaspoon celery salt
Salt
White pepper
Quick Hollandaise Sauce (see Sauces)
Watercress or parsley

Preheat the oven to 350 degrees F and put in a pan of water large enough to accommodate the mold or molds, which should be buttered. Remove any skin or bones from the salmon steaks and cut the flesh into pieces.

Break one egg white into the blender. Combine the cream, mayonnaise, onion, lemon juice and celery salt in a quart measure. Pour approximately 1/3 of the mixture and 1/3 of the salmon pieces into the blender. Spin at a moderately high speed until smooth. Put the mousse into a bowl and repeat the process until the egg whites and the rest of the ingredients have been used. Salt and pepper to taste. Fill the mold or molds and cover with buttered aluminum foil. Place in the pan of hot water and bake 45 minutes for the large mold and 25 minutes for the small ones. They should be firm on top. Remove from the oven and let stand 5 minutes. Unmold and cover with a little Hollandaise Sauce made with the 3 egg yolks. Garnish with watercress or parsley.

Fourth-of-July Poached Salmon with Egg Sauce

This dish and this custom are attributed to Mrs. Abigail Adams, wife of the second President of the United States, John Adams, and the first hostess of the White House. A typical Massachusetts meal for that season of the year—since in early July the salmon were running, new potatoes were being dug and fresh peas were in the garden waiting to be picked—it seemed to her to be the right choice for the dinner served on Independence Day in 1776. Since then it has been the traditional meal served in thousands of American homes every Fourth of July.

1 (5- to 7-pound) whole salmon or
    5 to 6 pounds center cut
1 bay leaf
2 sprigs thyme or ¼ teaspoon
    powdered thyme
Celery leaves
Salt
Cream Sauce (see Sauces)
2 teaspoons lemon juice
4 hard-cooked eggs, sliced
Chopped parsley

A whole salmon makes a pretty presentation. Leave the head on or not, as you choose. The eyes should be removed after cooking if you leave the head on. Wash it and wrap the salmon in a large piece of cheesecloth with extending long ends to make it easy to remove the fish once it is cooked. Allow enough water to cover the salmon in a deep kettle. Measure 1 teaspoon of salt for every quart of water. Add the herbs tied in a small bouquet and bring the water to a boil. Simmer 5 minutes.

Lower the fish into the water and simmer it for 40 to 50 minutes, allowing 8 minutes per pound.

Meanwhile make the sauce, adding the lemon juice and the egg slices. Season highly, using freshly ground black pepper.

Remove the salmon and let it drain on toweling for a few moments. Turn onto a heated platter, cover with the sauce and garnish with parsley.

Codfish Balls with Watercress Salad

Codfish balls, which in Boston takes second place only to baked beans as a native specialty, is the subject of some culinary controversy. Basically they are a simple mixture of salt codfish, potatoes and eggs. The controversy centers around the proportion of fish to potatoes, the enormity of making any additions and whether they are best panfried or dropped from a spoon into hot deep fat. We prefer the latter. Either way the watercress salad makes a refreshing accompaniment even at breakfast time and is far superior to the usual catsup bath.

¾ pound salt codfish (2 cups)
6 to 8 potatoes (4 cups)
2 eggs, slightly beaten
2 tablespoons butter or margarine
Black pepper
2 bunches watercress
French Dressing (see Sauces)

Soak the codfish in cold water for several hours, then rinse and drain. Place in a pan of fresh water, bring to a boil, and simmer 20 minutes. Flake the fish very finely. At the same time, pare and cube the potatoes. You should have 4 cups. Boil them in salted water until tender. Drain well and return to the heat for further drying, tossing them until they are mealy on the outside. The secret of good codfish balls is not to have the mixture soggy. Remove from the heat and mash the fish and potatoes together. This can be done by hand or by an electric beater. Add the butter and eggs. Taste for seasoning, being generous with freshly ground black pepper.

Heat the deep fat to 380 degrees F. While the fat is heating, wash the watercress, discarding any wilted leaves or hard stem ends. Make the French dressing with cider vinegar. Toss well just before serving.

Drop the fish mixture in ½ tablespoonfuls into the fat. Do not fry more than 5 or 6 at a time. Fry 1 minute. Drain on paper toweling and keep warm. Serve as soon as you have enough for the first serving. You will have to fry more.

Creamed Codfish

One of the earliest lessons the Indians gave the Pilgrims was how to catch, salt and dry codfish. Many dishes have been derived from this process. One of the favorites, at least in New England, is creamed codfish, which can be used for breakfast, lunch or supper.

1 pound salt codfish
Cream Sauce (see Sauces)
Butter or margarine
3 hard-cooked eggs
Chopped parsley

Soak the codfish for several hours in cold water. Rinse and place it in a pan of fresh water. Bring to the boil and simmer 20 minutes or until tender. Drain and run cool water through the fish. Flake into a shallow baking-serving dish. Meanwhile prepare the cream sauce but do not add any salt until after it has been mixed with the salt cod. Be generous with the pepper. Dot with a little butter and bake 30 minutes at 300 degrees F. Surround the edge with sliced hard-cooked eggs and garnish the center with parsley. Serve on toast for breakfast, but creamed codfish is really best with baked potatoes.

To broil T R O U T S.

AFTER having gutted, waſh'd and dry'd them with a Napkin, we bind them about with Packthread, ſprinkle them over with melted Butter and Salt ; then broil them over a gentle Fire and keep turning them from Time to Time. We ſerve them with a white Sauce made of Butter, a Pinch of Flower, Salt, Pepper, Nutmeg, ſome Capers, one Anchove, and a very little Water and Vinegar : We keep turning the Sauce over the Stove till it come to a due Thickneſs, then having laid the Trouts in a Diſh, pour the Sauce upon them and ſerve them.

Baked Shad with Roe Anchovy Sauce

Shad is a sign of spring which creeps up the coasts every year. In slavery times shad, like salmon, was so plentiful that records have been found in the East of agreements with slaves that shad, like salmon, had to be eaten only so many times a week. Now it is considered a great delicacy. It is very bony and is best bought already cleaned and boned.

3½-pound shad with roe,
  cleaned, split and boned
Butter or margarine
Salt and pepper
1 cup dry white wine
5 tablespoons flour
1 cup chicken stock or canned broth
1 teaspoon anchovy paste
½ pint heavy cream

Preheat the oven to 350 degrees F. Put the roe in a small buttered baking dish. Dot generously with butter. Sprinkle with salt and pepper and add the wine. Cover well with aluminum foil and bake 30 minutes.

Place the split shad, skin side down, on a well-buttered baking pan. Smear the surface lightly with butter and sprinkle with salt and pepper. About 10 minutes before the roe is cooked put the shad in the oven. Baste frequently.

Heat 4 tablespoons of butter and stir in the flour, letting it cook 2 to 3 minutes over low heat, stirring to prevent browning. Add the stock and the liquid from the cooked roe and stir until smooth. Add the anchovy paste and the cream and stir until hot but not boiling. Taste for seasoning.

Transfer the shad to a heated platter. Pour over some of the sauce and put the rest in a gravy boat. Serve with Steamed Potatoes (see Vegetables).

Sautéed Trout

The early settlers or the pioneers wending their way westward never thought of "sautéing" the trout they found so plentiful in river and stream, but modern culinary jargon uses the word to distinguish the process from frying in shallow or deep fat. Fresh-caught trout is one of man's most treasured prizes and the more simply it is cooked the better. Allow one 12-inch trout per person. One of the smaller variety will not satisfy the ordinary appetite. Frozen trout thawed before cooking are not the same thing but they make very good eating. Other small fish (smelt, small perch, small whitefish, etc.) can all be cooked the same way.

6 to 8 trout
Milk
Flour or cornmeal
4 tablespoons salad oil
Butter or margarine
Salt and pepper
Lemon wedges
Chopped parsley

The fish should be cleaned, washed, and dried inside and out. The head can be left on or not according to taste. Dip each trout in milk and then in flour or fine cornmeal. Prepare all the fish before cooking any of them. Put 4 tablespoons of oil and 4 tablespoons of butter in 1 large or 2 medium-size skillets. The pans should be well coated with fat. When they are hot, add the fish and brown them quickly on both sides.

At the same time, heat a metal platter so that it is almost too hot to handle. Transfer the fish to the hot platter, lining them up side by side. Heat butter, allowing 1 tablespoon per fish. While the butter is heating, garnish the fish with a lemon slice and sprinkle with parsley, salt and pepper. Pour the hot butter over the fish and carry it sizzling with protected hands to the table. The sizzle is music to the ears.

Cover painting, THE SATURDAY EVENING POST, *August 3, 1929.*

Baked Fish Steaks With Cream

2½ to 3 pounds fish steaks
   (halibut, haddock, etc.)
¼ cup butter
½ pound fresh mushrooms
1 medium onion
1 clove garlic
½ bay leaf
1 cup dry white wine
Salt and pepper
1 cup heavy cream

Preheat oven to 350 degrees F. Butter well the inside surfaces of a baking pan large enough to hold the fish steaks side by side. Sprinkle with salt and pepper, dot with butter, and bake 15 minutes.

Slice onions and mushrooms while fish is baking. At the end of 15 minutes remove fish from oven, add onions, mushrooms, bay leaf and garlic (do not break bay leaf or mince garlic clove). Pour over white wine. Cover (use buttered foil if the baking pan has no lid of its own) and bake 30 to 40 minutes until flesh flakes easily and has lost its translucent appearance. Discard bay leaf and garlic. Lift fish steaks out onto heated platter and keep warm. Add the cream to the juices in the baking pan and heat, stirring constantly. Correct seasoning and pour sauce over fish.

Escalloped Fish

2 cups cooked fish
2 cups White Sauce (see Sauces)
2 or 3 hard-cooked eggs
Buttered bread crumbs
Salt and pepper
Paprika

Flake the fish, inspecting carefully to remove any bones. Chop hard-cooked eggs, forcing yolk through sieve if desired. Preheat oven to 450 degrees F. Generously butter the inside of a medium-size baking dish. Place half the fish in the bottom of the baking dish, top with half the egg and half the sauce. Taste for seasoning and add a sprinkling of salt and pepper if it is needed. Repeat with the remaining ingredients, topping with buttered crumbs and a sprinkling of paprika.

Baked Stuffed Whitefish

Bluefish and striped bass may also be stuffed and baked whole, where they are available. For an impressive appearance on the table, leave the head and tail in place. You may, if you like, substitute dill seed for the tarragon in the stuffing.

3- to 3½-pound whole fish
Butter or margarine
Salt and pepper

Stuffing:
1½ cups bread crumbs
2 tablespoons chopped onion
½ cup chopped celery
1 tablespoon chopped parsley
½ teaspoon salt
½ teaspoon dried tarragon
3 tablespoons butter or margarine
Hot water

Lightly oil a baking dish or roasting pan large enough to hold the fish, then line the pan with heavy-duty foil or with two thicknesses of the lighter weight foil. The foil should be long enough that the ends extend beyond head and tail, to form handles with which the whole fish can be lifted. Generously butter the foil, and sprinkle with salt and pepper. Wipe the fish with a dampened paper towel and center it on the foil.

To make stuffing: Melt butter or margarine in a skillet. Add chopped onion and celery, and sauté until transparent but not brown. Remove from heat. Stir in bread crumbs, salt, tarragon or dill. Taste for seasoning—a dressing for fish should not be too highly seasoned or it will overshadow the naturally delicate taste of a good fish. Mix in beaten egg and a little hot water, just what is needed to make the stuffing stick together.

Preheat the oven to 325 degrees F. Spoon stuffing into the cavity of the fish, and dot the top of the fish with butter, salt and pepper. Turn the edges of the foil up, so as to hold juices inside.

Bake fish uncovered for 20 minutes, then remove from the oven and fit a second sheet of foil over the top, pinching the edges over the other so as to form a fairly close seal around the fish. Bake 20 minutes longer, or until the flesh of the fish flakes easily.

Fish Fillet Casserole

6 to 8 fillets (flounder, snapper,
   haddock, pompano, etc.)
Salt and pepper
4 tablespoons butter
1 bottle dry white wine
2 pounds fresh spinach
Cream Sauce (see Sauces)
1/8 teaspoon nutmeg
Grated Parmesan cheese

Season the fillets with salt and pepper.

Melt the butter in a large skillet. Add enough wine to measure ½ inch in the skillet. Bring to a boil.

Poach the fillets for just 5 minutes, spooning the wine over the fish. Remove from the liquid.

Wash the spinach removing the large stems. Put in a large pan, cover and cook until tender. Drain and reserve the broth.

Make the cream sauce but instead of milk use 1 cup of spinach broth and 1 cup of cream. Season well with nutmeg, salt and pepper.

Preheat the oven to 350 degrees F. Spread half the sauce in the bottom of a baking-serving dish. Place the fish fillets on the sauce. Cover with the spinach and pour over the remaining sauce. Sprinkle with grated cheese and bake 20 minutes.

Baked Fish Fillets

6 to 8 fish fillets
   (haddock, scrod, sole, etc.)
Salt and pepper
½ cup melted magarine
1 cup fine bread crumbs
½ cup sweet butter
1 small clove garlic, minced
2 teaspoons chopped chives
2 tablespoons chopped parsley
1 tablespoon canned pimiento, minced

Preheat the oven to 375 degrees F.

Sprinkle fresh or thawed fish fillets with salt and pepper. Dip in melted butter and then in the bread crumbs.

Place in an oven-serving dish and bake 15 to 18 minutes, depending on the thickness of the fillets.

Meanwhile cream the butter until soft with a fork and work in the garlic, chives, parsley and pimiento.

Just before serving top each fillet with a teaspoon of the herb butter.

Maryland Crab Cakes

Crab cakes have long been a specialty of Maryland and they can be very good. They can also be bland and soggy. The secret is to spice them up without hiding the wonderful flavor of crab.

1½ pounds crab meat
3 cups soft white bread crumbs
¾ cup peanut oil
2 tablespoons minced onion
2 tablespoons minced green pepper
3 egg yolks, slightly beaten
2 teaspoons Worcestershire sauce
2 tablespoons Dijon mustard
2 teaspoons lemon juice
¾ teaspoon salt
3 egg whites, beaten stiff
Fine bread crumbs

Pick over the crab to be sure there are no filaments.

Put the bread crumbs in a bowl and stir in 6 tablespoons of oil.

Heat 2 tablespoons of oil in a small skillet and cook the onion and green pepper slowly until soft.

Combine the beaten egg yolks with the Worcestershire, mustard, lemon juice, and ½ teaspoon salt.

Beat the egg whites stiff with ¼ teaspoon salt.

Combine the crab with all the other mixtures, folding in the egg whites gently but thoroughly. Shape the mixture into flat cakes and coat them with bread crumbs. Let the cakes rest in the refrigerator for at least 30 minutes. Heat 2 tablespoons of the remaining oil and sauté half the cakes until golden brown on both sides. Keep warm while repeating the process with the rest of the cakes.

Serve hot with wedges of lemon.

Dungeness Crab

Dungeness crab, the pride of the Pacific, is bought already boiled and cracked in strategic places. Serve it with nutcrackers, picks, plenty of Homemade Mayonnaise (see Sauces), crusty bread and cold white wine or beer.

Deviled Crabmeat

1 pound crab meat
4 tablespoons butter or margarine
2 tablespoons minced onion
2 tablespoons minced green pepper
2 tablespoons chopped parsley
Cream Sauce (see Sauces)
3 egg yolks, slightly beaten
3 tablespoons sherry
1 tablespoon Dijon mustard
2 teaspoons lemon juice
Salt and pepper
Fine bread crumbs
Parsley

Pick over the crab meat to be sure there are no filaments.

Heat 2 tablespoons of the butter in a small skillet and gently cook the onion and pepper just until soft.

Make the Cream Sauce, using 1 cup of milk and 1 cup of chicken stock or broth. Combine the onions, peppers and most of the parsley with the sauce. Save a little of the parsley for garnish.

Combine the beaten egg yolks with the sherry, mustard and lemon juice and add gradually to the hot sauce, stirring constantly. Taste for seasoning.

Place the mixture in a shallow baking dish. Cover with fine bread crumbs and dot with the remaining butter. This can be browned in a 400-degree oven and served immediately, or if it is to be served later in the day it can be kept refrigerated for several hours and heated for 30 minutes at 300 degrees F just before serving. Garnish with parsley.

Clambake

The Indians taught the early settlers how to heat the rocks along the shore and to steam their clams. That lesson is the ancestor of our elaborate clambake,. which used to be a uniquely coastal specialty but now, thanks to modern shipping, can be done any-where in the country. Clams and lobsters packed in seaweed are shipped everywhere. If you are going to the trouble of having a clambake, share it with at least 14 to 16 people. However, this recipe can be easily halved or for that matter doubled or tripled.

½ bushel soft shell clams
14 to 16 young lobsters (1¼ pounds)
2 to 3 dozen ears of corn
5 pounds medium potatoes
4 pounds onions
Butter or margarine
Salt and pepper

About 3 hours before the clambake is to begin, find a natural hole on coastal rocks or dig a hole 4 feet wide and 2 or 3 feet deep in the sand above the high water mark or in the backyard. Line the sand or backyard holes with smooth rocks, filling in the chinks with small stones. Fill the hole with firewood and start a brisk fire, feeding the fire for an hour. Allow the fire to burn itself out. Do not leave it unattended. Let someone else collect the ingredients for the clambake.

Put the husked corn, the clams and each type of vegetable—the unpeeled onions and the scrubbed potatoes—in loose woven bags such as onions are sold in. Provide plenty of aluminum pie plates, little indi-vidual tartlet tins for the butter and individual salt and pepper cartons, because no one wants to "pass the salt" once settled on the ground. An old coffee-pot is ideal for melting butter and a large coffeepot with campfire coffee is a necessity. These are placed on a hot stone next to the tarpaulin. Kosher pickles, watermelon and beer are also part of the picture. Some people provide a half lobster for each person, but that seems like gilding the lily.

When the fire is reduced to ashes, rake and sweep out the pit and put in a layer of wet seaweed. Put the clams and vegetables in the pit. Add a layer of lob-sters and cover the whole thing with a tarpaulin, weighted at the corner with stones. Steam 1¼ hours. To check for doneness pull a leg from one of the lobsters. If easily detached the rest of the meal is ready.

Soft Crabs

Soft crabs, as they used to be called, are soft-shelled crabs caught between shells, so to speak, since crabs shed their shells and acquire new ones several times during the growing process.

12 to 16 soft-shelled crabs
1 cup flour
1 teaspoon salt
Butter or margarine
Peanut or salad oil
½ cup chopped parsley
Salt and pepper
Lemon wedges
6 to 8 toasts

Buy the crabs cleaned. Combine the flour and salt on a plate and dip the crabs in the mixture to coat them lightly on both sides.

Heat 2 tablespoons of butter and 2 tablespoons of oil in each of 2 large skillets. When the fat is hot but not brown sauté the crabs, allowing 5 minutes to each side. They should be golden brown. Place on toasts on a heated platter. Sprinkle with parsley, salt and pepper. At the same time heat ¼ pound of the butter until it bubbles. Pour this over the crabs and garnish with lemon wedges. Serve immediately.

Baked Buttered Sea Scallops

This dish is delicious with either fresh or thawed frozen scallops. It can be prepared early in the day and cooked whenever convenient.

1½ to 2 pints scallops
1 to 1½ cups crushed butter crackers
8 to 10 tablespoons butter or margarine
1 tablespoon dry vermouth
2 teaspoons lemon juice
Salt and pepper

If the scallops are very large, cut them in pieces of about 1 inch square.

Crush the crackers (2 dozen 2-inch crackers yield 1 cup cracker crumbs).

Heat the butter in a skillet, and when it is bubbling add the cracker crumbs and stir until lightly browned. Remove from the heat and toss the scallops in the crumbs until well coated. Put in a shallow oven-serving dish and sprinkle with the vermouth, lemon juice, salt and pepper.

Immediately or anytime later in the day, bake 20 minutes at 350 degrees F.

Scallops in Garlic Butter

1 pound scallops, fresh or frozen
1 clove garlic, cut into 2 or 4 pieces
½ cup butter or margarine
Salt and pepper

Thaw the scallops if frozen, wash and pick over carefully if fresh. Melt the butter in a heavy saucepan over moderate heat and add garlic. Cook for several minutes, allowing the butter to absorb the garlic flavor, but do not brown. Remove the garlic and discard. Add the scallops and cook 5 minutes. Serve with lemon wedges and Tartar Sauce (see Sauces).

Martha's Vineyard Bay Scallops

Bay scallops are very choice. They are small and sweet and are delicious eaten raw after being sprinkled with lime juice. This recipe makes a good first course for a dinner party or a delicious luncheon or supper dish.

¼ pound butter
2 tablespoons chopped shallots
    or scallions (green onions)
1 teaspoon fresh tarragon or
    ¼ teaspoon dried tarragon
2 tablespoons chopped parsley
1 cup dry white wine
1 quart bay scallops
Salt and pepper
½ pint heavy cream
6 to 8 slices firm bread

Heat the butter in a skillet and add the shallots, tarragon and parsley. Simmer for a moment before adding the wine. Bring to a simmer and stir in the scallops. Cook gently for 3 to 4 minutes. Remove from the heat, sprinkle with salt and pepper and add the cream. Put back on the heat just until the sauce thickens slightly. Do not let the sauce boil. Serve on rather thick slices of buttered toast.

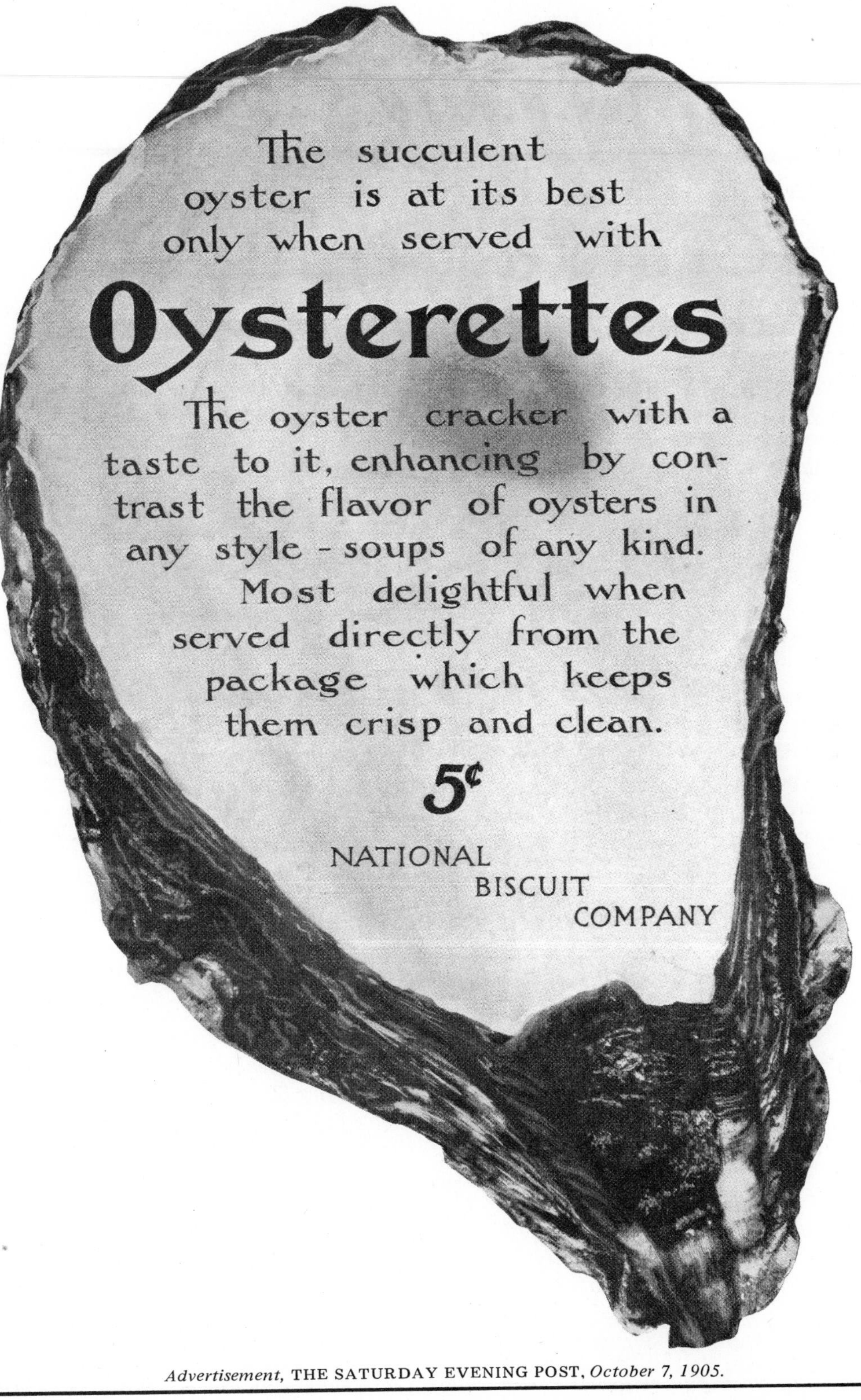

The succulent
oyster is at its best
only when served with

Oysterettes

The oyster cracker with a
taste to it, enhancing by con-
trast the flavor of oysters in
any style - soups of any kind.
Most delightful when
served directly from the
package which keeps
them crisp and clean.

5¢

NATIONAL
BISCUIT
COMPANY

Advertisement, THE SATURDAY EVENING POST, *October 7, 1905.*

Barbecued Shrimp

1½ to 2 pounds raw shrimp
½ cup chili sauce
2 tablespoons honey
¼ cup salad oil
1 small clove garlic, pressed
½ teaspoon salt
¼ teaspoon cracked black pepper
Lemons

Remove the shells from the shrimp and take out the black intestine running down the center of the tail.

Combine the remaining ingredients except for the lemons and mix until well blended or spin in a blender.

Thread the shrimp on skewers and broil them over hot coals or under the oven broiler, allowing 8 minutes to each side. Baste frequently with the sauce.

Serve very hot with lemon slices.

Spicy Shrimp in Butter Sauce

1½ to 2 pounds raw shrimp
6 to 8 tablespoons butter
½ teaspoon turmeric
½ teaspoon curry powder
¼ teaspoon dry mustard
2 teaspoons lemon juice
A few drops Tabasco
1 teaspoon Worcestershire sauce
1½ quarts water
1 bay leaf
½ teaspoon powdered thyme
2 slices onion
1 tablespoon vinegar
2 slices lemon
2 teaspoons salt

Remove the shells from the shrimp and take out the black intestines running down the middle of the tails.

Over low heat combine the butter, turmeric, curry powder, mustard, lemon juice, Tabasco and Worcestershire sauce. Simmer gently. In a large saucepan combine the other ingredients and simmer 5 minutes. Add shrimp and simmer 10 minutes. Drain and discard all but the shrimps. Place the shrimp in indi-

vidual heated ramekins or scallop shells. Cover with the butter sauce and garnish with a sprig of parsley. If there is any delay, slip the ramekins under the broiler. Serve with sopping bread.

Shrimp Jambalaya

There are many versions of this old recipe which hails from New Orleans as so many of America's good recipes do. Once it was all made in one kettle and stirred over the fire on the hearth, but this is an easier method.

4 tablespoons butter or margarine
¼ pound Canadian bacon, cut in strips
1 cup cooked chicken, cut in pieces
1 cup salami, cut in strips
½ cup chopped onion
4 tablespoons chopped green pepper
4 tablespoons diced celery
4 cups tomatoes, canned or stewed
1 teaspoon chili powder (optional)
1½ cups rice
1 pound cooked (medium to small) shrimp

In a deep kettle, heat the butter and cook the bacon, chicken, salami, onions, peppers and celery over moderate heat, stirring frequently. When the vegetables are soft add the tomatoes and simmer until most of the moisture has evaporated. Season with salt, pepper and chili if desired.

Meanwhile, cook the rice for 12 minutes in a large pan of boiling salted water. Drain and run cool water through the rice. Add it to the vegetables and stir well. Add the cooked shrimp and simmer 10 minutes before serving. Taste for seasoning.

Cover painting, THE SATURDAY EVENING POST, *October 25, 1947.*

Boiled Lobsters

Early travelers to these shores sent back to England accounts of lobsters of prodigious size and plenitude. Whether they were referring to the lobsters found in northern waters or the spiny or rock lobster caught in southern water is not certain. Both are delicious and can be cooked in the same way. Maine folk still talk about hearing of lobsters costing 5 cents apiece.

6 to 8 lobsters (1¼ to 1½ pounds)
Hot butter or Homemade Mayonnaise (see Sauces)

Put 4 to 5 inches of ocean water in a large kettle. Lacking sea water use fresh water, allowing a tablespoon of salt to a quart of water. Bring the water to a rapid boil and throw in the lobsters. Allow 15 minutes after the water reaches the boiling point the second time. Test the lobsters by pulling off a leg. If easily detached the lobster is done.

Serve with melted butter. A Maine man will tell you to put a little vinegar or lemon juice into the butter and to always have a jar of pickles on hand. Some connoisseurs will say that the best way to serve lobster is cold with real mayonnaise.

Bake-Broil Lobster

This is an answer to the controversy of whether the lobster is better baked stuffed or broiled. This recipe involves both baking and broiling, so everyone should be satisfied.

6 to 8 (1½-pound) lobsters
4 to 5 cups toasted soft bread crumbs
½ pound crab meat
1/8 teaspoon cayenne
3 tablespoons sherry
½ pound butter, melted
Salt and pepper
Dry bread crumbs
Lemon wedges

Lay the live lobsters down on their backs on a large board. Holding the claws flat with one hand, place a large pointed knife in the center of the head and cut down the center to the tail. If this seems too gruesome, throw the lobsters for just a moment into a large kettle of boiling water before splitting them, but that is for your sake, not the lobster's. Once the lobsters are split, remove the claws and lay them aside. Spread the bodies open and remove the green liver—the tomalley—and save it. Discard the stomach near the head and the long black intestine in the tail. Place the lobsters side by side on a grill in an open roasting pan. Six will fit nicely, two more will require another pan and grill. Tuck the tails under the outside grid to keep them from curling.

Toast the bread crumbs lightly on a baking sheet and mix them with the tomalley, tossing them with a fork. Add the crab meat, 1/8 teaspoon of cayenne, sherry and enough melted butter to moisten it. Season with salt and pepper to taste. Fill the body and tail cavities with the stuffing. Cover lightly with dry crumbs and sprinkle with butter. Bake 15 minutes at 425 degrees F and put on the broiler for the last 5 minutes so that the crumbs are dark brown.

At the same time, boil the claws in sea water or heavily salted fresh water (1 tablespoon to a quart of water) for 15 minutes after the water has come to the boil again. Serve the lobster bodies and claws on individual platters with small bowls of butter and wedges of lemon.

Lobster 'Newburg

Lobster Newburg became a fashionable chafing-dish sort of dish around the turn of the century. It is a delicious concoction and can be served in patty shells, with toast points or in a Rice Ring. We give you two ways of preparing them, one as the original formula indicates, for which you can buy the lobster meat, and the other a little less rich and made from live lobsters.

Lobster Newburg I

1 pound cooked lobster meat
  (3½ cups)
8 tablespoons butter
4 tablespoons brandy
½ teaspoon cayenne
½ teaspoon nutmeg
¾ teaspoon salt
1 pint heavy cream
1 tablespoon cornstarch
¼ cup milk
4 tablespoons sherry
6 egg yolks, slightly beaten
2 teaspoons lemon juice
½ pound mushrooms (optional)

Cut the lobster in good-size pieces. Heat the butter in a large shallow pan and sauté the lobster gently for 3 to 4 minutes or until the lobster is well coated with butter and hot. Add the brandy and touch it with a lighted match. Spoon the brandy over the lobster until the flames subside. Add the seasonings and stir for 1 minute. Transfer the lobster to the top part of a large double boiler. Combine the cream with the cornstarch mixed with milk, sherry, and egg yolks. Add to the lobster and cook over simmering water, stirring until the sauce is thick. Add the lemon and taste for seasoning. The mushrooms are not traditional, but sliced and sautéed in butter they stretch the size of the servings in a very pleasant way.

Lobster Newburg II

6 to 8 pounds live lobsters
2 cups fresh water
1 cup dry white wine
2 sprigs fresh thyme or
  1/8 teaspoon powdered thyme
½ bay leaf
1 teaspoon salt
½ pound mushrooms
8 tablespoons butter
6 tablespoons flour
4 tablespoons sherry
½ pint heavy cream
3 egg yolks, slightly beaten
½ teaspoon cayenne
2 teaspoons lemon juice
Salt

Allow at least 1 pound live weight of lobster to a person. Bring the water, wine and seasonings to a boil in a deep kettle and throw in the lobsters. Cover and boil 15 minutes or until a small leg easily detaches itself when pulled from the body. Remove the lobsters with large pincers and save the liquid. Cool the lobsters.

Clean, slice and sauté the mushrooms into 2 tablespoons of butter until they are dry and slightly browned. Set aside.

Shell the lobsters. Save the tomalley to use mixed with sweet butter for a spread at cocktail time. Discard the stomach and the intestine down the center of the tail. Take out the claw and tail meat and cut into bite-size pieces. Throw the carcasses back into the pot. Cover and simmer 20 to 30 minutes. Drain the liquid through a very fine strainer. If it measures more than 2 cups, boil it down to that amount.

Melt 6 tablespoons of the butter in the top of a double boiler and stir in the flour. Cook for 2 to 3 minutes without browning. Add the lobster liquor and stir until smooth. Place the sauce over hot water and add the sherry, and the cream mixed with the slightly beaten egg yolks. Stir until thickened. Add the lemon juice, cayenne, and salt to taste. Stir in the lobster and mushrooms and heat thoroughly. Serve as you would Lobster Newburg I.

Noodle Ramekins with Shellfish

The ancestor of this dish is macaroni and oysters, a favorite of President Arthur. The ramekins make a good luncheon dish or a first course for a dinner party. The recipe can be baked in one large dish if more convenient.

1 to 1¼ pounds small egg noodles
2 tablespoons salad oil
1 pint oysters
1 pint small cooked shrimp
1 tablespoon chopped parsley
4 tablespoons butter
4 tablespoons flour
¼ cup vermouth
1 cup milk
¼ teaspoon nutmeg
½ pint sour cream
Salt and pepper
Fine bread crumbs
Parmesan cheese
Butter

Put the noodles gradually into a large pan of boiling salted water, allowing 1 teaspoon of salt to a quart of water. Add the oil and boil 4 minutes or *just* until tender. Drain.

Drain the oysters, saving the liquor carefully. Unless the oysters are very small, cut them in pieces. Put the oysters, shrimp, parsley and noodles in one bowl.

Heat the butter and stir in the flour, cooking for 2 minutes without browning. Add the oyster liquor, vermouth and milk and stir until smooth. Add the nutmeg and season to taste with salt and pepper. Fold in carefully with the noodle mixture. Cool and fold in the sour cream. Divide the mixture into the ramekins. Cover with bread crumbs and dot with butter. Bake 20 minutes at 350 degrees F. Before serving garnish with a sprig of parsley.

Oysters on the Half Shell

Oysters bought by the half-bushel or bushel basket and opened at home are more economical than those bought by the dozen and opened at the fish store. Unopened oysters will keep in a cool place for weeks. As long as they are shut tight they are alive and well. Oysters should be chilled before opening and served on a bed of ice with nothing for garnish but a little lemon juice or a small dab of horseradish and some freshly ground black pepper. Dark bread, sweet butter and a lively white wine are all you need to have perfection.

Creamed Oysters

Creamed oysters, a favorite for generations, are delicious served on toast, in patty shells or in a deep dish topped with mashed potatoes.

1 quart shucked oysters
6 tablespoons butter or margarine
6 tablespoons flour
2 cups fish stock or chicken broth
1 cup oyster liquor
¼ cup sherry
1 teaspoon lemon juice
Salt
Black pepper

Drain the oysters over a bowl to catch the liquor. In a large saucepan heat the butter and stir in the flour, letting it cook for 2 to 3 minutes without browning. If you have got into the habit of keeping fish stock in your freezer (an excellent idea), stir that in. Otherwise add the chicken broth and the oyster liquor. If you do not have a full cupful, supplement with a little bottled clam juice. Stir until smooth.

Add the oysters and the sherry and cook just long enough for the oyster edges to curl. Season with lemon juice, salt and black pepper to taste.

Creamed Oysters

1 quart oysters
½ pound mushrooms
4 tablespoons butter
Cream Sauce (see Sauces)
4-ounce jar pimientos
Salt and pepper
Baking Powder Biscuits (see Breads)

Poach the oysters in their own liquid just until plump. Drain, reserving the liquid carefully.

Clean the mushrooms and slice them lengthwise, caps and stems together. Sauté in butter until almost dry.

Make the cream sauce replacing some of the milk with the oyster broth and using ½ cup of cream instead of one of the cups of milk. Season well with salt and pepper.

Dice the pimiento and cut the oysters if they are large. Add the pimiento, mushrooms and oysters to the sauce. Reheat in a double boiler.

Serve on large baking powder biscuits or on toast.

Oyster Pan Roast

In the days when the only cooking utensil other than the kettle was a skillet, this was a favorite way to cook oysters—simple, quick and good, quite what we look for in today's kitchen.

12 to 16 slices of bread
½ pound clarified butter
1 quart shucked oysters, drained
Salt
Black pepper
Lemon juice

Trim the crusts from the bread and toast them. At the same time, heat the butter in a heavy saucepan over very low heat. The clear fat will rise to the top and separate from the whey. Pour the clarified butter into a large skillet and heat until it is bubbling hot. Add the oysters and cook 3 to 4 minutes or just until they are plump and beginning to curl around the edges. Season with a little salt, a lot of freshly ground black pepper and the juice of ½ lemon. This will serve 6 bountifully and 8 generously. Have catsup and Worcestershire sauce on the table.

Oysters Rockefeller

This dish was invented in New Orleans by a Frenchman but America claims it for her own. A product of a famous restaurant, it is easy to reproduce in any kitchen. Pie tins or 2 aluminum foil pie plates, one fitted into the other to make them strong enough, serve as baking-serving dishes. Provide yourself with rock (ice cream) salt and fill each pie tin half full. Arrange two or three shelves in your oven and baking sheets to hold the pie tins.

¾ cup soft butter
1/3 cup finely chopped onion
1/3 cup chopped parsley
1/3 cup chopped celery
2/3 cup fine bread crumbs
3 cups spinach leaves
A few drops hot sauce
4 tablespoons Pernod or anisette
1 teaspoon salt
½ teaspoon black cracked pepper
3 to 4 dozen oysters on the half shell,
   opened

Melt 4 tablespoons of butter in a skillet and sauté the onion, parsley and celery just until soft. Remove from the stove and put the mixture, the bread crumbs, the well-washed spinach leaves (there should be no stems), a drop or two of hot sauce, the rest of the butter, the liquor, salt and pepper into a blender. Blend for 30 seconds.

Arrange the freshly opened oysters on the rock salt beds so that they will be secure. Put a generous teaspoonful of seasoning mixture on each oyster and bake in a 450-degree oven for 4 to 5 minutes or just until the butter is bubbling and the topping begins to brown.

Escalloped Oysters

Squeamish children who refuse the slippery oysters in stew may learn to like them served this way. This quantity will serve 8 to 10 persons, but it can easily be halved for serving 4 or 5.

1 medium onion, chopped
½ cup celery, chopped
1 clove garlic, chopped
¼ cup butter or margarine
2 cups toasted bread crumbs
1 quart oysters
2 hard-cooked eggs, sliced
1 tablespoon Worcestershire sauce
1 pint milk
Salt and pepper

Sauté onion, celery and garlic in small amount of butter until slightly brown; remove from pan. In baking dish, place a layer of bread crumbs, oysters, onion, celery, and garlic. Sprinkle salt and pepper over contents. Make a second layer of all ingredients, and top entire dish with sliced eggs. Add Worcestershire sauce to milk, and pour milk over entire dish. Place in oven at 325 degrees for a half hour, or until juice and milk are absorbed. Serve with a tossed salad and plenty of crusty bread.

Cooked Shrimp With Peas

Serve this dish on crackers and call it Shrimp Wiggle, or serve it on toast and call it Shrimp a la King. Add a chopped hard-cooked egg to make it a little heartier.

¼ cup butter or margarine
½ cup chopped onion
½ cup chopped celery
4 tablespoons flour
2 cups milk
2 cups small cooked shrimp
1 cup cooked peas
Salt and pepper
Fluffy Rice (see Rice)

Melt butter in a heavy saucepan, over moderate heat. Add onion and celery and sauté until transparent but not browned. Push vegetables to one side and add flour, blending it into the melted butter. Add milk and cook until thickened, stirring constantly. Add shrimp and peas and a little salt and pepper. Heat thoroughly, taste and correct seasoning. Serve on rice.

Beer Batter Fried Clams

Clams were an important food for the hungry Pilgrims. There is no record of their eating them this way, but fried clams, no matter what the batter, are certainly a part of the American food picture. If you can dig and shell your own clams that's not only cheaper but better. Otherwise order the shucked clams in advance.

1 (12-ounce) can beer
3 egg yolks
1 teaspoon salt
2 tablespoons salad oil
2 cups flour
3 egg whites, beaten stiff
1 quart shucked clams

Open the can of beer to let the initial fizz wear off. Beat the egg yolks until light. Add the salt, oil and flour. Stir in enough beer to give the consistency of very heavy cream. Cover and let stand 30 to 60 minutes.

Preheat the fat to 370 degrees F. Beat the egg whites and fold them in gently but thoroughly to the batter. When the fat is hot, pick each clam up separately with a long fork, dip it into the batter and drop it into the oil. Fry 8 to 10 clams at a time. They should be cooked in 3 or 4 minutes. Drain on toweling and serve very hot. Serve with lemon wedges, tartar sauce or catsup.

LEADING hotels, clubs, restaurants and cafés consider Snider's Catsup the best foundation for making their own oyster cocktail sauce. This is a very high testimonial in favor of Snider's as the perfect seasoning.

TRY THIS: Two tablespoonfuls of Snider's Tomato Catsup and one teaspoonful of finely grated horseradish as the cocktail sauce for each serving of raw oysters.

FRIED OYSTER RECIPE

1 pint large oysters   ½ cup milk
½ cup flour   ½ teaspoon salt
½ cup Snider's Tomato Catsup

Mix thoroughly the flour, milk, catsup and salt; dip oysters into mixture, then roll them in cracker crumbs. Fry in sweet, fresh lard until a dark brown. Serve very hot.
Mrs. Clara L. Street.

Advertisement, THE SATURDAY EVENING POST, *September 14, 1912*

EGGS & CHEESE: ARTFUL AFTERLIFE OF CACKLE AND MOO

There are certain occasions when a historian wishes to be a soothsayer or at least an astrologer so that what he has to say relates to the future and not to the past. That way, if things do not work out as predicted, the sage merely keeps out of the way for a while, keeps on soothsaying, and sooner or later *something* works out pretty much as predicted.

The chicken historian, on the other hand—and particularly the chronicler of the American chicken—is in deep trouble. The Pilgrims brought some chickens with them in 1620, and some birds had also traveled to Jamestown in 1607. Some of them were eaten, and some of them laid eggs. And there you have it. We can go back and reflect that, historically, chickens got their first start around 1400 B.C. in southeastern Asia. And also that by the sixteenth century the French king, Henry of Navarre, a nice monarch but a rather dull one, expressed a wish that there be a chicken in every Frenchman's pot every Sunday. Henry let it go just as a wish, however; he gave away no chickens to his subjects.

So that's it. You've got the chickens in Plymouth and Jamestown and they are laying eggs. That's all the egg historian has to say. Later on we'll hear from the expert on egg cookery.

But cheese!!! Here the historian licks his lips, sharpens his quill pen and sails in. The shelves of libraries are glutted with fantastic documentation about cheese.

Cheese has such style! There are at least 2,000 named cheeses in the world with 500 recognized varieties. France supports a society of cheese appreci-

ators which is regally dubbed *La Confrérie des Chevaliers du Taste-Fromage de France*. The society even has its Grand Commander for the United States of America, who recently outdid even the renowned eloquence of wine lovers by referring to "the robust cheeses of Germany, the solid cheeses of England, the earthy cheeses of Scandinavia, the distinguished cheeses of Switzerland, the amiable cheeses of Italy . . ." Mr. Winston Churchill himself reached some apex, even for his justly famous wit, with his reference to France: "No country that offers 325 varieties of cheese is capable of being governed."

Cheese has been extolled as "milk's leap into immortality," and is considered the only fit companion for the finest wines. *Formos* in ancient Greece, *forma* in Latin, *formaggio* in Italian, *fromage* in French, *Käse* in German, *kaas* in Dutch, *cais* in Irish, *caws* in Welsh, *quiejo* in Portuguese, *quese* in Spanish, it was *cese* or *cyse* in Anglo-Saxon, from which we derived our *cheese*.

Cheese, beloved by so many for so long, is made mostly from cow's milk, but you can also count, udderwise, on sheep, goats, buffalo, camels, reindeer and yaks.

And we all know how the most expert of photographers, tensed and lensed on the most beautiful female models in the world, must urge warmth into the wooden perfection of those flawless lips by pleading with the lady just to say: "cheese." The very word is a smile.

One cannot write about cheese without mentioning its discovery—since the very process of making it

July 31 1915

Five Cents the Copy

The
COUNTRY
GENTLEMAN

The OLDEST AGRICULTURAL JOURNAL in the WORLD

is inherent in the tale. The veracity of the story cannot be doubted because no one has ever dared to write about cheese without telling it. An Arab, at a time so long ago that one dares not even whisper it, set out on a trip across the desert. In his saddlebag, made from the sturdy insides of some defunct animal, he has placed milk with which to slake his thirst on the journey. But that night at the oasis, when he attempts to drink his milk, he discovers that it has separated into liquid whey and solid curd. He has invented cheese!—even to the fact that the milk was sloshed around in the stomach of an animal, thus supplying the *rennet* (a natural stomach chemical which will curdle milk). It is an interesting thing that every single reference book on cheese contains the same tale, sometimes told solemnly or sometimes with mild apology, but the Arab is always the hero. It would be somehow more appropriate if the rider were a Kurd: all of the necessary elements of the trip would be present, in addition to the pun. But then, you'd miss the oasis, and who wants to do that? Let the ancient Arab reign as the founder of cheese.

Cheese has been mentioned on tablets of cuneiform writing, and holds high favor in legends of the Romans, Greeks, Chinese, Sumerians, and Egyptians. Great value was always put upon cheese. The citizens of Cheshire, Massachusetts presented Thomas Jefferson with an enormous 1,235-pound cheese to celebrate his victory in 1801 over the Federalists. It is said that from that occasion sprang the custom of referring to somebody of note as a "big cheese." The farmers of Somerset in England made for Queen Victoria a wheel of cheese over a thousand pounds in weight, the results of one day's milling of some 800 pounds. The lady was not displeased. Country fairs seem to inspire feats of cheese. There was a four-ton cheese at the Toronto Fair at the turn of the century, and a New York State Fair even exceeded that in 1937.

Probably the biggest cheese binge of all was brought about by that most boisterous of our presidents, Andrew Jackson. Since Jackson was inordinately fond of cheese, he was mighty pleased when he was presented in the middle of his term of office with a 1,400-pound cheddar cheese from an upper New York State cheesemaker. Old Hickory took his time about things sometimes, so he let this cheese stand for twenty months in the White House vestibule while it acquired character. When it came time to end his term in office, the President decided to wheel out his cheese for a wingding like one he'd had on the way in. He threw this party, with the great cheese as the pièce de résistance. Everyone in Washington was invited. A local account tells the story:

"This is Washington's Birthday. The President, all departments, the Senate and we, the people, have celebrated by eating a big cheese. The President's house was thrown open. The multitude swarmed in. The Senate of the United States adjourned. The representatives of the various departments turned out. Representatives in squadrons left the Capitol, and all for the purpose of eating cheese: Mr. Webster was there to eat cheese, Mr. Woodbury, Colonel

Once more the liberal year
laughs out O'er richer stores
than gems of gold;
Once more with harvest song and
shout Is nature's boldest
triumph told.

J. G. Whittier

Berton, Mr. Dickerson, and the gallant Colonel Trowbridge were eating cheese. The court, the fashion, the beauty of Washington, foreign representatives in stars and garters; gay, joyous, dashing and gorgeous women all in the pride and panoply and pomp of wealth, were there eating cheese. Cheese, cheese, cheese, was on everybody's mouth. All you heard was cheese; all you smelled was cheese. It was cheese, cheese, cheese, streams of cheese were going up the avenue in everybody's fists; balls of cheese were in a hundred pockets; every handkerchief smelled of cheese. The whole atmosphere for a half mile around was infected with cheese."

The hungry guests ate the entire cheese in two hours. Old Hickory barely had a chance to nibble on a small piece. But a good time was had by all.

Cheese has always been a traditional American food habit, since those three cows arrived at Plymouth in 1624. A cheese factory was soon started, a modest beginning to a great industry. Every home and farm made its own, but the first big cheese factory was up in the New York State cow country, in Oneida, where one Jesse Williams gave his name and brand to history in 1851. Cheddar (and its relative Colby) is the most popular cheese in America. It dates as far back as 1655. Probably 80 percent of the cheese we eat is cheddar, also called store cheese, rat cheese, American cheese and what have you. Swiss is probably second, and our own variety of Muenster third. The greatest dairy states, of course, produce the most cheese—Wisconsin first, with probably half

of the total, then Minnesota, New York, Iowa, Missouri, and Illinois, in that order—but cheese comes from almost every state.

One last little story about cheese: The names of cheeses are, as we all know, little poems in themselves, haunts of places and people all over the world—Port-Salut, Bleu d'Auvergne, St. Paulin, Fontin d'Asti, Gorgonzola, Caccio-cavallo, Bel Paese, Edelpilzkaese, Gjetöst, Ekiwani, Danablu, and Fin de Siècle, just to name a few. But Liederkranz? Guess who discovered it? We did. A young Swiss cheese maker working in New York in the 1880's was instructed to try to duplicate the subtle flavor niceties of an imported cheese called Bismarck Schlosskaese, from guess what country, but which didn't travel very well. The young man, Emil Frey, gave it a try. He couldn't quite make the same kind of cheese as the Bismarck Schlosskaese, but he *did* come up with a nice smooth, tasty bit of stuff which was tried out on the unsuspecting members of the Liederkranz Singing Society in New York City. The songbirds approved, Bismarck was forgotten, and Liederkranz marches on into American cheese history. On the order of a French Camembert, it has a quality all of its own and is easily available in all food stores. Liederkranz does not lend itself to cooking but should be served with a good green salad or with crusty bread and sweet butter and a ripe chilled pear. Needless to say a full-bodied red wine is a must with a cheese of this caliber.

Say cheese and smile.

Say egg and exult. And for the last word on egg

cookery we quote from a definitive essay on the topic which appeared in *The Saturday Evening Post* in the Thirties. The author was George Rector, whose restaurant was famous for the elegant eggs (among other things) prepared and served there. A lot of things have changed since the Thirties but not eggs, and no one has better described the niceties of egg preparation. The words that follow are Mr. Rector's:

EGGS TO PERFECTION

The sermon begins with the obvious remark that anything as undecided as a raw egg escaped from the shell needs special measures to keep it from demoralization when dumped into so hostile an environment as a hot pan. Seeing eggs profaned by bad scrambling has always exerted an unholy fascination over me, just as some people can't look away from a bad accident on the street.

Each of the three major schools of egg scrambling disagrees with the other two as intolerantly as a third-party candidate always does. Two swear by the frying pan, but snarl between themselves over the method; the third pounds the table and insists that frying pans are fit only for cooking up proverbs and shouts the praises of the double boiler. The main lines of battle are crossed and recrossed by all kinds of minor schisms involving whether straight butter or a half-and-half mixture of bacon fat and butter is the right answer. In the old days at Rector's, our cooks would have walked out if we'd suggested anything but butter. But that undertone of husky bacon flavor has its

private points, and so has a little ham fat left in the pan.

The frying pan calls for a real cook, make no mistake about that—somebody with that sixth sense of culinary timing which defies written formulas like dancing and cocktail making.

This old-fashioned, bottled-in-bond country scrambling is a split-second operation like a matador's death thrust. A hottish frying pan, but not so that the butter starts smoking before you've lubricated the sides and bottom well. Crack the eggs in boldly, as if you were frying them, and watch them as suspiciously as a dog observing a tramp passing along the family fence. Just when the whites are beginning to "set"—cook's jargon for solidifying—dive in with fork or spoon and mix whites and yolks as frantically as the madman in the Spanish proverb about how to make a salad. Since the yolks are still practically raw and the whites as yet rather undecided—don't miss that critical moment or it's all over and you'd better breakfast on something else—you get the yolk as a binding, richening sauce. Add salt and pepper here and then indulge in a gentle stirring motion for a short while, just enough to keep traffic moving while the yolk cooks in and the whites make up their minds.

But you can't fool round and miss your boat. If they stay a second too long in the pan, the whites will be tough with that filmy toughness and the yolk will have passed the exact stage, between runny and gluey, where it surpasses itself. No kind of scrambled egg can sit round in a hot pan without damage—not least the other frying-pan variety, with the eggs mixed together in a bowl—just mixed, not whipped—before reaching the pan. This school insists that "setting" should be interfered with from the start by a mixing, scraping motion of the fork which keeps bringing the solidified egg up from the bottom and giving the hot pan a chance at the liquid on top. That motion never stops—it even slightly increases throughout—until the pan is full of a fluffy, moist yellowness that cries out for hot buttered toast to receive it.

The double boiler's great recommendation—and for this reason alone it's a favorite wherever housewives swap troubles over back fences—is that it tends to preclude toughness. So long as you don't let the water boil hard below the buttered upper part that holds the egg mixture—and if you're careful to get them out as soon as they're done—a boiler-scrambled egg will come right up smiling. To make sure of a delicate consistency, some people mix a little milk or cream in before starting that gentle stirring which eventually produces a solid and yet unobtrusive mass. I have learned to plug that system on the impregnable principle that it's much better to give the average cook a break than to set her trying something she'll probably bungle. With the double boiler it is almost impossible to bungle. If she's capable of a frying pan scramble, on the other hand, she doesn't need instruction from me.

It's logical that anything as subtle as the flavor of an egg close to the hen should call for finicky handling. Not that this flavor doesn't combine most politely with others—the dash of angostura in the scrambled eggs, or the half teaspoon of Worcester-shire sauce—for four eggs—or the drop of Tabasco find their rooters well distributed among hearty feeders. A teaspoon of chopped onion or chopped chives is another tactful stunt, and to fry a few mushrooms in the pan before introducing the eggs—you probably won't need any more butter—makes them a cracking fine luncheon dish.

Certainly no new marriage can be considered safely launched until she has learned—and also learned to observe—the exact second at which his boiled eggs should be snatched out of the water. The trouble is that, to most people, a three-minute egg is not a scientifically exact description of an egg in contact with boiling water for one hundred and eighty seconds, no more, no less, but a kind of general description of something ranging all the way from half raw to solid.

I say "boiled eggs" because the world thinks of them that way, whereas the best way to boil eggs is not to boil them at all—coddle them instead. Coddling suits epicures just as well as the doctors who lay our diets for babies. It consists of the glorious simplicity of pouring fast-boiling water over the eggs and letting them stand somewhere between eight and ten minutes—I can't be more definite without encroaching on your prerogative of doping out the exact time yourself. In any case, never introduce an egg fresh out of the icebox to boiling water without a chance to warm up beforehand, or its shell will crack like a thick glass tumbler under the same ordeal. The coddled egg, its white firm and yet tender, its yolk halfway between liquid and solid, properly bolstered with

> *At noon he bounded out for*
> *food, And nothing less than*
> *roast lion would content him.*
> *But by suppertime*
> *milk toast would do.*
>
> *Thoreau*

buttered toast and eaten with crisp bacon on the side, will strike anybody but a chronic victim of egg sensitivity as pretty close to what Nature had in mind when she invented the thing.

Now for omelets. No cook who takes this acid test of skill seriously ever flops one side of an omelet bodily over on the other or uses one of these folding omelet pans. The orthodox omelet pan is an iron frying pan, slightly hollowed on the bottom, and the folding is done with a dexterous waggle of the wrist, as slick as a billiard player's stroke. The pan is buttered, bottom and sides, the eggs are beaten up well with a tablespoon of milk for each egg and appropriate salt and pepper; a wooden fork and wooden bowl are best. The mixture goes in when the pan is average hot and cooks till the bottom is barely set, with the artist jostling it nervously all the while with a modified version of the corn-popping gesture to make sure it won't stick. A thick layer of cream is spread on top just before folding. In folding, the expert delicately loosens the outside edge with a silver knife, and then, holding the pan so the heat is concentrated on the unloosened half, gives that one championship flip which, as if by a docile miracle, makes the omelet climb over itself, the brown bottom eclipsing the white cream on top till the pan is half uncovered. Then he puts a hot platter over the pan, flops the works upside down, and there she is.

But that takes a lifetime to learn, like dancing on the slack wire, and the amateur can do pretty well by using a spatula as gently as he knows how in the encouragement of the folding process. A wife who can get the hang of it at all is the kind Solomon spoke of as more precious than rubies, for the consequences, plain, or *fines herbes,* or mushrooms, or cheese, or jelly, or Spanish, are the apotheosis of the egg. And a rum omelet is a prime way of showing off on occasion. After it's landed on the hot platter, coat it lightly with powdered sugar and baptize it with slightly heated rum—brandy will do. Then, having turned off the dining-room chandelier to make it more dramatic, light the rum with a match and fetch her in in state. Spoon the rum over and over the omelet as it runs down, burning with that ghostly blue flicker; and, by the time the grand pyrotechnic display is over, you have a caramelly sauce, impregnated with the soul of sugar cane, that would cheer the heart of Carry Nation herself.

Eggomaniacs will accuse me here of passing far too lightly over the ins and outs of frying. The hot pan is the principal criminal in this precinct—only a slowish heat will cook the yolk to the proper point by the time the white is solid. Otherwise you're doomed either to the top of the egg remaining raw or to that brown, crusty, harsh effect underneath, as if your egg had been fried on a lace-paper doily. And even slow heat won't help much unless you take a large spoon and baste the egg with the surplus fat from the moment it strikes until it's served. I've often wondered if the popularity of the fried-egg sandwich wasn't partly due to the fact that sandwiching will keep the egg's shortcomings out of sight. Otherwise there would be no excuse for concealing the white-and-gold beauties of a specimen of the first class.

THE SATURDAY EVENING POST

An Illustrated Weekly Magazine
Founded Aᵒ Dⁱ 1728 *by* Benj. Franklin

Volume 172, No. 28 | Philadelphia, January 6, 1900 | 5 Cents the Copy; $2.50 the Year

Copyright, 1900, by The Curtis Publishing Company

PUBLISHED WEEKLY AT 425 ARCH STREET

Entered at the Philadelphia Post-Office as Second-Class Matter

Three MEN *on* Four WHEELS

By Jerome K. Jerome

Author of Three Men in a Boat

A Good Fried Egg

A good fried egg is delicious, a bad one is a disaster. Allow 1 or 2 eggs per person but do not fry too many at once. Allow 1 tablespoon of butter or ½ tablespoon of bacon fat per egg. Heat over a low flame. Break the egg into a cup, using only the freshest eggs possible. Slide them one by one into the pan and cook gently. As the egg whites begin to form, cut them in several places to allow them to cook quickly. Transfer the cooked eggs to warm individual serving plates.

Shirred Eggs

Shirred eggs are a delicious way to serve eggs for 1 person or any number. They are baked in individual shallow baking dishes and have the advantage of keeping warm longer than other egg preparations. There are several variations of shirred eggs of which we give you a few. It is a wonderful way to use leftover sauce. This is the recipe for 1 serving.

Melted butter
1 or 2 eggs
Capers (optional)
Chopped herbs (chives, tarragon,
  parsley) (optional)
Salt and pepper

Heat the oven to 400 degrees F. Heat the baking dish with a teaspoon of butter. Break in 1 or 2 eggs. Add a teaspoon of melted butter and bake 5 minutes or until the whites are set. Sprinkle with salt and pepper and add a few capers or chopped herbs or both if desired.

Shirred Eggs with Mushrooms

Follow the recipe for shirred eggs. Once cooked cover with warm Mushroom Sauce (see Sauces).

Shirred Eggs With Cream

Follow the preceding recipe, but instead of adding the butter to the eggs, add 1 tablespoon of heavy cream. Sprinkle with salt, pepper, a dash of paprika and chopped herbs.

Shirred Eggs with Tomato

Follow the recipe for shirred eggs. Just after the egg whites are set, cover with Tomato Puree (see Sauces) and sprinkle with Parmesan cheese. Slip under the broiler for just a moment.

Shirred Eggs with Dish Gravy

If dish gravy is left in the platter after a roast is served, save it carefully. Follow the recipe for shirred eggs. Add 1 teaspoon of melted butter and 1 tablespoon of dish gravy to the eggs. Serve with capers and a little chopped parsley.

Scrambled Eggs

Scrambled eggs are good for breakfast, lunch or supper, especially the midnight variety. They are most often served with crisp bacon, or lightly fried slices of thin ham, but they are delicious made with a generous addition of mixed chopped herbs (parsley, tarragon, chives, dill, etc.).

12 to 16 eggs
4 tablespoons butter
4 to 6 tablespoons heavy or
  commercial sour cream
Salt and pepper

Beat the eggs until just blended. Melt the butter in a large skillet and add the eggs. Stir constantly with a fork over moderate heat. As the eggs begin to thicken, add the cream and keep stirring. Do not let them get dry and remember they will continue cooking even off the heat, so transfer them to a warm (not hot) platter immediately.

Chive Flower Scrambled Eggs

The Shakers liked to cook everything that was edible. This included the wild chives and their blossoms.

12 to 16 eggs
1 to 1¼ cups milk
1 teaspoon salt
¼ teaspoon white pepper
3 tablespoons chopped chives
2 dozen chive blossoms
4 tablespoons butter or margarine

Beat the eggs and milk just until blended. Add the salt, pepper, chives and blossoms, pulled into shreds.

Heat the butter in a large skillet. Add the egg mixture and cook over moderately low heat, stirring constantly with a fork. Serve plain or with bacon or fried ham.

Texas Skillet Scrambled Eggs

A dozen eggs cooked this way would feed 6 to 8 people of ordinary appetites, but add an extra dozen eggs if you are feeding large appetites, especially if you are cooking outdoors.

1 to 2 dozen eggs
¾ to 1½ cups milk or water
2 cups Tomato Puree, canned
  or homemade (see Sauces)
4 to 6 tablespoons bacon fat
1 large green pepper, seeded
  and chopped
1 onion, peeled and chopped
3 tablespoons chopped
  canned pimiento
Salt and pepper

Beat the eggs and milk or water just until blended.

Heat the tomato puree in a saucepan.

Heat the fat in a large skillet and cook the pepper and onion until soft. Do not brown. Add the beaten eggs and the pimiento and stir with a fork until cooked but still creamy and moist. Do not overcook. Taste for seasoning.

Add the puree and serve immediately in individual warm plates. Serve with plenty of toast, biscuits or corn bread.

Virginia Poached Eggs

This recipe is an adaptation of one that President Monroe's wife liked to serve at the plantation in Virginia. It is easier to make a few at a time as people present themselves for breakfast.

Hollandaise Sauce (see Sauces)
6 to 8 slices buttered toast
3 or 4 tomatoes, peeled
Salt and pepper
6 to 8 poached eggs
2 tablespoons chopped parsley
  and chives

Make the hollandaise and keep it warm over warm (not hot) water. The sauce need only be lukewarm.

Toast and butter thick slices of firm white bread. Cut the tomatoes into ½-inch slices and sprinkle with salt and pepper. Place the toast on individual plates and cover with a tomato slice.

Cook the eggs in buttered egg poachers or, lacking them, crack an egg into a cup and slip it into a pan of simmering water containing a teaspoon of salt and a teaspoonful of vinegar. Poach no more than 4 eggs at a time. Spoon the water over the eggs and the egg whites around the yolks so that they won't spread too far. Remove the eggs with a slotted spoon to the tomato slices. Cover with a spoonful of sauce and sprinkle with the chopped herbs. Serve immediately.

Omelets

Heaven knows who first invented the omelet--probably the Chinese or the French, but it is a universal food with thousands of variations. A thin omelet made simply with whole eggs and butter is considered a French omelet, but for generations Americans have cooked their omelets with separated eggs, and milk. Since the French have become so very influential in America's culinary habits in comparatively recent years, both methods are used. In both cases fresh eggs and butter and immediate serving are requisites of good omelets. A large omelet using 8 to 10 eggs can be made in a 12-inch omelet pan but it will be harder to handle and not quite as tender as the smaller variety. Fillings are added to omelets just before they are folded.

Thin Omelet

The best thin omelets are those made for 1 or 2 persons using 2 or 3 eggs. These are cooked in a thin 7-inch sloping-sided pan. They are made so quickly that it is easy to serve many guests in order and still sit down at table. In this case beat all the required eggs together, have a saucepan of clarified butter at hand and measure out a generous ½ cupful of egg mixture each time. Rebeat the eggs for a moment before measuring out each successive portion.

2 or 3 eggs
½ teaspoon salt
1/8 teaspoon pepper
1 tablespoon butter or margarine

Heat the butter in the omelet pan or skillet over very high heat. As soon as it stops sizzling tilt the pan to coat the interior. Add the eggs and stir while they thicken. With a fork or small spatula fold the near side over the far side of the pan, tilting the pan away from you as you do it. Cook a moment longer and turn out over a warm plate. Cut in half if this is to serve 2 people.

Puffy Omelet

8 to 10 egg yolks
½ cup nonfat milk
1 teaspoon salt
¼ teaspoon white pepper
8 to 10 egg whites
Chopped parsley

Preheat the broiler and set the rack 6 inches below the heat. Beat the egg yolks until blended, add the milk, salt and pepper. Beat the egg whites until stiff but moist and stir in a third of them gently but thoroughly with the egg yolks. Fold in the remaining egg whites.

Melt the butter over moderate heat in a large skillet with a heatproof handle. When it begins to sizzle add the egg mixture. Keep running a small spatula around the edge of the pan and over the top to keep it smooth, pricking down to the bottom with the tip to let the heat rise. When the bottom part is well set place the skillet under the broiler and cook 3 or 4 minutes longer or until golden brown but not dry. Fold one half over the other with a wide spatula or leave it flat as you prefer. Hold a platter close to the skillet and turn the omelet out on it. Garnish with chopped parsley.

Tomato Omelet

Tomato Puree (see Sauces)
Plain or Puffy Omelet
Parmesan cheese

Make the tomato puree and keep warm. Make the plain or puffy omelet and just before folding put some of the puree on the lower half of the omelet. Transfer to a plate or warm platter. Cover with more of the puree and sprinkle with Parmesan cheese.

California Oyster Omelet

During the Gold Rush, food in California made Alaskan prices today seem very low in comparison. A sign of success and wealth was to eat oysters and eggs which were at the top of the luxury items. This wasn't exactly the recipe they used, but it celebrates those days.

1 pint small oysters, drained
Butter or margarine
8 to 10 egg yolks
½ cup fat-free milk
¾ teaspoon salt
Freshly ground black pepper
8 to 10 egg whites beaten stiff
3 tablespoons chopped chives
½ pint heavy cream

Cook the oysters in 2 tablespoons of butter until they are plump and the edges begin to curl. The tiny west coast Olympia oysters are perfect for this. If the oysters are large cut them in pieces. Remove from the heat and keep warm.

Heat 4 tablespoons of butter in a large skillet with a heatproof handle. Make the omelet as in Puffy Omelet. As soon as the omelet has set on the bottom, strew the oysters on the surface and let the omelet continue to rise over them. Finish under the broiler. At the same time warm the cream with the chives. Do not boil. Turn the omelet out onto a platter, folded or not. Cover with the hot cream and serve.

Mushroom Omelet

Mushroom Sauce (see Sauces)
Plain or Puffy Omelet
Parsley

Make the mushroom sauce.

When the sauce is ready, prepare either omelet and just before folding add some of the sauce to the lower half of the omelet. Transfer to a warm plate or platter and cover with more of the sauce. Garnish with parsley.

Cheese Omelet

Cheese Sauce (see Sauces)
Plain or Puffy Omelet

Make the cheese sauce, saving out ¼ cup of grated cheese to sprinkle on the omelet.

Make either a large plain or puffy omelet. Just before folding pour 1 cupful of the sauce on the lower half of the omelet. Fold and transfer to a heatproof platter. Pour the rest of the sauce over the omelet. Sprinkle with cheese and run the omelet under the broiler just long enough to brown. Serve immediately.

EGGS *and* AMLETS.

Eggs with Juice of Orange.

BEAT up more or fewer Eggs according to the Size of the Diſh you would make; while you are beating them, ſqueeze in ſome Juice of Orange, taking care that none of the Seeds fall in among the Eggs. When they are well beaten, and ſeaſon'd with a little Salt, take a Sauce-pan, and put in it a little Butter or Gravy; pour in your Eggs, and keep them always ſtirring over a gentle Fire, that they may not ſtick to the Bottom: When they are enough, pour them into a little Diſh or Plate, and ſerve them warm.

Poach'd Eggs in Gravy.

Poach ſome new-laid Eggs in boiling Water and a little Vinegar. Have ſome good Gravy in readineſs, put to it ſome Salt and Pepper and a whole Leek, heat it over the Fire, and having laid your poach'd Eggs in a Diſh, ſtrain it through a Sieve upon them, and ſerve them hot in Plates or little Diſhes.

Creole Omelet

This kind of omelet makes a hearty but not-too-filling entree for luncheon or Sunday evening supper, or a substantial midnight snack to serve leftover guests who gather in the kitchen after a party. Prepare the sauce ahead of time and store in a covered jar in the refrigerator; it can be heated while you are assembling ingredients for the omelet.

½ cup chopped onion
4 tablespoons minced celery
2 tablespoons chopped green pepper
1 clove garlic, pressed
2 tablespoons olive or
    peanut oil
2 cups chopped, peeled tomatoes
    or canned tomatoes
1 small bay leaf
¼ teaspoon powdered thyme
Few drops Tabasco
½ teaspoon sugar
1 teaspoon salt
1/8 teaspoon freshly ground pepper
Plain or Puffy Omelet
Stuffed olives

Cook the vegetables in heated oil over a moderate heat just until soft. Add the tomatoes, bay leaf, and seasonings and cook until the sauce is quite thick. Remove the bay leaf.

Make the omelet of your choice. Just before folding, while the top of the omelet is still moist, put ¼ cup of the sauce on half of the omelet. Fold over the other half. Turn onto a warm platter and cover with the rest of the sauce. Garnish with a few stuffed olives.

French Toast

New Orleans taught all America one version of this concoction and called it "Pain Perdu" or "Lost Bread." The New England version is similar but simpler, and it is not unreasonable to suppose that it was thought up by some thrifty housewife for the same reason, which was to use up not-too-fresh bread. We give you both versions in one recipe and let you take your choice. One is more of a dessert; the other more of a breakfast dish. This will make 12 to 16 pieces.

4 eggs
¾ cup milk
¼ teaspoon salt
1 teaspoon grated lemon rind
    (optional)
2 tablespoons sugar (optional)
12 to 16 slices slightly stale
    white bread
Butter or margarine

Beat the eggs slightly with a flat whisk in a shallow dish and add the milk. Add the salt and, if desired, the lemon rind and sugar.

Heat 2 tablespoons of butter in a large skillet. Dip 3 slices of bread in the batter and brown them well on both sides. Keep warm while repeating the process until all the bread is used. Serve with maple syrup, jam or honey or cinnamon sugar, made of ½ cup of sugar mixed with 2 teaspoons of cinnamon.

While tradition decrees that French Toast be made with white bread, there is no law against using whole wheat bread in its place, on occasion. Omit the lemon rind and add a last-minute sprinkling of confectioners' sugar over the top slice.

Large Cheese Soufflé

Cream Sauce (see Sauces)
6 egg yolks
¾ pound mild or sharp cheddar cheese
Salt and pepper
2 teaspoons Dijon-type mustard (optional)
7 egg whites

Make the cream sauce, using 6 tablespoons of butter and 6 tablespoons of flour with the 2 cups of milk. Beat the egg yolks thoroughly and gradually add them to the sauce, stirring constantly. Cook until the eggs thicken. Season well with salt and white pepper. Add the mustard if you like a highly seasoned soufflé. Cool to lukewarm.

Preheat the oven to 375 degrees F. Butter a large, deep (3-quart) soufflé dish or casserole.

Beat the egg whites until stiff but still moist. Stir in a third of them into the sauce. Fold in the rest of the egg whites, lifting the whisk high as you do it to incorporate as much air as possible. Pour into the prepared dish and bake 40 to 45 minutes. Serve immediately. If there is a slight delay, don't panic. Turn down the oven to 200 degrees F. Keep the oven door slightly ajar. The soufflé will keep without falling perceptibly for up to 15 to 20 minutes.

Individual Cheese Mushroom Soufflés

Cheese Soufflé (preceding recipe)
½ pound mushrooms
2 tablespoons butter

Butter 6 to 8 ramekins or individual soufflé dishes.

Make the cheese soufflé mixture, excluding the mustard.

Clean and chop the mushrooms and sauté them in butter until they have lost their moisture. Add to the egg yolk sauce mixture before adding the egg whites.

Pour the soufflé mixture into the individual dishes, filling them approximately two-thirds full. Place in a pan of hot water and bake at 350 degrees F for 30 minutes. Serve immediately.

Tillamook Toasts

Tillamook cheese is one of Oregon's many good products. It is a rich cheddar type that has a flavor all of its own. Combined with ham and chutney, it makes a very tasty luncheon or late supper dish. Allow 1 or 2 toasts per person. Serve with very cold beer.

Cut Good White Bread (see Breads) or other firm bread in ½-inch slices. Toast on both sides lightly, butter well and trim the crusts. Top each slice with a 1/8-inch slice of cooked ham. Spread with a thin layer of chutney and cover with a slice of Tillamook. Bake in a 400-degree oven until the cheese bubbles and lightly browns.

Welsh Rabbit

Another culinary controversy that won't ever be solved is whether to call this dish "rarebit," as most of the British do, or "rabbit," as most Americans do. Legend has it that it was a dish invented by a Welshman to take the place of rabbit. Whatever its name, it makes a delicious luncheon or supper dish that can be made in the kitchen or at the table. Good cold beer and a tartly dressed green salad make good companions to the rabbit. This dish must be served the minute—no, the second—it is ready.

12 to 16 (½-inch) slices of bread
¾ cup beer
2 to 2½ pounds sharp cheddar
 cheese, cubed
1½ teaspoons salt
¼ teaspoon freshly ground pepper
½ teaspoon paprika

Toast thick slices of firm, preferably homemade, bread, trimming the crusts if desired.

Heat the beer in the top of a double boiler or chafing dish and add the cubed cheese. Stir with a wooden spoon until it melts. This will take 10 to 15 minutes. Add the seasonings and serve on the toast placed on warm plates. Allow 2 pieces to each person.

Fondues

The famous Brillat-Savarin, while in exile over here shortly after the French Revolution, gave this dish to a restaurant owner in Boston. The fondue was immediately adopted by Americans both as a name and as a basis for many cheese dishes.

Brillat-Savarin's Boston Fondue

8 eggs
4 tablespoons butter
¼ pound Gruyère cheese, grated
Black pepper

Break the eggs into a flat-bottomed pan or deep skillet. Beat with a fork until thoroughly blended. Add the butter and grated cheese. Stir over fairly high heat, stirring constantly with a wooden spoon until the cheese is melted. Season with plenty of freshly ground black pepper. Serve with French bread and your best dry white wine that has been properly chilled and decanted.

American Fondue

1 loaf unsliced white bread
1½ to 2 cups California Chablis
2 to 2½ pounds American Swiss
   cheese, cubed
4 tablespoons rum
¼ teaspoon black pepper

Cut the bread in ¾-inch slices and trim the crusts. Toast the bread and cut each slice into 1½-inch squares. Place in 1 or 2 baskets or bowls.

Heat the wine and cheese in the top part of a double boiler over boiling water, stirring with a wooden spoon. As soon as it is melted, add the rum and stir for a few minutes. Add the black pepper. Pour into the top of a chafing dish or fondue pot. Provide those assembled with long forks and plenty of the Chablis, chilled. The guests will dip the bread into the cheese.

Cheddar Fondue

12 to 16 slices firm white bread
Butter or margarine
2 cups grated cheddar cheese
   (medium or sharp)
½ to 1 pound cooked shrimp (optional)
4 eggs
2 teaspoons Dijon-type mustard
1½ teaspoons salt
½ teaspoon paprika
2 cups milk

Trim the crusts from the bread. Spread each slice with butter and cut into 3 strips. Butter a large deep rectangular baking-serving dish and put a layer of bread strips in the bottom. Sprinkle generously with grated cheese. Repeat the process until the bread and cheese are used, ending with a layer of bread strips, butter side up. If shrimp is added, strew the bread layers with shrimp before adding the cheese.

Preheat the oven to 350 degrees F. Beat the eggs and add the seasonings and milk. Blend well. Pour the mixture into the baking dish and bake 25 to 30 minutes or until golden brown. A good feature of this fondue is that the dish can be prepared in advance, adding the custard mixture just before baking at a convenient time.

Advertisement for General Motors, THE SATURDAY EVENING POST, *July 16, 1927*

VEGETABLES & SALAD: BIG DOINGS DOWN AT THE PLANT

The brave but foolish gold hunters who came to America from Spain even before the advent of the Pilgrims were never to realize that what they would send back to the Old World would benefit the peoples of this planet far more significantly than any puny yellow metal.

In a word, vegetables. Certain new kinds of food that ancient Europe and Asia had never dreamed existed. We can say with safety that these new foods came from "America" in a kind of general sense. The nomadic nature of most Indian tribes on the new continents as well as the offshore islands made possible exchanges in agri-culture as well as in their art culture in the course of time. Some vegetables originated in Mexico, some Peru, Guatemala or Brazil. But in due time they became universally American.

There is a kind of drama to the simple little tale of these new foods. Their overfamiliar names perhaps offset the tremendous impact they were going to have on the dietary habits of the entire world. *New!* Tomatoes. Sweet potatoes, Irish potatoes. Corn. Pinto beans, green beans, snap beans, navy beans, kidney beans. Hubbard squash. Pumpkin. Chili peppers.

Of course, when the captains and the conquistadores returned with these vegetables to their European ports of call, the food was often received by many merely as novelties. But there were others to whom they were a godsend almost in the literal sense of the word. These were the dedicated ones who did not eat flesh, sometimes for practical reasons and sometimes from religious conviction.

The idea that eating meat is distasteful to the gods harks back to centuries before Christ when flesh eaters were denounced in the Vedic literature of India. We have discovered in our time that a soybean burger has as much protein in it as an all-beef burger, but soybean culture had already become an art thousands of years ago in China. Six centuries before Christ, the genius who developed the basic mathematics of the science of geometry, Pythagoras, headed up a colony in Italy where they ate only vegetables to expound the philosophy of the sacredness of living things.

It is curious how many extraordinary individuals all across history have been imbued with the value of the vegetable diet and connected it with the moral purposes of a good life. Among them, such as Albert Einstein, Jean-Jacques Rousseau, Richard Wagner, Alexis Tolstoy, Mahatma Gandhi, Leonardo da Vinci, Percy Bysshe Shelley, Albert Schweitzer, and George Bernard Shaw. Shaw, with his usual ebullient Irish egomania, put the point right on the line: "It seems to me, looking at myself," quoth the bearded one, "that I am a remarkably superior person, when you compare me with other writers, journalists and dramatists; and I am perfectly content to put this down to my abstinence from meat." (Adolf Hitler was also an avid vegetarian, and although we can hardly classify him as one of the benefactors of mankind, it must in all fairness be admitted that beastlike as he was in his philosophies and actions, even in his brief orgy of destruction, he demonstrated powers of leadership beyond those of ordinary men.)

Whole groups of people all over the world have espoused vegetarianism, sometimes in a religious way,

Painted by Norman Rockwell for Green Giant Company advertising, 1940

as with the Seventh Day Adventists. Others, such as the 100,000 or so Abkhasians who are tucked away between the Black Sea and the crest of the greater Caucasus range in the northwestern corner of the Georgian part of the Soviet Union, simply demonstrate the sensibleness of a vegetarian diet by living longer than anyone else in the world. They are quite the darlings of magazine and Sunday supplement writers, but we cannot slide along into our vegetable recipes without at least a brief visit with the Abkhasians. They figure that a vegetable diet is the smartest one, on the whole, and they prove this by living to be over a hundred years old as a general practice. Hardly any Abkhasians suffer from arteriosclerosis, except when they begin to run into problems of extreme old age, which with them is somewhere past the century mark. Nobody retires in that country. People may slow down a little after they pass ninety, but they keep on producing for the community by active physical work. In Sukhumi, the capital city of Abkhasia, there is an example of a splendid cultural interest by this people. They maintain a famous musical ensemble there with an enormous repertoire of songs and instrumental accomplishments. They also feature on their frequent tours the very acrobatic native folk dances of the area. Well and good you may say: but—get this—you have to be at least ninety years of age to join this ensemble! They don't need any octogenarians messing things up with any youthful pranks or childish additions like rock 'n' roll.

The Abkhasians seem to have the formula down

right. But it isn't for lack of trying that vegetarianism hasn't made as much progress in our own country as you might expect. The British beat us to it by organizing the first vegetarian society in 1847, but our own American Vegetarian Convention met in New York in 1850, with Sylvester Graham as one of its chief cheerleaders. He was a gentleman of firm convictions, a man of fine grain, you may recall, for whom the Graham cracker was named. He actually may be the true founder of the health movement in America, although one may be sure that he would be highly grieved today to find that his cracker has emerged as a backslider—marketed with a chocolate covering.

Mr. Graham also talked Horace Greeley, founder of the *New York Herald Tribune*, out of drinking coffee, no small feat of persuasion if you have any idea of the inextricable linkage between coffee swilling and the publishing business. Long before Bernard Shaw, Mr. Greeley felt compelled to have his say in the matter: "Other things being equal, I judge that a strict vegetarian will live ten years longer than a habitual flesh eater, while suffering, on the average, less than half as much from sickness as the carnivorous must."

We may also take note of the fact that long before much was known about psychiatry, the author Samuel Butler in his *Way of All Flesh* (no pun intended in this particular reference) dealt with the psychic agonies of one of his characters in true vegetarian style. His hero, almost on the brink of insanity from the pressures of his life, is directed by his doctor to

Bread gained by deceit is sweet
to a man
But afterward his mouth
will be full of gravel.

Proverbs 20:17

take a course in zoo visiting. "Avoid the carnivores and the meat eaters," advised the medico in effect, "but try to give over a few hours each day to lingering in the company of the larger herbivorous animals. Observe the elephant, the hippopotamus, and the rhinoceros. Commune with their calm strength and great stature. Take some of their divine serenity for your own."

In the enormous literature about vegetables, probably the most interesting documents from our point of view might concern the tomato, because it really has such an amusing history, and corn, because it might be said to have saved the lives of our original forebears and could be in the long run the most valuable product of this nation.

If you have ever grown tomatoes, you know how lively and prolific a plant they can be. Once the tomatoes start to form on the vine, it seems as if more and more spring into shape every day as if by magic. A few rows of tomato plants can feed many families. But for a long time they were considered such an oddity that they were hardly regarded as a food at all. Some favored tomatoes in Europe as soon as the Spaniards brought the plants back from the New World, but not everyone ate them. The French called them "love apples" and considered them as a kind of costume jewelry—to be carried and fondled but not eaten. The British called the tomato "the wolf peach," believing it to be aesthetically as appealing as a peach, but positively as dangerous to eat as flirting with a full-grown wolf. Seed catalogues which may be found in early American libraries list tomatoes as

"annual ornamental flowers."

The naming of the tomato has a touch of romance. It was Hernando Cortez who first became intrigued in Mexico with the little red fruit the Aztecs called *tomati* or *tomatl*. He Iberianized it into *tomato*. The tomato then traveled to Portugal, then to Macao via the Portuguese trading captains, and thence to China. The Chinese have been great cooks from time immemorial, and there was no nonsense in their minds as to the value of the tomato as a food. They immediately made it the basis of a very delicious and tangy sauce, which they dubbed *kai-sup*. You may use *kai-sup* very often: the label on our bottles usually calls it catsup or ketchup.

Thomas Jefferson was one of the first Americans to enjoy tomatoes. He threw things into reverse by first discovering them in France when he was American Minister to the Court of King Louis XVI, and then bringing some seeds with him back to Monticello, Virginia, when he returned in 1789. His friend George Washington also enjoyed eating a love apple when he could get one.

But the old canard that it was poisonous clung to the poor tomato. (After all, botanically, tomatoes do belong to the poisonous nightshade family.) So one day in 1820 a tomato lover by the name of Robert Gibbon Johnson, of Salem, New Jersey, announced that he would prove that the "fruit" was nonpoisonous. He stood on the steps of the public courthouse in front of a huge crowd of citizens, each of whom was convinced that he was off his rocker and close to his demise, consumed one tomato after another.

> *The sluggard does not plow in*
> *the autumn*
> *He will seek at harvest and*
> *have nothing.*
>
> Proverbs 20:4

When they saw that he did not expire on the spot, word spread that love apples were not quite as dangerous as originally supposed. The fact is that Mr. Johnson had really hedged his bet a bit—he had eaten tomatoes in many parts of the world, and knew that he was going to survive his little bit of exhibitionism. But he converted our nation to the tomato.

By 1840 tomatoes were being cultivated everywhere. The first canned tomatoes appeared in 1870.

If you get right down to it, we should not be discussing tomatoes in this chapter at all, because botanically they are a fruit. But you'll find them on the vegetable stands in your supermarket. And the United States Supreme Court—which, it must be admitted, is usually presumed to have more important matters to decide—ruled in 1893 that the tomato was not a fruit but a vegetable. So there.

Have a sip of tomato juice before your meal, sir? Or perhaps a Bloody Mary? Just an old Aztec custom, that's all.

But the greatest food gift from the New World was, of course, corn. In the Americas, before European exploration, there were three main centers of civilization—the Aztecs in Mexico, the Mayas in Yucatan and Honduras, and the Incas in Peru. It is suspected that corn was known to these cultures some 6,000 years before Columbus landed. Indubitably it had had time to filter northward to our own Indian areas, and had thus become the main food staple of the tribes both in Virginia and Massachusetts when those first settlers arrived. Captain John Smith—to use a phrase delicately attuned to this chapter—made

no beans about what corn meant to them in Jamestown. His journal states that the settlers would have starved in 1607 had not the Indians brought them corn.

Up in Plymouth, they were doing well on another Indian vegetable—pumpkin; perhaps too well, as one of their seventeenth-century songs goes:

"We have pumpkins at morning,
Pumpkins at noon,
If it were not for pumpkins,
We should be undoon."

But it was corn that was at the kernel of their survival. At Plymouth, too, Bradford reported that certain baskets of corn found buried on Cape Cod by the Indians spelled the difference between life and death for the Pilgrims. They used it for their first planting in the spring:

"And being now come to the 25th of March, I shall begin the year 1621.

MAYFLOWER DEPARTS AND CORN PLANTED

"They now began to dispatch the ship away which brought them over, which lay till about this time, or the beginning of April. The reason on their part why she stayed so long was the necessity and danger that lay upon them; for it was well toward the end of December before she could land anything here, or they able to receive anything ashore.

"Afterward, the 14th of January, the house which they had made for a general rendezvous by casualty fell afire, and some were fain to

A CALIFORNIA CONTRIBUTION TO THE NATIONAL MARKET BASKET

Del Monte
BRAND QUALITY
REG. US.   PAT. OFF.
CALIFORNIA CANNED FRUITS AND VEGETABLES

Advertisement, THE SATURDAY EVENING POST, *January 26, 1918*

retire aboard for shelter; then the sickness began to fall sore among them, and the weather so bad as they could not make much sooner any dispatch. Again, the governor and chief of them, seeing so many die and fall down sick daily, thought it no wisdom to send away the ship, their condition considered and the danger they stood in from the Indians, till they could procure some shelter; and therefore thought it better to draw some more charge upon themselves and friends than hazard all. The master and seamen likewise, though before they hasted the passengers ashore to be gone, now many of their men being dead, and of the ablest of them (as is before noted), and of the rest many lay sick and weak; the master dared not put to sea till he saw his men begin to recover, and the heart of winter over.

"Afterward they (as many as were able) began to plant their corn, in which service Squanto stood them in great stead, showing both the manner how to set it and after how to dress and tend it; also he told them, except they got fish and set with it in these old grounds, it would come up nothing. And he showed them that in the middle of April they should have store enough come up the brook by which they began to build, and taught them how to take it, and where to get other provisions necessary for them. All which they found true by trial and experience. Some English seed they sowed, as wheat and peas, but it came not to good, either by the badness of the seed or lateness of the season or both, or some other defect."

It is pleasant to report as well that later the Pilgrims made gifts to the Pamet Indians who had buried the corn, in payment for their bounty. The Pilgrims even used corn for money—so important was it in their scheme of life—paid their rent, taxes, and debts with it. Nor were the Indians unaware of what corn meant to them: their very word for it, *maize*, translates both as "bread of life" and "grain of the gods." There are thousands of legends describing its origin. One of the more fanciful is the Iroquois tale of how in time of terrible famine, a spirit figure from the sky came down to walk the earth with pity and corn sprang up miraculously in the marks of her moccasins to feed the starving people.

Later on, as the country expanded, corn kernels went along with the settlers.

"We wouldn't have lasted long without cornmeal," reminisced one Hoosier pioneer. "Corn bread was our staff of life. For several years we had it in some form for breakfast, dinner and supper, never tirin' of it. Sometimes a few coals or a little ashes would get in the cookin', but that didn't matter; we thought it just helped season it some."

No wonder one historian flatly states that the Western Hemisphere was built on Indian maize. Today it is probably still one of the entire world's greatest two foods, being grown everywhere on our planet, second in volume only to wheat, ahead of rice and potatoes.

> *He who has a bountiful eye*
> *will be blessed, For he shares*
> *his bread with the poor.*
>
> *Proverbs 22:9*

What does corn do for us except perhaps get stuck in our teeth after we battle with it on the cob? We eat it canned, fresh, frozen, in baby foods, and as candy and chewing gum ingredients. We eat corn cookies, cornmeal, cornstarch, corn sugar, corn syrup, corn vinegar, corn margarine, corn yeast, and we cook our other foods in corn oil. We feed our livestock with corn bran, corn fodder and silage. Corn by-products include alcohol, antifreeze, ceramics, cosmetics, dyes, ether, explosives, insulating materials, medicines, paints, paper, paperboard, pastes and binders, photographic film, plastics, safety glass, soaps, solvents, textiles and varnishes.

And we pop corn. A gift from the gods, and fun besides. So, come next fall, with Thanksgiving near, do not fail that charming old custom. Hang an ear or two of corn on your front door. So fresh and decorative and meaningful. And perhaps it will say something of thanks in your own heart: this husk of corn, give or take a few million statistics and a few libraries full of history, could well be just the one basic reason that you are here today to enjoy America.

If we have been a bit corny in our story of the greening of America, or related with undue solemnity the decision by the highest judicial court in our land that a fruit is legally a vegetable, perhaps we can be forgiven for being impressed by, but also neglecting, others of the extraordinary multiplicity of vegetables not only originating in the Americas but also imported.

It is told how the Egyptians worshipped the onion as the symbol of the universe, an image of planetary oneness not too unlike the actual containment of planets within their own constellation and of constellations within their own galaxy, within a larger firmament of outer and inner skins. An inscription on the pyramids built nearly 5,000 years ago indicates that the workmen ate not only onions but garlic, proof that the Hero Sandwich is not a recent invention (the onion, however, was originally a native of Persia).

To be patriotic about it, we Americans have our own wild onion, not quite the thing for your dinner table, but a vegetable which lives on in the fantastic vigor of America's perhaps most extraordinary city. A meadow where the Indians found onions growing was known to them as Shi-kai-O. When white settlers moved to the Midwest and found themselves pleased to settle on that same spot of the wild onion, next to a huge body of water, they had little hesitation in naming it for the Indian term. Chicago—if you please.

Broad beans and limas were known to the Old World, but all the others—green beans, the navy beans used in bean soup and baked beans, the red kidney beans that go in chili and bean salad and the spotted pinto bean—are American through and through. Beans were being grown by the North American Indians when the first colonists arrived, and the colonists soon learned to plant, cook and eat them.

What a break! Because the humble bean is one of the most valuable of all vegetables. It is quick and easy to grow, requiring little space and producing edible fruit within fifty-five days of planting time. It also enriches the soil, by fixing nitrogen from the air, so that subsequent crops grow better. Beans are among

Let first the onion flourish
there, Rose among roots,
the maiden-fair, Wine-scented
and poetic soul
Of the capacious salad bowl.

R. L. Stevenson

the most nourishing of all vegetables since they contain proteins and carbohydrates as well as vitamins and minerals.

Potatoes? The sweet potato and the so-called Irish potato are both American-born and bred.

The Indians living in Virginia were cultivating the sweet potato when the first colonists arrived. This crop, however, requires warmth and a fairly long growing season, so it couldn't be adapted to the more rugged climate the Pilgrims found in New England.

The white or Irish potato came to North America from South America—by way of Europe! The Spanish explorers took it home to Spain, and from Spain it was introduced into England and then Ireland. The Irish brought it with them when they settled in New England—and that's how it got its name.

And so, on to that aesthetically pleasing role of the vegetable—salad.

After the musical comedy overtones of the tomato and the symphonic theme of corn's contribution to our world, "salad" comes on a little lightly, like someone whistling a rock tune.

Yet salad has had its place in our food's history. The word itself dates back to the Latin word *sal*, for *salt*. The English—that marvelous race of non-linguists who, for example, managed to call the wines of Juarez, Spain "Sherry" and believed they had it straight—grouped any number of uncooked tender leaves of herbs and plants under the world *sallet*.

There are hundreds of varieties of lettuce today, deriving from wild plants scattered all over Europe and Asia through the ages, fodder for both hungry man and beast. Chaucer mentions in the fourteenth century a chap who enjoyed a sallet of "garlic, onions, and lettuce." Tom Jefferson, who keeps popping up in every book about food, grew about twenty varieties of lettuce for his princely table at Monticello. But every New England housewife with a tiny plot of ground found a place to plant marjoram, thyme, sage, caraway and a garden of other herbs to spice up the sallets of lettuce, chicory, watercress, dandelion and other greens she primped up for her farmers and hunters, home after a day outdoors. A favorite in almost every New England home was a bowl of pickled beets, maybe mixed with sliced onions and cucumbers in vinegar and oil as something to sharpen up the appetite for the hearty fare to come.

How many hundreds of kinds of salads are there? As many as cooks who would like to make a new and different variety. Those that we suggest here have been tried and true throughout centuries of American cooking.

We pause only on our blithe way to hail Jack Bibb, soldier in the War of 1812, native of Frankfort, Kentucky, one-time legislator, who grew such bouffant and tasty heads of lettuce behind his house that from a tiny start in his neighborhood, now everybody calls his unique gastronomic gift to sallet Bibb lettuce. A crisp salute to Mr. Bibb—long may he be tossed in name and fame.

For more about salads and salad dressings, skip ahead to the essay on Garnishings and Blandishments and see what expert George Rector has to say on the topic.

Where Goodies Tempt Most

Advertisement for White Enamel Refrigerator Co., THE SATURDAY EVENING POST, *April 29, 1911*

Artichokes

Artichokes were commonly used in George Washington's time and the most popular way seems to have been as it is now, to have them boiled.

Count on one artichoke per person. Trim the coarse outer leaves from the bottom and snip the sharp ends of the leaves. For special occasions force the leaves apart and twist out the prickly choke. Boil in salted water for 45 minutes or until the outside leaves are easily torn from the artichoke. Drain thoroughly, squeezing out the water by holding the artichoke in a clean dish towel.

Serve simply with a sauce of melted butter seasoned with salt, pepper and lemon juice or with a Hollandaise Sauce (see Sauces). For those special occasions put a small glass containing sauce in the center of the artichoke.

Asparagus

Wild asparagus was found by the early settlers, but like the asparagus we eat now, what was eaten in the late seventeenth century in America was probably brought over from Europe. A favorite way of serving asparagus then was to scoop out the center of French rolls and fill them with creamed asparagus. The crust was put back and the whole roll fried in butter. Here is an easier method.

Cut the hard ends off very fresh asparagus and wash them well. Stand them in an asparagus cooker with the water coming halfway up the stalks. Steam in salted water for 12 to 15 minutes. Meanwhile make Cream Sauce (see Sauces) and add ½ cup grated fairly sharp cheddar cheese. Stir until the cheese melts. Drain the asparagus well and lay in a shallow baking dish. Cover with the sauce and sprinkle with a little more cheese. Brown in a 375-degree oven.

Asparagus with French Dressing and Dill

This is delicious as a first course or in place of a salad. Prepare 2 to 3 bunches of asparagus as in the previous recipe. Drain well and cool. Serve with French dressing and sprinkle with a little fresh dill.

California Refried Beans with Cheese

This is one of the best and heartiest dishes for which we have to thank the Spanish and the Mexicans. Now that pinto beans are sold everywhere, all America can enjoy them. They are especially good with barbecues.

20 ounces pinto beans
2 quarts water
1 cup bacon fat
2 cloves garlic, pressed
Salt
Pepper
1½ teaspoons chili powder
   (optional)
1½ cups diced cheese

Boil the beans in the water over a very gentle heat for 2 hours or until tender. Add more water if needed. In the bottom of a glazed earthenware pot, an enamel-lined casserole or an old iron pot, heat 2/3 cup of bacon fat. Put in the liquid from the beans and as many beans as it takes to absorb the liquid which you mash with a potato masher. When you have a moist paste, add the rest of the beans, the garlic, salt and pepper to taste and chili powder, if desired. Stir well. The beans are ready to refry at your convenience.

Reheat the beans, adding 1/3 cup of the bacon fat. Stir in a mild cheese—cheddar, Monterey Jack, coon cheese or other. Stir until well heated and the cheese melted. The beans should be quite dry, but add a little water if necessary.

Boston Baked Beans

This is a recipe that takes long, slow cooking. Special electric bean pots are on the market, but the old Boston Bean Pot seems to give a special flavor.

20 ounces pea or kidney beans
6 tablespoons brown sugar
½ cup molasses
2 teaspoons dry mustard
2 teaspoons salt
1 medium onion
6 ounces fat salt pork

Soak the beans overnight in a large bowl of cold water. Discard any imperfect ones. The following morning drain the beans, put them in a kettle, cover with cold water, and bring quickly to a boil. Drain the water from the beans, saving the liquid. Put the beans in a bean pot or in a deep casserole. Stir in the brown sugar, molasses, mustard and salt. Poke the onion down into the center. Divide the pork into 3 pieces. Stick 2 pieces down into the beans and place the third on top. Add enough liquid to cover the beans, adding more later if necessary. Bake covered all day, usually 7 to 8 hours, at 275 degrees. Check occasionally to be sure the beans are still moist, adding more liquid if necessary. Uncover the pot for the last hour of cooking. Remove the onion before serving the beans.

Canned Beans Bean Pot

Buy a 20-ounce can of pea or kidney beans and pour them—liquid and all—into a Boston Bean Pot. Follow the preceding recipe, but parboil the salt pork for 2 minutes before adding it to the pot and use 2 small onions instead of the larger one. Heat for 1 hour at 350 degrees, uncovered. Do not let them dry out.

Green Beans with Herbs

A big step forward on the American agricultural scene is the stringless green bean. Just snip the ends off and leave them whole or cut them in half according to their age and variety. Former cooks didn't have it that easy.

2 pounds fresh small green beans or
  2 boxes frozen beans
½ teaspoon sugar
4 tablespoons butter
1 teaspoon chopped tarragon
2 teaspoons chopped chives
Salt and freshly ground black pepper

Prepare the beans and put them in a saucepan with the sugar, butter, and herbs. If using the frozen beans, omit the water and add 1 more tablespoon of butter. Cover very tightly and cook over low heat for 8 minutes. Season with salt and pepper and serve.

Green Bean Salad

2 pounds fresh green beans or
  2 boxes frozen green beans
2 very small onions
French Dressing (see Sauces)
¼ teaspoon powdered vitamin C

Add ½ cup of water to fresh or frozen beans. Cover and cook 8 minutes over moderate heat. Drain the vegetables if necessary. Place in a shallow serving dish. Cover while hot with thinly sliced onion and French Dressing. Spoon the dressing over the beans occasionally while the beans are cooling. Refrigerate but do not serve too cold. Stir in vitamin C before serving.

Cider Beets

2 pounds red or yellow beets
1/3 cup light brown sugar
2 teaspoons cornstarch
1 cup hard cider
3 tablespoons butter
Salt and pepper

Scrub the beets and cut off most of the tops but not the roots. Boil in unsalted water for 45 minutes or until tender. Drain and cool in cold water. Slip off the skins and slice into a baking-serving dish.

Preheat the oven to 300 degrees F. Combine the sugar, cornstarch and cider in a small saucepan. Boil for 5 minutes and pour over the beets. Cover and bake 30 minutes. Just before the end of the cooking add the butter in small bits and heat until melted. Season with salt and pepper and serve.

Beet Greens

When beets are being thinned in the family garden the reward is a mess of beet greens. The beets are very tiny and the greens are fresh and tender. Some markets sell them. Wash them very carefully and put them in a pan with 2 cups of boiling salted water. Cook just until the tiny beets are tender, 10 to 15 minutes. Drain thoroughly. Chop coarsely. Reheat in butter. Sprinkle with a little cider vinegar and garnish with hard-cooked egg slices.

Broccoli with Hollandaise Sauce

2½ to 3 pounds broccoli
Hollandaise Sauce (see Sauces)

Cut off the tough stems and outer leaves of the broccoli, leaving 4- or 5-inch bunches of flowerets and tender stems. Soak in water while making the sauce.

Make either sauce and set aside.

Boil the broccoli for 12 minutes. Drain throughly. Place in a warm vegetable dish and cover with the sauce.

Broccoli Puree
 (Blender made)

3 pounds fresh or
  3 boxes frozen broccoli
3 tablespoons butter
3 tablespoons flour
1½ cups milk
1 teaspoon salt
¼ teaspoon white pepper
¼ teaspoon nutmeg
Buttered croutons

Cook the broccoli as in the previous recipe. Drain but keep very moist. Put the broccoli into a blender. Add the butter, flour, milk, salt, pepper, and nutmeg. Spin for 30 seconds. Place in the top of a double boiler or in an ovenproof serving dish. Thirty minutes before serving, cook over simmering water or set the oven dish in a pan of hot water in a 300-degree oven. Longer cooking will do no harm so that this makes a very convenient party dish. Top with hot buttered croutons before serving.

Broccoli Pudding

2 pounds broccoli or 2 boxes
    frozen chopped broccoli
3 tablespoons butter
3 tablespoons flour
1½ cups milk
3 eggs, beaten well
2 teaspoons grated onion
½ teaspoon salt
1/8 teaspoon white pepper
½ cup fine bread crumbs
3 tablespoons grated
    Parmesan cheese
2 tablespoons butter, melted

Fresh broccoli should be soaked in salted water for a little while in case anything is hiding in the leaves.

Heat the butter and blend in the flour and cook for a moment or two. Add the milk and stir until thick. Beat the eggs and slowly add them to the sauce (off the heat), stirring constantly. Add the onion, salt, pepper and broccoli. Mix well and put into a buttered casserole dish. Cover with a mixture of bread crumbs, Parmesan and butter. Bake 30 minutes in a 350-degree oven.

Cabbage in Sour Cream

3 or 4 cups shredded cabbage
3 tablespoons butter or margarine
½ teaspoon salt
1 teaspoon caraway seeds
¼ teaspoon white pepper
½ teaspoon dry mustard
2 tablespoons brown sugar
½ pint commercial sour cream

Boil the cabbage in a kettle of boiling salted water for 6 minutes or until just tender. Drain. Toss with the butter, salt, seeds and seasonings until well mixed. Reheat in the empty kettle and just before serving stir in the sour cream.

10 Minute Cabbage

6 cups shredded green cabbage
3 tablespoons butter
1 cup whole milk
½ cup heavy sweet
    or commercial sour cream
Salt and pepper
1 teaspoon caraway seeds
    (optional)
¼ teaspoon powdered vitamin C

Shred a firm, medium-size cabbage with a sharp knife or chop the cabbage in a wooden bowl with an old-fashioned food chopper. Boil in just enough salted water to cover for 10 minutes. Drain and reheat without boiling in the butter, milk and cream. Season with salt and pepper and caraway seeds if desired. Stir in vitamin C.

German Red Cabbage

6 tablespoons fat (chicken*,
    goose, duck or bacon)
1 large onion, chopped
2 tablespoons sugar
6 cups shredded red cabbage
4 cooking apples,
    peeled, cored and sliced
3 tablespoons cider vinegar
2 teaspoons salt
½ teaspoon black pepper
Bouillon or water

Heat the liquid fat in a deep pan. Add the onions and the sugar and cook until the onion is soft and the sugar slightly caramelized. Add the rest of the ingredients except for the bouillon and stir well. Add just enough bouillon or water to come to the surface of the cabbage. Cover and cook very slowly or in a 275-degree oven for 3 hours. For highest flavor let the cabbage stand in a cool place overnight and reheat in a serving casserole.

*Chicken, goose or duck fat can be melted (tried out) in the top of a double boiler over simmering water.

Carrot Cheese Custard

This recipe will serve to glamorize the carrot which is too often considered a lowly and ordinary vegetable, suitable only for everyday lunches and children's meals. Carrots deserve better, for they are wonderfully nutritious and add a bright and cheerful note to the culinary color scheme. Young, fresh carrots are, of course, much more tasty than large ones that have spent a lot of time in storage.

2 tablespoons butter or margarine
2 tablespoons chopped onion
2 tablespoons chopped green pepper
2 heaping cups grated carrot
1 cup grated mild cheese
1 tablespoon tarragon vinegar
¾ teaspoon salt
¼ teaspoon white pepper
1½ cups milk
3 eggs, slightly beaten
Paprika
Parsley

Heat the fat in a small skillet and cook the onion and green pepper over low heat. Meanwhile scrub and grate the carrots into a bowl. Combine the onion, pepper, carrots, cheese, vinegar, salt and pepper and mix well.

Preheat the oven to 350 degrees. Scald the milk and pour slowly into the eggs while beating them with an electric beater or whisk. Cook the egg mixture over hot water in a double boiler until thick and creamy, stirring constantly. Pour over the carrot mixture and stir until blended. Bake the custard in a buttered deep casserole set in a pan of hot water. Bake 40 to 45 minutes or until an inserted knife comes out clean. Sprinkle with a little paprika and garnish with parsley.

Creamed Parsleyed Carrots

2 pounds carrots
1 small onion, sliced
Cream Sauce (see Sauces)
1 tablespoon chopped parsley

Scrub or scrape the carrots according to age and size. Cut into thick slices or leave whole if they are very young. Boil covered in 2 cups of lightly salted water along with the onion for 15 to 20 minutes or until tender. Strain the carrot broth and save it. Remove the onion and place the carrots in a vegetable dish.

Make the sauce, using 1 cup of the carrot water to replace 2 cups of milk. Add the parsley, taste for seasoning and pour over the carrots.

Cauliflower Au Gratin

1 large head cauliflower
4 tablespoons butter
4 tablespoons flour
1 cup milk
1 cup chicken bouillon
½ cup grated medium-sharp cheese
Salt and pepper
2 tablespoons butter
½ cup fine bread crumbs
Chopped parsley

Let the cauliflower soak in salted water 15 to 30 minutes to allow any creeping object to emerge. Cut off the flowerets with an inch of their stems. Boil covered in a little salted water for 10 minutes. Drain.

Heat the butter and stir in the flour. Cook for 2 minutes before adding the milk. Stir well with a whisk until creamy and smooth. Add the bouillon and the cheese and keep stirring until smooth. Taste for seasoning. Spread the cauliflower in a shallow buttered baking dish. Pour the sauce over the cauliflower. Sprinkle with bread crumbs heated in the butter. Bake 30 minutes at 300 degrees. Garnish the edges with chopped parsley.

Creamed Celery with Nutmeg

4 cups sliced celery
Cream Sauce (see Sauces)
½ teaspoon nutmeg

Wash the celery and cut it rather coarsely. Boil in 1½ cups of lightly salted water for 10 minutes. Drain, saving the liquid. Make a well-seasoned cream sauce, substituting 1 cup of celery broth or 1 cup of evaporated milk or cream for the milk. Add the nutmeg and let the celery stand in the sauce several hours, if possible, before reheating and serving.

Braised Celery

3 or 4 bunches hearts of celery
3 tablespoons butter
3 tablespoons grated onion
3 tablespoons grated carrot
1 bay leaf
2 cups chicken broth
Salt and pepper
3 tablespoons grated Swiss cheese

Trim the celery evenly and cut lengthwise into quarters. Wash thoroughly. Boil 10 minutes in enough salted water to cover. Drain well. Sauté the onions and carrots in the butter and when soft, spread the vegetables in a shallow baking-serving dish. Lay the celery on top of the vegetables. Pour over the chicken broth, add the bay leaf, and season with salt and pepper, taking into account the saltiness of the broth. Cover with aluminum foil and bake 40 minutes at 300 degrees. Remove the foil and the bay leaf for the last 10 minutes and sprinkle with the cheese.

Individual Corn Soufflés

This is a refinement on the old-fashioned corn soufflé, but it is devised to go with the same dishes that complement the soufflé but shouldn't be on the same plate. You will need individual soufflé dishes or deep ramekins.

1½ cups fresh corn pulp
Cream Sauce (see Sauces)
2 tablespoons chopped onion
2 tablespoons chopped pepper
2 tablespoons butter
2 tablespoons chopped pimiento
5 egg yolks, beaten lightly
5 egg whites, beaten stiff
Salt and pepper

Prepare the corn as you would for Virginia Fresh Corn Pudding or, second best, use the canned variety. Make the cream sauce but use 4 tablespoons of butter and 4 tablespoons of flour with the 2 cups of milk in order to have a very thick sauce. Cook the onion and pepper in butter just until the onion is soft. Add this and the pimiento to the corn and the cream sauce. Add the beaten egg yolks gradually, stirring constantly, and cook until thick. Season highly with salt and pepper.

Remove from the heat. Up to this point the soufflés may be prepared in advance. Thirty minutes before serving preheat the oven to 350 degrees. Beat the egg whites stiff and fold them gently but firmly into the egg yolk mixture. Spoon the mixture into the buttered baking dishes. They should be two-thirds full. Place in the oven and bake 15 to 20 minutes. Have an extra buttered baking dish handy in case this is too much mixture for your size dishes.

Boiled Fresh Corn on the Cob

There are various hybrid corns for human consumption and the best one is your own favorite, provided it is freshly picked. Real corn lovers will pick the corn only when the kettle has been put on to boil—which just leaves time for husking. The number of ears to be consumed by 6 to 8 people is variable and cannot be prescribed.

Fresh corn
Butter
Salt and pepper

Fill a large kettle two-thirds full of water. Remove the husks and all the silk from the ears and rinse under cool running water. Add no salt to the water but some old-timers like to add 2 tablespoons of sugar. Put in the corn and bring the water back to a boil. Boil 5 to 10 minutes according to the age of the corn—large kernels take longer. Do not overcook. Serve in a large dish covered with a napkin. Butter, salt and pepper are the only seasonings.

Virginia Fresh Corn Pudding

This pudding can be made with canned kernel corn but it is particularly good when made with corn fresh from the cob. It will take 8 to 10 ears to provide a sufficient quantity of corn.

2½ cups corn pulp
2 teaspoons sugar
2 teaspoons salt
¼ teaspoon white pepper
1 tablespoon cornstarch
¼ teaspoon nutmeg
2 cups milk
3 large eggs
3 tablespoons butter
Parsley

Remove the husks and silks from the ears of corn. Cut off the tips of each ear and scrape off the corn with a sharp knife, getting as much pulp (without the cob) as possible. Mix the corn with the dry ingredients. Heat the milk with the butter and add gradually to lightly beaten eggs. Combine the two mixtures well and pour into a buttered soufflé dish or casserole. Bake at 350 degrees for 50 minutes or until an inserted knife comes out clean. Sprinkle with chopped parsley and serve at once.

Cucumbers

Cucumbers, not much longer than your middle finger, picked in the evening and chilled overnight, peeled and eaten plain at breakfast time, are food fit for the gods, but young fresh cucumbers are good in other ways too. The following dish, with French bread, makes a delicious first course but was designed as a side dish to counterbalance an otherwise heavy meal.

Cucumbers and Red Onions

3 cucumbers
1 red onion
¾ teaspoon salt
¼ teaspoon cracked black pepper
¼ cup tarragon vinegar
¾ cup olive oil
½ teaspoon oregano

Crisp cucumber slices and onion slices, both cut quite thin, in a bowl of salted ice water for 20 to 30 minutes. Drain and pat dry with toweling.

Spread the vegetables in a serving dish and cover with the dressing just before serving.

Canned Food-the Miracle on Your Table

Advertisement for National Canners Association, **THE SATURDAY EVENING POST,** *April 3, 1920*

Cucumber Shrimp Boats

3 to 4 cucumbers, 5 inches long
Salt and pepper
French Dressing (see Sauces)
1 pound tiny cooked shrimp
Mayonnaise (see Sauces)
Lettuce
Fresh tarragon

Choose cucumbers of equal size. Peel them and cut them in two lengthwise. Scoop out the seeds and discard them. Scoop out some of the cucumber, leaving about a ¾-inch shell. Sprinkle the shells with salt and pepper. Dice the scooped-out cucumber and mix it with the shrimp, which can be bought cooked and cleaned. Moisten with French Dressing made with white wine or tarragon vinegar. Pile the shrimp into the cucumbers. Place each one on a fresh leaf of garden lettuce. Spoon mayonnaise over the top and garnish each with 3 tarragon leaves. Serve for luncheon on a hot day with whole wheat popovers.

Wilted Dandelion Greens

3 to 4 quarts dandelion greens
8 slices bacon
1 teaspoon dry mustard
2 tablespoons sugar
6 tablespoons cider vinegar
1 teaspoon salt
¼ teaspoon cracked black pepper

Wash the greens very carefully, discarding the roots and tough stems. Dry between two towels. Tear the greens into small pieces. Fry the bacon in a large skillet over moderate heat until the bacon is very crisp. Remove with a bacon fork to paper toweling. Add the mustard, sugar, vinegar, salt and pepper to the fat in the pan. Bring to a boil and put in the dry greens. Cover and cook the greens for about 3 minutes, until just hot and wilted. Transfer to a warm vegetable dish and crumble the bacon all over the top.

Buttered Dandelion Greens

After a long winter of root vegetables housewives, particularly in Northern climes, used to look forward eagerly to greens, particularly dandelion greens, which seem to spring up overnight. They were thought to be good for the blood.

3 quarts dandelion greens
Butter
4 hard-cooked eggs
Salt and pepper
Cider vinegar

Wash the dandelion greens, preferably the young variety, very carefully, discarding the roots and coarse stems. Place them in a large kettle of boiling salted water. Bring back to the boil and boil 6 to 8 minutes, depending on the age of the greens. They should be just tender. Drain very well in a colander, extracting some of the water with the back of a spoon. Melt 4 tablespoons of butter in the kettle and return the greens to the kettle and toss just long enough to coat the greens. Season with salt and pepper. Serve in a warm vegetable dish covered with slices of hard-cooked eggs and a cruet of cider vinegar.

Mustard Greens

Growing wild in the open places, this is a plant that our forefathers gathered as a cooking green. They have to be picked young and green. Many farmers grow and market these greens.

3 to 4 pounds mustard greens
4 tablespoons butter
Salt and pepper
2 tablespoons vinegar
2 hard-cooked eggs

Wash the greens thoroughly, picking out any hard stems or wilted leaves. Place in a large kettle and add 1 cup of water. Cover and boil with vinegar. Serve in a vegetable dish garnished with wedges of hard-cooked eggs.

Sautéed Eggplant

Eggplant or what used to be known as Guinea Squash has been part of the American cooking scene at least since the time of George Washington and probably several decades before that.

2 medium eggplants
Salt and pepper
½ cup olive oil or
   2 tablespoons butter and
   2 tablespoons olive oil
1 large clove garlic, sliced
3 slices onion
2 egg yolks
1 cup fine bread crumbs
Chopped parsley

Cut the eggplant into 1-inch slices. Season well with salt and pepper. Heat the fat in a large skillet and sauté the garlic and onion over a moderate flame until both are soft. Remove them from the fat and discard. Pour out half the fat and save. Meanwhile beat the egg yolks with ¼ cup of water until just blended and place in a shallow dish. Spread half the bread crumbs on a plate.

Dip the eggplant slices first in the egg mixture and then in the bread crumbs, coating them well. Prepare as many as the skillet will hold. Fry the eggplant about 4 minutes on each side. Meanwhile prepare the remaining slices. Transfer the first batch to a baking sheet lined with paper toweling. Keep warm and fry the rest, adding more of the fat as needed.

Serve on a hot platter and garnish with chopped parsley and if you like, even if it isn't traditional, a fillet of anchovy.

Pacific Eggplant

Quick Tomato Sauce (see Sauces)
2 or 3 eggplants
2 eggs
2 tablespoons water
Fine bread crumbs
Olive oil or salad oil
Salt and pepper
1 cup grated Monterey Jack
   or cheddar cheese

Make the sauce and let it simmer while preparing the eggplant.

Choose eggplants that are not too large. Peel and slice them ½ inch thick, allowing 3 to 4 slices per person. Beat the eggs and water just until blended in a shallow dish. Spread the bread crumbs on a plate. Dip each slice in the egg and then in the crumbs and let them stand on a platter for 10 to 15 minutes.

Preheat the oven to 400 degrees F. Heat enough oil in a large skillet to cover the bottom by 1/8 inch. Brown quickly on both sides as many pieces of eggplant as the skillet can hold. Transfer the browned pieces to a slightly oiled shallow baking-serving dish. Continue browning and transferring the eggplant adding more oil to the skillet when necessary. Sprinkle the eggplant with salt and pepper and cover with 2 cups of tomato sauce. Cover the sauce with grated cheese and bake 15 minutes.

New England Fiddlehead Ferns

Fiddlehead ferns are found in early spring mostly in northern New England and Canada. Small, compact, dark green little sprouts, they have a flavor similar to asparagus and look like tiny fiddleheads. Markets in Maine sell them occasionally, and they are sold canned and frozen, but mostly they are gathered wild.

Wash the tiny ferns and boil them 5 minutes in salted water. Drain well and toss in butter. Season with salt and pepper. They are also delicious served cold in a French dressing.

Wilted Lettuce

2 heads garden lettuce
2 tablespoons chopped scallions
8 strips bacon
¼ cup cider vinegar
¼ cup cream
2 tablespoons sugar
½ teaspoon salt
1/8 teaspoon freshly ground
   black pepper
1 cup croutons

Wash the lettuce well and break into pieces in a wooden salad bowl. Sprinkle with the chopped scallions using the green tops as well. Fry the bacon over moderate heat until very crisp. Drain on toweling. Add the vinegar, cream, sugar, salt and pepper to the fat in the pan. Stir well and bring just to the boiling point. The sauce should be served hot and poured over the lettuce and tossed thoroughly just before serving, but this step can be done at the last minute. Sprinkle with croutons and crumbled bacon.

Braised Lettuce

Garden lettuce is too often overlooked as a hot vegetable. Braised lettuce is a great way to serve fresh lettuce that is past its small-head prime but still good.

2 large heads Boston lettuce
2 cups chicken broth
2 teaspoons sugar
3 tablespoons butter
1 tablespoon vinegar
Salt and pepper

Wash the lettuce well and place 3 to 4 large leaves one on top of the other. Roll them up and tie them securely with kitchen twine. Trim them evenly with kitchen scissors or, if too large, cut them in two. Continue to do this until you have 2 rolls per serving. Drop the rolls into boiling salted water and boil 3 minutes. Retrieve with a slotted spoon and drain on toweling. Place the rolls in a well-buttered shallow baking dish. Sprinkle with a little sugar. Add the chicken broth, butter and vinegar and sprinkle with salt and pepper. Cook covered for 30 minutes in a 350-degree oven. Remove the cover for 10 minutes more of cooking.

LETTUCE.

To farce Lettuce à la Dame-Simone.

TAKE ſome Cabbage-Lettuce, and but juſt dip them in ſcalding Water to blanch them, then take them out and drain them. Take the Breaſts of a roſted Capon or Pullet, haſh it with ſome boil'd Ham, and ſome Muſhrooms, a little Parſly and ſome Cives, a little blanch'd Bacon, the Crum of a *French* Roll ſoak'd in Cream, and the Yolks of four or five raw Eggs. Seaſon this with Salt, Pepper, ſavoury Herbs, and Spices:

To dreſs Larks in Ragoo.

Having drawn your Larks, toſs them up in melted Bacon, with an Onion ſtuck with Cloves, and ſuch Ingredients as you have to put to it, as Truſles, Muſhrooms, Capons-Livers, &c. Toſs it all up together, and if you have no Cullis, powder it with a little Flower: Then moiſten it with good Beef or Veal-Gravy: Let it waſte away to the Degree it ought; then beat up an Egg in a little Cream, with ſome ſhred Parſly amongſt it; pour this into your Stew-pan, give it a Turn or two over the Stove to thicken it,

Mushrooms Under Glass

This dish was considered fashionably elegant in days gone by. What made this comparatively simple dish extraordinary was the glass bell it was baked and served under. These have been antique collector's items but they can be found also in restaurant supply houses. Six-inch Pyrex bowls make a satisfactory, if not elegant, substitute although they are less easy to handle and should be left in the kitchen at serving time.

1½ pounds mushrooms
6 to 8 slices firm white bread
6 tablespoons butter
1 tablespoon chopped parsley
1 teaspoon chopped fresh tarragon or
  1/3 teaspoon powdered dry tarragon
2 teaspoons lemon juice
¼ teaspoon black pepper
1½ cups all-purpose cream
3 tablespoons Madeira or sherry
Parsley

Remove the stems from the caps. Wipe the caps clean. Cut the slices ½ to ¾ inch thick from a loaf of white unsliced bread, preferably homemade. Toast them.

Butter the center of 6 to 8 salad-size ovenproof serving plates. Work the herbs, lemon juice and freshly ground black pepper into the butter, using a small fork. When very creamy in texture, spread each piece of toast. There will be a little left over. Place a toast on each plate. Preheat the oven to 350 degrees F. Put the mushroom caps on the toasts and cover with 2 tablespoons of cream. Place the plates on 2 baking sheets and cover them with the bells or bowls. Bake 30 minutes.

Combine the rest of the cream with the wine and add any herb butter that remains. Heat but do not boil. Just before serving remove the bell and spread a spoonful of sauce over the top. Garnish with parsley. Replace the bell. This is a lovely beginning to an elegant dinner party.

Mushrooms in Cream

The Indians knew wild mushrooms and undoubtedly taught the early settlers which ones were safe, but there must have been some awful examples of mushroom poisoning when food was so scarce. Safe wild mushrooms have a wonderful flavor but in order to be sure we can recommend only the cultivated variety.

1½ pounds mushrooms
½ cup finely chopped onion
6 tablespoons butter
2 tablespoons flour
1/8 teaspoon nutmeg
¾ teaspoon salt
Black pepper
1 cup chicken stock or broth
3 tablespoons Madeira or sherry
½ pint heavy cream

Cultivated mushrooms are usually very clean, but just to be sure cut off the base of the stem and wipe them with a towel. Slice them lengthwise (cap and stem). Chop or grate the onion and cook both the mushrooms and the onion in butter, until the mushrooms are quite dry. Stir frequently. Add the flour and stir until the flour disappears. Add the nutmeg, salt and enough black pepper to season the mushrooms highly. Add the stock and simmer until slightly thickened. Add the cream and heat. All this can be made in advance except for the addition of the cream. Served with either toast or patty shells this makes a nice chafing dish supper.

Bacon-Stuffed Mushrooms

18 to 24 large mushrooms
¼ pound Canadian bacon
4 tablespoons butter
2 tablespoons grated onion
4 tablespoons sherry
½ teaspoon dried basil
Salt and pepper
Fine bread crumbs
Parmesan cheese

Cut off the ends of the stems and remove the caps, wiping them clean. Lay the mushrooms in a shallow, buttered baking dish. Chop the stems and cut the bacon into small pieces. Heat the butter in a small skillet and cook the chopped onion, mushrooms and bacon all together until the mixture is quite dry and lightly browned. Add the sherry, basil, salt and pepper to taste and continue cooking until the sherry has evaporated.

Preheat the oven to 400 degrees F. Stuff the mushroom caps with the mixture. Cover each cap with fine bread crumbs and with Parmesan cheese. Dot each one with butter and bake 20 minutes. Serve as a garnish around a roast or on toast for a luncheon dish.

Stuffed Mushrooms with Sour Cream

The hardest part of this recipe is finding the right size mushrooms. Some stores make a specialty of selling the large variety.

18 large mushrooms
1 cup soft bread crumbs
6 tablespoons minced onion
4 tablespoons finely chopped parsley
2 tablespoons sherry
½ pint commercial sour cream
Salt and pepper
6 to 8 slices of toast

Search for mushrooms of uniform size. Remove the stems and brush off any sand. Do not wash them. Place them in a buttered baking tin. Make the bread crumbs from day-old bread, chopping them quite fine. Chop the trimmed mushroom stems.

Sauté the onion and parsley in butter just until soft. Add the mushrooms and cook for 3 minutes. Add the sherry and bread crumbs and stir until blended. Remove from the heat and stir in the sour cream and season to taste with salt and pepper. Stuff the mushroom caps with the mixture.

Just before serving, bake 10 minutes at 425 degrees F. Serve on thin slices of lightly buttered toast.

Creole Okra

Okra came to America from Africa, possibly on the ships transporting slaves. It flourished in Louisiana and became an integral part of their cooking. This is the most typical way of serving it.

1¼ pounds small okra
3 tablespoons bacon fat
1 medium onion, chopped
1 medium green pepper, chopped
1 clove garlic
3 cups tomatoes, peeled and diced
1 tablespoon brown sugar
1 teaspoon lemon juice
1 bay leaf
1 teaspoon salt
¼ teaspoon freshly ground
  black pepper

Choose only the young green pods and wash them well, removing their stems. Slice them. You should have about 2½ to 3 cups. Heat the fat in a heavy skillet or pot and add the prepared vegetables, removing the seeds from both the pepper and tomatoes. Cover and simmer 5 minutes. Add the lemon juice, bay leaf, salt, pepper and okra and stew 30 minutes or until the okra is tender. Serve very hot.

Sweet Onions

14 to 16 small onions
4 tablespoons butter
2½ tablespoons white or
　brown sugar
Salt and white pepper

Peel the onions and pierce each one with the sharp tines of a small fork. Cover with salt water and boil gently for 15 minutes, or until tender. Drain and dry on toweling for 30 minutes, turning them occasionally. Heat the butter in a skillet. Add the sugar and cook 1 minute. Toss the onions in the mixture until well coated on all sides. Place in a shallow baking-serving dish and bake uncovered for 20 to 30 minutes. Serve as a garnish or in the baking dish.

Thanksgiving Creamed Onions

This was not served at the first Thanksgiving but it has been part of the Thanksgiving tradition for a long, long time.

1½ to 2 pounds medium to
　small onions
Cream Sauce (see Sauces)
½ cup heavy cream
¼ teaspoon nutmeg
½ cup fine bread crumbs
Butter
Chopped parsley

Peel the onions. If you hold them under cold water while you are peeling them you will not get teary. Boil them in salted water for 15 minutes or just until tender. Do not overcook. Drain very thoroughly.

Make the cream sauce. Add the cream and season with nutmeg and a little extra salt and pepper. Both the onions and sauce can be made a day in advance, but combine them just before the final baking. Place them in a buttered oven-serving dish. Cover with bread crumbs and dot with butter. Bake 20 minutes in 325-degree oven. Garnish with chopped parsley.

Buttered Fried Parsnips

The parsnip is a root vegetable that does its best growing in the late fall and according to many is best eaten in the spring after it has been touched by frost. Parsnips traveled well with those trekking westward and were added to many a stew. Because of their excessive sweetness, they are most delicious when they have been twice cooked—first boiled, then fried. Do not use the very large variety.

2 pounds parsnips
4 tablespoons butter
1/8 teaspoon fresh nutmeg
Salt and pepper
1 tablespoon chopped parsley

Wash, trim and scrape the parsnips. Cut into uniform pieces and boil in salted water 25 to 30 minutes or until tender. Drain well and let dry. Just before serving, heat the butter in a skillet and saute over moderate heat until light brown on all sides, letting the parsnips caramelize a little in their own sugar. Season with nutmeg, salt and pepper and serve in a warm vegetable dish garnished with chopped parsley.

Peas in Cream

Anyone who knows and grows peas will tell you that you shouldn't pick peas until a half hour before dinner time and if you do pick them ahead of that time, keep them in the refrigerator and shell them just before you cook and eat them. Americans prefer peas not tiny as the French do, and not big as the British do, but medium-size, boiled just until tender, and if you belong to the old school you put on a dollop of butter and a couple of tablespoons of heavy cream. Save the fancier ways of cooking for the times when you are using the frozen or the 2-day-old variety. One pound of peas will usually serve 2 people but there's a New England maxim that dictates one pound per person.

4 to 8 quarts peas
Butter
Heavy cream (room temperature)
Salt and pepper

Shell the peas and boil them covered in a very little lightly salted water, adding a teaspoon of sugar if the peas are not just picked. Cook 10 minutes or just until tender. Peas should not be overcooked. Drain and serve in a warm vegetable dish. Mix with butter, salt and pepper. The cream can be added at the same time or served separately.

Pokeweed

Southerners from presidents down have eaten pokeweed for generations.

Pokeweed is found mostly in the South and was exported long ago to Europe, because of its red dye potential, when its berries were full grown. But young and green, it is a delicious vegetable to be eaten in late May and early June. It should be boiled in very lightly salted water for 8 to 10 minutes, drained, tossed in butter with a little salt and pepper and served with hard-cooked egg wedges and a dash of cider vinegar.

Pigweed

Pigweed is one of those dividends that comes with a home garden and is rarely recognized for what it is—a delicious green vegetable. Eaten in the late spring or early summer and gathered during the first garden weeding, it can be served like spinach. Wash the pigweed in several waters, removing the tough stem bottoms. Cook 6 minutes in boiling salted water. Drain well and season with salt, pepper, butter, and a dash of cider vinegar.

Baked Potatoes

Baking potatoes is the most healthful and the simplest way to prepare them. Simply scrub Green Mountain, russet or Idaho potatoes. Prick them with a fork and bake in a 400-degree oven for 1 hour. Serve with butter, cream or commercial sour cream.

Steamed Potatoes

Nutritionists feel that potatoes retain more of their minerals and other good qualities if the potatoes are steamed rather than boiled. New potatoes do not need to be peeled, merely well washed. Older potatoes are better peeled. Steam the potatoes in the upper part of a steamer for 40 minutes or until tender. Serve like boiled potatoes with butter, salt and pepper, unless gravy is being served.

Tiny New Potatoes

Tiny new potatoes not much bigger than large marbles constitute another home garden dividend although they are sometimes found in the market. They must be well scrubbed but not peeled, and washed in several waters. Boil them in just enough salted water to cover for 15 to 20 minutes according to size. Drain well and serve swimming in melted butter and well sprinkled with chopped parsley.

Sweet Potatoes

The yam was one of the treasures that came with the land and although it was for years cooked principally in the South, it has become a universal favorite. Today sweet potatoes, a near cousin, are more common. Yams are sweeter and moister than sweet potatoes but they are usually both cooked the same way. Sweet potatoes are better for baking.

Baked Sweet Potatoes. Scrub the potatoes well. Bake 45 to 60 minutes at 400 degrees F, depending on size.

Sautéed Sweet Potatoes. Boil sweet potatoes or yams for 20 to 25 minutes or until soft. Cool, peel and slice. Sauté in a heavy skillet using either salt pork fat, bacon fat or butter. Brown well on both sides. For special occasions sprinkle with a little sugar and rum or bourbon and touch with a lighted match just before serving. In this case, sauté the potatoes in butter.

Tennessee Sweet Potato Pudding

This confection is not a vegetable but more of a dessert unless you happen to favor sweets with your meat.

3 cups grated sweet potatoes
3 eggs
½ cup sugar
½ teaspoon salt
½ cup raisins
½ cup currants
¾ cup chopped walnuts
¾ cup milk
½ cup molasses
¼ cup corn syrup
1 teaspoon cinnamon
½ teaspoon nutmeg
¼ teaspoon cloves
¼ pound butter

Peel and grate the potatoes. Beat the eggs until light and add all the ingredients except for the butter. Mix in the sweet potato thoroughly.

Preheat the oven to 350 degrees F. Heat the butter in a heavy iron skillet or in an ovenproof serving dish. When bubbling stir in the sweet potato mixture and stir until the mixture begins to boil. Put in the oven and bake for 45 minutes stirring every 15 minutes. Serve with Plum Preserves (see Sauces) and heavy cream.

Deep Dish Sweet Potatoes

5 tablespoons butter
1 medium-size onion
2 cups apple chunks
½ cup diced celery
3 cups boiled sweet potatoes, sliced
¾ cup brown sugar
1 teaspoon lemon juice
1 teaspoon salt
¼ teaspoon white pepper
2 tablespoons rum (optional)

Heat 2 tablespoons of the butter and sauté the onion until tender. Melt the remaining butter in a small saucepan. Butter a deep 8-inch baking dish and put in a layer of sweet potatoes. Cover them with apple chunks and celery and sprinkle with a little onion, half the brown sugar, lemon juice, salt and pepper and butter. Repeat the process using the rest of the ingredients and finish with a layer of apples and brown sugar. Sprinkle with lemon juice and with rum if desired. Bake uncovered in a 350-degree oven for 30 minutes.

Candied Sweet Potatoes or Yams

6 sweet potatoes or yams
½ cup butter
½ cup brown sugar
2 tablespoons rum or sherry
4 tablespoons water
Salt and white pepper

Boil the sweet potatoes or yams which have been well washed in their jackets for 20 to 25 minutes or until tender. Cool and skin. Cut lengthwise into 1/3-inch slices. Put a layer in a well-buttered baking dish that can be used for serving. Sprinkle with butter, salt, pepper and brown sugar. Repeat the process until the sweet potatoes are all used. Finish with a layer of brown sugar and sprinkle with rum or sherry and water. Bake 30 minutes at 350 degrees F.

Creamed Potatoes

Creamed potatoes used to be regular breakfast fare for the fortunate, along with lamb chops or fried ham.

3 to 4 cups boiled potatoes
Cream Sauce (see Sauces)
2 cups grated medium
   cheddar cheese (optional)
Salt and pepper

Slice or cube the boiled potatoes and put them in the cream sauce. Allow them to cook together over simmering water for at least 30 minutes. Be sure the sauce is highly seasoned with salt and plenty of freshly ground black pepper. If you prefer to serve the potatoes au gratin, add most of the cheese to the sauce, saving just enough to sprinkle over the top. Dot with butter and bake 30 minutes in a 375-degree oven.

Old-Fashioned Mashed Potatoes

There is nothing better than good mashed potatoes and nothing worse than the soggy variety, and it's so easy to make them good.

6 to 8 medium-size potatoes
5 to 6 cups boiling salted water
1 cup hot milk
4 to 5 tablespoons butter
1¼ teaspoons salt
¼ teaspoon white pepper

Peel and halve the potatoes. Boil them for 30 minutes or until tender. Drain them and return to the heat, tossing them over moderate heat until mealy on the outside. This is a matter of moments. Toss them during the drying process. With an electric beater or a potato masher and large whip, reduce the potatoes to a lumpless meal. Gradually add the milk and butter, beating all the time over very low heat. Season highly with salt and pepper.

Skillet Potatoes

¼ pound fat salt pork, diced
½ cup chopped onion
3 to 4 cups chopped boiled potatoes

Try out the salt pork over low heat until the pork is crisp and brown. This can take as long as a half hour if the pork bits are to be cooked properly. Stir occasionally. Remove all the pork with a slotted spoon and save. Add the chopped onion and cook just until tender. Add the boiled potatoes and mix well with the fat and onion. Pat down with the back of the spoon and cook over low heat for about 20 minutes. Sprinkle with the hot pork chips.

Cover painting, THE SATURDAY EVENING POST, *November 29, 1913*

German Hot Potato Salad

This is not a salad but a hot potato dish that the Germans brought. Eaten with slabs of ham or fried pork and some fresh cooked greens, it's a dish that will stick to the ribs and give you a lot of quick energy.

6 to 8 good-sized potatoes
3 tablespoons bacon fat
1 large onion, chopped
½ cup chopped celery
½ pint heavy cream
½ cup cider vinegar
½ teaspoon dry mustard
2 teaspoons salt
½ teaspoon cracked pepper
Salad greens

Wash the potatoes well and boil them in their jackets about 40 minutes or until tender. Meanwhile, gently fry the onion and celery in the bacon fat just until tender and heat the cream with the vinegar, mustard, salt and pepper. Do not boil.

Drain the potatoes. Peel them while they are hot and slice them into a wooden salad bowl. Mix well with the onion mixture and the dressing. Serve hot with a ring of salad greens around the edge of the bowl.

Eat lukewarm—never cold.

Delmonico Potatoes

This dish is attributed to Lorenzo Delmonico, who with his uncles dominated the food scene of the nineteenth century in New York and to whom America owes much for raising the standards of eating in this country.

3 to 4 cups boiled potatoes
4 hard-cooked eggs
¾ cup grated medium cheddar cheese
½ cup fine bread crumbs
2 tablespoons butter

Butter a baking dish or casserole with a tablespoon of butter. Slice the potatoes and the eggs. Make the

Cream Sauce, substituting ½ pint of cream for 1 cup of milk, if desired. Season highly with salt and pepper. Alternate layers of boiled potatoes and egg slices in the baking dish. Pour over the cream sauce and sprinkle the surface with the bread crumbs. Dot with the remaining butter and bake 30 to 40 minutes in a 350-degree oven until golden brown. Serve from the baking dish.

Mashed Rutabagas

Rutabagas have more aliases than any other vegetable. Known as Swedes, yellow turnips, cow turnips, and turnip-rooted cabbage, they have a stronger flavor than the white variety, but properly prepared they are delicious. Choose rutabagas that are not too large.

5 to 6 cups rutabaga chunks*
4 tablespoons butter
2 tablespoons brown sugar
2 tablespoons dry sherry (optional)
1½ teaspoons salt
¼ teaspoon freshly ground
   black pepper
Chopped parsley

Peel the rutabaga and cut into chunks. Cover with boiling water. Add a teaspoon of salt. Cover and cook for 25 to 35 minutes or until tender. Drain and return to the pan. Toss over low heat until the steam stops rising from the vegetable. Keep shaking the pan so that the rutabaga will not be scorched. Mash or puree in a blender or electric beater. If the rutabaga is still moist return to the pan and stir over moderate heat until quite dry. Add the seasonings and serve hot sprinkled with chopped parsley.

*Some cooks like to cook equal parts of potatoes and rutabaga to give a milder flavor.

Homemade Sauerkraut

Sauerkraut can be bought in bulk and in cans but for the adventurous it can be made at home. Sauerkraut is nutritionally excellent and very low in calories.

Measure 22 pounds of solid heads of cabbage. Discard the outer leaves and cut them in quarters, removing the core. Shred them as you would for cole slaw. Using 1 cup of salt, alternate layers of cabbage with a good sprinkling of salt in a deep earthenware or enamel crock, leaving room for fermentation. Pound the cabbage down with a potato masher so that the cabbage is well broken and tightly compressed. Weight it down with a plate or round board, holding a heavy object (like a meat grinder, or weight measures). Keep the crock in a warm place (about 85 degrees). Each morning remove the scum that rises to the surface. The cabbage must always be covered with liquid, so it is just a matter of pushing down the cabbage. Fermentation should take 10 to 12 days.

Pack the sauerkraut in sterilized pint or quart jars, with enough of the brine to cover the cabbage. To insure perfect keeping, put the covers on fairly tightly, simmer in a canning kettle over low heat for 20 minutes, remove from the water bath and seal tightly.

Baked Sauerkraut

3 pounds sauerkraut,
  fresh or canned
Bacon fat or butter
2 cups diced cooking apples
Black pepper
1 tablespoon caraway seeds
3 cups dry white wine

Wash the sauerkraut in plenty of water and drain. Rub a deep casserole with bacon fat or butter and put in 3 cups of sauerkraut. Cover with a cup of diced apple. Sprinkle with freshly ground black pepper and half the caraway seeds. Repeat the process and top with a final layer of sauerkraut.

Preheat the oven to 300 degrees F. Dot the surface with 2 tablespoons of bacon fat or butter and add the wine. Bring to a boil on top of the stove. Cover tightly and bake 1 hour.

Buttered Spinach

Spinach when it is green and young is sweet and delicious; old and tough, it is bitter and deserves its unpopular reputation. Use only fresh young spinach or the frozen variety.

3 to 4 pounds spinach or
  2 to 3 boxes frozen leaf spinach
4 tablespoons butter
1/8 teaspoon nutmeg
Salt and pepper
2 hard-cooked eggs (optional)

Wash the spinach in several changes of water, discarding the tough stem ends and wilted leaves. Tear into large pieces. Lift the spinach from the final wash water into a kettle. Cover and boil in its own water only 5 to 6 minutes over moderately high heat. Drain well. Toss with butter, nutmeg, salt and pepper. Serve in a warm vegetable dish. Egg slices are the traditional garnish for this dish, and for those who like it, place a cruet of vinegar on the table.

Blender Spinach Cream

3 to 4 pounds fresh young spinach
  or 2 to 3 boxes frozen leaf or
  chopped spinach
3 tablespoons butter
3 tablespoons flour
1 cup milk
½ cup cream
1/8 teaspoon nutmeg
Salt and pepper
¾ cup small croutons
2 tablespoons butter

Prepare and cook the spinach as in the preceding recipe. Save ½ cup of the spinach water. Place the cooked spinach in a blender. Add the remaining ingredients including the spinach water. Spin for 30 seconds. Place the spinach cream in the top of a double boiler or in a baking-serving dish which should be placed in a pan of hot water. Cook 20 to 30 minutes over boiling water or in a 300-degree oven. Garnish with buttered croutons.

Spinach Soufflé

2 cups finely chopped cooked spinach
3 tablespoons butter
3 tablespoons flour
2/3 cup milk
1/3 cup spinach water
1/8 teaspoon freshly grated nutmeg
4 egg yolks, beaten lightly
5 egg whites, beaten stiff
Hollandaise Sauce (see Sauces)

Prepare and cook the spinach as in Buttered Spinach. Drain well, reserving 1/3 cup of spinach water. Squeeze all excess water from the spinach with your fingers. Chop fine.

Heat the butter in a small saucepan and stir in the flour, cooking for 2 minutes without browning. Add the milk and spinach water. Stir until thick and smooth. Season highly with salt, pepper and nutmeg. Remove from the heat and beat in the egg yolks quickly and thoroughly. Stir in the spinach. This part of the soufflé may be made in advance.

Forty minutes before serving, preheat the oven to 375 degrees F. Beat the egg whites until stiff but not dry. Stir in a third of them until blended. Fold in the remaining egg whites very gently, lifting the mixture high with the whip as you do it. Pour into a buttered 1½-quart soufflé dish. Place the dish in a pan of hot water and bake 30 to 35 minutes. Just before serving cover with Hollandaise Sauce and sprinkle with a dash of paprika.

Swiss Chard

Swiss Chard is best eaten while the leaves are not too large nor the stalks tough. Cook as you would cook spinach.

Winter Squash

Some forms of squash were found here when the early settlers arrived. There are many descendants of the early varieties. The most popular are the Butternut, the Green and Blue Hubbard and the Green Delicious. When buying fresh unpeeled squash allow ½ to ¾ pound per person.

Break the squash in 3-inch-square pieces. Dropping it on the back steps is very satisfactory, but using a large knife or cleaver is perhaps more professional. Bake in a well-buttered covered dish for 30 minutes. Uncover and bake 30 minutes longer or until tender. Mash the squash with a potato masher or puree it in a blender. Season with plenty of butter and a little cream, salt and pepper.

Winter Squash with Bacon

3 to 4 pounds crookneck
 (butternut) squash
½ pound bacon
4 to 6 tablespoons butter or margarine
Salt and pepper

Cut the squash in quarters and remove the seeds and fibers. Pare the pieces and drop them into a pan of boiling water. Boil for 20 to 25 minutes or until tender. Drain thoroughly.

Meanwhile bake the bacon on a grill in a 400-degree oven (this takes no watching) or fry until crisp in a moderately heated skillet. Drain the bacon on toweling and keep warm.

Mash the squash with a potato masher or with an electric beater. If the squash is too liquid stir it over heat until the excess moisture evaporates. Season with butter, salt and pepper and serve in a heated vegetable dish with bacon crumbled all over the top.

Baked Stuffed Acorn Squash

3 to 4 acorn squash
Butter
Salt and pepper

Optional Fillings:
1) 12 to 16 frozen precooked thawed
   sausages and applesauce
2) 2 to 3 apples, sliced, nutmeg and
   brown sugar
3) Maple or brown sugar

Preheat the oven to 350 degrees F. Halve the squash and remove the seeds and fibers and place them cut side down in a baking dish. Add 1 cup of boiling water and bake 30 minutes. Turn them over, dot each one with a little butter and sprinkle with salt and pepper. Leave plain or add any of the fillings. For the first filling, put in a large spoonful of applesauce and cover with 2 pieces of either link or patty sausages. For the second filling, fill the cavities with apple slices and dot with more butter. Sprinkle with nutmeg and 2 teaspoons of brown sugar. For the third put a tablespoonful of brown or maple sugar and dot with more butter. Sprinkle with salt and pepper. Return the squash to the oven and bake until the squash is tender—about 30 minutes.

Winter Succotash

2 cups dried lima beans
3 strips bacon
3 cups canned or frozen
   corn kernels
1 teaspoon sugar
2 cups stewed tomatoes
1 teaspoon salt
1/8 teaspoon pepper

Soak the lima beans several hours. Drain and rinse once more, discarding any imperfect beans. Cut the bacon into 2-inch pieces and place in a heavy pan with the beans and enough water to cover by 1 inch. Cover and cook 30 to 40 minutes or until tender. Add the corn, tomatoes and seasoning and stew gently uncovered for 20 to 30 minutes.

Summer Succotash

2 cups cooked lima beans
4 cups cooked corn kernels or
   12 to 14 ears of corn
1 cup milk
½ cup cream
3 tablespoons butter
½ teaspoon sugar
1 teaspoon salt
1/8 teaspoon white pepper

Garden-fresh lima beans, boiled in a little salted water for 20 minutes or until tender, are incomparably good, but if they are not available use the large frozen variety. Similarly, very freshly picked corn, boiled on the cob and cut off with a sharp knife, is the best possible, but that too may have to be substituted by the frozen variety. Heat the cooked vegetables with the milk and cream, butter, sugar, salt and pepper. Serve in individual dishes.

Zucchini and Summer Squash

1 large onion, diced
1 large clove garlic, pressed
4 tablespoons butter
4 small summer squash
4 small zucchini
1 pint commercial sour cream
1 tablespoon chopped parsley
1 cup fine bread crumbs
Salt and pepper

Cook the onion and garlic in butter in a large skillet just until the onion is soft. Wash and trim the ends of young squash and zucchini about 8 inches long and quite thin. Slice them into the skillet. Stir well. Let them cook for 10 minutes. Cool completely. Season with salt and pepper and stir in the sour cream and transfer to a shallow baking-serving dish. Spread with fine bread crumbs and dot with the remaining butter. Bake in a 350-degree oven for 30 minutes.

Tomatoes

Tomatoes came to us through Spain and were suspect for a long time as being an aphrodisiac. While that attribute does not seem to be true, it remains one of the most versatile of all our vegetables. One farmer's favorite is Creamed Green Tomatoes. Use 2 skillets at the same time when making this for 6 to 8 people. Serve with johnnycake.

Creamed Green Tomatoes

3 to 4 large, almost ripe tomatoes
1 cup flour
1 teaspoon salt
¼ teaspoon white pepper
½ teaspoon sugar
12 to 16 slices bacon
Cream Sauce (see Sauces)

Cut the tomatoes in thick slices, allowing 2 to 3 slices to a serving. Combine the flour with the seasonings and spread on a plate. Cook the bacon in the skillets until quite crisp. Remove and drain on paper toweling.

Make the Cream Sauce. Dip each tomato slice in the flour mixture and fry in the bacon fat 2 to 3 minutes on each side or until golden brown. Turn with a broad spatula. Place on a piece of johnnycake. Cover with a little Cream Sauce and top with bacon.

Sliced Tomatoes in French Dressing

4 yellow tomatoes
4 red tomatoes
French Dressing (see Sauces)
Pitted black olives
Chopped parsley

Slice the washed tomatoes without peeling them. Put them on a pretty nonmetal platter, alternating the red and yellow slices. Chill in the refrigerator. Shortly before serving, spoon over the French dressing, garnish with black olive halves and chopped parsley.

Baked Stuffed Tomatoes

6 to 8 tomatoes
5 tablespoons butter
2 tablespoons onion,
  chopped very fine
½ cup finely diced celery
1½ cups soft white bread crumbs
½ cup cracker crumbs

Choose medium-size tomatoes as uniform in size and shape as possible. Cut a thin slice from the top of each one and scoop out the pulp, leaving a ½-inch shell. Force the pulp through a sieve to remove the seeds. Turn the tomato shells upside down on a rack to drain.

Heat 3 tablespoons of the butter in a small pan and sauté the onion and celery just until the onion is soft. Add the bread crumbs and tomato pulp and stir until well mixed. Preheat the oven to 375 degrees F. Sprinkle the inside of the tomatoes with a little salt and pepper and unless the tomatoes are garden fresh add just a trace of sugar. Fill with the stuffing. Top with crisp cracker crumbs and dot with a little butter. Bake 20 minutes.

Broiled Tomatoes

These are usually used as an accompaniment to a breakfast or dinner dish. If more convenient they can be baked along with the meat or fish they are to garnish, but broiled tomatoes seem to have a nicer consistency. Allow 1 or 2 halves per person.

Uniform sized tomatoes
Sugar
Fine bread crumbs
Chopped parsley
Butter

Halve the tomatoes and gently squeeze out the seeds. Place on a baking sheet and sprinkle very lightly with sugar. Combine the bread crumbs, allowing 1 teaspoon to each tomato half, with a little chopped parsley. Spread over the tomato halves. Dot with butter and sprinkle with salt and pepper. Broil 5 to 6 minutes or until crumbs are browned.

Turnips in Cream

2 to 3 pounds white or yellow turnips
4 tablespoons butter
Salt and pepper
2 tablespoons sherry
¼ teaspoon freshly grated nutmeg
1 cup cream

Peel and dice the turnips in ¾-inch cubes. Boil in salted water for 10 minutes or just until tender. The yellow turnips will take longer than the white variety. Drain and toss in butter and season with salt and pepper. Cover with the sherry, nutmeg and cream which have been heated but not allowed to boil.

Glazed Turnips

6 to 8 white turnips
4 cups chicken broth
   (canned or homemade)
2 tablespoons sugar
3 to 4 tablespoons butter
Salt and pepper
2 tablespoons sherry
¾ teaspoon salt
1/8 teaspoon white pepper
1/8 teaspoon nutmeg

Pare and slice the turnips into ¼-inch slices. Cook them in the chicken stock in a covered pan for 10 minutes or until almost tender. Remove the cover and add the remaining ingredients. Boil down slowly, uncovered, until the turnips are glazed. Keep an eye on them to see that they do not burn. Toss occasionally. These can be cooked in advance, transferred to a baking-serving dish and reheated in the oven.

Potato Salad

This can be the simplest or the most elegant dish imaginable.

6 medium-size potatoes
¾ cup French Dressing (see Sauces)
¾ cup chopped celery
1 clove garlic, pressed
1 tablespoon grated onion
½ cup Mayonnaise (see Sauces)
½ teaspoon powdered vitamin C

Peel and cube the potatoes. Boil them in well-salted boiling water for 10 minutes or just until tender. Drain them well and place in a large wooden bowl. While still hot, pour in ¾ cup of French dressing, the celery, garlic and onion. Toss well, cover and let cool. Stir in vitamin C.

When cool add the small amount of mayonnaise. Serve simply in a bed of lettuce leaves, or form in a mound on a handsome serving platter and garnish as fancifully as you will with hard-cooked eggs, parsley, tomato wedges, anchovy fillets and black olives, forcing mayonnaise through a pastry tube in pretty patterns and surrounding the platter with lettuce leaves and watercress.

Green Salad

Rules for making a good green salad are few but important:

1) Choose good greens. The greener they are the better they are. Boston, Bibb, oakleaf, loose leaf, escarole, endive, romaine and iceberg are America's best lettuces, but watercress, young dandelion greens, spinach and Chinese cabbage are also very good. Greens should be well washed and picked over to discard wilted leaves and chilled.
2) Variety is achieved by the addition of herbs. Parsley, chives, chervil, tarragon, borage, savory, thyme, garlic and onion tops are to be had in either fresh or dried form. Dried herbs should be

soaked in small quantities in vinegar before being used. Fresh herbs are preferable.
3) Raw and cooked vegetables make salads in themselves or mix with salad greens. The salad artist is the home cook who can let his or her imagination run riot. Serve tomatoes as a separate salad or if combining them with greens do so at the last moment since they tend to dilute the flavor of the dressing.
4) Add French or other dressing at the last minute and toss well just before serving.

New England Cole Slaw

6 cups shredded cabbage
½ cup grated carrot
4 tablespoons grated onion
1 teaspoon caraway seeds (optional)
¼ teaspoon powdered vitamin C
Boiled Creamy Dressing:
3 tablespoons flour
2 teaspoons dry mustard
1 teaspoon salt
1 tablespoon sugar
2 eggs, slightly beaten
6 tablespoons vinegar
¾ cup milk
3 tablespoons butter
4 tablespoons heavy sweet
  or commercial sour cream

Shred the cabbage into a large bowl. Fill the bowl with cold water and let stand in the refrigerator for at least 2 hours. Drain and dry well between towels. Place the cabbage in a salad bowl and mix well with carrot and onion and caraway seeds, if desired. Toss with Boiled Creamy Dressing shortly before serving.

Dressing: Combine all the ingredients for the sauce except for the cream and vitamin C in a heavy saucepan, using a sturdy whisk. Beat constantly and vigorously while cooking over medium heat until the mixture thickens. Remove from the heat, add the sweet or sour cream and allow to cool. Stir in the vitamin C. This may be stored in a covered jar for several days.

Lycopersicon esculentum

Painted for a Stokely-VanCamp, Inc., promotion that appeared in 1967.

Shrimp Cocktail or Salad

This versatile dish can be used instead of soup as a first course for a dinner or in a slightly larger quantity as a luncheon or supper dish. Served with Popovers or Johnnycake (see Breads), it makes a delicious meal.

1½ to 2 pounds raw shrimp
2 cups water
1 cup dry white wine
1 slice onion
2 sprigs parsley
1 small bay leaf
½ teaspoon powdered thyme
2 teaspoons salt
Cocktail Sauce (see Sauces)
Lettuce
Chopped parsley

Wash the shrimp. If the shrimp has been frozen, soak it in cool water for 20 minutes. Dry well.

Combine the water, dry white wine, onion, parsley, bay leaf, thyme and salt in a large saucepan and boil for 5 minutes. Reduce the heat and add the shrimp. Simmer gently for 3 to 5 minutes or until the shrimp are bright pink. Do not overcook. Drain, discarding the liquid and any remnants of the onion, parsley and bay leaf, and cool.

Remove the shell and the black intestine. Cover and store in the refrigerator until ready to serve.

Line stemmed dessert glasses or small plates with fresh garden lettuce. Place the shrimp on the lettuce and cover with the sauce. Garnish with chopped parsley and serve at once.

California Caesar Salad

This salad created in the West by an ingenious restaurateur has many versions, some of which the creator would not recognize. The fundamental ingredients are good lettuce, freshly fried croutons, Parmesan cheese and anchovies.

1 head Boston lettuce
1 head romaine
½ cup olive oil
½ cup peanut oil
¼ cup lemon juice
2 eggs
1½ cups bread cubes
½ teaspoon prepared mustard
1 large clove garlic, pressed
4 tablespoons Parmesan cheese
1 tin anchovy fillets
¾ teaspoon salt
¼ teaspoon black pepper
Tabasco sauce

Wash the lettuces. Tear the leaves into pieces and crisp in the refrigerator. Be sure they are well dried.

Heat 4 tablespoons of oil in a skillet and brown freshly cut or store-bought croutons. Drain on paper toweling and keep warm.

Dip the eggs in boiling water for just 30 seconds. Break them into a bowl and mix vigorously with the lemon juice and mustard. Add the remaining oil, the cheese, salt, pepper and Tabasco sauce to taste. Stir until well blended.

Toss with the salad greens and add the croutons and the anchovy fillets, cut in half. Serve immediately to appreciative guests.

Waldorf Salad

Waldorf salad is an American invention and makes a refreshing dessert salad. Do not combine the ingredients until just before serving.

3 to 4 cups cubed apples
Lemon
2 cups diced celery
1 cup Mayonnaise or
  1 cup Boiled Creamy Dressing (see Sauces)
¾ cup chopped walnuts
Salt and pepper
Garden lettuce

Choose and wash firm, crisp eating apples. Unless the peel seems tough leave it on. Core and cube the apples in rather small pieces. Sprinkle with lemon juice and toss lightly.

Mix with the celery, mayonnaise or boiled dressing and walnuts. Season to taste with salt and pepper and stir. Line a salad bowl with washed and crisped lettuce and fill with the mixture.

Fruit Salad

3 to 4 cups fresh or canned fruit
½ cup French Dressing (see Sauces)
1 cup Mayonnaise (see Sauces)
1 cup sour cream
Fresh lettuce

Cut oranges and grapefruit in half and carefully spoon out the flesh. This is easier than peeling off the white membranes. Cut cantaloupe, honeydew or other melons in small cubes or make balls with a small scoop designed for that purpose. Mix with the French Dressing made with the herbs of your choice and chill.

Combine the mayonnaise and sour cream and chill.

Just before serving combine the fruit and the mayonnaise mixture. Serve in a bowl lined with washed and chilled lettuce leaves. Garnish with a few pieces of uncoated fruit.

"One order 'Chef's Salad.'"

BREAD: AND KEY MEMBERS ON THE STAFF OF LIFE

One of the most charming stories in all of our food literature concerns two great Americans—Ralph Waldo Emerson and Henry Thoreau. During the nineteenth century Emerson was by all odds the reigning author-philosopher and litterateur of the day. His presence alone made the town of Concord the intellectual capital of America.

Oddly, we do not read much of Emerson today. Very few college graduates can admit to having read any of his works, much less knowing who he was. On the other hand, Thoreau has become something of a cult, largely because of his beliefs in the simple life and his anti-establishment viewpoints, which inspired even so elevated a personage as Mahatma Gandhi while he was developing the theory of nonresistance, something which made the little man more powerful in a certain sense than the whole British empire. Yet, in the mid-nineteenth century, Thoreau was an obscure eccentric, virtually a handyman in the house of Ralph Waldo Emerson. (Some of Thoreau's boasts as to the enormous economies of his little house on Walden Pond really should be examined more closely, by the way. It is true that he lived on lentil soup and the like and he wrote about nature exquisitely. But he was ever careful not to mention that he was living on Emerson's land, on Emerson's generosity, without cost. But that's another story.)

The story that concerns us here is a Thoreauly foodish tale. Seems the Emerson housekeeper had kneaded her dough for the baking of the next day's bread, and left it on the sill of the kitchen window in readiness for early morning baking, for the Emer-sonian breakfast of piping hot bread and fresh melting butter. But it was not to be. Thoreau's pet pussycat discovered the great wad of soft dough in the kitchen, and as cats will, decided that it was put there specifically for her comfort, a pillow of ineffable softness and smoothness. She spent the night there, and her feline body heat went to work on the dough. It rose, inch by inch, during the night, elevating the pussy to a higher pillow than she had ever imagined as she composed herself for sleep, and putting Thoreau once more—as he frequently was—in the doghouse as far as the master of the house was concerned, who breakfasted, perforce, breadless.

The breadbasket of this country today is not on the windowsill but on the plains of the Dakotas, Nebraska, Kansas and Oklahoma, where grows the wheat which, as we have previously observed, is getting to be more of an international tool of power than guns and oil. We shall pass over the fact that for some years now, the makers of American bread have done their best, it would seem, to remove the wheat germ, which is the very heart and soul of the grain. But they are beginning to bring back that heart-and-soul, we trust. Right now, the best way to get the perfect loaf of bread you are really going to enjoy purely for its own sake is to make it yourself, which we are about to help you to do.

Curious that life on the trail teaches so many people, both men and women, the truths of cooking. The art of sourdough cooking, closely connected with the frontier for so many years, on farms and cattle ranches in the West, in the logging camps of Alaska

Cover painting, THE COUNTRY GENTLEMAN, *February 16, 1918.*

and the Northwest and in the prospector's lonely search for the gold always beckoning around the corner, is coming back as one of the "discoveries" of our space age microbiology. We are beginning to understand why the cowboy cook valued his sourdough. His pot of "starter" was the secret of his success as a cook for a pretty rough gang of customers. Each day, he put the right amounts of water and flour into his "starter" and set the mess out into the sun to ferment. He baked his bread that night for the men around the campfire, but a little of the fermented dough—the starter—was always set aside to provide the next day's miracle. If he had to, he wrapped his "starter" in a blanket to keep it warm, and if it was going to get so cold that a blanket couldn't do any good, any self-respecting cook slept with his "starter." That was his homemade yeast, and if it froze, that was going to be the last of good bread in that camp, and probably the last of "cookie" in that six-gun outfit. (Incidentally, the value of yeast in the brewing industry—which is, in a manner of speaking, the making of a liquid bread with a touch of alcohol in it—is well understood in that craft. In a recent shipment of a small amount of their special base yeast from a home office brewery in the Midwest to a new plant opening up on the east coast, the precious basic was flown in an aircraft especially leased for that purpose; the pilot received solemn and forceful instructions on what altitudes he was to maintain; and the cargo—just some yeast, good friends!—was insured for a million dollars.)

The ingenuity of Americans seems to be challenged on all sides by the bread of life. St. Louis is where peanut butter came from. Can you *imagine* how many slices of bread have gone down youthful throats, sluiced along by that deliciously gooky and never-cloying kind of butter? In Battle Creek, Michigan, Dr. Sylvester Graham, mentioned earlier, expanded his theories on nutrition, and created his own memorial in the healthful graham cracker. What happened then? A gentleman called Post was a patient in a sanitarium founded by some of the Graham followers and became so enthused over nutritional values that he created Postum and Grape Nuts. Dr. John Harvey Kellogg, director of the same sanitarium, was distressed to discover that one of his patients had cracked his teeth on a piece of zwieback—delicious in its way, but, as its name indicates, "twice baked." Accordingly, the kindly doctor invented a thing called cornflakes so this poor fellow could munch away at breakfast and find life worth living, even with shattered molars.

Ah, bread—today it is the "with it" word for money. And yet it always was. Bread is the thing which changed a man's idea of what food should be. It made him a planter rather than a hunter. Civilization began at that moment: the nomad became the settler, the settler became a citizen in a growing community, and out of communities grew nations.

The story of the first loaf of bread is another "first," like the story of the cheese in the Arab's saddle bag we told a few chapters back in this book. The age-old method of baking bread had been to rub wheat or another grain between a couple of stones,

> *That all-softening,*
> *overpowering knell,*
> *The tocsin of the soul*
> *—the dinner bell.*
>
> *Byron*

mix the crushed grain with water and then bake it—into something no doubt resembling a health-giving rock—by smothering it with hot ashes. Our little "first" concerns an Egyptian who discovered leavening as an ingredient for bread. The Egyptians were great on beer and already knew how to use yeast to produce it. But it is told that an Egyptian baker, working on his bread, inadvertently mixed into it some brewer's yeast which he had on hand for his "HEK," the Egyptian word for beer. When he left the dough out in the sun, lo, it had fermented and the yeast produced the leavening gases which are the miracle of bread, that airy and priceless food, created in the oven's heat.

Wheat, oldest of the grains! The ancient Anglo-Saxons invented a word, *Lady*, which means "Giver of the Loaf": Could anything be more of a total compliment? Some 6,700 years ago they were baking bread in the clay ovens of Jarmo, Mesopotamia. The Egyptians devised more than fifty kinds of bread and cakes and gained a name for themselves around the then known world as "bread eaters." They offered bread to the gods in tribute. It was placed in their tombs for sustenance during the afterlife. Daily bread—the men who built the eternal pyramids were paid a daily wage of three loaves of bread and two jugs of beer.

Bread had a humble history. If a couple had dinner in their home in the Middle Ages, they ate from the same platter or pot. But if there were more guests, bread was used instead of plates. A piece of bread about two days old, nice and crisp, about six inches across and two or three inches deep, made a great platter for pieces of roast meat. Don't forget, it was heavy unleavened bread for the most part. The meat juices simply soaked into it. After you ate the meat, you ate the plate. We might try that again in our own day. It would save a lot of trouble, although it would be bad news for detergent, dishwashing, and china manufacturers.

Bread rises throughout history. The *croissant*, for example, has a fine historic pageantry about it. There are a couple of stories told how the bakers invented the croissant, the bread-crescent in the shape of the Turkish scimitarlike symbol when Budapest, Hungary was besieged by the Turks, in 1686. According to one tale the Hungarian bakers, working late at night to feed the besieged soldiers, heard the Turks tunneling under the battlements, warned the armed defenders, and thus saved the day and the city. As a reward the bakers were commissioned to design croissants in honor of their alertness. The second story has a sad ring of probability to it. The Turks, as it appeared at the time to any thinking Hungarian, were about to conclude their siege of Budapest by rushing the city on the following morning and probably slicing off the heads of every citizen with savage precision. The bakers decided to meet them with gifts of bread shaped in the Turkish crescent: not a bad move, if you think you've figured out in advance whose game plan is going to win. Anyway, the Turks were defeated and flung back. The bakers, stuck with their treasonable croissants, vaingloriously fed them to their fellow Budapestians, turning defeat into victory,

> *The history of the world*
> *is the record of man in quest of*
> *his daily bread and butter.*
>
> *Hendrik Van Loon*

as it were, in a time of knead.

The pancake itself is a kind of bread, ancient as the feast of Shrovetide, a kind of merrymaking and self-indulgent period entered into by Europeans prior to the sacrifices, spiritual and physical, of their Lenten season. Wrote an Englishman:

"There is a thing call'd wheaten floure, which the cookes do mingle with water, eggs, spice and other tragicall, magicall enchantments, and then they put it by little and little into a frying-pan of boiling suet, where it makes a confused dismall hissing, until at last . . . it is transformed into the form of a . . . Pancake, which ominous incantation the ignorant people do devour very greedillie."

The Spaniards brought wheat to this hemisphere, first sowing their seeds of bread in Mexico and Peru, even as they sowed the seeds of destruction in those two ancient civilizations. Maine and Massachusetts and Virginia took to the growing of wheat as soon as the first settlers could get a shovel off the first boat to land. One hundred years later, the great plains were covered with wheat.

Baking in Colonial times was by all accounts a formidable challenge. The early settlers had come from towns and cities across the sea where all the baking was done by a licensed town baker, so that the pioneer housewife was ill prepared. All the ingredients had to be readied. Corn had to be ground into flour; yeast, if any, had to be made and kept and that was at best uncertain; salt was scarce. Once the dough was mixed the only way to bake it was in a pile of hot ashes, in a preheated pit or on the open hearth. The results were neither very palatable nor easily digested, but they kept people alive.

Each generation brought improvements. Very soon rye, wheat and oats were turned into flour, ovens were built into chimneys and then into kitchen ranges and the inventiveness of Colonial housewives brought new recipes. Today, baking is a simple process with good flour at our disposal, dependable yeast and controlled oven temperatures. It is not only fun to make bread, it is economical, soul-satisfying and much healthier for the entire family.

Winston Churchill, a good trencherman of roast beef and brandy, always had a low opinion of the sandwich. But it was, after all, the invention of another Britisher, in the eighteenth century. John Montagu, Earl of Sandwich, was so fond of gambling and card-playing that he could not bear to give up time from the gaming tables even to eat. He simply ordered his roast meats brought to him wrapped between two slices of bread, so he could keep on playing while he munched. Churchill spoke scathingly of the Earl, being of the opinion that a better formula would have been to hold that the meat is the only thing worthwhile in a sandwich, and the thinner the bread the better. Would that restaurants would follow his idea. But if you've ever had really fresh bread, say, sourdough, with some thick slices of ham and some marvelously fresh cheese therein, you'll disagree even with a Churchill. For, as the Walrus said in *Through the Looking Glass,* . . . "A loaf of bread is what we chiefly need."

CRACKERS
10¢ a lb.

Cover painting, THE SATURDAY EVENING POST, *March 15, 1913.*

Good White Bread

It has taken generations to develop easy-to-make bread that anyone can do, given a little muscle and patience. It is a far cry from the hard and coarse hearth-fired loaves the pioneers made, but made with unbleached flour, milk and butter, it is indeed the staff of life. Lots of Americans are getting back to the once-a-week baking binge because homemade bread is far superior. It can be stored in the refrigerator or in the freezer very satisfactorily. Chances are that this bread won't last that long if you have family and friends in the house.

2 packages dry yeast
1½ cups lukewarm water
5 tablespoons butter or margarine
6 or 7 cups all-purpose flour
2 tablespoons sugar
1 cup whole milk
3 teaspoons salt

Stir the yeast with the lukewarm water in a deep bowl. Cover and set in a warm (80 to 85 degrees F) place (near a heat outlet perhaps) for 15 minutes.

Meanwhile prepare the pans. Melt 1 tablespoon of butter and grease 2 large (9-by-5-inch) bread pans (unless they are Teflon-lined) and a deep bowl for raising the bread.

Add 1 cup of flour and 1 tablespoon of sugar to the yeast. Stir well with a wooden spoon. Cover and let rise for 30 minutes.

Scald the milk, add 4 tablespoons of butter, tablespoon of sugar and the salt. Mix and cool to lukewarm. Put both mixtures in a large electric mixer bowl and start beating. Add 2 cups of flour and beat hard for 2 minutes. Then, still beating, add flour by half-cupfuls until you have a dough that is no longer sticky but soft and compact. When the dough gets too heavy for your particular type of mixer add the flour with a large wooden spoon or with your hands.

Turn the dough onto a lightly floured surface which can be a porcelain-topped kitchen table, Formica, marble or board. Start kneading with your hands, taking out a week's frustration on the innocent dough, pummeling, throwing it onto the board, punching it and kneading until you have a smooth elastic ball. This should take 10 minutes. Place in the greased bowl and turn it so that all sides are coated. Cover with a folded clean kitchen towel or plastic and let rise in a warm protected place until doubled (50 to 60 minutes). Punch down and cut in half, forming each half into a rectangular loaf. Place in the prepared pans. Cover and return to the same cozy spot for 35 to 45 minutes or until doubled. Bake in a preheated 400-degree oven for 25 minutes. Remove from the oven and turn out on a wire rack, brush lightly with butter and cool.

Anadama Bread

Legend has it that this bread was invented by a New England farmer who, tired of his daily ration of cornmeal and molasses, grabbed the porridge bowl from his patient but uninventive housewife, added wheat flour and yeast and baked it on the hearth. Tasting his new discovery, he is supposed to have said, "There, Anna, dammit this is what I like." True or not, the modern version of his discovery makes a delicious bread.

6 tablespoons soft butter or
  margarine
1 cup cornmeal
6 to 7 cups all-purpose unbleached flour
1 tablespoon salt
2 packages dried yeast
½ cup molasses
2 cups very hot water

With 1 tablespoon of butter grease 2 medium-size (8½- by- 4½-inch) bread pans and a large bowl for raising the bread.

Put the rest of the butter, the cornmeal, 2 cups of flour, salt and yeast in an electric mixer bowl. Mix the molasses and hot water until well blended. When lukewarm, add gradually to the ingredients in the bowl while beating vigorously with the electric beater. Gradually add more flour, still beating. When the dough gets too heavy for the beater, continue the process by hand until you have a soft, firm dough that no longer sticks to your hand. Turn onto a floured surface and knead with the palm of your hand, pushing the dough away and then reforming the ball, for 10 minutes. Place the ball of dough in the prepared bowl and turn it around to coat it with butter. Cover with a doubled clean dishcloth or with plastic and set in a warm place (80 to 85 degrees F). Let it rise until doubled (50 to 60 minutes). Punch down and cut in half. Cover and let rest 5 minutes. Shape into rectangular loaves and place seam side down in the pans. Cover again and put back in the same warm spot. Let rise again until doubled (40 to 45 minutes) and put into a preheated 425-degree oven. Reduce the heat to 375 degrees F and bake 35 minutes. Remove immediately from the pan and place on a wire rack to cool.

Whole Wheat Bread

Much that is sold in stores as whole wheat flour is not the true ground whole wheat, but such can be found in many specialty stores and is well worth finding. Not only is it far richer in protein, vitamins and minerals but it is far superior in flavor. Whole wheat bread is not as light as other varieties, but it has a nutty flavor that is delicious. Allow plenty of time to make this bread. It's easy to mix but the dough has to rise several times.

5 tablespoons butter or margarine
2 cups milk
2 tablespoons sugar
3 teaspoons salt
2 packages dry yeast
¼ cup lukewarm water
6 or 7 cups whole wheat flour

Melt 1 tablespoon of butter and grease 2 medium-size (8½-by-4½-inch) pans and a deep bowl for raising the dough.

Scald the milk with the rest of the butter, 1½ tablespoons of sugar and the salt. Stir until the sugar dissolves and cool until lukewarm.

At the same time, combine the yeast and lukewarm water with the rest of the sugar. Stir and cover until the milk is lukewarm. Combine the mixtures in an electric mixer bowl and add 2 cups of flour. Beat vigorously for 2 minutes. Add flour gradually until the dough is really thick and not sticky. Stop using the electric beater when the dough becomes too heavy and finish adding the flour with a wooden spoon or with your hands. Turn onto a floured surface and knead for 2 minutes or until you have a smooth ball. Place in the bowl and turn it around so that all sides are coated. Cover and let rise in a warm place (80 to 85 degrees F) until doubled (about 1 hour). Punch down and let rise again. Repeat this twice more. Turn onto a floured surface, knead down for a moment and cut in half. Shape into 2 rectangular loaves. Place them in the prepared pans. Let rise once more and bake 10 minutes in a preheated 425-degree oven. Reduce the heat to 375 degrees and bake 25 minutes more.

Turn onto a wire rack. Brush the tops with melted butter and cool.

Crusty Sourdough Bread

Sourdough starter is by no means an American invention, but it came to this country early in its history and was used by pioneers and their wives who were far from any source of yeast. Tales are told of prospectors going to Alaska carrying sourdough starter so that they could have bread of sorts whenever the spirit moved them. Once started, sourdough starter is self-perpetuating. Don't expect to make this bread in a hurry. Everything about it is slow, but the results are worth waiting for.

Starter:
1 cup unbleached flour
1 cup water
2 teaspoons sugar

Bread:
1 package dry yeast
1½ cups lukewarm water
2 teaspoons salt
6 to 7 cups unbleached flour
1 teaspoon sugar
½ teaspoon baking soda

To make starter, combine the unbleached flour, water and sugar in a quart jar. Mix well and put in a warm place (80 to 85 degrees F). It may be in the attic in the summer or the cellar or utility room in the winter, but keep searching with a thermometer until you find it. Let the mixture work 2 or 3 days or until fermented. Stir it down every day.

When the starter is ready, stir the yeast into the lukewarm water in an electric mixer bowl. Add 1 cup of the starter, the salt and sugar and 4 cups of flour. Beat hard for 2 minutes. Cover the bowl and put in the same warm place for 2 to 2½ hours or at room temperature (68 degrees F) for overnight. Stir down the sponge and add 1 cup of flour mixed with the soda, using the mixer, if it is a strong one, or your hands. Turn onto a floured surface and gradually work in more flour until you have a stiff dough. Knead for 10 minutes, incorporating more flour if necessary to give a smooth elastic ball of dough. Divide in half and let rest while preparing the oven. Put a roasting pan full of hot water on the bottom of your oven. Preheat to 400 degrees F.

Shape the dough into round or long loaves and place them on a lightly greased baking sheet, with seams on the bottom. Make a crisscross design on the round loaves with a very sharp small knife or diagonal slits in the long loaf. Brush with water and place in the oven. Bake 45 to 50 minutes. The loaves should be hard to the touch. If you hold the loaf to your ear and it is still "singing" it is not done. Give it a few more minutes.

To perpetuate the starter: Replace the starter with 2/3 cup of water and 2/3 cup of flour. Stir well and let it stand uncovered at room temperature for 24 hours. Cover and store in the refrigerator. A starter should be used every week or 10 days.

If You Love Peanuts

Steamed Boston Brown Bread

The inventor of this famous bread is unknown but not unsung. For generations in New England, Boston brown bread was as regular a part of Saturday night supper as church was of Sunday. It steamed all afternoon in a fireless cooker. Today most people buy the bread in cans and forget how good it is homemade. The bread is so tender that it used to be the custom to slice it by tying a string around the loaf and crossing the ends to give regular smooth-cut slices.

¾ cup seedless raisins
2 tablespoons all-purpose flour
1 cup rye flour
1 cup yellow cornmeal
1 cup graham flour
2 teaspoons baking soda
1 teaspoon salt
1 pint buttermilk
¾ cup molasses

Grease the insides of 2 (1-pound) coffee tins, including the top plastic lid. Cut out 2 circles of wax paper the size of the bottom of the can. Butter them lightly and place on the bottom of the insides. Put the raisins in a small bowl and stir with the white flour until coated. Set aside.

Mix all the dry ingredients in an electric mixer bowl. Stir the buttermilk and molasses until blended. Pour into the flour mixture gradually and beat slowly just until blended. Add the raisins and give one more stir. Divide the batter between the 2 cans. Cover and place on a rack in a kettle half full of warm water. Cover the kettle and bring to a slow boil. Steam 2½ hours, adding boiling water when necessary to keep the level up halfway on the cans. Remove the cans from the water and take off the tops. Put the cans in a roasting pan and allow the bread to dry out for 20 minutes in a 300-degree oven. Unmold onto 2 plates and serve one at each end of the table. Serve with butter, Boston Baked Beans (see Vegetables) and Codfish Balls with Watercress Salad (see Fish).

Oatmeal Molasses Bread

3 cups whole wheat flour
3 or 4 cups all-purpose unbleached flour, sifted
1 cup old-fashioned oatmeal flakes
2½ teaspoons salt
2 packages dry yeast
½ cup powdered milk
¼ cup wheat germ
4 tablespoons soft butter or margarine
2 cups very hot water
½ cup unsulfured molasses

Grease 2 medium-size (8½-by-4½-inch) bread tins.

Combine 3 cups of whole wheat flour with 3 cups of white flour in a bowl.

Put 2 cups of the flour mixture in a large electric mixer bowl with the oatmeal, yeast, milk, wheat germ and butter.

Mix the water and molasses and add it to the dry ingredients, beating at medium speed for 2 minutes. Add ½ cup of the flour mixture and beat at high speed for 2 minutes. Continue adding the flour mixture, until the dough is soft and workable. When the dough becomes too heavy for your particular mixer, stir in the flour with a wooden spoon. Turn the dough onto a floured surface and knead for 10 minutes until the dough is smooth and elastic, adding more white flour if necessary. Place in a greased bowl, turning the bread so that it is coated on all sides. Cover and let rise in a warm (80 to 85 degrees F) place for 1 hour. Knead down and cut in half. Shape each half and put into loaf tins. Cover and let rise 45 minutes or until doubled.

Preheat the oven to 350 degrees F. Bake 40 minutes. Remove from pan. Paint crust with a little butter or margarine. Cover with a clean cloth until cool.

Maryland Beaten Biscuit

Beaten biscuits are the pride of the South. In former times no Southern hostess would fail to be able to offer these at any and all times of day. To be good they have to be pounded unmercifully, traditionally for at least 30 minutes with a hatchet until the dough blisters. This was the daily duty of the plantation cook, but not many such jewels are left nor is culinary energy what it used to be. However, with a good meat chopper or one of the new high-powered food processing machines now available, beaten biscuits are still possible.

1 cup cold milk
4 cups all-purpose flour
½ teaspoon salt
½ teaspoon baking powder
½ cup cold lard or
   vegetable shortening

Pour the milk in a measuring pitcher and add enough ice to measure 2 full cups.

Sift the dry ingredients and work in the lard or vegetable shortening with fingers, pastry blender or electric beater until the texture is fine like white cornmèal. Add the milk gradually until the dough is very stiff and not sticky. Run the dough through a meat chopper 3 times. The dough will be firm but elastic.

Roll out the dough on a floured board to ½-inch thickness and cut with any size cookie cutter you wish and place on an ungreased baking sheet. Or break off small portions, roll them in your hands and flatten onto an ungreased baking sheet. The biscuits should be about ½ inch apart.

Preheat the oven to 450 degrees F. Prick each biscuit twice with a fork. Bake the larger ones for 20 minutes or until golden brown.

Don't forget that miniature beaten biscuits, split, buttered and filled with slivers of Maryland or Virginia ham make a perfect cocktail tidbit. They bake only 10 minutes.

Baking Powder Biscuits

The secret of making good baking powder biscuits is to work quickly and lightly. This will make about 14 biscuits. Double the recipe if necessary.

2 cups all-purpose flour
1¼ teaspoons salt
2½ teaspoons baking powder
4 tablespoons butter or
   vegetable shortening
¾ cup milk (approximate)

Preheat the oven to 450 degrees F. Sift the dry ingredients together. Work in the shortening with a pastry blender, fingertips or an electric mixer until you have a fine texture like white cornmeal. Add just enough milk to give a soft dough that is not sticky. Turn onto a floured board or other working surface and knead lightly just until smooth. Pat with floured hands to a thickness of 2/3 inch. Cut into small rounds with a floured cookie cutter or water glass. Place them on an ungreased baking sheet leaving an inch between the rounds. Bake 12 to 14 minutes.

Popovers

Popovers, sometimes called puff-pops in bygone days, have been and still are universal favorites. This recipe will make 12 to 24 popovers.

4 eggs
2 cups all-purpose flour
1 teaspoon salt
1½ cups milk
2 tablespoons clarified butter
   (see Sauces) or salad oil

Preheat the oven to 425 degrees F. Grease well Pyrex or earthenware custard cups or deep muffin tins.

Beat the eggs until light-colored. Add the flour, salt and milk and beat until very smooth. Stir in the butter or oil and pour into cups or tins filling them half full. Bake 30 minutes. Remove from the pans. If popovers are forced to wait, prick them with a fork and keep in a warm oven with the door ajar.

Hello! Hello!

"Give me the best Flour, please!" That's your order to the Grocer. But you may not get it – you are disappointed. Next time you order, specify GOLD MEDAL FLOUR– WASHBURN-CROSBY'S; because you want the finest bread, and bread can't be better than the flour it's made from.   Use–

WASHBURN – CROSBY'S
GOLD MEDAL FLOUR

Pancakes

Pancakes of various forms, ranging from the good thick flannel cakes of Northern fame, to the thinner variety made in New Orleans, have been standard American fare for generations. Our forefathers found them easy to cook on an open campfire, and housewives could fry them on special skillet pans. Our skillets are a little more sophisticated and easier to regulate. Served with bacon or sausage, with maple syrup, brown sugar, maple sugar, or just plain they are wonderfully good. Packaged mixes of every sort can be found on the grocery shelf and can make good pancakes, but making them at home is far more satisfactory. This recipe will make 2 dozen or more. Add more milk or water for thinner pancakes, if desired.

3 cups sifted flour
2 tablespoons baking powder
1½ teaspoons salt
2 cups milk
2 eggs, well beaten
Butter, margarine, or salad oil

Combine the dry ingredients in a bowl. Mix the milk and eggs with 4 tablespoons of melted fat or oil. Combine the two mixtures as quickly as possible to keep the pancakes tender.

Heat the griddle or skillet to 375 degrees F or until a few drops of water sizzle when dropped on the surface.

Lightly grease the surface. Spoon as many half-ladlefuls of the batter as the griddle or skillet will hold. Cook until the top of the pancake is full of bubbles. Turn and brown the other side. Keep warm until you have a good supply, allowing 2 per person to start. Grease the griddle or skillet occasionally. Keep right on frying or let someone else take over.

Waffles

Waffles rich with eggs and cream were one of Thomas Jefferson's favorite imports from Holland. The waffle irons were heated over burning coals on both sides and thoroughly greased before each cooking. Modern electric waffle irons are very simple to operate and require no greasing. A trick of the trade is to put a little water in the waffle iron before heating it. When the steaming stops the iron is ready to cook the waffles. This will make 16 or 24 waffles, depending on the size of the waffle iron.

Rich Waffles

2 cups sifted all-purpose flour
2½ tablespoons baking powder
¾ teaspoon salt
6 egg yolks
1 pint heavy cream
6 egg whites, beaten stiff

Sift the dry ingredients together in a bowl.

Beat the egg yolks until thick. Add the cream gradually, continuing to beat. Mix the liquid and dry ingredients. When smooth and creamy fold in the egg whites thoroughly so that all the whites are well blended. Cover and put in a cool place for an hour.

Heat the waffle iron. Pour ¼ cup of the mixture into the center or a little more if you have a large waffle iron. Lower the top and cook until the waffle stops steaming.

Serve for breakfast with sausages or bacon and maple syrup or with creamed chicken or creamed chipped beef for luncheon or supper. Individual bowls of tossed salad for each person to nibble at make the waiting easier while the waffles are being cooked either in the kitchen or at the table.

Cover painting, THE SATURDAY EVENING POST, *November 10, 1934*

Everyday Waffles

These waffles, while less historic, are not quite as rich or caloric and may seem better for ordinary breakfast fare. This recipe will make 12 to 16 waffles, depending on the size of the waffle iron.

3 large eggs
1 2/3 cups milk
2 cups all-purpose flour
4 teaspoons baking powder
1 tablespoon sugar
1 teaspoon salt
¼ cup melted butter or margarine

Beat the eggs well in an electric mixer bowl. Add the milk. Combine the dry ingredients and add them to the liquid. Beat just until blended. Add the melted shortening. Let stand while heating the waffle iron.

Put a tablespoon of water in the waffle iron. Close and heat until the steaming stops. Open the iron and put ¼ cup of the batter in the center or slightly more if the waffle iron is large. Cover and do not open again until the steaming has stopped. Remove to a warm place and continue cooking until you have one waffle for each person. Keep on making the waffles, preferably at the table, pouring the batter from a pretty pitcher.

Virginia Spoon Bread

4 tablespoons plus 1 teaspoon
  butter or margarine
1¼ cups white cornmeal
2½ cups boiling water
1¼ teaspoons salt
1¾ cups milk (lukewarm)
4 egg yolks, beaten well
5 egg whites, beaten stiff

Preheat oven to 350 degrees F. Melt the butter and grease a 1½-quart baking or soufflé dish.

Put the cornmeal into a bowl and stir while gradually adding the boiling water. Mix until smooth and cool to lukewarm. Stir in the salt, slightly heated milk, the melted butter, and the beaten egg yolks. Stir just until blended. Fold the egg whites into the mixture and pour into the baking dish. It should fill the dish two-thirds full. Bake 35 to 40 minutes or until an inserted knife comes out clean.

Carry to the table and serve with a spoon. This is delicious with bacon, ham or sausage and is eaten with lots of butter.
Try Skillet Ham and Eggs (see Eggs) but instead of serving eggs, remove the ham to a hot platter, add 1 cup of water (or coffee) to the fat in the pan and stir until the mixture boils. This is known as Red Gravy and tastes very good with spoon bread.

Hoe Cake

Hoe cake was probably one of the first breads eaten by the early settlers in Virginia. It was made by combining a cup of white cornmeal with ½ teaspoon of salt and enough boiling water to make a semi-stiff mush. It was then cooled and baked on a greased shovel—called a hoe—over glowing coals. It was also called "Ash Cake" because sometimes it was made a little thicker, shaped into a cake, wrapped with leaves and buried in hot ashes to bake. Today's version is to use the same ingredients, add a tablespoon of melted butter or margarine and bake about ¼ inch thick in a well-greased heavy pan at 375 degrees F for 20 to 25 minutes. Cut while hot and serve with plenty of butter.

Johnnycake

Johnnycake, which Rhode Island claims as its own, was originally called journey cakes because they were small cakes made of a coarse corn batter fried on a griddle and were hard enough to travel with a man on horseback for many a day without spoiling. They must have been difficult to digest and it's a far cry from the delicious baked version that we enjoy today.

2½ tablespoons melted butter, margarine
  or bacon fat
1 cup yellow cornmeal
1 cup all-purpose unbleached flour
1 tablespoon sugar
1 tablespoon baking powder
¾ teaspoon salt
2 eggs, beaten light
1 cup milk

Preheat the oven to 425 degrees F. Melt the fat and grease an 8-by-8-inch baking dish liberally. Save the rest of the fat.

Mix all the dry ingredients in a bowl. Combine the well-beaten eggs with the milk and add gradually to the dry ingredients, stirring *just* until blended. Add the remaining fat, give a quick stir and pour the batter into the prepared pan. Smooth the batter to the edges. Bake 20 minutes. Cut into squares and serve warm.

Southern Batter Bread

3 tablespoons butter or margarine
2½ cups white cornmeal
2 teaspoons sugar
1 teaspoon salt
2 teaspoons baking powder
2½ cups milk
4 eggs, well beaten

Preheat the oven to 350 degrees F. Put the butter into a 1½- to 2-quart baking-serving dish and place in the oven while preheating. Do not let the butter brown. Mix the dry ingredients in a bowl. Combine the milk and eggs. Stir the two mixtures *just* until blended.

Remove the dish from the oven. Tilt it so that the butter coats the sides. Pour in the batter and bake for 25 to 30 minutes. An inserted knife should come out clean but the bread should not be too dry. Serve with butter or margarine. This accompanies fish in place of potatoes.

Maryland Buttermilk Cornsticks

Maryland Buttermilk corn batter makes thin crisp cornbread, often baked in special cornstick pans, which sometimes come shaped like ears of corn or are rounded thin pans 4 to 5 inches long. Lacking these, the batter can be baked in an 8-by-10-inch baking tin or in shallow individual muffin tins. Make a double recipe if you are cooking for more than six people because one of these cornsticks is never enough.

1 tablespoon butter or margarine
2 cups white cornmeal
1 teaspoon baking soda
2 teaspoons salt
2 eggs, beaten light
2 cups buttermilk

Preheat the oven to 425 degrees F. Melt the butter and grease the pans liberally. Heat whatever you are going to bake in. Combine the dry ingredients in an electric mixer bowl. Combine the beaten egg and the buttermilk and pour gradually into the bowl, beating constantly. Pour the batter into the hot cornstick pans to about 1/3 inch. The use of a large measuring pitcher is handy for this process. Bake immediately for 20 minutes. Serve at once, hot, with plenty of butter.

Pumpkin Bread

3½ cups sifted all-purpose unbleached flour
1½ cups light brown sugar
1½ cups white sugar
2 teaspoons baking soda
1½ teaspoons salt
1 teaspoon cinnamon
½ teaspoon nutmeg
4 eggs
1 cup salad oil
2/3 cup water
2 cups mashed pumpkin (fresh,
   frozen or canned)

Preheat the oven to 350 degrees F. Grease 3 medium (8½-by-4½-inch) loaf tins and sprinkle them with a little brown sugar.

Combine all the dry ingredients in a large bowl and fashion a well in the center.

Break in the 4 eggs and add the salad oil, water and pumpkin. Beat thoroughly until well mixed. Pour into the prepared pans.

Bake 1 hour and 15 minutes. Cool for 5 minutes in the pans before turning onto wire racks to cool.

This bread can be wrapped in aluminum foil and frozen very satisfactorily.

Quick Orange Nut Bread

2 cups unbleached all-purpose flour
½ teaspoon salt
1 teaspoon baking powder
½ teaspoon baking soda
1 orange (rind and juice)
Boiling water
2 tablespoons melted butter or margarine
1 cup sugar
1 egg, slightly beaten
1 teaspoon vanilla
½ cup chopped walnuts

Preheat the oven to 350 degrees F. Grease a medium-size (8½-by-4½-inch) loaf tin. Mix the dry ingredients in a bowl.

Grate the orange and squeeze the juice into a measuring cup. Add enough boiling water to make a cupful. Combine with the orange rind, melted fat, sugar, beaten egg, and vanilla in a bowl and stir until blended.

Stir into the dry ingredients just until mixed. Add the nuts. Pour into the loaf tin.

Bake 1 hour. Turn onto a wire rack to cool.

Aunt Charlotte's Nut Bread

1 cup all-purpose unbleached flour
2 cups whole wheat flour
1 tablespoon baking powder
½ teaspoon soda
1 teaspoon salt
1 cup dark brown sugar
1½ cups milk
1 cup walnuts, coarsely chopped

Preheat the oven to 300 degrees F. Combine the flours, baking powder, soda and salt in a bowl. Stir the sugar in the milk until it dissolves. Stir the milk mixture into the dry ingredients just until mixed. Add the walnuts and bake in 2 greased medium loaf tins (8½ by 4½ inches) for 1 hour. Turn onto a wire rack and cool completely. Slice thin and spread with sweet butter.

Uneeda Biscuit

Muffins

Muffins of cornmeal, wheat flour or cereals are purely an American invention. Until recently they were part of ordinary breakfast fare, but now that life has speeded up and few people are willing to spend the time or the calories on a leisurely breakfast they have faded from the scene somewhat. This should be remedied because there is nothing more delectable nor more reminiscent of old-fashioned good cooking than a hot muffin fresh from the oven. The least possible beating is the secret of good muffins.

Plain Muffins

4 tablespoons melted butter
  or margarine
2 cups minus 2 tablespoons
  all-purpose unbleached flour
1 tablespoon baking powder
¾ teaspoon salt
1 tablespoon sugar
1 cup milk
2 eggs, well beaten

Preheat the oven to 400 degrees F. Melt the butter and grease the muffin tins. Combine the dry ingredients in a bowl. Mix the milk with the beaten eggs and stir in the melted butter. Combine the two mixtures as quickly and deftly as possible, stirring just enough to mix them. Spoon into the prepared pans. The muffin tins should be about half full. Bake immediately for 15 to 20 minutes, depending on the size of the tins. Turn out immediately. Muffins can be reheated or frozen for eating at a later date.

Blueberry Muffins

Take ¼ cup of the prescribed flour and sprinkle over 1½ cups of blueberries, stirring until the berries are coated. Follow the recipe for Plain Muffins and stir them in quickly just after the addition of the milk, eggs and butter.

Apple Muffins

Follow the recipe for Plain Muffins but increase the sugar to 4 tablespoons and fold in 1 cup of finely diced, peeled cooking apples just after the addition of the milk, eggs and butter.

Bran Muffins

Bran muffins are not only good to eat, they are good for you. Bran furnishes the kind of roughage and fiber that nutritionists say we need more of, and muffins will be acceptable to many people who don't care for bran cereals served the usual way with milk and sugar.

2 cups bran cereal
1½ cups milk
2 cups all-purpose flour
½ cup brown sugar
¾ teaspoon salt
4 teaspoons baking powder
1 large egg
4 tablespoons melted butter
  or margarine

Preheat the oven to 400 degrees F. Grease 18 large or 24 medium-large muffin tins. Soak the bran in the milk, while assembling the other ingredients. Combine the flour, sugar, salt and baking powder. Beat the egg for 1 minute and add the melted fat.

Quickly and lightly combine the 3 mixtures stirring *just* until blended. Fill muffin tins half full. Bake 20 to 25 minutes or until well browned.

Confederate Coffee Cake

¾ cup butter
1 1/3 cups sugar
3 large eggs
½ cup milk
1½ cups all-purpose flour
1 teaspoon baking powder
½ teaspoon salt
¼ teaspoon nutmeg
1 teaspoon cinnamon
¾ cup chopped pecans

Preheat the oven to 375 degrees F. Beat ½ cup of butter and 1 cup of sugar with an electric beater until well blended and fluffy.

Beat in the eggs and milk and continue beating just until blended. Stir in the flour, combined with the baking powder and salt: Pour into a 9-by-9-inch greased baking-serving dish.

Quickly melt the remaining butter and stir in the remaining sugar, nutmeg and cinnamon. Spread over the dough with a small spatula and sprinkle with the nutmeats. Bake 20 minutes.

Coffee Cake

¼ pound butter or margarine
1 cup sugar
2 eggs
½ pint commercial sour cream
1½ cups all-purpose unbleached flour
1 teaspoon soda
1½ teaspoons baking powder
1 tablespoon vanilla extract

Topping:
¼ cup sugar
½ teaspoon cinnamon
¼ teaspoon grated nutmeg
½ cup chopped pecans
1 tablespoon butter

Preheat the oven to 350 degrees F. Grease a 10-by-10-inch baking tin.

Beat the butter and sugar in a bowl with an electric beater until light and fluffy. Add the eggs one by one, beating hard after each addition, add the sour cream and the dry ingredients sifted together. Beat until smooth. Stir in the vanilla and pour into the prepared pan.

Mix all the ingredients for the topping except the butter. Sprinkle over the top and dot with the butter. Bake 45 minutes.

Serve warm with butter.

Doughnuts

4¼ cups sifted all-purpose flour
½ teaspoon cinnamon
¼ teaspoon allspice
¼ teaspoon nutmeg
1 teaspoon salt
1 cup sugar
2 eggs
1 cup milk
3 tablespoons melted butter
  or margarine
Deep fat

Mix the dry ingredients in a bowl. Beat the eggs until lemon-colored and combine with the milk and fat. Combine the mixtures, thoroughly beating with a wooden spoon or an electric beater. Cover and let the dough rest in the refrigerator for 30 minutes.

Preheat the fat to 375 degrees F. Turn the dough onto a well-floured surface. The dough should be very soft—just firm enough to cut and handle. Keep your hands and the working surface and the rolling pin well floured. Roll out to a thickness of 1/3 inch and cut with a doughnut cutter. Reform the uncut dough and roll it out again. The last of the dough can be dropped in bits into the hot fat.

Fry the doughnuts 3 or 4 at a time for about 3 minutes, turning once. Drain on paper toweling. Shake in a paper bag containing ½ cup sugar. This recipe will make about 2½ dozen doughnuts.

Advertisement for Russell-Miller Milling Co., 1915.

Peanut Butter Banana Bread

This is good made with the chunky kind of peanut butter.

1¾ cups flour
2 teaspoons baking powder
½ teaspoon baking soda
½ teaspoon salt
1/3 cup vegetable shortening
   or margarine
¾ cup peanut butter
2/3 cup sugar
2 eggs
1 cup mashed bananas

Preheat the oven to 350 degrees F. Combine flour, baking powder, soda and salt and sift together. Cream together the peanut butter and shortening, in large mixing bowl. Add eggs and beat well, then add dry ingredients alternately with banana pulp. Mix thoroughly but do not beat. Pour batter into a well-greased loaf pan and bake 1 hour or until done. Cool before slicing.

Oatmeal Muffins

¾ cup flour
2 tablespoons brown sugar
1½ teaspoons baking powder
½ teaspoon baking soda
½ teaspoon salt
¾ cup oatmeal (uncooked)
1 teaspoon cinnamon
¼ cup butter or margarine
¾ cup buttermilk
1 egg

Preheat oven to 425 degrees F. Combine flour, sugar, baking powder, soda, salt, cinnamon and oatmeal. Mix well. Add butter and cut in with two knives or with a pastry blender. In a small bowl, mix together egg and buttermilk. Add to dry ingredients and mix only until dry ingredients are moist. Pour batter into 12 well-greased muffin cups and bake 15 to 20 minutes. Serve warm, with butter.

Banana-Wheat Germ Muffins

1½ cups sifted flour
½ cup sugar
3 teaspoons baking powder
½ teaspoon salt
1 cup wheat germ
2 eggs, beaten
1 cup mashed banana
½ cup milk
¼ cup melted vegetable shortening,
   cooking oil or margarine
¼ cup chopped nuts (optional)

Preheat oven to 400 degrees F. Combine flour, sugar, baking powder and salt. Sift into a large mixing bowl. Stir in wheat germ and nuts. Add eggs, banana pulp, milk and shortening and mix just until dry ingredients are moistened. Spoon batter into 12 well-greased muffin tins. The cups should be 2/3 full. Bake 20 to 25 minutes and serve warm, with butter.

Whole Wheat Apple Nut Rolls

2 cups whole wheat flour
2 cups white flour
1¼ cups milk
¼ cup sugar
2½ teaspoons salt
¼ cup margarine or butter
¼ cup honey
½ cup warm water
2 packages yeast
½ cup finely chopped apple
½ cup chopped pecans

Mix the two kinds of flour together and set aside. Heat milk but do not boil. Stir in sugar, salt, margarine or butter and honey. Cool to lukewarm.

Measure warm water into a large mixing bowl. Stir in yeast. Add lukewarm milk mixture. Stir in flour; it should make a thick batter but be less stiff than regular bread dough. Cover with a clean dish towel and place in a warm place to rise until nearly doubled in bulk.

Stir batter down. Mix in apple and pecan bits. Grease 18 large muffin cups and spoon the batter into them. Cover and let rise until doubled. Bake at 400 degrees F about 20 minutes. Remove from pans and cool on wire rack.

Griddle Biscuits

These tasty little cakes are "baked" on top of the stove as English muffins are.

2 cups flour
½ teaspoon baking powder
½ cup butter or margarine
½ cup sugar
½ cup currants or raisins
1 egg
1 scant cup milk

Sift flour and baking powder into a large mixing bowl. Add butter and cut in with two knives or a pastry blender until mixture is evenly blended. Stir in sugar and currants or raisins. Mix milk and egg together in a smaller container and add, stirring into the dry ingredients. Turn dough onto a floured pastry cloth and roll to a thickness of ½ inch. Cut into 2-inch circles or squares. Cook on a medium hot ungreased griddle about 3 minutes, or until first side is lightly browned. Turn over and lightly brown the second side. Serve with butter and jam.

Buttermilk Potato Biscuits

This recipe comes from the South, where some old-time cooks consider this the best possible way to use up a small quantity of leftover mashed potatoes.

1 cup buttermilk
½ teaspoon soda
1 tablespoon honey
1 cup mashed potatoes
2 tablespoons butter or margarine, softened
2 cups flour
1 tablespoon brown sugar
2 teaspoons baking powder

Preheat oven to 400 degrees F. Combine buttermilk, soda and honey and set aside. Stir butter into the mashed potatoes, in a large mixing bowl. Combine dry ingredients—flour, baking powder and brown sugar. Add dry ingredients and buttermilk alternately to the potatoes, mixing just until all ingredients are moistened. Turn dough onto a floured pastry board and pat to a thickness of about ¾ inch. Cut round biscuits and bake 15 to 20 minutes or until lightly browned.

Banana Bread

Banana bread is a favorite because of its moist, tender texture, and it is a wonderful way to use up leftover bananas that are almost too ripe to eat. For an occasional variation, add ½ cup chopped pecans or walnuts, or 1 cup of raisins.

2 cups flour
2¾ teaspoons baking powder
½ teaspoon salt
2/3 cup sugar
½ cup vegetable shortening, margarine
  or butter
2 eggs
1 cup mashed banana pulp
  (2 or 3 ripe bananas)

Preheat oven to 350 degrees F. Combine and sift together the flour, baking powder and salt. Cream the shortening with the sugar and add the eggs. Add sifted dry ingredients and banana alternately to the sugar-shortening-egg mixture, beginning and ending with the dry ingredients. Stir in additional ingredients—nuts or raisins—if desired. Pour into a well-greased loaf pan. Bake 1 hour and 10 minutes, or until top is dry and glossy and sides pull away from the pan.

Poppyseed Bread

Rich and sweet, this quick bread needs no buttering. Slice it thin and serve, cold or toasted, with coffee or dessert fruits.

4 eggs, beaten
2 cups sugar
1 1/3 cups corn oil
3 cups flour
1 can condensed milk
1 teaspoon vanilla
1½ teaspoons baking soda
1 teaspoon salt
5 tablespoons poppyseeds

Preheat oven to 325 degrees F. Combine ingredients in a large mixing bowl, using an electric beater to blend well after each addition. Mix an extra 100 strokes by hand, or 2 minutes with an electric mixer, after all ingredients are combined.

Grease well and lightly flour 2 regular loaf pans, 3 miniature loaf pans or 3 (1-pound) coffee cans. Divide batter evenly and bake (about 1 hour in 3 pans, or 1 hour and 15 minutes in 2 pans) till top looks dry and edges pull away from the sides of the pan.

Buttermilk Soda Bread

Traditionally Irish, soda bread deserves a place in any and every American kitchen. Toast and butter it for breakfast, or serve it with soup and salad at lunch time.

4 cups flour
1 tablespoon sugar
1 teaspoon salt
1½ teaspoons baking soda
1 teaspoon baking powder
1¾ cups buttermilk
1 cup raisins
2 tablespoons caraway seeds

Preheat oven to 350 degrees F. Combine flour, sugar, salt, soda and baking powder and sift together. Add buttermilk and stir until just blended. Fold in raisins and caraway seeds. Turn dough out onto a floured pastry board and knead, turning and stretching the dough, for 3 minutes. Shape into a round ball and bake on a greased cookie sheet 1 hour and 10 minutes, or until loaf sounds hollow when tapped with a knuckle.

Cottage Cheese Bread

1 package yeast
½ cup warm water
½ pound cottage cheese (1 cup)
2 tablespoons sugar
2 tablespoons minced onion
2 teaspoons dill weed
1 teaspoon salt
¼ teaspoon baking soda
1 egg
2½ cups flour

Dissolve yeast in warm water (it should be very warm) in a large bowl and let stand for 10 minutes.

Warm cottage cheese in a saucepan, then add it to the yeast and water mixture. Add the sugar, onion, dill weed, salt, baking soda and egg, beating well after each addition. Add half the flour and mix until smooth, then add the remaining flour. Add a little more flour if it is needed to make a soft dough (some

cottage cheese is moist, some dry, and this will make a difference in the amount of flour needed).

Cover bowl with a clean dish towel and set in a warm place to rise until nearly double in bulk. Punch dough down and spoon it into four miniature loaf pans or 6 custard cups or 8 large muffin cups (pans should be generously greased). Cover and let rise 1 hour or until nearly doubled in bulk. Preheat oven to 350 degrees F. Bake 30 minutes, then cover with foil and bake 10 to 15 minutes longer, or until loaf sounds hollow when tapped with a knuckle.

Cranberry Bread

This can also become prune bread or apricot bread; just replace the 1 cup of cranberries with 1 cup of cooked, mashed prunes or 1 cup of raw apple, finely chopped or grated.

3 cups flour
3 teaspoons baking powder
¾ teaspoon baking soda
1 teaspoon salt
½ cup vegetable shortening, butter
   or margarine
2 eggs
1 cup chopped cranberries
1¼ cups milk
Chopped pecans (optional)
Grated orange rind (optional)

Preheat oven to 350 degrees F. Combine the flour, baking powder, soda, salt and sift together. Cream the shortening with the sugar and mix in the eggs. Stir in the cranberry pulp (fresh cranberries can be put through a food mill or grinder on coarse setting). Add dry ingredients and milk, alternately, to the cranberry-sugar-egg mixture, stirring until smooth after every addition. Stir in ½ to 1 cup chopped pecans (or walnuts) and the grated rind of one orange, if desired. Pour batter into a generously greased and floured loaf pan and bake 1¼ hours.

FARINACEOUS FUN: YANKEE NOODLE DANDY

The vocabulary of *pasta* rolls off the tongue with all of the Italianate bravura of a Verdi opera libretto. *Cannelloni. Ziti. Mezzani. Macheroncelli. Vermicelli. Capellini. Fettuccine*, which legend avers was designed to honor the divinely golden curls of Lucrezia Borgia. Butterflies, *farfallini*. Seashells, *conchiglie*.

One of the varieties of pasta has an interesting origin. It is made up of infinitesimal little squares and the tale goes that no one had quite thought up this particular shape until a nobleman clad in his chain mail rather carelessly sat down on some pasta dough. When he rose, lo! the pasta was shaped into tiny cubits. Others of the thirty or forty varieties and shapes of pasta seem to have been created with almost childish glee: *alfabeto* (letters), *astri* (in star shapes), *crocette* (of little crosses), and *elefanti* (surprise, elephants), all among the tiny pasta bits tossed into soups to delight the eye as well as the palate.

Yet one of the most beguiling tales of pasta belongs to our own American history, although in a way which most schoolchildren are apt to learn in reverse. Who cannot recite:

"Yankee Doodle went to town,
Riding on a pony,
Stuck a feather in his hat
And called it macaroni!"

We tend to think of this as an American ditty, most frequently played as the accompaniment to a group of marching Revolutionary soldiers, tootled on their way by a fife and drum corps.

Not so, actually. The song originated before the Revolution in upper New York State. Seems a British doctor by the name of Richard Shuckburgh was visiting Fort Crailo in 1758, and watched derisively as the eager and untutored bumpkins of the local colonial militia went through their so-called military paces. Our soldiery of the day, as George Washington himself was to learn later, was hardly the material to throw against the trained Hessians or the redcoats, best fighters on the battlegrounds of Europe. These raw kids, fresh from the farm, literally did not know right from left. So that, to give them their marching orders, their despairing officers tied hay to one foot and straw to the other. The land echoed with "hayfoot, strawfoot," as the militia marched ever closer to combat, but at least in cadence, if somewhat hampered by all the fodder strapped to their ankles.

It was Dr. Shuckburgh who wrote "Yankee Doodle," after seeing this parade of bumpkins, and his use of the word *macaroni* in it bears a double thrust of derision to it. The English, in the glory of their growing empire, were openly contemptuous of the artistic and elegantly dressed Italian nobility. But some of the younger bloods of London, much as our youngsters today do their level best to outrage the Establishment, had formed a club devoted to two high-level principles. One was a form of rowdyism which consisted of night forays in which they captured rotund and dignified old gentlemen and rolled them in barrels down the steepest and longest flights of steps available, of which there are thousands in London. The other was to dress in the elaborate and foppish fashion of Italian dandies—hence these young London hotbloods called themselves *macaroni's* after the fa-

182

Cover painting, THE SATURDAY EVENING POST, *October 9, 1948*

vorite food of Italy.

What had happened up at Fort Crailo was that our militia, dressed in homespun without so much as a uniform among them, had attempted to lend a little style to the occasion by sticking cock's feathers in their hats. According to the good doctor, looking down his long British nose at the militia, this hardly entitled them to be dubbed macaroni.

The ditty was sung to a catchy tune, and strangely enough, the colonial population, although the butt of the joke, took it over as their own, even as they were ultimately to take over the proud English battle standards at Yorktown.

If you ever have the good fortune to visit the tap-room of the Nassau Inn at Princeton University in New Jersey, you will see Norman Rockwell's famous mural showing Yankee Doodle Dandy riding through the town astride his new pony, a gawky fellow indeed with a feather in his cap, so ridiculous a figure, in fact, that a British soldier cannot restrain his laughter.

An Italian food, yet not only part of our Revolutionary musical heritage but also an item on our table which is now thoroughly an Americanized staple.

The English brought apple pie to America; the French, chowder, a word derived from *chaudière* or fish kettle. The Dutch brought us cookies, *kookjes*, and the Germans *sauerbraten*. And the Italians their pasta, and the marvelous ways of cooking it, which chiefly came to pass during the great immigration waves of sons and daughters of Italy to America in the 1890's, although, naturally, Thomas Jefferson had imported it to his private table at Monticello a

century before. We have settled here in our book for a number of our own Americanized specialties which give you, we believe, the supreme experience of *pasta* cookery.

Marco Polo, indubitably one of the best public relations experts who ever lived, with himself as chief client, is generally credited with having brought pasta back to Italy with him from his travels in China, where civilization had been flourishing for thousands of years before Englishmen painted themselves blue and danced around trees in worship of Druids. But some histories suggest that the Etruscans knew about pasta long before Marco. Also, it seems likely that the sea traders of Venice and Genoa had long since covered the relatively short water routes to China before Polo and brought back Oriental slaves who were handy at preparing Chinese pasta specialties which soon became the staple food of Italians, both rich and poor.

Pasta is basically wheat flour and eggs, often mixed with butter and salt. From there, the original takes wing like a flight of birds—in tubular macaroni, elbow macaroni, lasagne in wider strips, all the way down to the exquisite vermicelli, whose diameter does not exceed one-fourth inch.

Pasta has given rise to stories of the miraculous as well as to American colonial ditties. One of the more charming concerns a fourteenth-century hermit saintly enough to be beatified by Pope Paul. The good man was dining at a neighbor's, a creature so unfortunate as to have a wife already in league with the devil. To mock the holiness of her guest, this satanic

*Honor the Lord with your
substance and with the first
fruits of all your produce;
Then your barns will be filled
with plenty, and your vats will
be bursting with wine.*

Proverbs 3:9,10

trollop served him pasta stuffed with chaff. Her guest quietly said grace with saintly modesty, and then proceeded to eat his *ziti* which now was filled not with chaff but with delicious ricotta. Plainly, it was not the devil's day. And, as our soldiers learned, discovering the joys of *pizza* during World War II forays into Italian cuisine, pasta continues to be on the side of the angels.

Rice and hominy grits belong in this section of the book because they do have a great deal in common with the pastas. Like the pastas they are cereal products derived from grains (yes, rice is a grain) and all are "go with" foods. They go with meats, and they go with vegetables, and they go with highly seasoned entrees and sauces. If the pastas are the special "go with" foods of the Italian tradition, and rice of the Oriental tradition, they have become, over the years, as Americanized as ham and eggs. And, of course, the special cereal food that goes with ham and eggs is cooked grits, piled in a snowy, steaming mound midway between the fried ham and the fried eggs, and topped with melting butter and pepper.

Rice is the fantastic grain food which is the chief source of nourishment of more than half of the world's population—the main item of the diet of six out of every ten people on this planet. About 95 percent of the world's rice supply is grown and eaten in the Orient—China, India, Japan, and the Philippines. Once more, the Chinese seem to have been the originators of record: a rice-planting ceremony is recorded in the year 2800 B.C. with the Emperor Chin-Nung himself in attendance. Since then, members of

the imperial court were required to do their bit for the rice crop, which had acquired an almost religious symbolism in China. Each year, as the planting came around, the Chinese nobility planted their appointed rows, three for the emperor, six for his sons, and but a few more rows for each relative according to his distance from the royal throne.

Rice followed the westward path of civilization, to the river cultures of the Middle East, and then into the developing lands of Europe. We tend to think of ourselves as masters of communication. Before the electronic age, we glorified our Pony Express in the West, and indeed with good reason. But Genghis Khan had the idea perfected some centuries before us. He cleared a bridle path racing across Asia from China to the European frontiers, and its stable depots were stocked with a million—a *million*!—of the fleetest horses in the world. When old Genghis wanted to spread the word, horsemen rode like the wind, changing horses, changing riders, with never a second lost in transit, until the word arrived at its destination halfway across the face of the earth. Not quite our electronic speed of light, 186,000 miles per second. But the old G.K. got the word through. And the rice too.

It came to America under perhaps less romantic clouds of glory, but, in its own somewhat humble way, quite dramatically. Captain Thurber, bound out of New England in 1686 for Madagascar on his world-flying brigantine, was pushed into the port of Charleston, South Carolina by hard weather. Laying over in Charleston until the storm subsided, they enjoyed the

It is the part of a wise man to feed himself, with moderate pleasant food and drink, and to take pleasure with perfumes, dress, music, sports, and theaters.

Spinoza

hospitality of a surgeon, Dr. Henry Woodward. Captain Thurber's gesture in return was a bag of golden rice seed he had acquired on previous voyages to Madagascar. Dr. Woodward and his friends gave the rice a try in their own fields, and the sunny south did the rest. The city of Charleston prospered on its rice crop, as South Carolina remained the leading rice-producing area of the United States until around 1840. By then, rice was being grown in all the states south of the Ohio River and east of the Mississippi, and, by 1889, Louisiana became the number-one rice producer. In the early 1900's Arkansas and California became important rice-growing areas, and today Texas leads in production. Illinois and Virginia are the northernmost states that ever tried growing rice; it is a crop that requires a mild climate with a long growing season as well as a special kind of moist, heavy soil.

Rice products have proliferated in recent years, as you will learn when you look on the grocer's shelves. There are preseasoned rice mixes and several different kinds of processed rices that save cooking time. Some are fully precooked, but with all the water removed, and you just add boiling water to reconstitute them. Purist rice cooks find these "instant" rices an abomination, saying that they never acquire the proper body with fluffy texture.

Nutritionists and natural food addicts swear by brown rice, which is the unpolished grain—only the inedible outer hull is removed in milling. Brown rice is richer in natural salts and vitamins than polished rice, true, and it has a nice, nutty flavor. But it takes a lot longer to cook brown rice—40 or 50 minutes, at least—and it is hard to get it light and fluffy.

We mustn't overlook our own "wild rice," which we owe to the Indians rather than to Captain Thurber and the Chinese. This is the long-grain coarse variety so prized by the lake-country Indians, the Chippewa and the Winnebago, which they valued as money, much as the Eastern Indians did their corn. The rice grew all along the shores of the Great Lakes, but the largest and best fields were on Lake Superior's shores, growing right at the edge where the water was a couple of feet deep. The Indians used to glide along in their canoes through the tall-growing rice and shake off their grains right into the canoe, a method still used in the harvesting. As an American dish, often served as accompaniment to fowl or game birds, our Indian rice is still as highly prized by the discriminating cook.

Highly prized . . . and high-priced. As the price has gone up, in recent years, the packages in which wild rice is sold have become smaller and smaller. For most of us, wild rice has become a special treat served only on special occasions—but that only makes it taste better. Keep in mind that 1 cup of wild rice equals 3½ or 4 cups cooked and ready to serve, and you'll feel a little better about the high price you pay for a tiny box of the delectable stuff.

So much for background, history and economics. Now, on to the recipes for preparing pastas and the other foods derived from the cereal crops—the amber waves of grain that flourish below America's spacious skies.

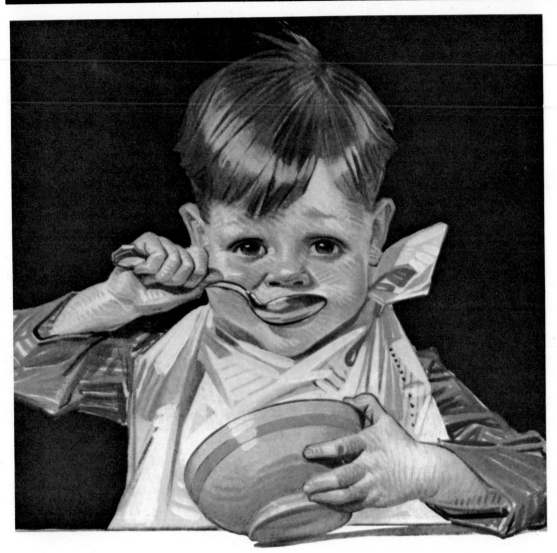

AT your house, perhaps, there is some important member of the family who should be enjoying Kellogg's Toasted Corn Flakes—with good milk poured in the side of the dish —not on top—just enough to float the crispy flakes and bring out their delicate flavor. *Spare the sugar.*

Then too there is the WAXTITE package that keeps the fresh, good flavor in—and all other flavors out.

Copyright, 1915, Kellogg Toasted Corn Flakes Co.

Oh, you'll *all* be eating them—and repeating oftener than with any other breakfast food—these golden flakes with the ever-alluring fresh-from-the-oven taste!

And remember *please* that you don't know corn flakes unless you know *Kellogg's*—the original Toasted Corn Flakes—with the pride of the originator to keep the delicate process *complete.*

Even Baby can tell the difference!

W.K.Kellogg

Kellogg's TOASTED CORN FLAKES

W. K. Kellogg

KELLOGG TOASTED CORN FLAKE CO. BATTLE CREEK, MICH

Advertisement, THE SATURDAY EVENING POST, *May 29, 1915*

Macaroni and Cheese

1½ to 2 pounds elbow or
  broken macaroni
2 cups grated cheddar cheese
  (mild or sharp)
2 cups Cream Sauce (see Sauces)
Nutmeg
Salt and pepper
1 cup fine bread crumbs
Butter or margarine

Boil the macaroni in a large kettle of boiling salted water (1 teaspoon to each quart of water) for 8 minutes or just until tender. Drain in a colander and run cold water through it. Drain well.

Grate the cheese and make the cream sauce.

Lay half the macaroni in the bottom of a large greased baking dish (12 by 9 inches). Sprinkle lightly with salt, pepper and a dash of nutmeg. Cover with 1/3 of the cheese. Repeat the process. Pour over the cream sauce. Cover with the remaining cheese. Sprinkle with fine bread crumbs and dot with butter.

Bake 30 minutes in a 350-degree oven.

Macaroni and Chipped Beef

Most pastas, though widely enjoyed by Americans, must be considered natively Italian. This humble dish is not in the Italian repertoire but it has been eaten for generations by New Englanders.

Creamed Chipped Beef (see Meats)
1¼ to 1½ pounds macaroni
2 tablespoons salad oil
2 cups grated medium cheddar cheese
Fine bread crumbs
Butter

Make the creamed chipped beef and season it highly.

Slowly add broken pieces of macaroni to a large kettle of boiling salted water (1 teaspoon salt and 1 quart of water) so that the water will not stop boiling. Add 2 tablespoons of oil. Stir once and boil, partially covered, for 8 minutes or just until tender. Drain well.

Preheat the oven to 375 degrees F. Put a layer of half the macaroni in a large buttered baking dish. Cover with half of the chipped beef. Cover with a layer of grated cheese. Repeat the process and sprinkle with a thin layer of fine crumbs. Dot with butter and bake 30 minutes.

"Now, what were we talking about—oh, yes—marriage."

Spaghetti

While spaghetti cannot be traced to the early col-
onists, it is certainly in the mainstream of Amer-
ican eating today and deserves a place in this
collection. It must be properly cooked and served,
which is not, alas, the usual case. The fundamental
rule is to allow 1/3 to ½ pound of thin or very thin
spaghetti per person and to boil it just until tender (5
or 6 minutes) in a large amount of salted water to
which a tablespoon or two of salad oil has been add-
ed. The spaghetti is then thoroughly drained, reheated
with a little butter in the empty kettle (toss lightly
while reheating) and served in a hot tureen or deep
bowl or in individual heated soup plates or large
bowls. Serve with one or more of the following
sauces, letting each person serve himself accompanied
by a generous supply of Romano or Parmesan
cheese, freshly grated.

Spaghetti Meat Sauce

1 medium-size onion, chopped fine
1 clove garlic, minced
3 tablespoons butter or margarine
½ pound ground veal or beef
½ pound sausage meat
1 (20-ounce) can plum tomatoes
1 (6-ounce) can tomato paste
1 teaspoon salt
¼ teaspoon black pepper
½ teaspoon sugar
½ teaspoon powdered oregano
2 cups red Chianti
1 quart water

Sauté the garlic and onion in butter in a heavy saucepan just until soft. Add the meat and sausage and
brown lightly, stirring. Add the remaining ingredients
and stir until the mixture comes to a boil. Reduce the
heat and simmer partially covered 1 hour.

Butter Anchovy Spaghetti Sauce

12 to 16 tablespoons sweet butter
3 or 4 teaspoons anchovy paste
2 or 3 tablespoons chopped parsley

Combine the ingredients in a small saucepan and heat
until the butter is bubbling hot. Serve in a preheated
bowl.

Lobster Spaghetti Sauce

½ pound sweet butter
1 tablespoon chopped shallots or scallions
2 cups diced cooked lobster meat
   (fresh or frozen)
2 tablespoons chopped parsley
Salt
Black pepper

Simmer the shallots and diced lobster meat in the
butter over very low heat for 10 minutes. Add the
parsley. Season to taste with salt and pepper and
serve in a preheated bowl.

Clam or Mussel Spaghetti Sauce

½ pound sweet butter
2 cloves garlic, pressed
1 cup minced steamed clams or
   mussels, fresh or canned
2/3 cup fine bread crumbs
½ cup chopped parsley
2 teaspoons fresh chopped tarragon or
   ½ teaspoon dried tarragon
Black pepper

Simmer the garlic in the butter without browning for
2 to 3 minutes. Stir in the drained clams or mussels
and the bread crumbs. Stir for 1 minute. Add the
herbs and plenty of freshly ground black pepper. This
must be well mixed with the spaghetti.

Hominy

Preparing hominy was one of the many lessons the Indians—in this case the Algonquin tribe—taught the early settlers. It is made from white hulled corn and ground in various degrees of fineness. It is most commonly ground fine and used as grits. Sold in several ways—natural, precooked or "instant," or canned—it is used, particularly in the South, for breakfast as porridge, as a vegetable or side dish, or sweetened, as a dessert.

1½ cups hominy grits
1½ cups cold water
2 teaspoons salt
1 quart boiling water

Stir the hominy, cold water and salt in the top part of a double boiler. Add the boiling water gradually, stirring constantly over direct heat. Bring to a rapid boil, still stirring, and cook for 10 minutes. Place over simmering water and cover. Stir occasionally. Cook 1½ hours.

Breakfast Hominy

Prepare the hominy as in the preceding recipe, or follow the directions on the package for "instant" grits, or heat a No. 2½ can of hominy grits in a double boiler. Add a generous amount of butter or margarine to the hot grits and serve with white or brown sugar and cream.

Fried Hominy

Put prepared hominy (see Breakfast Hominy) in a small loaf tin, smoothing the top evenly. Chill covered in the refrigerator. Turn out the loaf and cut in ½-inch slices. Coat lightly with flour and brown well in butter, margarine or bacon fat. Serve with corn or maple syrup and with sausage or bacon.

Hominy Cakes

3½ to 4 cups prepared hominy
4 to 5 tablespoons butter or margarine
3 tablespoons flour
2 medium eggs, slightly beaten
Salt and pepper
2 tablespoons grated onion
  (optional)
2 tablespoons chopped parsley
  (optional)
Butter, margarine or bacon fat

Combine the hot prepared hominy (see Breakfast Hominy) off the heat with the butter, flour and eggs. Season with salt and pepper and the onion and parsley if desired. Stir well. Form the mixture into patties with your hands. Sauté the patties in fat until well browned. Serve with syrup if the onion and parsley are omitted; with catsup if they are included.

Hominy Soufflé

Hominy Soufflé is like spoon bread and can be eaten as a main dish with butter or gravy or as a side dish with fried ham.

2½ cups hot hominy grits
3 tablespoons butter or margarine
4 egg yolks, beaten well
¾ cup white cornmeal
1 teaspoon salt
¼ teaspoon white pepper
1 tablespoon baking powder
5 egg whites, beaten stiff

Preheat the oven to 375 degrees F. Prepare the hominy grits as in Breakfast Hominy. Place the grits in a bowl and stir in the butter, egg yolks, cornmeal, salt, pepper and baking powder. Stir until very well blended. Cool slightly. Stir in a third of the beaten egg whites thoroughly and fold in the rest. Pour into a well-buttered 2-quart baking-serving dish. Bake 45 to 50 minutes or until an inserted knife comes out dry. Spread the top with a little melted butter. Serve with more butter or margarine.

Advertisement, THE SATURDAY EVENING POST, *July 1, 1922*

Hasty Pudding

Hasty Pudding is another name for Cornmeal Mush, which is the name for one of the oldest recipes in Massachusetts. It was a natural for daily fare when a kettle hung from a hook over a fire on the open hearth. Serve very hot in individual cereal bowls. Make a well in the center and put 2 teaspoonfuls of butter, along with brown sugar or maple syrup, in the well.

1 cup cornmeal
1½ teaspoons salt
1 cup cold water
3 cups boiling water

Mix the cornmeal, salt, and cold water in the top of a double boiler.

Add the boiling water gradually, stirring constantly over direct high heat to prevent lumps. When well blended cook, still stirring, until thick. Place over simmering water and cook for at least 1 hour.

Pour leftover hasty pudding into a greased bowl or loaf pan and chill in the refrigerator. At breakfast-time cut into thin slices, dredge with flour and sauté in butter till crisp. Serve with syrup.

Hush Puppies

According to legend the strange name for these deep-fried cornmeal morsels comes from the fact that when yelping dogs gathered around the plantation kitchen door, they were thrown some of these to hush them. They are almost always served with fried catfish in the South but they are also a good substitute for potatoes with ham, sausage or with many kinds of fish.

2 cups white cornmeal
2 teaspoons baking powder
1 teaspoon salt
2½ tablespoons grated onion
1 cup milk
2 eggs, well beaten

Mix all the ingredients, adding more milk if necessary to give the mixture the consistency of heavy pancake batter. Let the mixture stand while heating the fat.

Preheat oven to 400 degrees F. Drop from a spoon in the size of a large egg and fry 3 or 4 at a time for 1 minute. Drain on paper toweling and keep very hot in the oven until the frying process is completed. Serve immediately. This will make 12 to 16, depending on size.

"I tried counting sheep and remembered the leg of lamb."

Rice

Rice growing was started in this land when a Captain Smith brought a bag of "paddy" or rough rice to these shores and presented it to a Charleston merchant, who planted it. Rice has been grown in the South ever since but in comparatively small quantities until the beginning of this century. Most of the rice used in America was imported before that, but in the early 1900's the business was expanded to its present enormous size with most of the rice being grown in Texas, Louisiana and Arkansas. There are many theories about making rice so that it is fluffy. This is our preferred method.

Fluffy White Rice

Pour 1½ cups of long-grain white rice into a large pan of boiling salted water. Stir once and partially cover the pan, leaving about an inch for the steam to escape. Boil the rice for 12 to 14 minutes or *just* until tender. Turn into a colander and run cold tap water through the rice, fluffing it up with a fork or with your fingers. Put into a buttered baking-serving dish. Thirty minutes before serving bake covered in a 300-degree oven. This will yield 6 cups of rice.

Baked Rice with Water Chestnuts

1½ cups long-grained rice
4 cups chicken broth, canned or
   homemade
1 cup sliced water chestnuts
½ cup chopped parsley
1 cup chopped scallions
   (green onions)
8 tablespoons butter
1½ teaspoons salt
¼ teaspoon white pepper

Preheat the oven to 350 degrees F. Combine all the ingredients in a deep baking-serving dish. Stir well and bake 45 minutes.

Brown Rice and Red Beans

This hearty dish has variations. It is natively southern but eaten country-wide. When it is cooked in Louisiana it is more highly spiced than it is farther north.

1 pound kidney or southern red beans
1½ cups long grain brown rice
½ pound lean salt pork
4 tablespoons chopped onion
2 tablespoons chopped green pepper
4 tablespoons chopped celery and leaves
1 clove garlic, minced
Salt and pepper
½ teaspoon chili (optional)
Few drops hot sauce (optional)
Butter
Chopped parsley

Soak the beans for several hours or overnight. Discard the imperfect beans. Drain and place in a heavy kettle. Cover with water. Bring to a boil. Cover, reduce the heat and simmer for 30 minutes.

Bring 3¾ cups of water to a boil in a deep saucepan. Add the rice slowly so that the water will continue to boil. Add 1½ teaspoons of salt and 1½ tablespoons of butter. Cover, reduce the heat and simmer 40 to 50 minutes or until quite dry.

Meanwhile sauté the pork slices in a heavy pan, browning them lightly on both sides and letting them give up about 3 tablespoons of fat. Add the pork to the beans. Cook the vegetables in the fat until tender but not brown. Add the vegetables and the desired seasonings at the end of 30 minutes and cook 30 minutes longer or until the beans are really tender.

Put the rice in a deep serving dish. Taste the beans for seasoning. Pour over the rice and sprinkle with chopped parsley.

Carolina Red Rice

6 to 8 slices lean bacon, cut
   1/8 inch thick
1 large onion, chopped
1 cup diced celery
½ cup diced green pepper
2½ cups stewed tomatoes
   (canned or fresh)
1 (7-ounce) can tomato paste
2 cups long grain rice
1 teaspoon sugar
¼ teaspoon powdered thyme
¼ teaspoon powdered sage
1 teaspoon salt
1/8 teaspoon black pepper

Fry the bacon in a heavy pan over slow heat until lightly browned on both sides. Remove the bacon to paper toweling and put in the prepared vegetables and cook them slowly in the fat until the onion is transparent. Add the tomatoes and the tomato paste and enough water to wash out the tomato paste can, the rice, the sugar, herbs, salt and pepper. Mix well. If the rice isn't covered with liquid add enough boiling water so that it is. Bring the mixture to a boil. Reduce the heat to low and cover the pan. Cook for 40 minutes or until all the moisture disappears or bake in a 300-degree oven for 35 to 40 minutes. Cut the bacon into pieces (it should be cooked but not crisp) and stir into the rice. Serve as a main dish or as an accompaniment to fried chicken.

Hopping John

Some southern states have different versions of this recipe using the local variety of peas; but they always use rice.

2½ cups fresh or dried black-eyed peas
¾-pound piece of bacon
1 large onion
1½ cups rice
2 tablespoons butter
1/8 teaspoon cayenne
Salt

Soak the dried peas overnight. Drain and use like the fresh variety. Put the peas in a deep pan and cover with 4 inches of water. Add the onion, peeled, and the bacon cut into ¼-inch slices. Boil 30 to 40 minutes or until the peas are tender.

Put the rice in a heavy pan with 3 cups of cold water. Add 1 teaspoon of salt. Bring to a boil, stir just once with a fork. Lower the flame and simmer 18 to 20 minutes or until the water is absorbed and the rice kernels are separate.

Drain all but about 2 cupfuls of liquid from the peas. Stir in the rice. Steam until almost dry. Add the butter, cayenne and salt to taste.

Oven-Cooked Rice

3 tablespoons butter or margarine
4 tablespoons finely chopped onion
2 cups uncooked long grain rice
4 cups chicken broth
½ teaspoon salt

Preheat oven to 400 degrees F. Melt 4 tablespoons butter or margarine in large skillet over moderate heat. Add onions and sauté until transparent but not browned. Add rice and cook, stirring frequently, for about 3 minutes. Add chicken broth (homemade, canned, or made with chicken bouillon cubes) and salt. Heat, stirring to mix well. Transfer to a baking-serving dish. Cover (use foil if dish does not have a close-fitting lid) and bake 20 minutes. Add more butter, toss with a fork and serve.

New Orleans Hot Rice Cakes

This is an adaptation of one of the oldest known recipes in New Orleans, one that is said to have been a favorite of President Zachary Taylor. It's a good way to use up leftover rice.

2 cups flour
2 teaspoons baking powder
4 tablespoons sugar
1/8 teaspoon nutmeg
¾ teaspoon salt
1 cup boiled rice
2 egg yolks, beaten well
2 egg whites, beaten stiff
Powdered sugar

Mix all the dry ingredients. Mix the rice with the beaten egg yolks. Stir the two mixtures until thoroughly blended. Fold in the beaten egg whites.

Heat deep fat or 1½ inches of salad oil or vegetable shortening in a skillet to 365 degrees F. Drop tablespoonfuls of the mixture into the hot fat, frying not more than 4 or 5 at a time. Fry until golden brown, turning them once. Drain on paper toweling, keep hot, and just before serving sprinkle with powdered sugar or serve the hot cakes with syrup.

Wild Rice

Wild rice is a luxury but it is particularly good with certain dishes, especially game. It is not a member of the rice family despite its name but the product of a perennial wild grass that the Indians knew long before the arrival of the white man.

Boiled Wild Rice

Wash 2 cups of wild rice in several waters. Place in a heavy pan with enough boiling water to cover by 1 inch. Add 1½ teaspoons of salt. Simmer over a low heat for 45 to 60 minutes or until all the water is absorbed and the grains are separate and dry. This will yield 6 cups.

Wild Rice with Mushrooms

2 cups wild rice
8 tablespoons butter
½ pound mushrooms, thinly sliced
3 tablespoons flour
¼ teaspoon nutmeg
2 cups chicken stock or canned broth
Salt and pepper

Wash the rice in several waters. Cover with water in a bowl and soak for several hours. Drain and cover with boiling water. Add a teaspoon of salt and soak 30 minutes.

Heat 4 tablespoons of butter and sauté the mushrooms until almost dry. Add the rest of the butter and heat. Add the flour and stir gently until the flour disappears. Season with nutmeg, salt and pepper. Add the chicken stock and stir until slightly thickened.

Drain the rice and put in a buttered baking dish. Cover with the mushroom sauce. One hour before serving preheat the oven to 350 degrees F. Bake the rice in a covered dish for 45 minutes.

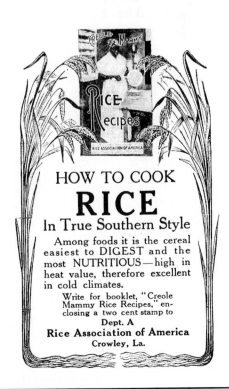

OLD-TIME DESSERTS: AMERICA LOVES A HAPPY ENDING

A youngster we know recently described dessert as what you have to eat all that other stuff to get to. And Americans in general have always had a fondness for desserts.

Desserts seem to have interested the Colonial housewife much more than meat, vegetables and bread because for every savory recipe in old cookbooks there are twice as many or more sweet recipes. Perhaps desserts were a kind of status symbol since they all involve some kind of sugar and sugar was costly. In the seventeenth and eighteenth centuries most refined sugar was sold in blue paper cones. The manager of the household snipped off with special shears the amount needed for the day's use and carefully stored the rest in some safe place. Other sweetening like corn and maple syrup, maple and unrefined brown sugar were also used.

Names for some of these desserts—Bettys, Cobblers, Slumps and Grunts—are hard to explain, but the desserts using fruits combined with flour-based pastries or breadstuffs are delicious and nourishing. There were less humble desserts, especially in elegant homes and in the White House, but it is interesting to note that many of the presidents seemed to prefer the homely American desserts to the fancier ones offered by imported chefs.

Once again, Tom Jefferson was the exception. He was especially fond of Baked Alaska, a confectionary inspiration he had brought back from his days in France—the first ever served in this country. George Washington was never that much of an epicure, but the cake that Martha baked for him quite often at his request has some rich ingredients as well as some hefty dollops of ingredients. The wife of the new country's leader was not one to flinch at even so solid a task as this recipe for her George's favorite cake, here given in her own words.

"Take twenty eggs and divide the whites from the yolks and beat the whites to a froth, then work two pounds of butter to a cream and put the whites of eggs to it, a spoonful at a time until well worked; then put two pounds of sugar, finely powdered, in it in the same manner, then add the yolks of the eggs, well beaten, and two and a half pounds of flour and five pounds of fruit. Add to this one-quarter ounce of mace, a nutmeg, a half pint of wine and some French brandy. Five and a half hours will bake it."

Abe Lincoln's law partner, Billy Herndon, once said: "Abe can sit and think longer without food than any man I have ever met." But there is some documentation of the fact that Lincoln was a frequent pecan-pie customer at a special Washington, D.C. bakery. He is also reputed to have annoyed wife Mary by a kind of absentminded disregard of her very finest White House dinners, and she was by all odds a lady of cultured dining tastes. But there was always the memory of the time before their marriage when Mary Todd found the sweet tooth of her giant husband with a cake he declared to be "the best in Kentucky." The original recipe once upon a time found its way into the pages of *The Saturday Evening Post*, and here it is:

O beautiful for spacious skies,
For amber waves of grain,
For purple mountain majesties
Above the fruited plain

Katharine Lee Bates

Advertisement for Peerless Ice Cream Freezer, THE SATURDAY EVENING POST, *August 12, 1922*

1 cup butter
2 cups sugar
1 cup milk
3 cups flour
2 teaspoons baking powder (double-acting)
1 teaspoon vanilla
1 cup chopped blanched almonds
¼ teaspoon salt
6 egg whites

Cream butter and sugar lightly. Sift flour and baking powder together and add alternately with milk (to the first mixture). Add well-floured nuts, then vanilla. Fold in stiffly beaten whites of egg, to which salt has been added. Bake in three layers (9-inch or 8-inch pans) in moderate (350 degrees F) oven. Ice with boiled icing, to which add ½ cup candied pineapple and cherries, chopped fine.

Imagine the feminine ingenuity which created this robust recipe for a *beer* layer cake:

1 cup beer
1 teaspoon baking soda
½ cup shortening
1¼ cups sugar
2 eggs
1 teaspoon salt
1 teaspoon cocoa
1 teaspoon vanilla
1-ounce bottle red food color
2½ cups sifted cake flour

Mix about a tablespoon of beer with baking soda and let settle. In mixing bowl beat shortening, sugar, eggs, salt, cocoa, vanilla and red color until light. Alternately beat in flour and beer. Stir in dissolved baking soda. Pour into 2 greased 9-inch round pans. Bake at 350 degrees F for 30 to 35 minutes.

Cool and split layers to make 4 layers. Spread frosting, below, between layers, on top and sides.

Frosting:
½ cup milk
2 tablespoons flour
1½ cups sugar
1½ cups butter
1 tablespoon vanilla

Stir milk and flour over medium heat until thick. Cool. Beat sugar, butter and vanilla until fluffy. Add cooked mixture, 1 teaspoon at a time, beating until smooth. Frosting should be consistency of whipped cream. After cake is frosted, keep in refrigerator.

Recipes were generous in those old days. One of the favorites was pound cake—as good a test of a fine cook as preparing a light and fluffy omelet—and one old-fashioned recipe simply called for a pound each of butter, sugar, and flour; ten eggs, and half a wine-glass each of wine and brandy.

American country cooking was always at its best in fruit desserts, pies, dumplings, cobblers, pandowdy, especially if the base was apple. The first apple trees were planted in 1629 and they had a hard

> *A man will pass his summers in health, who will finish his luncheon with black mulberries.*
>
> *Horace*

time at first in the rough New England weather, those British seedlings. But they made it, survived and grew healthier. The Colonial housewife had about two dozen recipes for apple desserts—and in those days deep-dish apple pie was *deep*.

Pie! To most people pie is *the* great American dessert, as witness the phrase "as American as apple pie and Mother."

In the Old World pie (spelled pye in the antique cookbooks) was primarily a main dish composed of meat, vegetables and gravy, all baked inside a crust of some kind. The fruit pie wasn't invented in America—cherry pie was served at the court of Queen Elizabeth I and was such a success that Bess ordered a cherry orchard planted immediately. Still, it was in America that the word "pie" came to stand for a dessert concoction of light, rich pastry filled with sweetened fruit or custard.

Fruit pie was well established by 1755 when the following directions appeared in a cookbook:

To Make Paste for Pies

"Take a Quarter of a Peck of Flour, rub fine Half a Pound Butter, a little Salt, make it up into a light Paste with cold Water, just stiff enough to work it well up; then roll it out, and stick Pieces of Butter all over, and strew a little Flour; roll it up, and roll it out again; and so do nine or ten Times, till you have rolled in a Pound and a Half of Butter. Beat it with a Rolling-pin well, then roll it out thin."

To make different Sorts of Pies

"If you bake in Tin-patties, butter them and you must put a little Crust all over. Lay fine Sugar and the Bottom, then your Plumbs, Cherries, or other Sort of Fruit, and Sugar at Top; then put on your Lid, and bake them in a slack Oven. Apple, Pear, Apricot, etc., make thus: Apples and Pears, pare them, cut them into Quarters, and core them; cut the Quarters across again, set them on in a Sauce-pan with just as much Water as will barely cover them, let them simmer on a slow Fire just till the Fruit is tender; put a good Piece of Lemon-peel in the water with the Fruit. Apricots do the same way but don't use Lemon."

Two pounds of butter in pie pastry! That's not such a lot when you realize that the quarter peck of flour equaled 8 cups; this quantity would make 4 double-crust pies.

Actually, only a raw beginner would bother to measure the ingredients she used. As a cookbook of 1859 counsels:

"After a little practice and observation, it will be just as well to omit weighing the materials for pastry. One very heaping handful of flour will make a common-size pie; not, however, allowing for the flour to be used in rolling the paste."

Up until around 1900 measurements were generally given in picturesque but inaccurate terms: a hand-

ful of flour, a pinch of salt, a piece of butter the size of a walnut, a wineglass of cider. The famous *Boston Cooking School Cookbook* by Fannie Farmer, published in 1896, was the first to give all measurements in terms of spoons, cups or ounces. We like to think that this improved the apple pie, along with the other staples of American cuisine.

We can thank a man named John Chapman for spreading so many of those dessert recipes across the country. He came to be known as Johnny Appleseed, for on his way at a slow walk from his home in Massachusetts to Fort Wayne, Indiana, where he died in 1845, Johnny zigged through the countryside of Pennsylvania, and Ohio, and over the course of forty years is supposed to have planted thousands and thousands of apple trees. The apple, next to corn, became the staple of frontier farm life. They ate it fresh or preserved, cooked or dried, fermented it for cider, applejack, and vinegar—it was always there, bending down the branches of the tree with the autumn weight of goodness.

Then there were the wonderful berries of the burgeoning new world. Roger Williams, after noting the Rhode Island Indians' strawberry beds, wrote: "In some parts where the natives have planted, I have seen—within a few miles—as many strawberries as would fill a good ship."

The Spaniards found the Indians of South America growing strawberries as big as pears, some red, some white, and others yellow. These were not as tasty as the northern variety; in fact, they were terribly pulpy. But finally, when crossed with the smaller English and North American strawberries, the large and red and juicy varieties of today evolved.

The land was full of wild plums to delight the settlers. Marvelous wild cherries. Blueberries, cranberries, raspberries, salmon berries, and blackberries in profusion. The Indians found them for the colonists, and out of that came the marvelous wild strawberry johnnycakes your great-great-great-great-grandmother used to make. In fact, at that very Thanksgiving in Plymouth, the dinner of succotash, oysters, clams, shellfish, venison, and turkey was launched at the very outset with an enormous baked Indian whortleberry pudding. Interesting idea, that—for many years, puddings of Indian corn, butter and molasses were set on the table before the main courses of meat and vegetables. One thing, though—it takes us back to that kid we mentioned at the beginning of this chapter. If you gave him his dessert first, how could you keep his attention on the rest of the meal?

No tribute to America's sweets would be complete without a paean to maple syrup, and the definitive paean was written some years ago by Vermonter Vrest Orton. The following is quoted from an article he wrote for *The Saturday Evening Post* some years ago.

SUGARING

Whatever way you care to look at it, as a craft, trade, business, art, science or pastime, maple sugaring in Vermont remains one of the most inviting and

*C_holds that a man cannot
have a pure mind who refuses
apple-dumpling . . .
Only I stick to asparagus, which
still seems to inspire gentle thoughts.*

Charles Lamb

Cover painting, THE SATURDAY EVENING POST, *October 28, 1905*

colorful of our American rural folk processes. With an original integrity intact, its basic principles are no different from those practiced in some remote past by the unknown Indian squaw who, stumbling upon a broken maple tree, had sense enough to catch the flowing juice in a wooden trough and, using the liquid to cook her chief's haunch of venison, unintentionally gave him something new in the world's cuisine. For sugaring, amateur or scientific, is simply the process of taking sap from the maple tree and then taking from the sap its 95 percent water content. What you have left is one of the most delicate-tasting and longest remembered natural flavors known to man.

A few can remember the barefoot boy on a hot June day, picking those small but sweet wild strawberries in the upper pasture, and occasionally stopping to eat a few crushed berries from fingers tired with picking. But no man alive who has tasted new maple syrup, fresh from the evaporator in an old aromatic, weather-beaten sugarhouse in the spring woods, can ever forget the delicate taste and fragrance that linger so long as memory lasts. Although the sugar maple grows in twenty-six other states, and New York produces great quantities of maple products—though not so much as Vermont—the Green Mountain people defend fiercely the superior flavor of their syrup that comes from the right combination of soil, elevation, precipitation and the sharply fluctuating temperature changes that prevail, by divine grace, in their country. This quality has, over the years, won for Vermont a reputation so that the words "Vermont maple" now go together as naturally as Boston baked beans, Virginia ham and Long Island duck.

The tourist has only to notice the myriad of farmhouse signs, MAPLE PRODUCTS FOR SALE, and the richly wooded hills, to realize how indigenous a Vermont product maple is, and how much it means to the hard-working Green Mountain native. John Godfrey Saxe demonstrated just about where Vermonters stand on maple when he wrote:

Men, women, maple sugar and horses;
The first are strong, the latter fleet;
The second and third are exceedingly sweet,
And all are uncommonly hard to beat.

Unlike other agricultural products raised on individual farms and processed in large centralized factories, you visualize the maple business by seeing little individual factories scattered all over the land, one to each farm and each farmer a raiser as well as processor. From 500 to 5,000 maple trees on a sidehill form what Vermonters call a "sugar bush." And among, or at the border of, the tall maples is the sugarhouse—usually a pitched-roof, single-room building, with a ventilating cupola on top and cords of wood piled inside or under a lean-to at one end.

When the first warmer days have come, and the temperature alternates sharply from freezing nights to snow-melting days, and the sap buckets and other utensils have been thoroughly washed—for here cleanliness is more important than godliness—then you are ready to "tap out." Although the pioneers used to tap by cutting gashes in the tree and catching the sap in wooden troughs, now the modern bit is used to

> *On turnpikes of wonder Wine*
> *Leads the mind forth,*
> *Straight, sidewise, and*
> *upwards, West, southward,*
> *and north.*
>
> *Hafiz*

bore a shallow hole in the outer core of the tree, about two feet above the ground. Into this is driven a sap spout or spile–a small pipe with a hook–and on the hook the sap bucket is hung. Men and boys distribute the buckets from the horse- or ox-drawn sled, walking gingerly on the frozen crust, or on snowshoes in case the crust breaks through. Now, buckets hung, you have to wait for Nature to make the sap run.

And Nature is very finicky about this. If a cold northwest wind blows after a night of frost, and the day is warm, the life juice of the maple is excited to flow through the tree and some drops out through the sap spout. But let a southerly wind come up, a storm approach, or the day turn cold, and sap will dry up in a jiffy. So sensitive is the tree that sap will sometimes flow sooner on the south and west sides than on the other two sides of the same tree! Here is where the Vermont weather–that so many cuss –comes in for its reward, because it is those very ups and downs from cold to warm that make good runs of sap.

Like milk, sap sours in the hot sun, and must be gathered often. As soon as a few quarts drip into the buckets, through the sugar bush comes the gathering tank, hauled on a sled by horses or oxen. Directly into it, scurrying men and boys pour the sap or, if impossible to drive near enough to the tree, pour it into big pails carried on old-fashioned neck yokes.

Inside the sugarhouse, on the cool north side–for sap, again like milk, is a cordial host to bacteria–is the storage tank. From this a pipe runs to the evaporator over the fire. In early times the evaporator was a plain metal pan, about eight inches deep, set over the arch, or long narrow furnace built of brick on a ledge foundation. But now it has been improved by upright partitions, dividing it into compartments to facilitate the flow of sap and to give greater heating surfaces. And today the arch is usually iron and factory-made. Through the automatic regulator, like a carburetor float, comes the sap. The fire going strong, the evaporator bottom covered, we are now ready to boil. Great clouds of savory steam scent the room and escape slowly through the cracks between the boards and the ventilator above. Then in and out of the compartments flows the sap, becoming thicker all the while, and being pushed around the partitions by constantly incoming cold sap. Finally, having been pursued through this labyrinth, and having lost most of its water by heavy evaporation, the increasingly dense liquid enters the last compartment, beside which the farmer stands waiting.

In the old days practically all maple syrup was boiled down to sugar at a "sugaring-off." Usually this process was made an excuse for a party. Neighbors were invited in, and as grandfather stood at the small hearth in the sugarhouse tending the boiling syrup in the sugaring-off pan, grandmother stood nearby with some cream or fresh butter to dash in to quiet down the stuff when and if it got too rambunctious and tried to boil over. As soon as it was thick enough to wax–at about 230 degrees F–some was dished out to each person. Grandfather went right on boiling until the syrup reached about 245 degrees F, then poured it off into molds or buckets as sugar.

In the meantime, picking a spot outdoors, the others spooned the syrup onto the clean snow, waited for it to harden and then lifted the brittle, curiously shaped but fine-tasting stuff to eager mouths. With this went sour pickles—so you could eat more syrup—plain doughnuts and eggs boiled in the sap. Later, big pans of snow were substituted for the snowbanks of the woods, and sugaring-off parties were held in the farm kitchen.

Charming as such native festivities are, there is a dastardly impression being bruited about the land that maple syrup is good only for sugar-on-snow or for dousing pancakes. In truth, there are a thousand and one delectable ways for using maple sweetening in cooking and in daily eating.

Many Vermont families keep a syrup jar on the table for sweetening breakfast food, coffee and tea, grapefruit and other daily rations. There are some, including this writer, who turn up a nose at rhubarb and squash, considering such provender fit only for neat cattle. But when you bake squash, liberally sprinkled with maple sugar, or sweeten rhubarb with maple syrup, you may also change your mind about these vegetables. And if you want to venture into the field of pure ambrosia, try maple for candied sweet potatoes, baked beans or baked carrots. Some of the most interesting uses of maple are for sweetening cornbread, johnnycake, waffles, fritters, and muffins made from stone-ground cornmeal, for then one is combining two of the best natural foods known. Old-timers still swear by hasty pudding, or cornmeal mush—some call it samp—which is stone-ground corn-

meal cooked twelve hours and eaten as morning cereal with maple sugar, or cooled, sliced, fried on a hot griddle and polished off with maple syrup.

The higher realms of maple cookery reveal such toothsome dishes as Maple Sugar Biscuit, described by Bob Brown as follows:

1½ teaspoons salt
2 cups pastry flour
½ pound maple sugar
5 teaspoons baking powder
3 tablespoons lard
1 cup milk

Sift flour, salt and baking powder; work in lard, add sugar crushed in lumps, and stir in milk to a soft dough (which is not to be rolled out). Toss on floured board, pat into shape, cut into small rounds and bake 10 minutes on buttered baking sheet in hot oven (450 degrees F). Eat hot.

I could go on making my own mouth water with hints of grandmother's maple-sugar cookies, maple-and-blueberry muffins, maple fruit cobbler, and cakes, sauces and drinks made with maple. But I shall only mention mincemeat. Locked in our cellar, we are hoarding about twenty-five jars, made four years ago. My wife made the mincemeat, using maple sugar to sweeten, and when she wasn't looking I put in a quart of old Armagnac brandy and another of Burgundy. The mincemeat, I figure, will easily mature in four years more and at that date pies may be eaten with something approaching gastronomical exuberance.

*Behold, I have given you
every herb bearing seed, which
is upon the face of all the
earth, and every tree, in the
which is the fruit yielding
seed; to you it shall be for meat.*

Genesis

Cover painting, THE SATURDAY EVENING POST, *December 20, 1952.*

Pie and Tart Pastry

Pie is America's second most popular dessert and has been since the beginning of this country's culinary history. Some accounts of early pie making, when the housewife had to make do with whatever fat and flour were at her disposal, do not make the pies sound very good or even digestible but they were made often and in large quantities and served for breakfast as well as for other meals. Today's pies are a great improvement over the earlier variety. Cold ingredients, speedy mixing and a light touch with the rolling pin are what give a tender flaky crust.

Two-Crust Pie

½ cup cold margarine,
  vegetable shortening or lard
4 tablespoons butter
2½ cups all-purpose flour or
  2¼ cups pastry flour
1 teaspoon salt
¼ cup ice water (approximate)

Combine the flour and salt in a bowl and cut the margarine and butter in with a pastry blender, 2 knives, your fingertips or an electric mixer until the combination has a mealy texture about the size of peas. It must not be a paste. Gradually add just enough ice water to form a ball. The less water you use, the better the pastry. Wrap in a sheet of wax paper or plastic food wrap and refrigerate for at least 1 hour. Remove from the refrigerator 5 minutes before rolling out.

Divide the pastry in two parts with one just a little larger than the other. Roll out the larger part on a lightly floured surface or pastry board using a chilled and lightly floured rolling pin. If you prefer, place it between two large sheets of wax paper. Press in the center and lightly roll out toward the edges until you have a circle 1½ inches larger than the circumference

of the pie tin. Roll the pastry up on the rolling pin and unroll it over the pie tin, letting it fall into place, or if using wax paper, take off the top sheet and turn the lower sheet upside down over the pie tin and gently pull the wax paper away. There should be a ½-inch overhang. Put the pie shell in the refrigerator while rolling out the top crust.

Preheat the oven to 450 degrees F. Moisten the rim with cold water. Spread a teaspoonful of flour on the lower crust and pat it in with your fingertips. Fill the pie as the recipe directs. Cover with the top crust and press the edges together with thumb and forefinger or with the tines of a fork. Trim the edges evenly with a sharp knife. Make incisions in the top crust as decoratively as you like. Bake 10 minutes in the hot oven. Reduce the temperature to 375 degrees and bake 35 to 40 minutes.

One-Crust Pie

Prepare half a recipe of pastry, allowing time for resting. Roll out pastry to a thickness of ¼ inch or a little less and roll it out as for a bottom crust, leaving a margin of 1½ inches. Fold the margin underneath the pastry and flute it with your fingers making it stand upright all the way around, or fold it once more and press it to the edge of the pie plate, pinching the dough between forefinger and thumb. Spread a teaspoonful of flour on the lower crust and pat it in with your finger tip. Fill and bake as for a two-crust pie.

Baked Pie Shell

Line a pie tin as for a One-Crust Pie (see above). Prick the bottom well with the tines of a fork. Cover with wax paper and weight it down with dried peas or beans or with rice. Bake 12 minutes at 450 degrees F. Remove the paper and the beans, peas, or rice and return to the oven for a few moments to brown lightly.

Cream Cheese Pastry

This pastry is so quick to make, delicious to eat and certain to be a success that it is indispensable, especially to the novice cook.

8 ounces cream cheese
8 ounces butter or margarine
2 cups all-purpose unbleached flour
1/8 teaspoon salt

Mix the ingredients in a bowl, using an electric beater or fingertips. Form quickly into a ball and wrap it in wax paper or Pliofilm and chill in the refrigerator for 2 to 24 hours. This will keep for several days.

Roll out, line the pie tins and bake just as you would for Pie and Tart Pastry (preceding recipe).

Cookie Crumb Crust

1½ cups cookie crumbs
  (vanilla, chocolate, graham or ginger)
½ cup light brown sugar
8 tablespoons (¼ pound) butter or
  margarine, melted
2 tablespoons milk, rum or brandy

Spin the cookies in a blender or crush in a paper bag with a rolling pin. Mix in a bowl with the sugar and beat in the melted butter and the liquid of your choice. A teaspoon of cinnamon or ½ teaspoon of nutmeg (or both) can be added if desired.

Press the mixture into a 9-inch springform tin. Bake 15 minutes at 300 degrees F. Cool before filling.

Real Apple Pie

Two-Crust Pie
6 to 8 tart cooking apples
2 tablespoons flour
¾ to 1 cup sugar
¼ teaspoon grated nutmeg
¼ teaspoon ground cloves
½ teaspoon cinnamon
¼ teaspoon salt
½ large lemon
2 teaspoons butter or margarine

Follow the recipe for preparing the pie crust, allowing time for resting the pastry.

Core, peel and thinly slice the apples until you have 6 cups. Place them in a bowl. Combine the flour, sugar, spices, salt and the grated rind and juice of ½ lemon. The amount of sugar will depend on the tartness of the apples. Toss the apples lightly until well coated.

Preheat the oven to 450 degrees F. Fill the lower, lightly floured bottom crust with the apples and dot with butter. Cover with the top pastry as directed and place on a baking sheet. Bake 10 minutes. Reduce heat to 350 degrees F and continue baking for 40 minutes. Serve warm with good chunks of cheddar cheese or with vanilla ice cream or just plain.

Note: An old Maine custom is to hold the apple pie under the cold water spigot for just a moment before popping the pie into the hot oven. It makes a very flaky top crust.

Deep-Dish Green Apple Pie

The first sign of fall in the Northeast is the turning of the goldenrod and the first picking of green apples, which are turned into deep-dish pie. This is a one crust pie but the crust is on top.

Pie and tart pastry
10 to 12 green apples
2 tablespoons flour
1 cup white sugar
½ cup brown sugar
½ teaspoon each—cinnamon,
  allspice and nutmeg
½ lemon, grated rind and juice
2 tablespoons butter
3 tablespoons rum
Hardsauce or heavy cream

Prepare half a recipe of pie pastry, allowing time for resting.

Peel and core the apples and cut them into eighths. Mix the flour, sugars and spices and toss with the apples until well coated. Place in a well-buttered deep 9-inch baking dish. Dot with the remaining butter and sprinkle with the lemon rind, lemon juice and rum.

Preheat the oven to 425 degrees F. Roll out the pastry 1 inch larger than the top of the baking dish and ¼ inch thick. Cover the baking dish, turning under the 1-inch edge and pressing the edge to the rim. Make several cuts in the pastry. Place in the oven and bake 5 minutes, then reduce the temperature to 350 degrees F. Bake 40 minutes. Serve warm with either Hardsauce (see Dessert Sauces) or cream.

Mince Pies

In Colonial times mincemeat was made with venison. Today it is made with either beef or venison or sometimes with green tomatoes. Whatever the filling, mince pie is part and parcel of Christmas and Thanksgiving dinner. Make the mincemeat in September and rejoice when the holiday season comes.

Follow directions for making Two-Crust Pie doubling the recipe. Fill each pie with 2 pints of mincemeat. When the top crusts are in place, cut out little leaf designs from the trimmings, moisten them on the bottom and place them around the edge of the pies. Brush with very cold water and put on a baking sheet in a 450-degree oven. Bake for 10 minutes and reduce the heat to 350 degrees. Bake 40 minutes or until golden brown.

Applejack Mincemeat

This recipe will make 10 pints of excellent filling for pies or tarts. It may be packed and sealed in hot sterilized jars or frozen.

2 pounds lean venison or
  beef, chopped or ground
1 pound suet, chopped or ground
6 cups cubed apples
1 pound currants
1 pound seedless raisins
1 pound muscat raisins
1 pound store-bought diced candied
  fruit (orange, citron, cherries, lemon)
3 cups brown sugar
2 teaspoons salt
1 teaspoon cinnamon
½ teaspoon cloves
1 teaspoon allspice
1 teaspoon nutmeg
2 to 3 cups water
2 cups applejack

Combine all the ingredients except for the applejack in a heavy kettle or casserole. Stir well and add enough water to make the mixture quite moist. Cover and barely simmer for 2 to 3 hours. Stir occasionally, adding more water if necessary. When cooked, the mincemeat should be fairly dry. Stir in the applejack and pack into pint jars or cool and pack into containers for freezing.

THANKSGIVING

Southern Pecan Pie

Serve this pie in thin wedges. It is devastatingly rich but very delicious.

One-Crust Pie
3 eggs
1 teaspoon vanilla
1 cup light brown sugar
  (tightly packed)
6 tablespoons melted butter or margarine
¾ cup light corn syrup
1/8 teaspoon salt
1 cup pecan pieces
Pecan halves

Prepare the pie crust and let it rest in the refrigerator while making the filling.

Preheat the oven to 400 degrees F. Beat the eggs and vanilla for 3 minutes. Add the sugar and continue beating until well blended. Stir in the butter, corn syrup, salt and pecan pieces.

Pat the bottom crust with a little flour and pour in the filling. Smooth it evenly and place the pecan halves, daisy fashion, on the center of the pie. Place on a baking sheet and bake 10 minutes. Reduce the heat to 300 degrees and continue baking 25 to 30 minutes or until firm. Serve cold.

McDougall Kitchen Cabinets

Cherry Pie

Two-Crust Pie
4 cups red cherries (tart)
2 teaspoons quick cooking tapioca
¼ cup flour
1 1/3 cups sugar
4 teaspoons lemon juice
1/8 teaspoon almond extract
1 tablespoon butter

Roll out the bottom crust and line the 9-inch pie tin. Let it rest in the refrigerator while you prepare the filling.

Remove the pits from the cherries and put them in a bowl. Mix the tapioca, flour, and sugar and toss the cherries in the mixture until the cherries are coated. Sprinkle with the lemon juice and extract. Let stand while rolling out the rest of the pastry.

Preheat the oven to 450 degrees F. Roll out the top crust to the right size. Cut cherry and stem shapes from any pastry trimmings, using a ¾-inch pastry tip as a cutter.

After patting in the flour, fill the pie shell with the cherries. Cover with the top crust, pressing the edges together very firmly. Make the incisions in the center of the crust and moisten the backs of the cut-out cherries and stems and press them around the edge. Put the pie on a baking sheet and place in the oven. Bake 10 minutes. Reduce the temperature to 350 degrees and bake 40 minutes longer. Cool before serving.

Serve with cheddar cheese or vanilla ice cream or just plain.

Pumpkin Pie

Pumpkin sauce is one of the first recorded American dishes which the early settlers in Virginia made from the wilderness staple that had helped to sustain them through the first bitter years. The bridge from that to pumpkin pie was not long.

One-Crust Pie
1½ cups pureed cooked pumpkin
  (fresh, frozen or canned)
½ cup brown sugar, tightly packed
½ teaspoon salt
1 teaspoon cinnamon
1 teaspoon powdered ginger
½ teaspoon nutmeg
3 eggs, well beaten
1 cup milk
½ pint all-purpose cream
4 tablespoons sherry

Make the pastry shell and let it chill in the refrigerator while preparing the filling.

Preheat the oven to 350 degrees F. Combine the pumpkin with the sugar, salt and spices and stir until well blended.

Beat the eggs well and add the milk, cream and sherry. Mix well with the pumpkin.

Pour into the shell and bake 45 minutes or until an inserted knife comes out clean. Cool on a wire rack.

Serve plain, with cheddar cheese or with vanilla ice cream.

King Lemon Meringue Pie

Baked pie shell or cookie crumb crust
  (vanilla wafers)
3 egg yolks
1 cup sweet white wine
½ cup water
1 cup sugar
1/8 teaspoon salt
6 tablespoons cornstarch
6 tablespoons lemon juice
1½ teaspoons coarsely grated lemon peel
2 tablespoons butter

Meringue:
3 egg whites
1/8 teaspoon salt
¼ teaspoon baking powder
6 tablespoons sugar

Allow time for making and baking the pie shell.

Beat the egg yolks until pale yellow. Beat in the white wine, water, sugar, salt and cornstarch and pour the mixture into the top of a double boiler. Cook over simmering water, stirring, until the mixture is thick and smooth. Remove from the heat and stir in the lemon juice, lemon peel and butter. Cool to lukewarm.

Preheat the oven to 350 degrees F. Beat the egg whites and salt until stiff and quite dry. Still beating, add gradually the baking powder and the sugar. Continue beating until the meringue is glossy and stiff.

Fill the shell with the custard mixture, smoothing it with a spatula. Cover the surface with the meringue, either by forcing it in a decorative way through a pastry bag fitted with a large cannellated tip or by using a spatula to smooth a layer of meringue over the entire surface and dropping "clouds" from a spoon all over the pie. Bake 15 minutes. Serve cold.

Date Rum Pie

Cream Cheese Pastry
1 (14-ounce) package pitted dates
1¼ cups water
1 cup brown sugar
½ cup chopped walnuts
½ tablespoon butter
2 tablespoons rum
Cinnamon sugar

Make the pastry, giving it time to rest.

Cut the dates in small pieces with a pair of kitchen scissors. Rinse the scissors in very hot water frequently to keep them from sticking. Put the dates and water in a small saucepan and cook until soft. Add the sugar, walnuts, butter and rum and stir until well mixed. Cool.

Preheat the oven to 450 degrees F. Roll out the pastry as directed on page 206. Fill with the date mixture and cover with the top crust. Make a few incisions in the crust and sprinkle with 2 teaspoons of sugar mixed with ½ teaspoon of cinnamon. Bake 10 minutes. Reduce the temperature to 350 degrees and bake for 40 minutes or until the crust is golden brown.

Easy Fruit Cobbler

Sliced fresh peaches or other
  fruit or berries (about 2 cups)
½ cup sugar
1 cup flour
2 teaspoons baking powder
1/8 teaspoon salt
½ cup milk

Topping
1 cup sugar
1 cup boiling water

Preheat oven to 375 degrees F. Place fruit in the bottom of a well-greased and fairly deep baking-serving dish. Mix together ½ cup sugar, flour, baking powder, salt and milk. Pour this thin batter evenly over the fruit. Sprinkle the cup of sugar over the top and pour the cup of hot water over all. Do not stir. Bake till top is crusty and delicately brown, about 1 hour, but time will vary with shape of baking dish used. Serve warm, with cream, whipped topping or ice cream.

Pennsylvania Dutch Shoofly Pie

One-Crust Pie
1½ cups sifted unbleached all-purpose flour
½ cup brown sugar, tightly packed
½ teaspoon cinnamon
¼ teaspoon cloves
¼ teaspoon nutmeg
½ teaspoon salt
¾ cup unsulfured molasses
¾ cup boiling water
1 teaspoon baking soda

Make the shell for One-Crust Pie and let it chill in the refrigerator while preparing the filling.

Preheat the oven to 450 degrees F. Put the flour, sugar, butter, spices, and salt in one bowl. Cut in the butter with a pastry blender, 2 knives, your fingertips or electric mixer, working lightly and rapidly until you have a fine crumb mixture. Combine the molasses, boiling water and soda in a 2-cup measuring pitcher.

Put a layer of a third of the crumbs in the pie shell and pour in half of the molasses mixture. Cover with another layer of crumbs and the rest of the molasses. Cover the top with the remaining third of the crumbs.

Bake 10 minutes. Reduce the heat to 350 degrees and bake for 20 minutes. Place on a cake rack to cool.

Baked-in-the-Shell Cream Pie

Many people can remember seeing their grandmothers make this kind of pie without using a mixing bowl or measuring the ingredients. They poured the cream (rich cream was plentiful on farms, in those days) directly in the unbaked shell, added the sugar and other things, and mixed with one clean finger. Some thought it was important to open the oven door from time to time and give the pie a shake, to keep the ingredients mixed while baking. Serve small slices to those who are watching their calories.

Pie shell, unbaked
2 cups all-purpose cream
1 teaspoon vanilla
½ cup flour
¼ teaspoon salt
½ cup light brown sugar
½ cup granulated sugar
¼ teaspoon nutmeg
1 tablespoon butter

Combine cream and vanilla and let stand 10 minutes without stirring. Mix flour and salt together in mixing bowl. Gradually add 2/3 cup of the cream mixture, stirring constantly. When smooth, add sugars and mix well. Stir in remaining cream mixture and let stand 20 minutes for sugars to dissolve.

Preheat oven to 300 degrees F. Sprinkle nutmeg in pie shell and dot with butter. Pour cream mixture into shell. Bake 10 minutes at 300 degrees F, then turn oven up to 350 degrees F and continue baking for 50 minutes or until filling is set and crust lightly browned.

Pecan Gems

Use the tiniest muffin pans you can find to bake these miniature pastries—they should be less than 2 inches in diameter. Single bite size, but very rich and sweet.

Pastry
1 (3-ounce) package cream cheese
½ cup butter or margarine
1 cup flour

Filling
1 egg
1¾ cup dark brown sugar
1 teaspoon vanilla
2/3 cup broken pecan halves

Let butter and cream cheese soften at room temperature, then cream them together. Mix in the flour, form into a ball and chill in the refrigerator for at least 1 hour.

To line muffin tins, take a 1-inch portion of the dough and press it against the bottom and sides, using the fingers or thumb. Do not roll the dough. There should be enough to make 24 tiny tarts.

Preheat the oven to 325 degrees F. Beat the egg and stir in the vanilla and brown sugar. In each muffin cup place a few nuts and a spoonful of the egg mixture. For extra richness add a tiny piece of butter to each. Bake until filling is set and pastry delicately browned—about 20 minutes, but this will vary somewhat with the size of the muffin cups and the depth of the egg filling.

Rhubarb-Strawberry Pie

Pie pastry for a Two-Crust Pie
1 pint strawberries
2 cups sliced raw rhubarb
¾ cup light brown sugar
½ cup white sugar
2 tablespoons flour
1 teaspoon grated lemon rind

Make the pastry, allowing time for it to rest. Roll it out and line a 9-inch pie plate.

Wash, hull and slice the strawberries and combine them with the sliced rhubarb. Combine the sugar, flour and lemon rind and toss lightly with the fruit.

Preheat the oven to 375 degrees F. Fill the pie shell and cover with the top crust. Bake 50 minutes.

Lemon Chiffon Pie

Baked pie shell
1 tablespoon unflavored gelatin
½ cup cold water
4 eggs, separated
1 cup sugar
1/8 teaspoon salt
Juice and grated rind of 1 large lemon

Stir the gelatin into the cold water and set aside. Combine the egg yolks, ½ cup sugar, salt, lemon juice and grated rind in the top of a double boiler. Cook over boiling water, stirring continually, for 3 minutes. Remove from heat, add the softened gelatin and allow to cool. Beat the egg whites until stiff, adding gradually the other ½ cup sugar. Fold cooled lemon-gelatin mixture into the beaten egg whites, heap into pie shell, and refrigerate until time to serve.

Lemon Tarts
(12 tarts)

Pie Pastry
Lemon Butter (see page 223)

Make the pastry of your choice, allowing time for resting. Roll out the pastry ¼ inch thick and cut in 4-inch circles with a floured cookie cutter. Line shallow tartlet tins, pressing the pastry circles into place with floured fingertips, or drape them over the backs of muffin tins. Prick the pastry well with the tines of a fork. If using tartlet tins, cover each one with wax paper circles and weight them down with dried beans or rice. Chill in the refrigerator for at least 30 minutes.

Make the Lemon Butter.

Preheat the oven to 450 degrees F. Bake the tarts for 8 minutes. If using the tartlet tins, remove the wax paper and beans or rice and slip the tarts back for just a moment to lightly brown the centers. Cool the pastry and put the shells on a dessert platter. Fill with the Lemon Butter.

Apple Walnut Custard Tart

One-Crust Pie
1 large egg
1 cup milk
1¼ cups Spicy Applesauce
¾ cup chopped walnuts
8 walnut halves

Prepare the pie crust, allowing time for resting the pastry.

Preheat the oven to 425 degrees F. Beat the egg well. Add the milk, applesauce and walnuts. Blend well and pour into the prepared pie shell after patting it with a little flour. Bake 20 minutes, reduce the heat to 350 degrees and bake 20 minutes longer or until a silver knife inserted in the custard comes out clean. Cool and decorate with the walnut halves.

THE SATURDAY EVENING POST

An Illustrated Weekly Magazine
Founded A? D? 1728 by Benj. Franklin

NOVEMBER 18, 1905   FIVE CENTS THE COPY

Floating Island

Floating Island appears often in the records of White House menus. Abigail Adams served it in 1801 and it is supposed to have been a great favorite of Andrew Jackson's, but this is not an elegant dessert. It is a basic custard presented in a fanciful manner.

5 eggs
1¼ cups sugar
1 teaspoon almond extract
2 cups milk, scalded
½ pint light cream
1 teaspoon vanilla extract
Salt

Separate 4 eggs, putting the whites into an electric mixing bowl. Add 1/8 teaspoon salt and slowly beat the egg whites to a froth. Increase the speed and beat until stiff. Still beating, gradually add ½ cup of sugar and continue beating until the whites are glossy and firm. Add the almond extract.

Bring a shallow panful of water to a boil and reduce the temperature so that the water is simmering. Drop tablespoonfuls of the mixture into the water and poach for 3 or 4 minutes, turning each meringue once. Poach only 3 at a time. With a slotted spoon remove them to paper toweling to dry.

Beat the 4 egg yolks and the remaining egg well, gradually adding the remaining sugar and 1/8 teaspoon salt. Beat in the milk, cream, and vanilla and cook in the top of a double boiler, stirring until the mixture thickens enough to coat the stirring spoon. Pour into a shallow dessert bowl, cool and chill.

Make little indentations in the cooked meringues. "Float" the meringues on the custard and fill the indentations with currant jelly.

Cottage Pudding

1/3 cup butter
2/3 cup sugar
1 large egg
2¼ cups all-purpose unbleached flour
4 teaspoons baking powder
½ teaspoon salt
1 cup milk
1 teaspoon vanilla

Preheat the oven to 375 degrees F. Beat the butter and sugar together with an electric beater until light and fluffy. Break in the egg and beat vigorously for 3 minutes. Sift the dry ingredients together and add half of them to the butter-sugar mixture. Add half the milk and repeat the process, beating constantly. Beat in the vanilla and pour the batter into a greased 10-inch-square baking pan. Bake 25 to 30 minutes. If you press the top of the cake with your finger and the imprint does not remain, the cake is done.

Serve from the baking dish in squares and cover with Chocolate Sauce, Dessert Lemon Sauce or Fresh Strawberry sauce.

Vermont Maple Mousse

3 egg yolks
1 cup maple syrup
1/8 teaspoon salt
3 egg whites, beaten stiff
1 cup heavy cream, whipped
½ cup chopped walnuts

Heat the maple syrup almost to the boiling point. Put the egg yolks and salt in the top of a double boiler and start beating over simmering water with an electric or rotary beater. When the eggs begin to rise, add the hot maple syrup very gradually, beating continuously. Continue to beat until the mixture thickens and coats a spoon. Remove from the stove. Cool completely, stirring occasionally. Chill for 10 minutes in the refrigerator before folding into the egg whites. Fold in the whipped cream and put in a freezing-serving bowl. Freeze 2 hours and serve in the bowl covered with chopped walnuts.

Christmas Pudding

The English plum pudding has a glorified descendant in American Christmas pudding. This recipe will fill a 2-quart melon mold (or a 2-pound coffee can) and will serve 16 people. Make it several weeks in advance. It improves with age.

½ pound chopped beef suet
1 (11-ounce) package currants
1 (15-ounce) package muscat raisins
1 (11-ounce) package seedless raisins
½ pound mixed diced candied fruit peels
½ pound diced candied orange peels
3 cups coarse bread crumbs
1½ teaspoons cinnamon
1 teaspoon nutmeg
½ teaspoon allspice
½ teaspoon ground cloves
½ teaspoon salt
6 eggs
1 cup dry white wine
½ cup brandy or bourbon
Cointreau

Put all the dry ingredients in a large bowl or kettle and toss them with large salad spoons. Beat the eggs until light and add the wine and brandy. Mix into the dry ingredients until thoroughly blended. Pack into a buttered mold and let stand overnight in a cool place.

The next day, put the mold on a trivet in a deep kettle. Fill with enough boiling water to come two-thirds up the mold. Cover and simmer 4 hours, adding boiling water when necessary. Remove from the water and cool. Turn out the pudding. Wash and dry the mold and line it with aluminum foil or cheesecloth. Replace the pudding and poke it in several places with a skewer or knitting needle. Sprinkle generously with Cointreau. Cover and keep in a cool (not cold) place. Repeat the sprinkling once a week, using Cointreau, brandy or both. On Christmas Day reheat in simmering water. Unmold the pudding onto a metal platter. Decorate with sprigs of holly, and just before serving pour over 1/3 cup heated brandy. Touch with a lighted match and spoon the brandy over the pudding until the flames subside. Serve with Hardsauce well laced with brandy.

Baked Indian Pudding

5 cups milk
6 tablespoons yellow cornmeal
½ cup molasses
¼ cup sugar
¼ teaspoon baking soda
1 teaspoon salt
1 teaspoon ground ginger
¾ teaspoon cinnamon
½ teaspoon nutmeg

Scald 4 cups of milk in a heavy saucepan or in the top of a double boiler. Gradually pour the cornmeal into the milk, stirring briskly to avoid lumps. When well blended add the molasses, sugar, baking soda, salt and spices and continue stirring for about 15 minutes or until thick.

Preheat the oven to 300 degrees F. Pour the cornmeal mixture into a buttered baking-serving dish. Smooth it evenly in the dish and place in the oven. Pour over 1 cup of cold milk and bake 2 hours.

Persimmon Pudding

2 cups persimmon pulp
2 cups sugar
2 eggs
1 teaspoon vanilla
1 cup buttermilk
1 teaspoon baking soda
½ cup butter or margarine
1¾ cups flour
1 teaspoon cinnamon
1 teaspoon baking powder
1 cup milk

Preheat oven to 350 degrees F. Mix together persimmon pulp, sugar, eggs and vanilla. Stir baking soda into the buttermilk and add. Melt the butter or margarine in the baking pan you will use (8 by 8 or 9 by 13 inches) and add it to the mixture. Sift flour, cinnamon and baking powder together and add alternately with milk to the batter. Beat with an electric mixer until smooth. Pour into pan and bake about 55 minutes. Serve warm or cold, with whipped cream.

Fresh Fruits

This nation abounds in fruits of endless varieties both wild and cultivated, and thanks to the marvels of transportation, local fruits can be distributed nationwide. There is no better dessert than fresh fruit and no cookbook long enough to describe all the ways it might be served. America's sweet tooth often masks the fruit's unique flavor with too much sugar. On the other hand, there are fruits like strawberries and blueberries whose essence is captured in a little sugar, so this too cannot be prescribed in a general way. The addition of powdered vitamin C (ascorbic acid) to freshly sliced fruit prevents it from darkening and enhances its nutrition. One of the earliest fruit recipes in America is a southern dessert often made at Christmas time. We give you that and a few other favorites.

Ambrosia

6 navel oranges
Shredded coconut (preferably fresh)
Sugar
Sherry (optional)

Peel and slice the oranges removing all the white membranes and any seeds. Put a double layer in the bottom of a pretty glass bowl. Sprinkle lightly with sugar and cover with a layer of coconut. Repeat the process until all the fruit is used and finish with a layer of coconut. Sprinkle with sherry if desired. Serve *very* cold.

White Grape Cup

3 to 4 cups seedless white grapes
½ to ¾ cup commercial sour cream
Maple or brown sugar
¼ teaspoon vitamin C

Pick the grapes from the stems, discarding any imperfect ones. Wash them well and pat dry in a towel. Mix in a bowl with sour cream and vitamin C. Place in a dessert bowl or individual sherbet glasses. Chill. Serve with a side dish of maple or brown sugar, which should be spread liberally on top.

Watermelon Bowl

This is a good way to serve fruit to a large number of people, especially at a cookout. The size of the watermelon and the amount of fruit depends on the head count of guests.

½ watermelon
1 small honeydew melon
1 cantaloupe or other melon
1 pound nectarines
1 pound peaches
Sugar
Lemon juice
1 pint sweet white wine or
  1 cup sherry (optional)
1 pint blueberries
¼ teaspoon powdered vitamin C

Scoop out all the red part of the watermelon with a melon ball cutter. Discard the seeds and put the balls in a large bowl. If possible, chill the watermelon shells.

Halve and seed the other melons and cut them into balls with the same cutter and add them to the watermelon balls. Slice the nectarines without peeling. Peel and slice the peaches. Sprinkle all the fruit with sugar to taste but do not oversweeten. Sprinkle with lemon juice to taste. Add the wine or sherry if desired. Mix gently. Cover and chill in the refrigerator.

Just before serving fill the melon shell with the mixed fruits and sprinkle all over with vitamin C and with blueberries.

Honeydew Cup

1 large honeydew melon
1 lemon
4 tablespoons sugar
2 cups sweet white wine
Mint leaves
¼ teaspoon powdered vitamin C

Choose a ripe melon. Halve and seed it and cut into small balls with a cutter designed for the purpose. Place the fruit in a nonmetal bowl and sprinkle with the juice of the lemon and the sugar. Pour in the wine. Cover and chill for at least an hour, stirring gently occasionally. Sprinkle on vitamin C just before serving.

Serve in glass dessert goblets garnished with a sprig of mint.

Cantaloupe Special

3 or 4 cantaloupes
Sugar
1 quart Lemon Orange Sherbet
Black cherries

Choose ripe cantaloupe. Slice off the tip of each end to give a flat bottom. Halve and seed them and sprinkle lightly with sugar. Chill in the refrigerator.

Just before serving fill in the cavities with sherbet (homemade or store-bought) and cover with pitted black cherries.

Irish Moss Blancmange

Along the coasts the early settlers found clinging to the rocks at low tide Irish moss which, when boiled with milk, made a palatable dessert. This moss is now gathered commercially to make soluble capsules for medicine, but amateurs still like to gather it and use it for desserts and aspics. The moss should be gathered and dried in the sun. Then it is picked over to remove any marine creatures or seaweed. Packed in airtight bags it will keep indefinitely. Three-fourths cup of Irish moss equals 2 tablespoons of plain gelatin in strength.

¾ cup Irish moss
1 quart milk
¼ teaspoon salt
½ cup sugar
2 teaspoons vanilla

Soak the moss in cold water and remove any foreign substance. Drain well and put in the top of a double boiler with the milk and salt. Simmer 30 minutes. Strain into a dessert bowl. Stir in the sugar until it dissolves and add the vanilla. Cool and chill. Serve with Fresh Strawberry Sauce (see Dessert Sauces).

Chocolate Blancmange

Make Irish Moss Blancmange and while it is cooking: Melt 2 squares of bitter chocolate in a heavy saucepan. Add ½ cup of boiling water and stir until smooth.

Orange Sherry Jelly

Abraham Lincoln was not very interested in food and preferred simple fare and not much of it, but this was a dessert he liked especially.

2 envelopes (2 tablespoons)
  plain gelatin
½ cup cold water
¾ cup boiling water
1 cup sugar
2 cups orange juice, strained
4 tablespoons lemon juice
½ cup sherry

Soften the gelatin in cold water in a small saucepan. Add the boiling water and stir until the gelatin dissolves. Add the sugar and continue stirring until the sugar dissolves. Put in a bowl and cool slightly before adding the fruit juices and the sherry. Pour into a dessert bowl or in a decorative large mold or in individual molds. Chill thoroughly before unmolding. Cover or surround with Sweet Whipped Cream and garnish with slivered almonds.

Coffee Rum Jelly

2 packages (2 tablespoons) gelatin
½ cup cold water
3 cups strong coffee, brewed or instant
½ to ¾ cup sugar
½ cup dark rum
Sweet Whipped Cream

Soften the gelatin in the water in a bowl. Add very hot coffee, which can be regular or decaffeinated. Sugar to taste, remembering that the rum is sweet. Add the rum and stir a moment.

Pour into dessert mold, individual dessert glasses or into a bowl. Chill until firm.

Garnish a turned-out mold or a dessert bowl with Sweet Whipped Cream. If serving in individual glasses, pour in a little unwhipped cream. In either case sprinkle with the chopped nuts.

Cranberry Nut Surprise

2 cups cranberries
½ cup brown sugar
½ cup chopped walnuts
2 eggs
1/8 teaspoon salt
1 cup sugar
1 cup unbleached, all-purpose flour, sifted
8 tablespoons melted butter or margarine
4 tablespoons salad oil
Vanilla Ice Cream (optional)

Preheat the oven to 325 degrees F. Wash the cranberries and spread them in a 10-inch greased pie plate. Sprinkle with the brown sugar and nuts.

Beat the eggs until light and fluffy and, still beating, gradually add the sugar. Stir in the flour, butter and oil. Pour over the cranberries and bake for 50 minutes. Cool. Cut in 6 to 8 wedges and serve with ice cream, if desired.

Raspberry Parfait

1 quart raspberries
1 cup sugar
2 teaspoons lemon juice
1 pint all-purpose cream, whipped
1/8 teaspoon almond extract

Reserve 1 cup of raspberries. Put the rest in a blender and add the sugar and lemon juice. Spin to a puree and strain through a stainless steel strainer or a tin one lined with cheesecloth so as not to get the metal taste. Measure out ½ cup of the puree. Cover and chill in the refrigerator.

Fold the rest of the puree into the whipped cream and flavor with the extract. Put in a plastic container and chill 2 or 3 hours or longer in the freezer.

To Serve: Put a spoonful of raspberry cream in the bottom of parfait glasses. Top with a tablespoonful of the puree. Add another spoonful of raspberry cream and garnish with fresh raspberries.

JELL-O
America's most famous dessert

LAND of romance—proud and haughty dons —brave matadors—lovely señoritas—the gayety of lurid color everywhere—Spain.

How the old grandees, epicures in the art of food, would have enjoyed Jell-O. Its delicious pure fruit flavor and sparkling crystalline colors would have greatly appealed to their discriminating tastes. But today Jell-O is within the reach of even the modest purse; in our recipe book you will find many suggestions for economical desserts and salads.

THE JELL-O COMPANY Inc.
Le Roy, New York

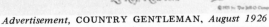

Advertisement, COUNTRY GENTLEMAN, *August 1926*

Blueberry Grunt

1 quart blueberries
1 cup brown sugar
1 cup white sugar
1 teaspoon cinnamon
3 cups water
1½ cups sifted unbleached all-purpose flour
2 teaspoons baking powder
1/8 teaspoon salt
½ cup all-purpose cream (approximate)
Dessert Lemon Sauce

Wash the berries, discarding any imperfect ones or tiny stems. Mix with the sugar, cinnamon and water in a shallow heatproof covered serving dish. Cook over low heat just until the berries are soft.

Meanwhile mix the flour, baking powder, salt and cream lightly with a fork just until it sticks together. Drop by spoonfuls onto the berries. Cover and cook for 15 minutes. Serve directly from the dish and pass a bowl of the sauce.

Peach Brown Betty

5 cups coarse bread crumbs
10 tablespoons butter or margarine
  (¼ pound plus 2 tablespoons)
1 teaspoon cinnamon
1 cup brown sugar
1/8 teaspoon salt
5 cups sliced peaches
1 teaspoon lemon juice
4 tablespoons rum (optional)

Make the bread crumbs from slightly stale slices of white bread. They should not be too fine. Mix them with the butter, cinnamon, brown sugar and salt in a bowl.

In another bowl, slice the peaches and sprinkle with lemon juice and rum if desired.

Preheat the oven to 350 degrees F. Butter a 2-quart baking dish and cover the bottom with the bread crumb mixture. Put in a layer of peaches. Continue this process until all the ingredients are used, ending with a layer of bread crumbs. Bake 45 minutes. Serve warm with cream or with Hardsauce.

Blueberry Buckle

¼ pound soft margarine
½ cup sugar
1 egg, well beaten
2 cups sifted all-purpose unbleached flour
2½ teaspoons baking powder
½ cup milk
1 pint fresh blueberries

Topping:
4 tablespoons white sugar
4 tablespoons light brown sugar
½ cup flour
1 teaspoon cinnamon
½ teaspoon nutmeg
4 tablespoons butter

Preheat the oven to 350 degrees F. Grease well an 8-by-8-inch baking-serving dish.

Beat the margarine and sugar together until light and fluffy. Add the beaten egg and, when well mixed, add the flour sifted with the baking powder alternately with the milk. Place in the dish and cover with the blueberries.

Put all the ingredients for the topping in a bowl and work them together with your fingertips until crumbly. Sprinkle over the top. Bake 1 hour and serve with Dessert Sauce or cream.

Spicy Applesauce

5 pounds cooking apples
2 cups water
1½ cups sugar
¼ teaspoon salt
½ teaspoon cinnamon
¼ teaspoon cloves
¼ teaspoon nutmeg
1 teaspoon vanilla

Core, peel and slice the apples. Put them in a heavy kettle with the water, sugar and spices. Cover and simmer until the apples are tender. Put them through a food mill. If the sauce is too liquid, boil it down over a moderate flame, stirring constantly, until thick. Add the vanilla.

Lemon Butter

This recipe is from Pennsylvania, and people there say it was brought from England by the William Penn family. It can be used as a filling for a jelly roll, or in tarts. In England lemon butter is spread on white bread and served with afternoon tea.

6 tablespoons butter
2 lemons, the grated rind and juice
3 eggs, beaten well
1 cup sugar

Melt the butter in the top of a double boiler and add the rest of the ingredients. Cook over simmering water, stirring constantly, for 5 or 6 minutes or until the mixture thickens. Pour immediately into a bowl and cool, then cover. This butter will keep quite a long time in the refrigerator.

New England Apple Slump

6 to 8 cooking apples
1¼ cups sugar
1 teaspoon cinnamon
¼ teaspoon nutmeg
¾ cup cider, apple juice or water
Baking Powder Biscuits (see Breads)

Peel, core and slice the apples into eighths. Arrange them in the bottom of a deep baking dish that has a tight cover. Combine the sugar and spices and sprinkle over the apples. Cover and place over moderate heat and bring slowly to the boil.

Preheat the oven to 300 degrees F. Prepare the baking powder biscuit dough and drop like dumplings onto the hot apples. Cover tightly and bake for 1 hour. Serve with lemon sauce or heavy cream.

Tipsy Parson

Sponge Cake
4 egg yolks
½ cup sugar
1 teaspoon cornstarch
1/8 teaspoon salt
2 cups milk
1 teaspoon vanilla
Sherry
Sweet Whipped Cream
½ cup slivered almonds, toasted
Candied cherries

Make the sponge cake and, when it is cool, slice it and let it stand at room temperature overnight to become a little stale. (This is a good way to use up stale cake.)

Beat the egg yolks until lemon-colored and add the sugar gradually while beating. Add the cornstarch and salt and, still beating, add the hot milk slowly. Add the vanilla. Pour into the top of a double boiler or a heavy saucepan. Cook and stir until the mixture is thick enough to coat the stirring spoon. Set aside to cool, stirring occasionally.

To Assemble: Line the bottom of a dessert bowl with the cake. Sprinkle liberally with sherry and cover with some of the cold custard. Cover with more sherry-soaked cake and then more custard. When all the cake and custard have been used, cover and chill in the refrigerator. Just before serving cover with Sweet Whipped Cream. Strew the top with the almonds and decorate with candied cherries.

Colonial Benne Cake

Benne seeds are a southern specialty, but lacking these, you can make this cake with the more available caraway seeds.

5 egg whites
¼ teaspoon salt
1½ cups sugar
½ pound butter or margarine, softened
5 egg yolks
2 teaspoons benne or caraway seeds
¾ teaspoon orange extract
1 2/3 cups all-purpose unbleached flour
Confectioners' sugar

Preheat the oven to 300 degrees F. Grease a Bundt pan or a 10-inch tube pan and dust with flour. Beat the egg whites and salt until stiff. Add ½ cup of the sugar, still beating. Set aside.

Beat the butter with the remaining sugar until light and fluffy. Add the egg yolks one at a time, beating hard after each addition. Add the benne or caraway seeds, extract and flour and beat until well blended. Fold in half of the meringue thoroughly and then add the mixture to the rest of the meringue, folding as gently as possible.

Turn the mixture into the pan and cut through the batter with a knife or spatula. Bake 60 to 70 minutes or until firm.

Cool 10 minutes before turning it out of the pan onto a wire rack to cool.

Frosting:
1 cup sugar
1 tablespoon corn syrup
½ cup water
½ teaspoon vanilla
Confectioners' sugar
Benne or caraway seeds

Boil the sugar, syrup and water for 4 minutes or until it spins a thread when you drop it from a spoon. Cool 3 minutes and add enough confectioners' sugar to give it a spreading consistency. Spread over the cooled cake and sprinkle with a few benne or caraway seeds.

Vermont Chiffon Cake

1 cup all-purpose unbleached flour, sifted
¾ cup sugar
1½ teaspoons baking powder
1/8 teaspoon salt
7 tablespoons cold water
4 tablespoons vegetable salad oil
4 egg yolks
5 egg whites
¼ teaspoon cream of tartar

Preheat the oven to 325 degrees F. Grease a 10-inch tube pan and lightly dust it with flour.

Sift the dry ingredients together. Combine the water and salad oil with the egg yolks and beat hard for 2 minutes. Combine with the dry ingredients and beat again until smooth.

Beat the egg whites and cream of tartar until very stiff. Add to the other mixture a third at a time, mixing the first third in thoroughly and folding the last two batches very gently.

Bake for 1 hour. Let the cake rest upside down on a wire rack in the pan until cold before turning it out.

Date Nut Tea Cakes
(2 dozen)

2 large eggs
1 cup light brown sugar
½ cup unbleached all-purpose flour
1/3 teaspoon baking powder
½ teaspoon salt
½ cup chopped walnuts
½ cup chopped dates

Preheat the oven to 450 degrees F. Grease miniature muffin tins.

Beat the eggs just until blended. Beat in the sugar. Stir in the flour, mixed with baking powder and salt, the walnuts and the dates.

Put a generous teaspoonful of the mixture in each tin. Bake 10 minutes. Turn out of the pans while hot. Cool on a wire rack.

Cover painting, THE SATURDAY EVENING POST, *January 3, 1953*

Election Cake

Election Cake, later known as Hartford Election Cake, first appeared in Amelia Simmon's American Cookery *in 1800 and was very popular with Andrew Jackson and Martin Van Buren. It was originally a yeast-based spiced fruit bread, but modern versions which appear every election year are more like a large fruitcake. Eaten with Port, sherry or whiskey, it makes for a good celebration or a solace for disappointment.*

6 egg whites
1 cup white sugar
1 cup light brown sugar
½ pound soft sweet butter
6 egg yolks, well beaten
½ teaspoon nutmeg
¼ teaspoon ground cloves
1 teaspoon cinnamon
1 teaspoon salt
1 teaspoon soda
1 cup milk
4 cups flour
2 cups chopped pecans
1 cup raisins
1 cup seeded muscat raisins
2 teaspoons baking powder
4 tablespoons brandy

Preheat the oven to 275 degrees F. Grease a large tube or deep cake pan and line the bottom with wax paper.

Beat the egg whites until stiff and gradually add ½ cup white sugar. Set aside.

In another bowl, beat the remaining sugar and brown sugar with the butter until light and fluffy. Add the egg yolks and spices and mix well. Add the salt and soda to the milk and stir well.

Put the nuts and fruit in a bowl and toss with 1 cup of flour. Add the baking powder to the rest of the flour. Add the flour and milk alternately to the egg mixture, beating until well blended. Fold in the fruits, nuts and brandy. Finally fold in the egg whites gently but thoroughly. Pour into the prepared pan and bake from 1 hour and 15 minutes to 1 hour and 30 minutes. Insert a cake tester or long skewer to be sure it is done. Cool in the pan inverted on a wire rack before turning out. This can be covered with a Sugar Glaze or sprinkled with powdered sugar.

Angel Cake

1 cup sifted flour
1½ cups sugar
1½ cups egg whites
¼ teaspoon salt
1 teaspoon cream of tartar
¾ teaspoon almond extract
¾ teaspoon vanilla extract

Preheat the oven to 375 degrees F. Resift the flour twice and put it in a measuring cup. Sift the sugar through a fine strainer and put it in a 2-cup measuring cup.

Beat the egg whites and salt with an electric or rotary beater until frothy. Add the cream of tartar and beat until very stiff.

Fold in the sugar, 3 tablespoons at a time, folding just enough to incorporate the sugar. Do not overmix. When all the sugar is mixed in, do the same thing with the flour, adding it by ¼ cupfuls. Fold in the combined extracts and pour the batter into a 10-inch tube pan. Cut the batter in several places with the spatula. Bake 40 minutes.

Turn upside down on a wire rack and cool completely before turning out of the pan. This may be left plain, sprinkled with powdered sugar or frosted with a Chocolate Frosting, Maple Frosting, Orange Frosting or Lemon Frosting.

Chocolate Cake I

2 squares bitter chocolate
4 tablespoons butter
4 tablespoons margarine
1 cup sugar
3 egg yolks
1½ cups unbleached, all-purpose
   flour, sifted
¼ teaspoon salt
1 tablespoon baking powder
½ cup room temperature milk
1 teaspoon vanilla extract
3 egg whites, beaten stiff

Preheat the oven (see below). Grease the pan or pans and dust with flour.

Melt the chocolate with 2 tablespoons of water in a heavy saucepan or in a double boiler. Blend well and cool to lukewarm.

Beat the butter and margarine together and slowly add ½ cup of sugar, beating with an electric beater until fluffy. Add the egg yolks one by one, beating hard after each addition.

In another bowl beat the egg whites until stiff and, still beating, add the rest of the sugar.

Resift the flour with the salt and baking powder and mix the milk and vanilla. Beat the chocolate into the butter-sugar mixture and then add the dry and liquid ingredients alternately, beating until blended. Fold in the egg whites thoroughly and pour into a 10-by-10-inch or 9-by-13-inch pan, or into 2 round layer cake tins.

Bake 25 to 30 minutes at 400 degrees F if you are making a layer cake. Bake 40 to 45 minutes at 350 degrees if you are making a square or rectangular cake.

Frost with White, Chocolate, or Mocha Frosting.

Chocolate Cake II

This cake has a chewy consistency and should be eaten with vanilla, coffee or chocolate ice cream.

1 cup plus 2 tablespoons Crisco
   or other hydrogenated shortening
¼ pound butter
3 cups sugar
3 cups flour
½ cup cocoa
1 teaspoon baking powder
½ teaspoon salt
5 eggs
2 teaspoons vanilla extract
1¼ cups milk

Preheat the oven to 300 degrees F. Grease a large (10-inch) tube pan and dust it with flour.

Beat the shortening and butter together until blended. Add the sugar gradually and beat with an electric beater until fluffy. Add the eggs one at a time, beating constantly. Beat in the vanilla.

Sift the flour with the rest of the ingredients and add in thirds alternately with thirds of the milk.

Pour the batter into the cake pan and bake for 1½ hours.

Sprinkle with powdered sugar or top with a Sugar Glaze.

Strawberry Shortcake

Strawberry shortcake is part of New England's observance of the Fourth of July, because that is when both wild and cultivated strawberries ripen. A wild strawberry shortcake is a once-a-year event, but with frozen strawberries available strawberry shortcake is possible all year round. These can be made and served as individual shortcakes or one large enough to serve 6 to 8 people.

1¾ cups sifted all-purpose unbleached flour
4 teaspoons baking powder
1 teaspoon salt
3 teaspoons sugar
4 tablespoons butter or margarine
Milk
1 quart wild or cultivated strawberries
   or 2 large packages frozen strawberries
2 cups sugar
1 pint whipping cream

Sift the dry ingredients together into a bowl. Slice the butter or margarine over the mixture and cut it in with a pastry blender, fingertips or an electric mixer until the combination has a mealy texture. Add just enough milk to give a soft workable dough. Work quickly so that the biscuit will be tender.

Preheat the oven to 425 degrees F. For a large cake, divide the dough in two parts and roll into two equal circular layers about 1 inch thick. Bake them one on top of the other on a greased baking sheet for 15 to 20 minutes or until lightly browned. For small shortcakes, roll out the dough on a lightly floured surface, using a lightly floured rolling pin, to a thickness of ¾ inch to 1 inch. Cut in 3-inch circles with a cookie cutter. Transfer with a spatula to a greased baking sheet. Bake 12 minutes.

The shortcake should be served warm, so it should be baked just before serving or reheated in a slow oven.

To make the filling: Pick out 6 to 8 of the finest berries and set them aside. Wash, hull and slice the rest of the berries and cover them with the sugar, stirring them gently to dissolve the sugar.

To Serve: Split the large or individual warm shortcake and spread the lower layer with butter or margarine. Cover with a generous layer of sugared berries. Put on the top part of the biscuit and spoon on whipped cream. Garnish with the reserved berries or with more strawberry sauce. Serve immediately.

Rich Marble Cake

½ cup sweet butter
12 tablespoons (1½ sticks) margarine
2½ cups sugar
5 eggs
2½ cups sifted cake flour
1¼ teaspoons baking powder
½ teaspoon salt
1 cup less 2 tablespoons milk
2 teaspoons vanilla
4 tablespoons sifted cocoa
Confectioners' sugar

Take the butter, eggs and milk out of the refrigerator 1 hour before making the cake.

Preheat the oven to 350 degrees F. Butter a Bundt pan or a 10-inch tube pan.

Blend the butter and margarine. Add the sugar gradually, beating until light and fluffy. Beat in the eggs one at a time, beating hard after each addition.

Sift together the dry ingredients and combine the milk and vanilla. Add the dry ingredients and the milk alternately to the butter-sugar mixture, beating until well blended and smooth.

Put 2 cups of the batter in a small bowl and stir in the cocoa.

Spoon the 2 cake batters alternately by large spoonfuls into the prepared pan.

Bake 1 hour and 10 minutes for the tube pan, 1 hour and 30 minutes for the Bundt pan. Cool the pan 10 minutes before turning out on a wire rack. Sprinkle with sifted confectioners' sugar.

Maple Nut Cake

4 tablespoons butter
1 cup soft maple sugar
1 egg
¾ cup milk
1 cup sifted cake flour
1 cup whole wheat flour
¼ teaspoon salt
2½ teaspoons baking powder
1 cup chopped walnuts

Preheat the oven to 350 degrees F. Grease an 8-by-8-inch cake tin.

Beat the butter and soft maple sugar until well blended. Add the egg and beat hard for 1 minute. Add the milk and when well mixed stir in the dry ingredients sifted together. Stir in the chopped nuts.

Pour into the prepared tin and bake 30 to 35 minutes or until an inserted broom straw or skewer comes out clean. Frost with Maple Frosting.

Note: If maple sugar is hard, spin it in a blender with a tablespoon of water.

Sponge Cake

This cake may be baked in a French loaf tin or in a 10-inch tube pan.

5 egg yolks
1 cup sugar
3 tablespoons lemon juice
1 cup plus 2 tablespoons sifted cake flour
1 teaspoon baking powder
3 egg whites, beaten stiff
¼ teaspoon salt

Preheat the oven to 325 degrees F. Beat the egg yolks well. Still beating, add the sugar gradually, beating until light. Add the lemon juice.

Resift the cake flour and fold it into the batter until thoroughly mixed. Fold in the egg whites, beaten stiff, with the salt. Pour into the ungreased pan and bake for 1 hour.

Turn the cake upside down on a wire rack and cool before removing from pan.

Fruit Cake

For generations fruitcake has been made at Christmastime and often presented to friends and neighbors as a gift. It should be made several weeks in advance in order to mellow.

1 cup sweet butter, softened
1½ cups sugar
6 egg yolks, well beaten
6 egg whites, beaten stiff
2 cups sifted all-purpose unbleached flour
½ cup cognac
½ cup Madeira
1 (12-ounce) package seedless raisins
1 (11-ounce) package currants
1 (12-ounce) package seeded raisins
½ pound citron, finely cut
½ pound candied orange peel
1 teaspoon cinnamon
½ teaspoon each cloves, nutmeg and allspice

Preheat the oven to 275 degrees F. Grease 1 large or 2 medium-size deep baking tins. Dust with flour.

Cream the butter and sugar together with an electric beater and gradually add the sugar until light and fluffy. Add the beaten egg yolks. When well blended fold in the beaten egg whites alternately with 1½ cups of flour. Stir in the cognac and Madeira. Combine all the fruits and spices and toss them with the remaining ½ cup of flour. Stir into the egg mixture gently but thoroughly.

Pour into the prepared tin or tins. Cover with buttered aluminum foil and bake 4 to 5 hours. Cool completely before turning out.

Wash the pan and replace the cake. Prick it in several places and sprinkle with cognac and Madeira. Repeat this process every week. Keep in a cool place. When the holiday arrives, frost with White Frosting and decorate with candied cherries and green angelica.

Brandy Cheesecake

Cookie Crumb Crust
2 envelopes (2 tablespoons)
  plain gelatin
2 egg yolks, well beaten
1 cup sugar
1 cup milk
4 teaspoons lemon juice
4 tablespoons brandy
1/8 teaspoon salt
3 cups (24 ounces) creamed cottage cheese
2 egg whites
½ pint heavy cream, whipped

Make and bake the Cookie Crumb Crust using graham cracker crumbs. Save out enough of the crumb mixture to make a topping.

Combine the gelatin, the beaten egg yolks, ¾ cup of sugar and the milk in the top part of a double boiler. Stir over simmering water until the mixture is slightly thickened. Remove from the heat and stir in the lemon juice, brandy and salt. Cool slightly.

Meanwhile puree the cottage cheese in a blender until free from any lumps. Combine with the gelatin mixture. Place in the refrigerator (or in the freezer if you are in a hurry). Stir every 5 minutes until it thickens.

Beat the egg whites until stiff. Still beating, gradually add the sugar. Fold the egg whites and the whipped cream into the cold cheese mixture and put into the prepared crust, smoothing the top with a spatula. Sprinkle with the crumb topping and chill several hours.

Cream Cheese Pound Cake

½ pound sweet butter
8 ounces cream cheese
5 large eggs
2 cups sugar
2 cups cake flour, sifted
1/8 teaspoon salt
1 teaspoon vanilla

Take the butter, cheese and eggs out of the refrigerator at least 1 hour before making the cake. Grease a 9-inch tube pan or a loaf tin and dust it lightly with flour.

Preheat the oven to 350 degrees F. Beat the butter and cheese in an electric mixer bowl until thoroughly blended. Add the eggs one at a time, alternating first with sugar and then with the flour mixed with the salt. Beat hard and continuously. Add the vanilla. Bake 50 to 60 minutes.

Lady Baltimore Cake

3 cups sifted cake flour
1 tablespoon baking powder
¼ teaspoon salt
10 tablespoons sweet butter
1 2/3 cups sugar
1 cup milk
5 egg whites, beaten stiff
1 teaspoon vanilla extract
White Frosting
1½ cups chopped seeded dark raisins
1½ cups chopped pecans

Preheat the oven to 375 degrees F. Grease 3 (9-inch) layer cake tins and line the bottoms with circles of waxed paper cut to fit.

Resift the flour with the baking powder and salt, using a very fine sifter.

Beat the butter and sugar together until light and fluffy. Add the milk and flour alternately, beating continuously. Fold in a third of the beaten egg whites thoroughly. Fold in the remaining egg whites and vanilla gently. Divide the batter between the 3 pans, smoothing the batter evenly in the pans with a spatula. Bake 25 minutes or until firm to the touch. Let stand 5 minutes before turning out on a wire rack. Cool completely before filling. Baking the layers a day in advance makes them better able to handle the heavy frosting.

Make the White Frosting. Mix a little over half of the frosting with the chopped raisins and nuts and spread between the 2 bottom layers. Pile them on a pretty dessert plate. Put the top layer in place and cover the top and sides evenly with the remaining frosting. Decorate with pecan halves.

Advertisement for Adams Gum, THE SATURDAY EVENING POST, *June 12, 1920*

Grandmother's Crumb Cake

This recipe turns up, with only minor variations, in many old collections. Quick and easy to assemble and requiring no frosting, it produced a cake that satisfied the sweet tooth without being very rich. You can, if you like, serve it in the morning and call it coffee cake.

2 cups light brown sugar
2 cups flour
½ teaspoon salt
½ cup vegetable shortening, margarine
   or butter
½ teaspoon baking soda
1 cup buttermilk
2 teaspoons baking powder
½ teaspoon cinnamon
½ teaspoon nutmeg
2 eggs, slightly beaten
Chopped pecans, ¼ cup or more

Mix together the sugar, flour and salt. Cut in the shortening with two knives, then work with a fork till the mixture is evenly colored and crumbly. Reserve ½ cup of these crumbs for topping. Stir the baking soda into the buttermilk and add to the larger quantity of crumbly mixture. Add the other ingredients except the pecans and mix well.

   Preheat the oven to 350 degrees F. Grease and flour two 8-inch layer cake pans or one large baking pan. Pour in the batter and top with the crumbs and nuts. Bake 30 minutes if in two pans, slightly longer if in one large pan.

Frosted Applesauce Cake

8 tablespoons butter or margarine, softened
2 cups sugar
2 cups Spicy Applesauce
3 cups sifted all-purpose unbleached flour
1¾ teaspoons baking soda
1 cup chopped walnuts
1 cup seedless raisins
1 teaspoon vanilla

Preheat oven to 350 degrees F. Grease a 9-inch tube pan and sprinkle with flour. Beat the butter and sugar until fluffy. Add the cold applesauce, which should be thick. If using canned applesauce, season it with a teaspoon of cinnamon and ½ teaspoon each of nutmeg and cloves. Stir in 2¾ cups of flour. Toss the walnuts and raisins in the remaining flour and add along with the vanilla to the cake mixture. Mix well and pour into the prepared pan. Bake 1½ hours. Cool 5 minutes and turn out on a wire rack to cool.

Frosting:
1½ cups light brown sugar
4 tablespoons heavy cream
3 tablespoons butter
1/8 teaspoon salt
1 teaspoon vanilla
¾ cup confectioners' sugar

Bring the sugar, cream, butter and salt to a full boil in a small saucepan over moderate heat, stirring constantly.

   Remove from the heat and beat in the vanilla and sugar with an electric beater, until it is thick but still runny. Pour over the applesauce cake quickly before it thickens too much.

Gingerbread Boys and Girls
(18 to 24)

½ cup butter
½ cup margarine
1½ cups sugar
1 egg
2 tablespoons dark corn syrup
4 teaspoons grated orange rind
3 cups all-purpose unbleached flour
2 teaspoons soda
2 teaspoons cinnamon
1 teaspoon ginger
½ teaspoon nutmeg
½ teaspoon cloves
½ teaspoon salt

Blend the butter and margarine and gradually beat in the sugar until light and fluffy. Add the egg and beat until smooth.

Add the corn syrup and orange peel and mix.

Sift all the dry ingredients and stir into the butter mixture. Form the dough into a ball and wrap it in wax paper. Chill in the refrigerator.

Preheat the oven to 375 degrees F. Roll out the dough on a lightly floured surface to a thickness of ¼ inch. Cut with a gingerbread-boy cutter. To differentiate between the sexes, cut out small triangular pieces and put on the sides of some of the heads to look like hair ribbons.

Place on ungreased baking sheets 1 inch apart. Bake 8 to 10 minutes. Allow to stand 2 minutes on the pans before transferring to a wire rack to cool.

Old-Fashioned Soft Gingerbread

½ cup soft butter
½ cup sugar
1 egg
1 cup unsulfured molasses
1 cup sour milk or buttermilk
1¾ teaspoons soda
2¼ cups unbleached all-purpose flour
2 teaspoons powdered ginger
1 teaspoon cinnamon
¼ teaspoon clove
½ teaspoon salt

Preheat the oven to 350 degrees F. Beat the butter and sugar until fluffy. Add the egg and beat well. Combine the molasses, milk and soda. Sift together the flour, spices and salt. Add the two mixtures alternately, still beating continuously. Pour into a greased 9-by-9-inch baking-serving dish. Bake 30 to 35 minutes. Press the surface with your finger. If it leaves no imprint it is done.

Serve warm with any of the following toppings:
Sweet Whipped Cream
Whipped cream cheese mixed with
  crystallized ginger
Marshmallow fluff
Sweet butter

Frostings

All the frostings are designed to frost a large 10-inch cake or a 2-layer cake.

White Frosting

2 cups sugar
1 tablespoon light corn syrup
1/8 teaspoon salt
½ cup water
2 egg whites
1 teaspoon vanilla extract

Mix the sugar, corn syrup, salt and water in a small saucepan. Stir over heat until the sugar dissolves. Boil until it reaches 238 degrees F on a candy thermometer or until it forms a soft ball if a little syrup is dropped into cold water.

Beat the egg whites with an electric beater until almost stiff. Add the syrup in a small steady stream into the egg whites, beating continuously until it is smooth, glossy and of a spreading consistency. Beat in the extract and spread immediately.

Chocolate Frosting I

4 squares bitter chocolate
¼ pound butter
2 eggs
1 pound confectioners' sugar
¼ cup boiling water
2 tablespoons sherry

Fill a large bowl half full of ice cubes.

Melt the chocolate in a small heatproof bowl over hot water. Transfer the small bowl to the bowl of ice and beat in the remaining ingredients, beating until the frosting is smooth and creamy.

Chocolate Frosting II

10 tablespoons butter
  (¼ pound plus 2 tablespoons)
2 cups sifted confectioners' sugar
3 squares bitter chocolate melted
  and slightly cooled
1 teaspoon vanilla

Beat the butter until soft. Add the sugar gradually, still beating. Add the chocolate and vanilla slowly and continue beating until the frosting has a spreading consistency.

Maple Frosting

1 cup maple syrup
2 egg whites
¼ teaspoon almond extract

Boil the maple syrup until it registers 238 degrees F on a candy thermometer or until it drops from the end of a teaspoon in a long thread. Beat the egg whites until stiff and add the syrup slowly but steadily in a thin stream, beating continuously. When the frosting is thick enough to spread, beat in the extract and spread immediately.

Orange Frosting

4 tablespoons concentrated frozen
  orange juice, thawed
2 cups sifted confectioners' sugar
2 tablespoons soft sweet butter
1/8 teaspoon salt
1 teaspoon lemon juice

Beat everything in a mixing bowl with an electric beater for 5 minutes. Prolonged beating takes away the raw taste of uncooked frosting. Add more sugar if necessary to give a smooth spreading consistency.

Lemon Frosting

4 tablespoons soft sweet butter
2 tablespoons lemon juice
1/8 teaspoon salt
1 tablespoon Cointreau or other
  orange liqueur
2 cups sifted confectioners' sugar

Combine everything in a mixing bowl and beat with
an electric beater for 5 minutes. Add more sugar if
necessary to give a good spreading consistency.

Mocha Frosting

6 tablespoons sweet butter
1 teaspoon instant coffee
3 tablespoons boiling water
2 cups sifted confectioners' sugar
2 tablespoons cocoa
2 tablespoons sherry
1/8 teaspoon salt

Beat the butter with the instant coffee dissolved in
the boiling water. When well blended, gradually add
the sugar mixed with the cocoa, beating constantly.
Beat 5 minutes. Add the sherry and salt and add more
sugar if necessary to give spreading consistency.

Sugar Glaze

1 cup sugar
2 teaspoons corn syrup
½ cup water
Confectioners' sugar

Boil the sugar, water and corn sugar for 5 minutes.
Cool 3 minutes before beating in just enough con-
fectioners' sugar to give a spreading consistency.
Spread while warm.

Lemon Sauce

¾ cup sugar
1/8 teaspoon salt
1½ tablespoons cornstarch
1½ cups boiling water
1 lemon
3 tablespoons butter or margarine

Combine the sugar, salt and cornstarch in a small
saucepan. Add the boiling water gradually, stirring
constantly to prevent lumps. Boil the mixture until
thick and clear, still stirring. Remove from the heat
and add the grated rind and the juice of the lemon.
Stir in the butter and serve warm.

Dessert Sauce

2 egg yolks
1 cup confectioners' sugar sifted
1 cup heavy cream, whipped
2 tablespoons brandy or
  1½ teaspoons vanilla extract

Beat the egg yolks until thick and lemon-colored.
Fold in the sugar and the whipped cream and add the
flavoring of your choice.

Fresh Strawberry Sauce
(2½ cups)

1 pint strawberries
1 cup sugar
1 teaspoon lemon juice

Wash, hull and slice the strawberries. Put in a shallow
nonmetal dish and cover with sugar. Sprinkle with
lemon juice. Cover and let stand in the refrigerator
for 1 to 2 hours or more.

Butterscotch Sauce

2/3 cup light corn syrup
1½ cups light brown sugar
4 tablespoons butter
1/8 teaspoon salt
1 teaspoon vanilla extract
½ pint heavy cream

Combine the syrup, sugar, butter and salt and boil until quite thick or about 10 minutes. Remove from the heat and add the vanilla. Cool and stir in the cream. Serve cold or reheat in a double boiler.

Chocolate Sauce

4 squares bitter chocolate
1 cup white sugar
1 cup brown sugar
1/8 teaspoon salt
1 cup boiling water
3 tablespoons butter or margarine
1 teaspoon vanilla

Melt the chocolate in the top part of a double boiler. Put the sugar and salt in a small saucepan and add the boiling water. Stir until the sugar dissolves. Remove the melted chocolate from the heat and stir in the sweet water. Whisk until well blended. Boil for 2 minutes. Remove from the fire and stir in the butter and vanilla. Cool slightly before using. This will keep well in the refrigerator for several weeks.

Hardsauce

½ cup sweet butter, softened
1½ to 2 cups confectioners' sugar
1/8 teaspoon nutmeg
1/8 teaspoon salt
2 teaspoons rum, brandy or sherry

Beat the butter and 1 cup of sugar with an electric beater until well blended. Add the nutmeg, salt and flavoring and enough additional sugar to make a firm paste. Put in a small bowl or decorative mold and chill. Unmold and dust slightly with nutmeg.

Claret Sauce

1½ cups sugar
6 tablespoons water
½ cup red Bordeaux wine
2 drops red coloring

Mix the sugar and water in a small saucepan. Stir over heat until the sugar dissolves. Boil 5 minutes. Cool until lukewarm. Add the wine and coloring. Store in a covered jar in the refrigerator.

Sweet Whipped Cream

1 cup whipping cream
6 tablespoons confectioners' sugar, sifted
1 teaspoon vanilla

Whip the cream until stiff and fold in the sugar and flavoring.

THE SATURDAY EVENING POST

An Illustrated Weekly Magazine
Founded A°. D! 1728 *by* Benj. Franklin

DECEMBER 2, 1905   FIVE CENTS THE COPY

Jeffersonian Vanilla Ice Cream

Ice cream is not an American invention although it is the favorite of all American desserts. It is known to have been eaten in this country in the mid-eighteenth century. George Washington's household accounts record the purchase of a "cream machine for ice." The first written recipe for ice cream in this country is in Thomas Jefferson's handwriting, and Dolley Madison served it often. But it was a dessert that demanded a lot of time and hard work and was therefore reserved principally for those who had servants until an ingenious lady, Nancy Johnson of Philadelphia, invented the hand-cranked home freezer and an enterprising businessman started producing ice cream commercially in Baltimore. Since then ice cream has become increasingly popular and enjoyed by everyone. Unfortunately, commerce has not improved ice cream, generally speaking, and Jefferson would not recognize his prize dessert. His recipe, made with the freshest possible eggs, rich cream and pure vanilla extract, is a historical as well as gastronomical experience. If you have a home freezer, electric or hand turned, try it.

6 egg yolks
¼ teaspoon salt
1 cup sugar
2 pints heavy cream, scalded
1 tablespoon vanilla extract

Beat the egg yolks and salt until thick and lemon-colored. Still beating, add the sugar, gradually followed by the hot cream. Pour the mixture into the top of a double boiler and cook over simmering water until the mixture thickens enough to coat the spoon. Stir constantly. Cool the mixture thoroughly and pour into the freezer can. It should be about two-thirds full. Place in the freezer bucket and attach the crank. Surround completely with 3 parts crushed ice to 1 part rock salt. Start turning the crank slowly and gradually increase the speed until the ice cream is fairly stiff. Carefully remove the salt and ice on top of the freezer can and wipe off the lid to prevent salt water from getting into the ice cream. Remove the paddles, scraping the ice cream into the freezer can, and pack it well. The ice cream can be kept in the freezer bucket packed in ice or it may be transferred to the freezer and packed in a decorative mold, plastic containers or freezer trays. Cover with a piece of wax paper before putting on the lid.

Serve with Chocolate Sauce, Fresh Strawberry Sauce or with a combination of 1½ cups of maple syrup and ½ cup of chopped walnuts.

Plain Vanilla Ice Cream
(Freezer method)

1 quart whipping cream
1 cup sugar
1/8 teaspoon salt
2 teaspoons vanilla extract

Pour ½ cup of cream into a small saucepan. Add the sugar and salt and stir over moderate heat with a wooden spoon until the sugar dissolves. Remove from the heat. Cool and mix with the rest of the cream. Freeze as in the preceding recipe.

Vanilla Ice Cream
(Refrigerator method)

1 pint all-purpose cream
½ cup sugar
1/8 teaspoon salt
3 eggs, slightly beaten
1½ teaspoons vanilla extract
¼ teaspoon almond extract
1½ cups heavy cream, whipped

Heat the cream without boiling either in a double boiler or in a saucepan. Remove from the stove and stir in the sugar and salt until the sugar dissolves. Add the cream slowly to the beaten egg yolks, beating constantly. Cook in a double boiler over simmering water until the custard thickens enough to coat the spoon. Do not stop stirring. Remove from the heat and add the flavorings. Fold in the whipped cream and pour into 2 freezing trays. Freeze for 3 hours, stirring frequently during the first hour of freezing. Repack and cover with wax paper or foil.

Chocolate Ice Cream

Follow any of the recipes for Vanilla Ice Cream but heat the cream in a double boiler with 2 squares of bitter chocolate—and omit the vanilla.

Maple Ice Cream

Substitute maple sugar for white in any of the recipes for Vanilla Ice Cream. For extra flavor add a little maple flavoring. Serve with hot maple syrup.

Grapenut Ice Cream

Add 1½ cups of grapenuts to any of the Vanilla Ice Cream mixtures before freezing.

Peppermint Stick Ice Cream

Add 1 cup crushed peppermint stick candy to any of the Vanilla Ice Cream mixtures before freezing. Serve with Chocolate Sauce.

Strawberry Ice Cream

Add 1 pint of fresh strawberries, washed, hulled and crushed, or 2 small packages frozen strawberries, thawed, drained and crushed, to any of the Vanilla Ice Cream mixtures. Substitute 1½ teaspoons of lemon juice for the vanilla extract.

Peach Ice Cream

Add 2 cups of crushed peach pulp to any of the Vanilla Ice Cream mixtures. Substitute ½ teaspoon almond extract for the vanilla. Serve with 2 cups of freshly sliced peaches sprinkled with ¼ teaspoon vitamin C (ascorbic acid) and sweetened very lightly.

Coffee Ice Cream

Dissolve 1 teaspoon instant coffee into ½ cup boiling water. Add to the cream in any of the recipes for vanilla ice cream.

Frozen Pudding

1 cup dark seeded raisins
¼ cup rum
1 cup slivered almonds
½ cup diced candied fruits
1 cup macaroon crumbs
1 quart vanilla ice cream

Soak the raisins in rum until plump. Stir the raisins and rum, the slivered almonds, candied fruits and macaroon crumbs into slightly softened vanilla ice cream. Mix well and pack into a 1½-quart decorative mold. Cover with wax paper and then with a lid or a double thickness of aluminum foil. Freeze for several hours.

To serve: Unmold on a dessert platter after dipping it in hot water for just a moment. Serve with Claret Sauce.

Cranberry Sherbet

In the days of elegant meals with a great many courses, it was the custom to serve a refreshing sherbet after the main course. It had to be cool, tart and invigorating. The custom still survives in some places for the Thanksgiving and Christmas feasts, but more often we eat sherbet as a dessert.

1 quart cranberries
1 pint water
2 cups sugar
¾ cup water
1 envelope (1 tablespoon)
  powdered gelatin
¾ cup strained orange juice
2 egg whites
1/8 teaspoon salt

Wash the cranberries, discarding any imperfect ones. Combine with the water in a saucepan and boil until the cranberries are very soft. This should take 5 minutes or less. Spin the berries in a blender for 30 seconds and strain or force through a food mill and strain. Mix the juice with the sugar and water and boil 4 to 5 minutes.

Soften the gelatin in the orange juice and stir into the hot cranberry juice. Cool completely. Pour into a refrigerator tray and freeze until almost hard. At the same time chill the electric mixing bowl and beaters.

Beat the egg whites and salt until stiff, just before beating the frozen fruit mixture. Put the frozen fruit mixture into the chilled bowl and beat at high speed until mushy. Gently fold in the egg whites and put the mixture in 2 ice trays. Freeze 3 hours or longer, stirring occasionally in the trays. Serve in individual punch or dessert glasses.

Roman Punch Sherbet

A mid-meal refresher! An afternoon pick-me-up! A good dessert!

1 quart Lemon-Orange Sherbet
1 cup light Jamaica rum
Mint

Mix slightly softened sherbet with the rum and refreeze for at least 2 hours. Serve in punch cups or dessert glasses topped with a sprig of mint.

Lemon Orange Sherbet

1 packet (1 tablespoon) gelatin
1/3 cup cold water
2 cups water
1 cup sugar
1 teaspoon grated lemon rind
2 teaspoons grated orange rind
¾ cup lemon juice
1 cup orange juice
3 egg whites, beaten stiff
1/8 teaspoon salt

Soften the gelatin in the cold water. Bring the 2 cups of water and sugar to a rapid boil and boil 8 minutes or until it threads from the spoon. Remove from the heat and stir in the gelatin until dissolved. Add the grated rind and fruit juices. Mix well and cool. Put the mixture into a freezer tray and freeze until almost hard. At the same time chill an electric mixing bowl and beaters.

Just before beating the sherbet, beat the egg whites until stiff. Quickly beat the frozen sherbet until mushy. Fold in the egg whites and place the mixture in 2 trays. Freeze 3 to 4 hours, stirring occasionally in the freezer trays.

Baked Alaska

Dolley Madison and Thomas Jefferson have both been credited with the forerunners of this spectacular dessert, but it was in the New York restaurant run by the fabulous Delmonicos that the dessert achieved its present form which, somewhat simplified, becomes very possible for the home kitchen. It takes courage and organization to attempt it, but once conquered it is hard to resist making it for all important dinners. Start to assemble the dessert a day in advance. With a little cooperation the final part can be done while someone is clearing the table.

Sponge Cake
1 quart strawberry ice cream
4 egg whites
1/8 teaspoon salt
1 cup sugar
½ teaspoon baking powder
Kirsch or Cointreau

The day before:
1. Measure a bread board. It should be approximately 10 inches by 8 inches. Find a rectangular baking pan approximately the same size, preferably about 1 inch smaller on both sides.
2. Make the sponge cake and pour ½ inch of batter into the prepared pan. Bake until firm. Use the rest of the batter for a small loaf or for cupcakes. Turn the cake onto a wire rack to cool. Leave uncovered overnight.
3. Make or buy the ice cream and pack it in a bread loaf tin. Cover with wax paper and a double thickness of aluminum foil. Freeze.

The day of the party:
1. Beat the egg whites and salt until stiff and dry. Slowly add the sugar, still beating, until the meringue is glossy and smooth. Beat in the baking powder. This will be safe for 25 to 30 minutes. If dinner is a protracted affair it will have to be done just before dessert.
2. Cover the bread board with brown paper. If the board has a handle protect it with aluminum foil.
3. Have a thick table protector and a large platter or tray ready so that they can be put on the table at the appropriate time.
4. Time the oven so that it will be heated to 500 degrees F at dessert time.
5. Place the sponge cake on the board. Unmold the ice cream in the center of the cake.
6. Quickly cover the ice cream and cake thickly with meringue, using a small spatula and giving it peaks and swirls as you do it.
7. Bury 2 eggshell halves in the meringue on top of the cake to hold the liqueur.
8. Bake the cake 3 to 5 minutes or until lightly browned on top.
9. Fill the egg cups with heated kirsch or Cointreau. Light with a match and carry triumphantly to the table or, if that is difficult, light it at the table.

Tutti Frutti Bombe

Credit for this dessert is given to President McKinley's wife. If all the ice creams were home frozen it would be complicated, but we recommend buying high-quality ice creams and making this dessert in a matter of minutes.

1 pint vanilla ice cream
1 pint raspberry sherbet
1 pint pistachio ice cream
½ pound mixed candied fruits

Soften the ice creams and sherbet a little. Stir the candied fruits into the vanilla ice cream and line a 1½-quart mold with the mixture, using the back of a large spoon to do it. Fill the center with the raspberry sherbet and spread the pistachio ice cream over the top. Cover with wax paper and with the lid or, lacking a lid, with 2 sheets of aluminum foil. Put in the freezer for several hours or several days.

To serve: Remove the lid and wax paper and dip the mold momentarily in a pan of very hot water. Turn on to a dessert platter.

Pipe Sweet Whipped Cream around the base of the mold using a large fluted tip and pour a little maraschino liqueur over all.

Grandmother's Cookies
(About 4 dozen)

3 cups unbleached all-purpose flour, sifted
1 cup sugar
1/8 teaspoon salt
1 tablespoon baking powder
½ cup butter
½ cup margarine
2 eggs, slightly beaten
2¼ teaspoons vanilla extract

Combine the dry ingredients in a bowl and slice the butter and margarine over the top. Using a pastry blender, 2 knives, your fingertips or an electric mixer, cut the fat in until you have a mealy texture.

Add the eggs and vanilla. Mix and shape into 2 long rolls. Wrap in wax paper and chill.

Preheat the oven to 400 degrees F. Grease 2 baking sheets. Slice the rolls ¼ inch thick and bake for 10 minutes.

Note: This cookie dough can be frozen for several weeks and sliced frozen and baked on demand.

Raisin Cookies
(About 3 dozen)

½ cup sweet butter
½ cup margarine
2/3 cup sugar
2 eggs well beaten
1½ cups unbleached all-purpose flour
½ teaspoon salt
1½ teaspoon vanilla extract
Large seeded raisins

Preheat the oven to 375 degrees F. Grease 2 baking sheets.

Blend the butter and margarine together with an electric beater and gradually add the sugar. When soft and fluffy add the eggs, flour, salt and vanilla. Beat until well blended.

Drop by teaspoonfuls onto a baking sheet and smooth them into rounds. Place a large raisin in the center of each one. Bake 8 to 10 minutes.

Ginger Snaps
(About 4 dozen)

½ cup molasses
¼ cup sugar
3 tablespoons butter or margarine
1 tablespoon milk
2 cups flour
½ teaspoon soda
½ teaspoon salt
1 teaspoon ginger
½ teaspoon cinnamon
½ teaspoon ground cloves
Granulated sugar

Bring the molasses, sugar, butter and milk to a boil.

Combine all the dry ingredients except for the granulated sugar and mix with the liquid. Shape into a ball and wrap in wax paper. Chill in the refrigerator.

Preheat the oven to 375 degrees F. Roll out the dough on a working surface lightly sprinkled with sugar. Cut with a 2-inch cookie cutter. Place the cookies on greased baking sheets and bake 8 minutes. Let the cookies stand 2 minutes before transferring them to a wire rack to cool.

Walnut Kisses
(40 to 50)

3 egg whites
1/8 teaspoon salt
2 cups sifted confectioners' sugar
¾ teaspoon vanilla
¼ teaspoon almond extract
2 teaspoons water
1 cup chopped walnuts

Preheat the oven to 225 degrees F. Use Teflon-coated baking sheets or line metal baking sheets with brown paper.

Beat the egg whites and salt until stiff but moist. Add the sugar slowly and alternately with a mixture of the extracts and water which is added drop by drop. When thick and glossy fold in the nutmeats.

Drop by half-teaspoonfuls onto the baking sheet. Bake 40 to 45 minutes. Remove from the pan while hot.

Cinnamon Butter Cookies
(About 6 dozen)

½ cup butter
½ cup margarine
1 cup sugar
3 eggs
2 teaspoons cinnamon
½ teaspoon nutmeg
3½ cups unbleached all-purpose
   flour
1 teaspoon vanilla extract

Beat the butter and margarine together and gradually add the sugar. When light and fluffy add the eggs and continue beating until well blended. Stir in 1 teaspoon of cinnamon, the nutmeg, the flour and the vanilla extract. Stir until thoroughly mixed. Fashion into long rolls, 2 inches in diameter. Chill 4 hours.

Preheat the oven to 350 degrees F. Grease 2 baking sheets.

Cut the dough in ¼-inch slices and place an inch apart on the baking sheet. Bake 10 minutes. While still hot sprinkle with the sugar mixed with the remaining teaspoon of cinnamon. Transfer to a wire rack to cool.

Apricot Bars

1½ cups flour
1 teaspoon baking powder
1 cup brown sugar
1½ cups uncooked oatmeal
¾ cup butter or margarine
¼ teaspoon salt
1 cup apricot jam (or a little more)

Mix together all the dry ingredients. Add the butter or margarine, cutting it in with two knives and then working with a fork till the mixture is evenly colored and crumbly.

Preheat the oven to 300 degrees F. Spoon about 2/3 of the mixture into a 9-by-13-inch baking pan and pat it down firmly. Spread the apricot jam over the top and evenly out to the edges. It should be about ¼ inch thick. Sprinkle the rest of the crumbly mixture evenly over the jam and bake for 35 minutes.

Oatmeal Cookies
(About 5 dozen)

6 tablespoons butter
6 tablespoons margarine
1 cup light brown sugar,
   tightly packed
½ cup white sugar
2 eggs
4 tablespoons water
1 teaspoon vanilla
1½ cups all-purpose unbleached
   flour sifted
1 teaspoon salt
½ teaspoon baking soda
1 teaspoon cinnamon
2½ cups old-fashioned oatmeal flakes
1 cup seedless raisins
1 cup chopped walnuts

Preheat the oven to 350 degrees. Grease 2 baking sheets.

Blend the butter and margarine and beat in the brown and white sugar until light and fluffy. Beat in the eggs one at a time, beating hard after each addition. Add the water and vanilla.

Combine the flour, salt, soda and cinnamon and add to the butter mixture. Stir in the oatmeal flakes, raisins and walnuts.

Drop from a teaspoon onto prepared baking sheets, 2 inches apart. Bake from 8 to 10 minutes or until the bottom of the cookie is lightly browned. Let the cookies stand before transferring them to a wire rack to cool. Repeat the baking process.

Harriot's Frosted Date Nut Brownies
(30 brownies)

1 cup boiling water
1½ cups chopped dates
½ cup margarine
½ cup sweet butter
1 cup sugar
2 eggs
1 teaspoon vanilla
1¾ cups unbleached all-purpose flour
4 tablespoons regular cocoa
½ teaspoon soda
½ teaspoon salt
¾ cup chopped walnut meats
1½ cups chocolate chips

Stir the boiling water into the chopped dates and let stand for 30 minutes.

Beat the margarine and butter together and add the sugar gradually. Beat in the eggs one by one and add the vanilla. Stir in the date mixture. Sift the dry ingredients together into the egg mixture and beat until well blended.

Preheat the oven to 325 degrees F. Grease a large (13-by-9-inch) baking pan. Pour in the brownie mixture and sprinkle with the chocolate chips and walnuts. Bake 40 to 45 minutes. Cool 5 minutes before cutting into squares.

Pine Tree Shillings

1 cup light unsulfured molasses
½ cup butter or margarine
½ cup brown sugar
3 cups flour
½ teaspoon soda
½ teaspoon salt
1 teaspoon cinnamon
½ teaspoon ginger

Heat the molasses and butter until the butter melts. Stir in the sugar and remove from the heat.

Sift the dry ingredients together and add to the sugar mixture. Beat thoroughly and shape into 2 rolls. Wrap them in wax paper and chill in the refrigerator for 8 hours.

Preheat the oven to 375 degrees F. Slice thin and bake on ungreased baking sheets for 10 minutes.

Note: The dough will keep in the refrigerator for several weeks and can be baked on demand.

Butterscotch Squares
(16 squares)

¾ cup 100 percent whole wheat flour
1 teaspoon baking powder
½ teaspoon salt
1 cup brown sugar, tightly packed
1 teaspoon cinnamon
4 tablespoons melted butter
1 egg, well beaten
¾ cup chopped walnuts

Preheat the oven to 325 degrees F. Grease an 8-by-8-inch baking pan.

Put all the ingredients in a bowl and beat until thoroughly mixed.

Spread into the pan with lightly floured fingers. Bake 25 minutes or until an inserted cake tester or toothpick comes out clean. Cut into squares while warm.

Short'nin' Bread
(4 dozen)

4 cups unbleached all-purpose flour
1 cup light brown sugar
1 pound sweet butter
1 egg yolk
1 tablespoon water

Preheat the oven to 325 degrees F. Mix the flour and sugar. Cut the butter in slices over the flour mixture and work it in with your fingertips until blended into a paste. Pat on a floured surface to a thickness of ½ inch. Cut into squares and place on ungreased baking sheets.

Paint each square with egg yolk blended with the water. Bake 20 to 25 minutes.

Hermits
(About 4 dozen)

½ cup milk
¾ cup raisins
½ cup corn oil
1 cup sugar
3 cups flour
1 teaspoon cinnamon
½ teaspoon nutmeg
½ teaspoon ground cloves
1 teaspoon soda
½ teaspoon salt
½ cup molasses
½ cup chopped walnuts

Preheat the oven to 350 degrees F. Grease 2 baking sheets or large baking pans with rims.

Pour the milk in a small bowl and add the raisins to plump them a little. Measure all the remaining ingredients into a large mixing bowl. Add the milk and mix well with a wooden spoon or a heavy-duty electric mixer.

Either spread the dough in a large baking tin; patting it smooth with lightly floured hands, or drop it by spoonfuls onto a baking sheet. Bake 20 minutes.

Whole Wheat Brownies
(16 brownies)

4 tablespoons margarine
4 tablespoons sweet butter
½ cup regular cocoa
1 cup brown sugar, tightly packed
1 cup 100 percent whole wheat flour
½ teaspoon salt
2 eggs
1 teaspoon vanilla
½ cup chopped walnuts

Preheat the oven to 325 degrees F. Grease an 8-by-8-inch baking pan.

Melt the margarine and butter in a small saucepan and stir in the cocoa. Put in an electric beater bowl and add the sugar gradually, beating well. Add the eggs one at a time, beating hard after each addition. Stir in the flour mixed with the salt and beat until thoroughly blended. Add the vanilla and chopped nuts.

Pour into the prepared pan and bake 25 minutes. Remove from the oven. Cool 5 minutes and cut into squares.

OUR HERITAGE OF AMERICAN WINES AND BEVERAGES

The rugged demands of Colonial life were considerably softened by the liberal use of alcoholic beverages on the part of all but a comparative few whose religious scruples would not allow them that solace. Hard cider was available to rich and poor alike and was thought suitable for young children. The flourishing molasses business brought rum from the West Indies and the southern distillers soon learned how to distill whiskey from corn, wheat and rye. Beer making was a chore of the housewife and some wines were made, but Madeira and sack (sherry) and other fine wines as well as beer were imported. Distilled liquors such as aquavit, rum, whiskey and gin were most often obtained at the local tavern which was the social center in many towns and cities. There were strong drinks served hot to counteract the chill on long winter evenings and to warm the traveler. These were considered to have an excellent medicinal effect. For the hot summer days there were shrubs, bounces and juleps. Some of these have stood the test of time.

The names of some of the "mixed drinks" would indicate that it was as much fun to think up the names as it was to concoct them. Slings, Toddies, Calibogus, Rumbullions, Rumfustian, Syllabub, Whistle Belly Vengeance (a Salem drink of sour homemade beer, simmered, sweetened with molasses, filled with the crumbs of brown bread, and drunk piping hot), Rattleskulls and a Yard of Flannel are some that make our modern nomenclature seem very dull.

We might tend now to think that the colonists were lucky to have clear streams of running water available to them over every hill, unsullied by years of pollution. But water was then held in very low esteem.

Thomas Jefferson is said to have spent over $11,000 on imported wines merely in the time he occupied the White House. He was such a connoisseur that George Washington, who knew a bit about wines himself, usually asked Jefferson's advice and on occasion in 1790 permitted his good friend Thomas to purchase sixty bottles of wine for him. When James Monroe was elected to the White House, Jefferson wrote him a letter of congratulation, but amusingly enough most of the letter was given over to advice on what wines should be served in the White House.

Solid chaps in those days. John Adams every day of his adult life drank a tankard of hard cider before breakfast. Everyone, but everyone, drank, that's about it. There was nothing unusual at all, for example, at the ordination of the Reverend Joseph McKean in 1785, in Beverly, Massachusetts, for a group of eighty people to wash down thirty bowls of spiked punch prior to the ordination ceremony. At the celebration dinner afterward they consumed forty-four bowls of punch, eighteen bottles of wine, eight bowls of brandy and a spanking amount of cherry rum.

Of course, tea, coffee and hot chocolate were all part of the food scene for those who could afford them. There was sweet cider, milk, and nonalcoholic fruit punch for the few blue-nosed backsliders found in every crowd.

For the most part, though, beverages had clout—along with variety, imagination and a touch of the

Cover painting, THE SATURDAY EVENING POST, *December 19, 1936*

unusual. The Colonists and the founding fathers seem to have found ways to concoct drinkables from almost every botanical specimen available to them, and the old books contain directions for alcoholic beverages from cowslips, roses, sassafras, violets and a good many other unlikely things.

There were grapes, too, of course, and there were always men who knew how to use them properly to make good wines. For the story of wine in this country, a story of trials, tribulations and eventual triumphs, we quote professional winetaster and gourmet Charles Turgeon:

Our Vinicultural Heritage

Legend has it that Leif Erikson discovered America and, on seeing the profusion of wild grapes, called this continent Vineland. Today we are less certain that the great Norse explorer was the first European to see these shores. There is no doubt, however, about his perception of the New World as one of the great natural homelands of the vine.

Scientific studies have shown that of the world's thirty-two families of grapes, twenty are native to North America. Practical experience has demonstrated that across the vast reaches of the United States there are combinations of soil and climate suitable for every nonnative grape with wine-making potential. From this splendid endowment American vintners have developed a wine industry that now stands sixth among the forty-four nations that report their production to the Paris office of *Wines and*

Vines, the wine industry magazine.

All the world's wines can be grouped into three broad categories. First in importance are the *natural* or table wines, i.e., the familiar red, white and rose wines that result from simple fermentation of fresh grapes and are most often used to accompany a meal. Next come the *fortified* wines like sherry, port or vermouth. These are natural wines to which something has been added, like extra alcohol or herb flavorings. They are customarily used before or after a meal and thus sometimes called aperitif or dessert wines. Finally, there are the *sparkling* wines, the best known example being champagne. They are made by introducing carbon dioxide gas into natural wine under pressure and are used on all occasions before, during or after meals.

American vineyards yield hundreds of examples of all of these three basic types of wine. From sherry to champagne, from Aurora to Zinfandel, from basic jug wines for everyday use to elegant vintages to be cellared for the next generation, this country's wineries make them all. In addition to producing impressive replicas of the world's classic wines from European grapes, they turn out a significant number of uniquely American wines made from native vines.

Grapes are grown in every state of the Union and over half boast commercial wineries. The giant of the American wine industry, however, is California. It produces 80 percent of all the wine made in this country and seven out of every ten bottles sold in the United States from foreign as well as domestic sources.

> *Let the mistress of the house see*
> *to it that the coffee is excellent,*
> *and the master that the liqueurs*
> *are of the first quality.*
>
> *Brillat-Savarin*

Despite these remarkable achievements, viniculture remains an obscure activity to many Americans, and regular use of its products has only recently begun to become a significant part of our national lifestyle. In Europe, annual adult consumption of wine has averaged about twenty gallons per person for generations. But in the United States, it was not until 1970 that wine purchases rose to a level which indicated that the average American adult was consuming two gallons a year. The reason for this remarkable disparity in the degree to which wine is used in this country and in its closest counterparts in the rest of the western world is a now unthinkable national experiment in abstinence: Prohibition.

From 1919 to 1933, the law of the land forbade "the manufacture, sale or transportation of intoxicating liquors within, the importation thereof into, or the exportation thereof from the United States." This stern denial, enshrined in the 18th Amendment to the Constitution and backed by a strictly worded enforcement law called the Volstead Act, was born of noble motives but yielded nightmarish results. The first casualties, of course, were the farmers, manufacturers and tradesmen who made and sold alcoholic beverages. That was intended. What had not been foreseen was the way Prohibition would tear at the social, economic and political fabric of the United States.

Denied the right to purchase beer, wine, or spirits, millions of Americans turned to making often unwholesome beverages at home or buying them from illegal sources. Until the mid-Twenties, some of

the nation's vineyards stayed alive by supplying the grapes that were bought in enormous quantities to make wines and brandies at home. Increasingly, however, the demand turned toward higher proof drinks supplied by a growing army of bootleggers. Today it is clear that Prohibition, probably more than any other factor, created the conditions in which organized crime got its start.

As the Twenties came to a close, it was apparent to many that Prohibition was an unenforceable law. Moreover, it was becoming clear that its defiance by a rapidly escalating percentage of the population was changing the key issue from one of whether the nation should be "wet" or "dry" to one of whether the rule of law could survive. That was a challenge to which most lawmakers could readily respond, and the first year of the Roosevelt Administration was marked by the passage of Repeal.

More subtle and enduring, however, than these issues of law and order were the effects of Prohibition on public taste. Before undertaking the "noble experiment," Americans appeared to be developing a tradition of using alcoholic beverages that was similar to what obtained in most Western countries. That is, most people preferred moderate drinks like wine or beer to strong spirits like whiskey or gin. But it is one of the great ironies of Prohibition that when it was over more people were interested in alcohol than ever before and that their preference had shifted to "stiffer" drinks. In this great metamorphosis of national taste, wine was the principal loser.

Part of the reason for this loss was the failure of

Day and night my thoughts incline To the blandishments of wine, Jars were made to drain, I think; Wine, I know, was made to drink.

R. H. Stoddard

the Volstead Act to distinguish between the two great classes of alcoholic beverages, i.e., those that are *fermented* and those that are *distilled*. It defined any drink with more than one-half of one percent alcohol as "intoxicating." Thus the public came to see such fermented beverages as beer and wine which normally range from 3 percent to 13 percent alcohol, as much the same thing as distilled spirits whose alcohol content averages over 40 percent. In the eyes of the law it was all just "booze" and the penalties were the same whether you had a bottle of "dago red" wine or a flask of "bathtub" gin. For citizens willing to run the risks and concerned with concealment, the low-volume high-proof liquors became the obvious choice. It was a change in taste that hung on after Repeal and soon became institutionalized in that peculiarly American contribution to the world's drinking habits: the cocktail party.

Another reason for wine's losing out in the aftermath of Prohibition is the time required for its manufacture. Beer and spirits can be made almost overnight. New grapevines, however, require four years before they bear sufficient fruit and most new wines need a year or two of aging before they can be sold. The nation's wine industry was in a shambles after fourteen years of neglect and misuse. Vineyards had been abandoned or turned over to other crops. Of those that were still functioning, many had been replanted in grape varieties more suited for the fresh fruit and raisin markets than for wine-making. In the wineries, machinery was in disrepair and the great wooden fermenting vats and aging casks had dried out and had thus become unusable.

The upshot was that America's vintners could not respond quickly enough after Repeal to catch what might have been a revived public interest in wine. They tried hard, to be sure, but most of the early vintages produced by the crippled industry of the Thirties probably did more to hurt the reputation of wine than help it. As a result, this healthful, moderate beverage was virtually absent from the American scene for more than two decades and beer and bourbon, later Scotch and gin, solidified their hold on the nation's taste. Alcoholic beverage consumption became an activity focused in the corner tavern or hotel bar rather than at the family dinner table and a whole generation of Americans grew up without a taste for wine—that hallmark of Western civilization which their country was uniquely equipped to provide.

We have dwelt at some length with the Prohibition experience and its lingering effects because it is the single most extraordinary event in our vinicultural history and serves to explain why America is still only a modest consumer of wine though a leader in wine production. Like the coming of the glaciers, this strange experiment scarred our land, but it would be wrong to imply that it erased everything that had existed before or to insist, as some wine writers have, that our vinous heritage dates back only to 1933. On the contrary, it is increasingly evident that the United States has a vinicultural history to match that of most great wine-producing nations and that understanding that history is directly relevant to the purchases we make at our hometown wine shops.

The COUNTRY GENTLEMAN

The OLDEST AGRICULTURAL JOURNAL IN THE WORLD

Cover painting, THE COUNTRY GENTLEMAN, *November 22, 1919*

In the first place, it is important to recognize that the long and colorful saga of American wine-making is a story in two parts. Basically, it is a story of East and West or, more precisely, of California and virtually all the other states where vineyards have been planted. The difference is that California's environment proved from the outset to be hospitable to the classic grape varieties of Europe while vintners elsewhere in the United States have had to make their wines from grapes more closely related to those seen by Leif Erikson. Thus the first practical fact to be gleaned from knowing the wine history of this country is that there is a fundamental difference in the character of American wines, depending upon their origin.

The first records of wine making in the East are sketchy, but it is likely that viniculture was underway long before the Pilgrims arrived. French colonists in Florida are known to have been making wine from some sort of grapes in the mid-1500's. The first English settlers of Virginia and Massachusetts harvested native grapes for wine making almost as soon as they arrived and shortly thereafter began experimenting with imported European vines. A letter of 1606, attributed to Captain John Smith, relates the making of twenty gallons of wine in Virginia. Governor's Island in Boston Harbor was set aside in 1632 for wine vineyards. Throughout much of the seventeenth century, the Virginia House of Burgesses promoted the development of viniculture through ordinances requiring home vineyards and the sponsoring of wine-making competitions. Similar efforts

were underway in Maryland, Pennsylvania, New York, New Jersey and several of the Southern colonies where the vines were established.

Much of the activity of the eastern vintners during the seventeenth and eighteenth centuries was focused on trying to get European grapes to grow in the New World. They found the wines made from native vines tasted "savage" or "foxy" and believed that in a countryside so overlaid with grapes the vines of their homelands would flourish here as well. It was not to be. Everyone from William Penn to Thomas Jefferson, both ardent wine enthusiasts, gave it a try but the sophisticated European vines were soon cut down by weather conditions or plant diseases.

With the coming of the American Revolution and the nation-building period that followed, most of the experimenters gave up the foreign grapes as a lost cause and turned to domesticating the native varieties through cross-breeding. Soon Eastern vintners had a respectable family of wine grapes with which to establish major vineyards. These included the Alexander, Catawba, Isabella and, by the mid-eighteenth century, the Concord, Delaware, Elvira and Diamond. The taste of the wines made from these fruits was still "foxy" by European standards, but Americans increasingly showed an affection for it and a healthy wine industry began to grow in New York and Ohio, down into the Carolinas and Georgia, and even out into Michigan, Missouri, Iowa and Illinois.

In the Far West, winemaking got started a bit later and on a far different footing. The first vineyard in what was to become California is generally agreed to

> *Give strong drink to him who*
> *is perishing, and wine to*
> *those in bitter distress;*
> *Let them drink and forget their*
> *poverty, and remember their*
> *misery no more.*
>
> *Proverbs*

have been planted by Spanish missionaries at San Diego in 1769. The Franciscan fathers brought European grapestock which they had already used with success in Mexico. Over the next fifty years they established vineyards for sacramental purposes and as part of their colonizing effort at a chain of twenty-one missions stretching from Baja California to San Francisco Bay. In doing so, they experienced none of the environmental problems that had plagued Eastern vintners, and their wine, while not very sophisticated, was hearty, abundant and European in character.

By the 1830's, Spanish and ecclesiastical power were on the wane in the West and commercial wine-makers began to appear from France, Italy and Germany. Their efforts were centered initially in the Los Angeles and San Diego areas but, like the missionaries, some gravitated north to San Francisco Bay. With the coming of the Gold Rush in 1849, San Francisco became a boom town and winemakers flocked there to meet the new demand. Most important among them was Agoston Haraszthy, a sometime Hungarian nobleman of extraordinary energy and talent, who recognized that in the Bay Area America had her Bordeaux, Burgundy and the Rhine all combined in one spectacular setting. By the time Haraszthy left California, during the 1860's, the foundations for America's principal wine industry had already been established.

From these beginnings, the nation's vintners both East and West sailed on until their near disaster on the shoals of Prohibition. This is not to say that it was all smooth sailing until 1919, for the wine busi-

ness was periodically afflicted with overproduction, plant diseases, cruel weather and fluctuating markets. But basically, American viniculture developed and matured as might be expected in an increasingly civilized and successful Western nation. Given the strength of this movement, it may seem strange that it did not snap back sooner after Prohibition was abandoned. But in addition to the crippling of the wine industry and the nation's taste for wine, it is important to remember that after Repeal America faced long years of economic depression followed by World War II. These were hardly days for wine or roses, and it is not surprising that the first real stirrings of new life in the nation's vineyards came only in the Fifties.

Today the American fascination with wine seems so fervent that one would think we were trying to make up for lost time. Certainly, we appear to be indulging our national predilection for taking up new causes with a vengeance once we are aroused. But the reasons for today's wine boom are more fundamental. First, the United States, despite some buffeting by inflation and recession, is affluent as it has never been before and can afford all the elements of what has been traditionally seen as the good life. Its citizens have been exposed to the dining and drinking habits of other lands to an unprecedented degree and have an expanded awareness of the pleasures of the table. Perhaps most important, the portion of the population that lived through Prohibition or was subsequently affected by it has finally become a minority.

To give some idea of how vigorously America is

*No nation is drunken where
wine is cheap;
and none sober where the
dearness of wine substitutes
ardent spirits as the common
beverage.*

Thomas Jefferson

bouncing back toward wine, a few figures drawn from the industry statistics may be helpful. In 1960, only about 165 million gallons of wine—both foreign and domestic—were sold in the United States. Ten years later that figure had jumped by 100 million gallons, and preliminary data from 1975 indicate total sales of about 400 million gallons. Responsible projections suggest that Americans will be buying more than 600 million gallons per annum by 1980.

To meet this unprecedented demand, the American wine industry has been expanding as never before. In California, for example, the land devoted to wine grapes has jumped from about 110,000 acres in 1965 to more than 250,000 acres in 1975. Dozens of new wineries have sprung up in that state and across the nation while established firms have been engaged in dramatic improvements and enlargements of their facilities. Major national corporations have entered the wine business by buying small family-owned vineyards and supplying them with needed capital and organizational skills. At the nation's enological institutions, student enrollments are at an all-time high and research specialists are breaking new ground.

Probably the most important technological development of the recent past is the emergence of new grape varieties and pesticides which should make it possible—at long last—for Eastern vintners to compete more directly with the wines of California and Europe. This breakthrough offers all sorts of interesting economic as well as vinicultural possibilities, and the day may come when the vineyards along the Atlantic Coast and throughout the Midwest will be regarded as equal partners with those of California. Substantial replanting with the new hybrid grapes has already been accomplished in New York's established wine districts, and new vineyards are cropping up everywhere from New Hampshire to Kentucky.

For the time being, however, the bipolar nature of American wine productions persists and, in attempting to devise a tabular presentation of the bounty from our nation's vineyards, it was necessary to develop one chart for Eastern wines and one for those of the West. Both charts present the major types of American wines in terms of their best known European equivalents and show wines sold under *generic* as well as varietal names. In American wine nomenclature, generically labeled wines are usually the vintner's standard quality products for everyday use which are named after famous European vineyard regions such as Burgundy or the Rhine Valley. They are made from a wide range of grapes whose high productivity permits the vintner to keep his costs low and are often sold in gallon or half-gallon jugs. Varietally labeled wines usually represent the industry's best efforts, those premium wines for special occasions which are named for the high-quality, low-yield grape variety from which they are principally made, e.g., Cabernet Sauvignon or Chardonnay. In the following tables, the varietal wines are listed opposite the generics to which they most closely relate. We will also attempt to indicate what wines are good with particular foods, although we emphasize that no hard and fast rules govern such a choice. Your particular preference is the best guide.

Cover painting, THE SATURDAY EVENING POST, *September 16, 1922*

THE MAJOR WESTERN WINES

	International Equivalent	Generic Name	Varietal Names	Especially Good With
REDS	Burgundy	Burgundy	Pinot Noir	Beef and
			Pinot St. George	Turkey
	Beaujolais	None	Gamay Beaujolais	Chicken and
			Gamay Noir	Veal
	Bordeaux	None	Cabernet Sauvignon	Steak and
			Ruby Cabernet	Lamb
	Rhône	None	Petite Sirah	Duck, Goose
			Zinfandel	and Venison
	Italy	Chianti	Barbera	Pasta and
			Grignolino	Cheese Dishes
WHITES	Burgundy	Chablis	Chardonnay	Chicken and
			Pinot Blanc	Veal
	Loire (Vouvray)	None	Chenin Blanc	Light Luncheon
			Fumé Blanc	Grilled Oceanfish
	Bordeaux (Graves)	None	Dry Sémillon	Oysters and Clams
	Bordeaux (Sauterne)	Sauterne	Sweet Sauvignon	Fresh Fruits
	Rhine	Rhine	Johannisberg	Trout and
			Riesling	Salmon
			Traminer	
	Italy	None	Moscato di Canelli	Rich Desserts
ROSES	None	Vin Rosé	Grenache Rosé	Picnic Fare
			Gamay Rosé	

THE MAJOR EASTERN WINES

	International Equivalent	Generic Name	Varietal Names	Especially Good With
REDS	Burgundy	Burgundy	Concord	Stews and
			Ives	Casseroles
			Baco Noir*	Roast Meat
			Foch*	Roast Meat
WHITES	Burgundy	Chablis	Delaware	Poultry
			Diamond	Poultry
			Seyval Blanc*	Oceanfish and
			Villard Blanc*	Shellfish
	Bordeaux (Sauternes)	Sauterne	Catawba	Rich Desserts
			Concord	
	Rhine	Rhine	Dutchess	Fresh Fruits
			Elvira	
			Aurora*	
ROSES	None	Vin Rosé	Catawba	Picnic Fare
			Cascade*	

*Wines from new French-American hybrid grapes.

Martinis

The martini is no newcomer to the scene. It was invented in the 1860's in San Francisco. The early recipe called for equal amounts of vermouth and gin with a little maraschino liqueur or sugar syrup to make it sweet. A dash of bitters was also added.

Today martini lovers, who are legion in numbers, usually consider the accepted formula of 3 parts gin to 1 part dry vermouth not quite dry enough, but that is a variable of personal taste. Real connoisseurs shudder at the prevalent custom of drinking martinis poured over ice cubes or "on the rocks" in modern parlance. They claim the perfect martini is served in a pre-chilled stemmed cocktail glass.

When hosting a large cocktail party, buy gin by the half gallon. Pour out a cup of gin and replace it with 1 cup of vermouth. This will make a very dry martini and can be made less dry be increasing the vermouth. This will make 30 drinks.

Manhattan

3 parts rye or bourbon
1 part Italian sweet vermouth
Dash of Angostura bitters

Stir well with ice until thoroughly chilled. Strain into a cocktail glass or serve "on the rocks."

Bloody Mary

1 teaspoon lemon juice
1½ to 2 ounces vodka or gin
4 ounces (½ cup) tomato juice
2 drops Tabasco
1/8 teaspoon cracked black pepper
½ cup shaved ice

Mix all the ingredients. Stir well or spin in the blender for 30 seconds. Serve in an old-fashioned glass. For additional nutrition stir in 1/8 teaspoon powdered vitamin C.

Whiskey Sour
(1 cocktail)

1 tablespoon lemon juice
1½ to 2 ounces bourbon or rye
1 teaspoon sugar
½ cup shaved ice
1 slice orange
1 maraschino cherry

Put the lemon juice, whiskey, sugar and ice in a pitcher or in a blender. Stir well or spin for 30 seconds. Strain into a wineglass and garnish with an orange slice and a cherry. For extra nutrition stir in 1/8 teaspoon vitamin C.

Daiquiris

1 tablespoon lemon juice
1½ to 2 ounces light rum
1 teaspoon sugar
½ cup finely shaved ice

Combine the ingredients, multiplied as many times as necessary. Shake well in a cocktail shaker or spin in a blender for 30 seconds. Strain into a cocktail glass or serve with the ice in an old-fashioned glass with small straws.

Hot Buttered Rum

Rum distilled from molasses was being made in considerable quantity by the early eighteenth century. When and where the particular drink was invented is a mystery but it's popular today, particularly with winter sports enthusiasts.

Into each heated mug, put 1 lump of sugar, 4 tablespoons of boiling water, ½ teaspoon allspice, 4 tablespoons of dark rum and 2 teaspoons of butter or margarine. Stir well. Fill the mug with boiling water and serve very hot.

Kentucky Mint Julep

The best way to make a mint julep is the subject of a continuing argument that will never be solved, but everyone agrees that the pint-sized metal mug or glass in which it is to be served must be icy cold. The modern home freezer is perfect for this. For each serving, put a teaspoon of sugar dissolved in a tablespoon of water in the bottom of each glass or mug. Crush a small mint leaf against the rim and drop it in. Fill with shaved ice and pour in enough bourbon to cover the ice. Garnish with sprigs of mint.

Raspberry Shrub

Shrubs are fruit-based drinks with or without the addition of rum or brandy. Raspberry Shrub can be served either way.

2 quarts raspberries
2 cups white vinegar
Sugar
Light rum (optional)

Pick over the washed berries and put them in a non-metal bowl. Add the vinegar. Cover and let stand for 2 days. Mash them well and put in a jelly bag and let the juice drip without pressing it. Combine equal amounts of sugar and juice and boil for 20 minutes. Pour into sterilized bottles and cap immediately.
To Serve: Put 2 tablespoons of raspberry syrup in each glass. Add the light rum if desired. Fill the glass ¾ full with cold water. Stir briskly and add ice cubes.

Stone Fence

This is another drink the name of which seems to make no sense, but the drink itself carries a message.

Applejack or bourbon
Sweet cider

Put 4 tablespoons of applejack or bourbon in each tall glass. Add 1 cup of sweet cider. For extra nutrition, add 1/8 teaspoon powdered vitamin C. Stir well and fill with ice cubes.

Tom and Jerry
(8 mugs)

Like most things alcoholic, the story of the naming of this drink has many versions. The drink itself is a hot one planned for cold winter nights.

8 egg whites
3 tablespoons sugar
8 egg yolks
1½ cups brandy
1½ cups Jamaica rum
1 quart rich milk, scalded
Freshly grated nutmeg

Beat the egg whites until stiff, adding the sugar gradually while beating.

Beat the egg yolks until thick and pale. Fold in the egg whites gently but thoroughly. Pour the mixture into a punch bowl or large crockery pitcher. Add the brandy, rum and hot milk. Stir briskly and dust with nutmeg. Serve in large heated mugs.

A Yard of Flannel

This drink was designed to ward off the cold weather on New England winter nights. A bartender who could flip a flip with debonair dexterity was a much-admired man.

3 pints of ale
6 eggs
6 tablespoons sugar
½ teaspoon ginger
1 teaspoon nutmeg
¾ cup New England rum

Beat the eggs hard, adding the sugar, spices, and rum. Put the mixture into a pitcher. At the same time heat the ale almost to the boiling point and put in another pitcher. Pour some of it slowly into the egg mixture, whisking briskly. Then pour some of the egg mixture back into the ale pitcher. To be traditional, flip the mixtures back and forth between pitchers until well blended. Serve in heated mugs.

Eggnog
(24 glasses)

Eggnog is a drink that has been used by generations of Americans. It was sometimes thought of as a medicine to build strength in convalescing patients, but it was just as often used as it is today for wintertime festivities.

1 dozen eggs
¾ cup sugar
1 pint bourbon or rye
½ pint rum
1½ quarts milk
1 pint heavy cream, whipped
Fresh nutmeg

Separate the eggs. Beat the egg yolks, adding the sugar gradually until the mixture is thick and lemon-colored. Add the liquors and the milk and mix well.

Beat the egg whites until stiff. Fold them and the whipped cream into the egg yolk mixture and serve in a punch bowl. Ladle into punch glasses and sprinkle each one with freshly grated nutmeg.

Spicy Mulled Cider
(24 mugs)

1 gallon sweet cider
2 cups brown sugar
1 cup lemon juice
2 teaspoons cinnamon
1 teaspoon cloves
1 teaspoon nutmeg
1 teaspoon ground ginger
1 teaspoon allspice
Orange slices

Bring all the ingredients except for the orange slices just to a boil over moderate heat. Remove from the stove and let the cider stand for several hours in a cool place. Reheat before serving. Pour into a punch bowl and float orange slices on the cider. Serve in warm mugs.

Syllabub

A syllabub is a ladylike version of eggnog which was considered mild enough for the whole family, including the youngest child, to drink on a festive occasion. Its chief characteristic is a frothy top which was eaten with a spoon before the rest of it was drunk. One method of achieving this froth was to place the punch bowl filled with wine and seasonings directly under a cow's udder and to milk directly into the bowl; this gave a fine froth. The modern method uses egg whites to achieve a similar effect.

1 bottle chilled wine or sherry
3 lemons
2 cups sugar
2 quarts milk
1 pint all-purpose cream
6 egg whites
Fresh nutmeg

Mix the white wine or sherry with the grated rind of the lemons and ½ cup of lemon juice. Stir in 1¼ cups of sugar until it dissolves. Add the milk and cream and put in a punch bowl.

Beat the egg whites until almost stiff. Add the remaining sugar, still beating. Spoon the egg whites over the surface of the milk-wine mixture and sprinkle with freshly grated nutmeg.

Hot Toddy

Fill an old-fashioned glass half full of boiling water. Add 1 teaspoon of sugar and stir until it dissolves. Add 1½ to 2 ounces of brandy, rye or bourbon and serve with a small slice of lemon. Serve very hot.

Cherry Bounce

The "bounce" and "shrub" seem to be interchangeable.

2 quarts pie cherries
1 quart New England rum
Sugar

Remove the pits from the cherries and put them in a stone crock or large glass jar. Cover with the rum. Let stand in a cool place for 1 week. Strain in a jelly bag. Add as much sugar as needed. It should not be too sweet.
To serve: Put 2 tablespoonfuls of the syrup into a tall glass. Fill ¾ full with cold water. Mix well. For extra nutrition, stir in 1/8 teaspoon powdered vitamin C. Add ice cubes and a slice of orange.

White Wine Punch
(50 glasses)

1 quart weak tea
2 cups cranberry juice
2 cups orange juice
2 cups lemon juice
1 gallon California Chablis
1 pint brandy
1 quart sherry
2 quarts soda water
Sugar
1 lemon
1 orange

Combine the tea, fruit juices, wine, brandy, and sherry. Taste to see if it is sweet enough to suit you. If not, dissolve some sugar in a little hot water and sweeten to taste. Divide the punch between 2 gallon jugs.
To Serve: Pour 1 jug of wine mixture in a punch bowl over a large block of ice, which can be made by filling a bread pan with water and freezing it for several hours. Add 1 quart of soda water and garnish with small lemon and orange slices. Repeat as often as necessary.

Fish House Punch

This punch has been the pride of Philadelphia since the early part of the eighteenth century when Washington's officers made it their favorite.

1½ to 2 cups sugar
4 cups lemon juice
½ gallon Jamaica rum
1 quart brandy
½ cup peach or apricot brandy

Dissolve the sugar in ¼ cup of water. Add the remaining ingredients and pour over ice cubes. Place in the refrigerator for several hours, stirring occasionally. Serve in small punch glasses or cocktail glasses. Three (12-ounce) cans of frozen lemonade concentrate may be substituted for the sugar and lemon juice.

All Fruit Punch

1 (12-ounce) can frozen lemonade
2 (6-ounce) cans concentrated frozen
  orange juice
1 pint white grape juice
1 pint pineapple juice
1 cup cranberry juice
2 quarts iced ginger ale
2 pints iced soda water
1 pint strawberries, washed and sliced

Dilute the lemonade and 1 can of the orange juice according to directions. Add the other can of orange juice without diluting. Add the grape, pineapple, and cranberry juice. Mix well. Divide between 2 half-gallon jugs and keep in a cool place until ready to serve.

Pour the contents of one of the jugs into a punch bowl and add ice cubes. Stir well to chill the punch. Add 1 bottle of ginger ale and 1 bottle of soda. Put in half the strawberries and ladle the punch into punch glasses. Repeat the process when necessary.

Frozen strawberries can be used, but they will sweeten the punch.

THE SATURDAY EVENING POST

An Illustrated Weekly Magazine
Founded A°. D! 1728 by Benj. Franklin

JULY 29, 1905   **FIVE CENTS THE COPY**

Dandelion Wine

The time to make dandelion wine is when the dandelion blossoms first carpet the lawn. For some reason dandelion wine used to be considered proper even by some of those who abstained from alcohol. It takes 5 weeks to make it.

12 cups dandelion blossoms
7 pints boiling water
2 oranges, sliced
4 lemons, sliced
1 package dry yeast
1 pint lukewarm water
10 cups sugar

Pick only blossoms that are young and full. Use no stems or leaves. Put the blossoms in an earthenware crock or deep enamel kettle. Add the boiling water and stir well. Cover and let stand 4 days, stirring from time to time.

Strain the liquid through a jelly bag or a cheese-cloth-lined strainer. Wash out the crock or kettle. Put the strained liquid back and add the oranges and lemons, the yeast dissolved in a pint of lukewarm water and the sugar. Stir until the sugar dissolves. Cover and let stand 3 more days. Strain the liquid again the same way.

Wash the crock out again and put back the liquid. Cover and keep in a cool place for a month without stirring. Strain once more and pour into sterilized quart bottles. Screw the caps on very tightly. Chill before serving. Dandelion wine is better if it is allowed to stand several months before using.

Switchel

This brew is a nonalcoholic drink invented to quench the thirst of farmers working in the hay field. Some farmers were known to add a little hard cider or whiskey just to make the work seem easier, but even without such an additive it is a refreshing and very healthful beverage.

1 cup unsulfured molasses
¾ cup cider vinegar
1 teaspoon powdered ginger
2 quarts spring water
¼ teaspoon powdered vitamin C

Mix the ingredients together in a jug and refrigerate until very cold. Serve with ice cubes.

Perfect Tea

Tea was known in this country as early as 1680, but it was regarded as a highly suspicious drink leading to public debauchery and moral indiscretions as well as ill health. Writers and preachers were strong in their protest about it in the early years, but that period gave way to one of enormous consumption of tea which still exists. The rules for making good tea are few but essential.

1. Bring fresh cold water rapidly to the boil.
2. Heat a nonmetal teapot by rinsing it out in boiling water.
3. Put in 1 teaspoon or 1 tea bag for every cup of water.
4. Pour in 1 cup of water. Cover and let steep for 2 minutes.
5. Add the rest of the requisite amount of water. Cover with a tea cozy or a double thickness of a tea cloth for 2 more minutes.
6. If the teapot does not have a strainer, provide yourself with a small tea strainer.

Serve with lemon slices, sugar, milk (not cream) and rum if desired.

Café Brûlot

4 cups strong fresh coffee
Peel of 1 small orange
Peel of 1 small lemon
6 cloves
2 sticks cinnamon
6 lumps sugar
½ pint brandy

Make the coffee, using, if possible, the kind of coffee that is ground with a little chicory.

Heat water under the chafing dish so that the top part will be hot. Peel the orange and lemon peel very thin so that none of the white is attached. Put in the cloves, cinnamon, and sugar and add the brandy, letting it heat before touching it with a lighted match. Once the brandy is burning, ladle it with a small silver ladle to keep the brandy burning while slowly adding the prepared hot coffee. When the flames subside ladle into demitasses and serve at the table.

Old Fashioned Hot Chocolate

A wedding gift that brides used to cherish was a chocolate set complete with a graceful pot and cups to match.

5 cups milk
3 ounces bitter chocolate
2 cups boiling water or hot coffee
1/8 teaspoon salt
2/3 cup sugar
1 tablespoon vanilla
½ pint cream, whipped

Scald the milk in the top of a large double boiler. Melt the chocolate in a small pan. Add the hot water or coffee gradually, whisking until well blended. Add the salt and sugar and boil for 5 minutes, stirring until the sugar dissolves.

Pour the chocolate mixture and the vanilla into the scalded milk and keep whisking until well blended. Cover and cook for 10 minutes. Beat again just before serving.

Put a little dab of unsweetened whipped cream on each filled cup.

Café Au Lait

This morning coffee, while French in origin, has been adopted by many Americans, particularly in those sections of the country where there are French descendants. Two coffeepots of similar size and shape make this a pleasant presentation at breakfast time.

3 or 4 cups freshly brewed strong coffee
3 or 4 cups whole or skim milk
Sugar

Brew the coffee by your favorite method, using, if possible, a coffee ground with a little chicory. Put in a heated coffeepot.

At the same time scald the milk to the boiling point and pour into another pot.

Holding a pot in each hand as high as you dare, pour from both pitchers into a cup so that the top is frothy. Let each person sweeten to taste.

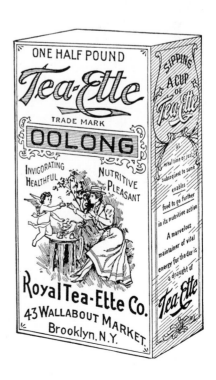

Jeff Davis Punch

1½ pints lemon juice
3¼ pounds sugar, dissolved in water
12 bottles claret
1½ bottles sherry
½ bottle brandy
½ pint Jamaica rum
1 cup maraschino liqueur
3 bottles ginger ale
6 bottles mineral water or soda

Garnish with 2 lemons sliced thin; half of a cucumber sliced with peel on; one orange sliced.

If too strong, water may be added till the quantity reaches 5 gallons. Best if made 24 hours before using, adding ice, the ginger ale and mineral water just before serving.

Ale Flip

Beat separately 2 egg whites and 4 yolks. Combine them, adding 4 tablespoons of moistened sugar, and ½ nutmeg, grated. Put 1 quart ale in saucepan and bring to boil. Pour into it the egg-sugar mixture, gradually, stirring as you add.

Transfer the steaming result to robust pitcher and pour back and forth rapidly between this pitcher and its twin brother, each time holding the pourer high above the receiver, till a handsome froth is attained.

Serve in mugs or large goblets.

New Orleans Fizz

Juice of ½ lime and ½ lemon
1 ounce sweet cream
2 ounces dry gin
White of 1 egg
3 dashes Orange Flower Water
½ teaspoon powdered sugar (optional)

Prepare a tall glass by dipping the rim in a saucer of lemon juice and then in powdered sugar. Combine ingredients and pour into a shaker with cracked ice (use any glass jar with a screw-top lid, if you haven't a special cocktail shaker). Shake very vigorously—some recommend 12 minutes of shaking to achieve the proper froth. Add a dash of seltzer, if desired, and pour into the prepared glass.

Mulled Wine

1 pint Burgundy or claret plus
   1 glass of the same
½ nutmeg
Yolks of 4 eggs
Sugar to taste

Grate nutmeg into pint of wine and sweeten to taste. Heat to the boiling point and set aside. Beat the egg yolks and strain them into the glass of cold wine. Add the cold mixture gradually to the hot, stirring constantly, and then pour back and forth, from one container to another, 5 or 6 times. Reheat, stirring constantly, till mixture thickens. Serve in mugs.

Advertisement, THE SATURDAY EVENING POST, *1904*

FINISHING TOUCHES: GARNISHINGS AND BLANDISHMENTS

It may not be such a long way, except in memory, from the days of the Pilgrims to the scientifically prepared food of the astronauts.

We have not in this book worked our way patiently through 200 years of American cookery with an eye cocked for a final chapter in which to have at you with a dramatic package of prepared capsulated goodies, weighing two ounces, which will sustain a man in flight through the Milky Way for six months.

But we cannot help being diverted by the little cranberries which appeared as part of that first Thanksgiving meal in 1621, which is the same table setting on which this book virtually began. "The Indians and English use them much," wrote a voyager who visited Plymouth in 1663, "boiling them in sugar for sauce to eat with their meat and it is a delicate sauce."

From 1663 in the bogs of Massachusetts, where the Pilgrims first found them, to the laboratories of science today, is not such a far cry after all, we suddenly discover.

The Indians knew nothing about medicine, but they knew that the cranberry, which they called *sassamanesh*, was good to eat both raw and cooked. They also pounded the berries together with meat and then added a bit of melted animal fat to hold the thing together. It was called pemmican—and they knew that pemmican would help keep them healthy through winter. (They even used cranberries on wounds, to help cure the possible infection.)

Cranberry juice, which New Englanders have been quaffing for lo these 356 years, it now turns out, is just crammed full of vitamin C, which authorities are becoming increasingly convinced is one of the wonders of dietary protection and nutrition. Vitamin C eliminated scurvy, which had plagued the navies of the world for centuries, and, as a medical preventive in this role, may be said to have made possible most of the great voyages of discovery following the sixteenth century.

So hearken to this amazing link, then, between colonial Indian lore and the modern laboratory. We know that fruits contain vitamin C and we are urged on all sides to make them a regular part of our diet . . . so on a comparative basis, on a value listing based on products with label stating 30 milligrams per six-ounce serving, well-known vitamin C providers such as apple juice hit at 2; raw apricot, 10; raw blackberries at 30; *and cranberry juice hits 40!*

This brings us to the simple sensible modern point of view that a solid intake of vitamin C insures health and increases resistance to infectious diseases. On that basis, we have a few final observations in this review of American cooking concerning a scientifically contemporary judicious use of vitamin C in your household cooking. The natural fact is that except for liver, foods such as meats, poultry and fish contain no vitamin C. Vegetables may be naturally rich in vitamin C but lose it in the cooking process. Vitamin C is not altogether stable in storage. So you're not really too far off in deciding that one of the latter-day blandishments you can add to your All-American cooking is a little vitamin C. Stir it in, or sprinkle it on, just before serving. If you like smoked and cured

*He causeth the grass to grow
for the cattle, and herb for the
service of man, that he may
bring forth food out of the
earth, and wine that maketh
glad the heart of man.*

Psalms

Cover painting, THE SATURDAY EVENING POST, *April 11, 1908.*

meat dishes you can add one-half teaspoon of powdered vitamin C per six servings of these dishes—ham casseroles, chipped beef on toast, beans and franks, and so on. Sprinkle it on fresh fruit or stir it into salad dressings, as suggested in the recipes that follow this section.

Anyway, since this little *finale con espresso* is our way of bowing offstage on our presentation of American cooking, we have one final fillip to add to our work of love and taste. These are words of the incomparable George Rector, without doubt the most distinguished gourmet and chef d'oeuvre ever to have been associated with American cooking. Rector for so many years, and over the course of dozens and dozens of articles on the culinary art in *The Saturday Evening Post*, instructed us in the wherewithals and the whatwithals. And, so as a final word of esprit on the delicate art of making salads and salad dressings, the sonatina to the full symphony of a complete meal, we quote from the master himself:

"People always quote at you the old Spanish recipe for salad: 'A spendthrift with the oil, a miser with the vinegar, a wise man with the salt—and a madman to mix it.' Very sound as far as it goes, but only the beginning of wisdom. It leaves out the pepper, which, if possible, should be freshly ground in coarse flakes out of one of those intriguing little French pepper mills which look like an old-fashioned wooden inkstand. It also leaves out the garlic, which is about like leaving the rum or brandy out of a plum pudding.

"If you're one of those people who can't stand even the idea of garlic, skip this next paragraph. But, if you recognize the subtler virtues of that vegetable vanilla which is the heart and soul of so much good eating, remember that it should be used sparingly for most tastes, with the care of a medieval alchemist mixing powdered unicorn's horn into the elixir of life. My own way of getting that tinge of Italian railway guard into your salad is to rub the inside of the bowl with a clove of garlic. The French method is to take the crusty nubbin off the end of one of those three-foot cigars of French bread, rub it briskly with garlic and then throw the nubbin into the bowl while mixing, removing it before serving. To slice garlic into the bowl, as some do, is a dirty trick, since anybody who gets one of the slices in his plateful is going to be a social pariah for the next three days, not to mention waking up the next morning with a taste in his mouth as if he has planted the grandfather of all onions there the night before. I do, however, know salad fiends who make their dressing in pint lots and soak a sliced clove of garlic in it for twenty-four hours before using, then fishing out the slices and throwing them away. The subtlest touch I know of is the procedure of the old-time chef who said he used to chew up a clove of garlic and then breathe lightly into the bowl. I wouldn't seriously recommend that, but the other dodges will enable you to vary the garlic tang to suit your own taste, not forgetting the public menace you may turn into if you overdo it.

"No two people can ever come to an agreement on just what ought to go into a French dressing. Several experts of my acquaintance have driven themselves

*Man can live without poetry,
music and art; We may live
without heart; We may live
without friends; we may live
without books; But civilized
man can not live
without cooks.*

Edward Lytton

practically out of their minds trying to write down a formula which will give the same results as an inspired impromptu. This is the nearest I've ever been able to come to it: Rub two teaspoons of salt, a teaspoon of freshly ground pepper, a teaspoon of paprika, a half teaspoon of powdered sugar—not absolutely necessary—a half teaspoon of powdered mustard, good and fresh, and a few grains of cayenne all together in the bottom of a bowl. Then slowly drip in a cup of olive oil, stirring briskly all the time until the dry stuff is thoroughly emulsified. Into that drip a quarter cup of vinegar, also stirred and beaten vigorously. Then taste it, making sure your sample is thoroughly mixed, for oil and vinegar don't take long to separate, and make your own personal improvements on that base.

"Variations will range all over the reservation. You may prefer a dash of Tabasco instead of the cayenne, or a quarter teaspoon of Worcestershire sauce as a suggestion of richening, or a little more vinegar if your tastes run to the sharp; say, a half cup of vinegar to your cup of oil. The sour ingredient, in fact, gives room for all kinds of ingenuity. The Frenchman insists on red-wine vinegar, which is hard to beat, but also hard to get in this country, and a good cider or malt vinegar goes very smoothly. Combining cider vinegar with a little tarragon vinegar gives an added tang, but I have never been able to approve of using all tarragon, for that chokes off all the other flavors except the garlic—you can't extinguish garlic with anything but sulfuric acid. Some people use fresh lemon juice for souring, with a teaspoon of tarragon for flavor. Lemon juice is a lot sourer than vinegar

and so dilutes the oil less, giving a better body—one part lemon juice to four of oil is plenty sour for any taste. Any and all of those dodges are worth trying as you explore after your own heart's desire.

"If you feel thrifty, you'll find that a good clean cottonseed or corn oil makes a fair dressing, but step up the sour a little to match its heavier body. A nice creamy effect is produced by rubbing the yolks of a couple of hard-boiled eggs into the dry ingredients before mixing, and it also adds that suggestion of egg flavor which fits very comfortably with good crisp greens. I have even got good results out of beating up a couple of raw egg yolks with the dry seasonings before dripping in the oil and vinegar.

"Knowing the hang of a good dressing is as convenient for emergencies as knowing how to swim. Very few restaurants make a really good salad and most of them haven't the vaguest notion where to begin, or else won't take the trouble to do the thing right. The usual consequence of ordering a plain salad is a china bowl containing several cold hunks of head lettuce, rubbery and discouraging, dripped over with a small quantity of watery stuff the color of what you drain off boiled cabbage and just about as flavorsome. The man who knows his way about among dressings, and has reason to suspect that he is in for that kind of mistreatment, can always bully the waiter into bringing him oil, vinegar, pepper, salt and mustard, get the lettuce properly separated in a bowl and, with a fork and a saucer, concoct himself a salad that the other patrons would sell their souls for. That not only gets you something fit to eat, it also makes

They say fish should swim
thrice . . . first it should swim
in the sea, then it should swim
in butter, and at last, sirrah, it
should swim in good claret.

Swift

the waiter respect you as he never did before.

"Back in the old days at Rector's any number of our customers went so far as to keep their own salad setups on the premises—special carafes of vinegar and oil and special brands of paprika and special pepper grinders. The moment they uttered the word salad the waiter tore off and brought along the outfit. It was just like keeping your own shaving mug with your name on it in the old-fashioned barbershop. As for one's domestic life, the man who lays in a salad bowl and convinces himself that he is the sole author of a good salad dressing is not only putting on a show that does his own ego a great deal of good, he is also saving his wife a great deal of spare trouble. I can't blame a woman, wife or cook, engaged in preparing a whole dinner, for yielding to the temptation to scamp the salad course. Any man who feels rebellious about that scamping has only to follow these words of wisdom, give his own sense of taste a chance to spread itself, and enjoy himself doing the job right.

"Of course salad making involves more than a bowl, a dressing and properly prepared greens. You need the right kind of soul and a knowledge of how to bring the ingredients together under the best possible auspices. We left the lettuce in the bowl, dry and disorganized and crisping in the refrigerator. Fetch it out and give it plenty of dressing, being careful to stir and stir as you pour, so oil and vinegar will stay in the right proportions. Then mix with the wooden fork and spoon, over and over again, using the same motion as an Italian cook lifting spaghetti out of the pot. Gently, though—don't take that madman business too

seriously. Keep it up until every leaf of greens is well coated on both sides and there is no dressing loose in the bottom. A good many people would consider it ready to serve at this point and, provided the dressing is good, it would be very pretty eating too. But it lacks the last refinement—that dressing should have more of a chance to soak into the greens. So, after mixing, put the bowl back into the refrigerator for twenty minutes or so before serving. Then out she comes, chilled and crisp again and yet chewy and wilty as well. That sounds like a contradiction, and I can't explain why it isn't gone. All I can say is, follow those gems of good advice and you'll see what I mean.

"For each leaf will both crunch and linger on the tongue and the imperceptible bitter savor of the greens will be playing ring-around-a-rosy with the tang of the garlic and the sweetness and body of the oil and the bite of the vinegar and the rasp of the pepper and the pucker of the tarragon and the tickle of the salt. Cataloguing it off that way fails to do justice to the beauties of the six-cornered blend, smooth and pungent at the same time. It's as exultant an effect as the harmonizing in a Gilbert and Sullivan finale, and as solidly satisfying as diving through a wave. You can go on from there ad infinitum. Try throwing in a little chopped parsley or chopped chives or both. And, if you just don't give a hoot about your social standing, a few chopped scallions. Chopped fresh tarragon, provided you haven't used tarragon vinegar, is also a beautiful idea.

"I quite understand that, at this point, I shouldn't

Cover painting, THE SATURDAY EVENING POST, *January 9, 1954*

give the impression that a plain greens-and-dressing salad is the only frog in the salad puddle. My pet hot-weather lunch, especially if I've made it myself, is a salad of cold cooked vegetables, string beans, peas, carrots, beets, whatever is left in the icebox, tossed up with lettuce and liberal quantities of a good Thousand Island dressing. For all that it looks so complicated, a Thousand Island dressing is merely a mayonnaise mixed two to one with chili sauce, a teaspoon of Worcestershire, a cup of whipped cream, and discreet proportions of chopped green peppers, chopped chives, and chopped stuffed olives. But that doesn't interfere with my expressing my conviction that a salad is a salad composed fundamentally of green stuff.

"The combination of pineapple, cream cheese and maraschino cherry is pretty to look at and pleasant enough to eat as a kind of subdessert. Properly chilled and daintily served, it has its own high virtues. But it isn't a salad and it doesn't belong in the salad spot, which is following the heavy course of a meal with something light and yet emphatic.

"It's much the same with cocktails, which should be equally emphatic and yet anything but cloying. Every man knows that there are only four or five kinds of cocktails worth drinking—the simplest and probably the driest. It's the female influence which produced the weird and syrupy concoctions with fancy names which clutter up every big bar's list and drive bartenders into the delicatessen business. The other day I was looking down a list of salads in a big cookbook, and I couldn't tell whether I was reading about fancy drinks or the entrants in a show of prize dahlias: Chiaroscuro Salad, I read, Exotique, Fandango, Frou-Frou, High Life, Ladies' Delight, Lollipop, Maiden Blush, Oh My, Yvonne, Wedding Ring and Mona Lisa. I didn't have the moral courage to look up what a Lollipop salad was made of. The one that brazenly called itself Marshmallow Dream Salad was all too self-evident, and a worthy peer of a salad I once met consisting of fresh violets and whipped cream.

"Fruit, on the other hand, has a definite place in the salad sun. Three hundred years ago, when the English understood salads a lot better than they do now, a piece of lemon rind was often included in the dressing—not a bad idea either. Thin-sliced orange or chunked-up grapefruit, lying on a bed of romaine, and well soused in a sharp dressing, is one of the best possible follow-up dishes for something hot and heavy, like curry. I'm not sure whether an alligator pear is fruit or vegetable, but I do know that half of one with the seed out and the hollow containing a teaspoonful of good French dressing is a beautiful experience. It also slices well in combination with some citrus fruit and lettuce. Raw carrots, cut shoestring style, and tomatoes have a prescriptive right along with the lettuce, if you wish. But a word of warning about tomatoes—unless you use caution, they drain so much juice into your pet dressing that it will be miserably watered down. Cut them in quarters, not in slices, and don't put them in the bowl until the final mixing, just before serving.

"Potato salad, that worthy running mate of the

> *Let the stoics say what they please, we do not eat for the good of living, but because the meat is savory and the appetite is keen.*
>
> *Emerson*

cold cut and the frankfurter, is very special business requiring forethought and loving care. The term usually means cold sliced potatoes with slabs of raw onion mixed in, the whole mixed with mayonnaise or an old-fashioned boiled dressing. That does all right for a slapdash dish, but it is to the real thing as a soda cracker is to a hot biscuit. Here is my private method—so far as I know it has never been exhibited before any of the crowned heads of Europe, the few of them that are left, but it should have been. Since I didn't invent it, I can say what I really think of it. I got the idea originally from the technique employed by the best artist in creamed potatoes who ever approached a stove on this side of the Atlantic.

"You boil potatoes with their jackets on till tender, then peel them quickly and put them in a bowl. Dive into them with a couple of big forks, stabbing and pulling crosswise until they've all broken up coarse and grainy. Give them our special family French dressing to drink, in proportions of a third of a cup to six medium potatoes and let them marinate—cook's slang for soak. When the French dressing has permeated every atom, throw in a half cup of blanched almonds sliced very thin, a couple of tablespoons of fine-chopped onion—a meat grinder does this job without so much eye watering—and another couple of tablespoons of fine-chopped green peppers. Mix it thoroughly and chill it off in the refrigerator. Just before serving, mix in a whole cup of chilled mayonnaise and a tablespoon of fine-chopped parsley, and serve it on lettuce, with paprika sprinkled here and there for garnish. If you like eggs in your salads in general, three or four hard-boiled specimens cut into businesslike chunks introduced along with the onions add both color and flavor. Mutilating your potatoes while they're still hot and "floury" gets rid of that appalling toughness to which the cold boiled potato is generally subject when sliced with a knife. And your cold boiled spuds needn't go to waste because you don't use them in potato salad—cold boiled is the best possible start on hashed brown, and I have yet to meet anybody who looked cross-eyed at hashed 'brown.

"The Frenchman, whose knowledge on these matters commands all possible respects, never bothers with variety in salads. He eats the same type of dressing twice a day all his life and wouldn't know what you were talking about if you suggested that that would be monotonous. Still, such variety as you can introduce with things like Roquefort dressing is all to the good. That is a man's-size variation, although you'd hardly want it every day. A little less pepper and salt in the dressing this time, then, after it's all made, a discreet quantity of Roquefort cheese crumbled up with a fork, say a quarter of a pound to a pint of dressing. The one disadvantage is that leftover dressing has to be kissed good-bye, since Roquefort is husky stuff and plays queer tricks when left in conjunction with oil and vinegar. There is another beauty of straight French dressing. It stays put till next time without a whimper. In fact, ardent dressing hounds of my acquaintance make up theirs in quart lots and use it along for a week or more, insisting that, like whisky, it improves with age."

Handmade Mayonnaise
(2½ cups)

2 egg yolks
1 tablespoon salt
1 teaspoon Dijon-type mustard
1/8 teaspoon white pepper
2 cups salad oil or 1 cup olive oil
    plus 1 cup peanut oil
3 tablespoons wine or cider vinegar
2 tablespoons boiling water

Combine the egg yolks, salt, mustard and pepper in a bowl placed on a rubber mat so that it won't slip. Whisk well before starting to add the oil drop by drop. Continue until the mixture begins to thicken. Continue adding oil ½ teaspoon by ½ teaspoon until half the oil is incorporated. Still beating, add the vinegar. This makes a fairly sharp mayonnaise, so use less vinegar if you prefer a blander taste. Add the last cup of oil tablespoon by tablespoon, still beating hard. Finally add the boiling water and beat until blended.

    Put in a jar. Cover and keep in refrigerator.

Beater Mayonnaise
(2 cups)

3 egg yolks
1 teaspoon salt
1 teaspoon Dijon-type mustard
1/8 teaspoon white pepper
2 cups salad oil or 1 cup olive oil
    plus 1 cup peanut oil or corn oil
2 tablespoons wine or cider vinegar
2 tablespoons boiling water
¼ teaspoon powdered vitamin C

Beat the egg yolks with the salt, mustard and pepper until thick. Start adding the oil in a very thin stream, never stopping the beater. When ¾ cup of oil has been added, add the vinegar slowly and continue with the rest of the oil at a slightly more rapid pace. Beat in the water. Put in a jar, cover and store in the refrigerator. Stir in vitamin C just before serving.

Variation: Herb Mayonnaise. Use tarragon vinegar and add 2 tablespoons of mixed chopped herbs (tarragon, chives, parsley). Do not store this very long. It is delicious with cold salmon.

To Users of DURKEE'S SALAD DRESSING
"A thousand different shapes it bears,
Comely in thousand shapes appears."— *Cowley.*

Blender Mayonnaise
(1½ cups)

1 egg
2 tablespoons lemon juice
1 cup salad oil or ½ cup olive
   oil plus ½ cup peanut or corn oil
½ teaspoon salt
1/8 teaspoon pepper
½ teaspoon dry mustard
1 tablespoon boiling water
¼ teaspoon vitamin C

Put the egg, lemon juice, 4 tablespoons of oil, the salt, pepper, and mustard in a blender. Cover and spin while you are counting to six slowly. Remove the center of the cover and gradually pour in a thin stream of oil. Immediately after the oil is used add the boiling water and stop blending. Place in a jar, cover and refrigerate. Stir in vitamin C just before serving. This is a lighter dressing.

Boiled Creamy Dressing

3 tablespoons flour
2 teaspoons dry mustard
1 teaspoon salt
1 tablespoon sugar
2 eggs, slightly beaten
6 tablespoons vinegar
¾ cup milk
3 tablespoons butter
4 tablespoons heavy sweet or
   commercial sour cream
¼ teaspoon powdered vitamin C

Combine all the ingredients except for the cream in a heavy saucepan, using a sturdy whisk. Beat constantly and vigorously while cooking over medium heat until the mixture thickens. Remove from the heat, add the sweet or sour cream and allow to cool. This may be stored in a covered jar for several days. Stir in vitamin C just before serving.

French Dressing and Variations

Many dressings are named "French" but don't deserve the title. Real French dressing is classically oil, vinegar, salt and pepper. There are legitimate variations with such additions as herbs, mustard, garlic, and onion, but the general rule of being miserly with vinegar and generous with oil will give the right basis.

2 teaspoons salt
½ teaspoon freshly milled pepper or
   cracked black pepper
¼ to 1/3 cup vinegar (wine, cider, tarragon)
1 cup olive oil or 1 cup peanut or
   vegetable oil or ½ cup each
¼ teaspoon powdered vitamin C

Put all the ingredients except the vitamin C into a small covered jar and shake well. The dressing can be stored in the refrigerator. Add the vitamin C and shake again just before serving.

Variations:
   Add 1 clove pressed garlic or 1 teaspoon scraped onion or
   2 tablespoons chopped herbs (parsley, chives, tarragon) or
   1 teaspoon Dijon-type mustard or
   all the variations together.

Tartar Sauce
(1¼ cups)

1 cup mayonnaise
1 tablespoon capers
1 tablespoon chopped parsley
1½ tablespoons chopped dill pickle
1 tablespoon scraped onion
¼ teaspoon powdered vitamin C

Mix the ingredients and chill for several hours in a covered jar. Stir in vitamin C just before serving.

Cream Sauce
(2 cups)

4 tablespoons butter
4 tablespoons flour
2 cups cold milk
Salt and pepper

Heat the butter in a saucepan. Stir in the flour and cook the mixture 2 minutes, stirring with a whisk. Add half the milk and stir hard while it comes to a boil. When the sauce is smooth, add the remaining milk, still stirring. Stir until the sauce is thick and smooth. Season with salt and pepper.

This can be doubled or halved. It can be refrigerated in a covered container for several days and in the freezer indefinitely, ready for use. If it separates in the freezer spin it in a blender or whisk vigorously for a moment.

Cheese Sauce

Cream Sauce (see preceding recipe)
2 cups grated cheddar cheese
1 teaspoon Dijon-type mustard (optional)
¼ teaspoon paprika

Make the cream sauce. When it is smooth reduce the heat and stir in the grated cheese, mustard and paprika. Stir until the cheese melts.

Clarified Butter

Clarified butter is sometimes called for in a recipe. It is simply pure butter distilled from its own whey. To obtain this, place the requisite amount of butter in a heavy saucepan or small double boiler and melt slowly. Carefully pour off the clear butter, leaving the milky sediment in the bottom of the pan.

Mushroom Sauce

Butter
1 small onion, peeled and sliced
1 clove garlic, peeled and sliced
3 tablespoons flour
1½ cups beef stock or canned bouillon
1 teaspoon tomato paste
2 tablespoons Madeira or sherry
½ pound mushrooms
1 teaspoon lemon juice
1/8 teaspoon nutmeg
Salt and pepper

Heat 3 tablespoons of butter in a saucepan. Add the onion and garlic and cook until lightly browned. Remove the vegetables with a slotted spoon and discard. Add the flour and stirring slowly let the mixture brown. Add the stock or bouillon, tomato paste and wine. Stir until smooth. Reduce the heat to low and simmer covered for 20 minutes.

Meanwhile clean and slice the mushrooms lengthwise and sauté them in 3 tablespoons of butter until almost dry. Add the lemon juice and nutmeg and combine with the sauce for the last few minutes of cooking. Season to taste with salt and pepper.

Quick Brown Sauce

4 tablespoons butter
3 tablespoons minced onion
4 tablespoons flour
1 teaspoon salt
¼ teaspoon black pepper
2 tablespoons catsup
2 cups beef stock or
  canned bouillon

Heat the butter in a saucepan and cook the onion over moderate heat, stirring with a wooden spoon until light brown. Add the flour and continue stirring until the flour has browned. Add the remaining ingredients and stir until the sauce boils. Spin in a blender or force through a sieve, adding a few drops of gravy coloring if the sauce is not a rich brown.

Detroit Vapor

Tomato Catsup
(4 pints)

2 dozen large ripe tomatoes
4 large onions, peeled and sliced
3 red peppers, seeded and cut in pieces
1 tablespoon salt
1 bay leaf
1 small red hot pepper
1 tablespoon celery seed
1 tablespoon mustard seed
1 cinnamon stick
8 peppercorns
3 cups cider vinegar
1 cup brown sugar
1 cup white sugar

Peel the tomatoes by dipping each one into boiling water for a moment and slipping off the skins. Put the peeled tomatoes in a large kettle and add the onions, red peppers and salt. Cover the kettle and bring to a boil over moderate heat. Boil until all the vegetables are tender. Force the vegetable juices through a food mill into another deep pan, preferably Teflon-lined or enameled.

Put the bay leaf, hot pepper, celery and mustard seeds, cinnamon stick and peppercorns into a small bag made of cheesecloth and tied with kitchen thread in the kettle. Boil the juice down by half, stirring frequently to prevent scorching. Stir in the vinegar and sugar and bring to a boil again. Cook for 20 minutes, watching it carefully. Taste for sweetness. Some people prefer catsup sweeter than others. Add more sugar if desired. Remove the spice bag. If the sauce is not thick enough, dissolve 1 or 2 tablespoons of cornstarch into 2 to 4 tablespoons of water and add to the catsup. Boil another minute or two. Pour into hot sterilized pint jars and seal.

Quick Tomato Sauce

Tomato sauce is traditionally simmered on the back of the stove for hours, but this sauce takes much less human or fuel energy and serves as an excellent substitute.

2 tablespoons butter
2 tablespoons olive oil
½ cup chopped onion
1 large clove garlic, pressed
1 large (20-ounce) can plum tomatoes
1 (6-ounce) can tomato paste
½ cup red wine
1 cup water
1 teaspoon salt
½ teaspoon sugar
¼ teaspoon black pepper
2 teaspoons chopped fresh basil or
  ½ teaspoon dried basil
½ teaspoon oregano

Heat the butter and oil and sauté the onion and garlic just until soft. Add the remaining ingredients and whisk over high heat until the mixture comes to a boil. Reduce the heat and cook gently for 30 minutes, stirring frequently.

Cocktail Sauce

1½ cups tomato catsup
  bought or homemade
½ cup chopped scallions
  (green and white parts)
1 small clove garlic, pressed
1 tablespoon horseradish sauce
2 teaspoons lemon juice
2 tablespoons Worcestershire sauce
1 tablespoon soy sauce
¼ teaspoon cracked black pepper

Combine all the ingredients in a pint jar. Shake well. Taste to see if more salt is needed. Cover and refrigerate for several hours before using.

Tomato Puree
(Blender made)
(3 cups)

1½ pounds (4 or 5) tomatoes
1 small onion, grated
¼ teaspoon powdered thyme
¼ teaspoon powdered basil
1 clove garlic, minced
3 tablespoons butter
½ teaspoon sugar
¼ teaspoon white pepper
¾ teaspoon salt

Dip each tomato at the end of a long fork into boiling water for a moment. Slip off the skins and halve them, gently squeezing out the seeds. Chop the tomatoes coarsely. There should be 3 cups.

Combine the tomatoes with the onion, herbs and garlic and simmer gently until the tomatoes are cooked. Spin in the blender with the remaining ingredients. This may be reheated for immediate use or stored in a covered container in the refrigerator and reheated later.

N.B. One-half cup of this sauce combined with a full recipe of hollandaise sauce is a delicious combination.

Cranberry Sauce

Cranberries are native to Massachusetts and are grown in large quantities in bogs not far from the sea. They are an integral part of a New England Thanksgiving and Christmas dinner.

1 pound cranberries
1 cup water
2 cups sugar
1 orange

Put the cranberries in a bowl of water and pick out any imperfect ones and any little sticks.

Combine the water and sugar. Stir over medium heat until the sugar dissolves. Boil 5 minutes. Add the cranberries and cook for about 5 minutes or just until the skins pop. Remove from the stove and while still hot add the juice and rind of 1 orange. Stir well. Cool, cover and refrigerate. Serve in a pretty bowl.

Barbecue Sauce
(2½ cups)

This sauce can be kept in a covered jar in the refrigerator for several weeks. It is excellent with pork.

1 medium onion, chopped
2 large cloves garlic, minced
½ cup olive or salad oil
4 tablespoons Worcestershire sauce
1 cup red wine
2 tablespoons soy sauce
4 tablespoons honey
½ teaspoon dried rosemary
¼ teaspoon powdered thyme
1 small bay leaf
2 tablespoons chopped parsley

Simmer the onion and garlic in the oil just until soft. Add the rest of the ingredients. Bring to a boil. Cover, reduce the heat and simmer for 15 minutes. Spin in the blender. Cool. This will keep in the refrigerator for several weeks in a covered jar.

Hollandaise Sauce
(1 cup)

This is probably America's favorite sauce. While Dutch in origin it is American by adoption.

3 large egg yolks
2 tablespoons lemon juice
8 tablespoons (½ cup) butter or margarine
½ teaspoon salt
Cayenne

Beat the egg yolks and lemon juice in the top part of a small double boiler until blended. Set over simmering water and whisk until the mixture begins to thicken. Add 2 tablespoons of the butter and continue beating. When the sauce thickens again add 2 more tablespoons of butter. Continue the process until all the butter has been used. Add the salt and a dash of cayenne. Beat hard for a few moments. Cover and keep warm. Hollandaise never needs to be served hot. It will get its heat from the food it accompanies.

Quick Hollandaise
(6 to 8 servings)

The convenient characteristic of this hollandaise is that it can be made for any number of people. One egg yolk and the proportionate ingredients will be sufficient for 2 people. Four egg yolks will provide enough for 8 servings. Fresh unsalted butter is the best for hollandaise.

3 or 4 egg yolks
3 or 4 tablespoons cream
3 or 4 teaspoons lemon juice
6 to 8 tablespoons butter or margarine
Salt
White pepper
Paprika

Whisk the egg yolks and cream over moderate heat until it starts to thicken. Remove from the heat, and, still whisking, add the lemon juice and a third of the butter. Whisk over heat, adding the rest of the butter in thirds. Never stop whisking. Remove from the heat and season with salt, pepper and a dash of paprika.

This can be made in advance, stored in the refrigerator and heated moderately, whisking hard, just before serving.

Béarnaise Sauce

Hollandaise Sauce
  (preceding 2 recipes)
1 tablespoon chopped parsley
1 teaspoon chopped fresh tarragon
2 teaspoons chopped chives

Make the hollandaise by either method. Stir in the herbs. If fresh tarragon is not to be had, soak ½ teaspoon of the dried herb in a tablespoon of white wine for a few minutes before adding it to the sauce.

Cumberland Sauce
(1½ cups)

1 (6-ounce) glass of currant jelly
1 egg yolk
¾ teaspoon dry mustard
4 tablespoons Port wine
2 tablespoons sugar
2 tablespoons wine vinegar
½ teaspoon salt
1/8 teaspoon cayenne

Melt the jelly over hot water. Stir in the remaining ingredients and keep stirring until the sauce thickens slightly. Serve with ham or venison.

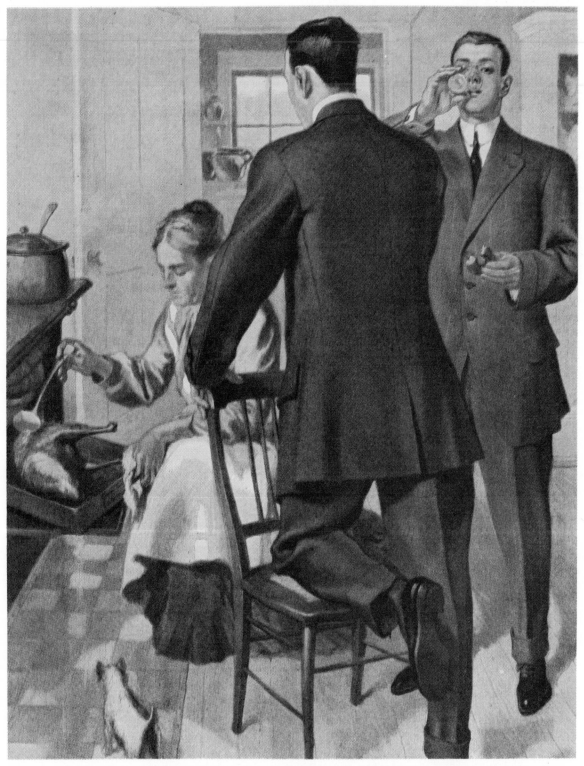

Advertisement for Hart Schaffner & Marx, THE SATURDAY EVENING POST, *November 13, 1909*

Sweet Apple Slices

4 cooking apples
1 cup sugar
½ cup water
½ teaspoon cinnamon
¼ teaspoon nutmeg
¼ teaspoon salt
1 teaspoon vanilla
A few drops red coloring

Peel, core and slice the apples in eighths. Combine the remaining ingredients in a small deep skillet or saucepan and stir over moderately high heat with a wooden spoon until the sugar dissolves. Boil 2 minutes and add half the apple slices. Return to the boil and boil 5 minutes, turning the apple slices once. Remove the apples to a plate with a slotted spoon and put in the rest of the apples and repeat the cooking process. The apples should be just tender and they must preserve their shape. If the syrup gets too thick add a tablespoon or two of boiling water.

Arrange the slices on a pretty glass plate or jelly server.

Apple Butter

1 dozen medium-size cooking apples
1 pint hard cider
Sugar
1 lemon
½ teaspoon powdered cloves
½ teaspoon nutmeg
½ teaspoon allspice
½ tablespoon cinnamon
½ teaspoon salt

Wash the apples and remove the stems. Cut them in chunks without removing skins or cores. Place them in a Teflon-lined or enameled pan and add 1 pint of hard cider. Cover and cook until the apples are soft. Let them cool completely before forcing through a food mill or strainer.

Measure the pulp back into the pan and add half as many cupfuls of sugar. Add the juice and grated rind of the lemon and the spices. Stir with a wooden spoon over moderate heat until the sugar dissolves.

Continue cooking, stirring frequently to prevent burning, until the mixture measures 220 degrees F on a thermometer or until it passes the "sheeting" test which is made by dipping a spoon into the hot butter. If it falls in small drops from the end of the spoon it is not ready, but when it collects in one large drop at the end of the spoon it is ready for bottling. Pour into sterilized 6-ounce jars and cover with paraffin at once. This will make 9 or 10 jars.

Spiced Crab Apples
(3 pints)

18 crab apples
4 cups sugar
1½ cups water
1 pint hard cider
½ teaspoon ginger
2 small sticks cinnamon
10 cloves
Red vegetable coloring

Wash the crab apples well but do not remove the stems. Take off the blossom ends and pierce each apple with a skewer.

Combine the sugar, water, cider and ginger and bring to a rapid boil. Tie the cinnamon and cloves in a small bag and put in the syrup. Boil 3 minutes. Reduce the heat and put in 6 apples. Simmer 6 to 7 minutes after they reach the boiling point. They should be just tender but keep their shape. Transfer the cooked apples with a slotted spoon to a bowl. Repeat the process twice more. Add a few drops of red coloring to the syrup and boil down for 3 more minutes. Pour over the apples, spice bag and all. Cool, cover and refrigerate for at least 24 hours.

Place the crab apples in 3 hot sterilized jars set in a pan of very hot water. Quickly boil down the syrup for 3 more minutes. Hold a silver knife in each jar as you pour in the syrup. Remove the knife and the syrup will be at the right level. Seal the jars tightly and process them by boiling 20 minutes.

Crab Apple Jelly

Crab apples were native to the land and were found everywhere. Too bitter to be eaten by themselves, they had to be sweetened before eating. It is safe to suppose that crab apple jelly was one of the first jellies made by our early housewives.

4 to 5 pounds crab apples
Water
Sugar

Wash the crab apples carefully and remove the stems. Cut them into pieces, removing any worm holes or bad spots. Do not peel or core. Put in a kettle and cover with water. Cover the kettle and cook slowly for 20 minutes or until the apples are very soft. Place in a jelly bag or in a stainless steel strainer lined with cheesecloth and let the juice drip into a deep bowl. Do not press the pulp. Let drip for several hours.

Measure the fruit juice and add an equal amount of sugar. Cook over high heat until the jelly registers 220 degrees F or until it coats a silver spoon. Pour into sterilized 6-ounce jars. This will make 10 to 12 glasses.

Pear Rum Butter

7 or 8 large pears
Water
Sugar
1 lemon
½ teaspoon cinnamon
¼ teaspoon allspice
¼ teaspoon cloves
2 tablespoons dark rum

Peel and core the pears and cut them into chunks. Add 2 cups of water. Cover and simmer just until soft. Mash with a potato masher until smooth. Measure into a bowl. Measure half the amount of sugar, the juice and rind of a lemon, the spices and rum. Cook slowly, stirring frequently, until the sauce is very thick. Seal in sterilized jars.

Wild Grape Jelly

8 cups wild grapes
2 cups bottled grape juice
1 lemon, sliced
Sugar

Wash the grapes and pick the fruit from the stems. Crush in a flat-bottom Teflon-lined or enamel-coated pan. Add the grape juice and bring just to the boil. Simmer for 15 minutes. Put in a jelly bag to drip or in a stainless steel strainer lined with cheesecloth. Let it drip for several hours into a nonmetal bowl. Do not press the pulp. Measure the juice and allow ¾ cup sugar to each cup of juice. Heat the sugar in the oven for 10 minutes.

Bring the juice to a boil and simmer 10 minutes. Add the sugar gradually and cook until the jelly measures 220 degrees F on the thermometer or until it falls in one large drop from the end of a spoon that has been dipped in the jelly.

Plum Preserves

4 pounds Damson or greengage plums
8 cups sugar
1 orange
1 lemon
1 teaspoon cinnamon
½ teaspoon cloves
½ teaspoon cinnamon

Preheat the oven to 300 degrees F. Wash the plums and cut them in half, removing the pit. Slice thin the orange and lemon. Mix the sugar and the spices in a bowl. Put a layer of plums in the bottom of a large baking dish. Cover with a layer of sliced oranges and lemons. Sprinkle with the sugar mixture so that you have a good even layer. Repeat the process, finishing with a layer of sugar. Cover with aluminum foil and bake for 2½ hours. Put into hot sterilized jars. This will make 12 (6-ounce) jars.

Cucumber Relish

18 small cucumbers
8 cups chopped onion
1 cup diced green pepper
1 cup diced red pepper
2 tablespoons salt
1 teaspoon turmeric
2 teaspoons mustard seed
1 teaspoon celery seed
1 cup brown sugar
1 cup white sugar
1 quart cider vinegar

Choose fresh green cucumbers about 5 inches long. Chop them and the other vegetables in a wooden bowl, an electric chopping machine or run them through a food chopper using a coarse blade. Stir in the salt. Cover and let stand 2 hours. Drain in a strainer lined with a piece of wet cheesecloth.

Mix in a kettle with the remaining ingredients and bring to a boil. Cook gently for about 20 minutes or until the vegetables are tender and the mixture quite thick. Put into sterilized hot jars and seal at once.

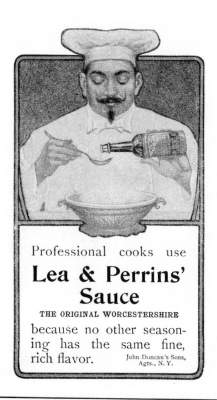

Grandmother's Watermelon Pickle

8 pints prepared watermelon rind
5 cups cider vinegar
5 cups water
10 cups sugar
1 ounce ginger root
1 lemon sliced thin
4 (3-inch) pieces of cinnamon stick
2 tablespoons whole cloves
2 tablespoons whole allspice

Cut the rind into 1-inch strips and then into 1-inch squares. Pare off the green rind and the red fruit. Cover the squares with cold water and let stand in the refrigerator overnight. Drain and put into a kettle of boiling water. Boil 12 minutes. Drain and cover with very cold water while preparing the syrup.

Combine the remaining ingredients, tying the cinnamon sticks, the cloves and allspice into a little cheesecloth bag, tied with kitchen string. Boil 5 minutes or until the syrup is slightly thickened. Add the drained watermelon rind and cook slowly until the syrup is slightly thick and the rind is almost transparent. Transfer the rind with a slotted spoon to hot sterilized jars. Cover with the boiling syrup and seal at once.

Easy Dill Pickles
(12 pints)

4 dozen 3- to 4-inch pickling cucumbers
1 bunch of dill
1 quart cider vinegar
8 cups water
1 cup salt
12 to 16 cloves garlic, peeled

Wash the cucumbers and remove any stems. Cover with cold water and refrigerate overnight or for several hours. Pack the cucumbers in pint jars as tightly as possible. Poke in 2 sprigs of dill. Bring the cider, water, salt and garlic cloves to a boil. Fish out the garlic cloves with a slotted spoon and put one in each jar while the brine cools slightly. Pour the hot brine into the jars and seal tight.

Advertisement for R. Wallace & Sons Mfg. Co., THE SATURDAY EVENING POST, *November 15, 1919*

THE PRUDENT HOUSEWIFE: FREEZING & CANNING

The home preservation of foods is a joy which goes hand in hand with the equally "in" idea of growing your own fruits and vegetables. Country dweller or city soilsport with only a few square yards of earth to nourish and flourish, somehow or other there is a gift lurking here for you, the green gift of nature yielded in exchange for a little thought and care.

What joy to serve those golden peaches in December, those tender green beans in January, and enjoy the harvest all over again.

Preserving garden and orchard surplus has come a long way since a 1755 cookbook:

"Take a quantity of water proportionable to your Number of Artichokes, and boil it with as much Salt as you judge necessary. Then pour it into the Vessel in which you intend to keep your Artichokes. Blanch them in boiling Water, and wash them in two or three several Waters, till you are sure they are very Clean. Then put them into the Vessel, pouring on top of it some Oil or good Butter, that no Air may enter. And if you will, you may put a little Vinegar to your pickle. Cover very carefully with Paper and lay a Board over it, that the least Breath of Air may not get in."

If the artichokes remained edible, it was because the "pickle" of brine and vinegar discouraged the growth of bacteria. True canning wasn't done until after 1810, when Napoleon ordered a means to be found to preserve food for his marching armies and Nicholas Alper, a French candymaker, found the answer—sterilization and sealing airtight in jars. For this, Alper won a prize of 12,000 francs. Not till later did Louis Pasteur reveal that food spoilage was caused by invisible bacteria, and that heat could kill bacteria. Only then did anyone understand home canning.

Home food preservation came of age in America where, in 1858, tinsmith John L. Mason invented a screw-top lid that could reliably seal a glass jar and where, beginning in 1917, Clarence Birdseye pioneered food freezing techniques.

Preserving! We cannot leave so domestic a subject without preserving for posterity this gem of a recipe from a church group in Muncie, Indiana:

How to Preserve A Husband

First, take care in selecting one who is not too young, but tender. Make your selection carefully and let it be final.

Otherwise, they will not keep.

Like wine, they improve with age. Do not pickle or keep them in hot water. This makes them sour.

Prepare as follows:

Sweeten with smiles, according to variety. The sour kind are improved with a pinch of salt of common sense.

Wrap well in a mantle of charity.

Preserve over a good fire of steady devotion.

Serve with peaches and cream.

The poorest varieties may be improved by this process and kept for many years in any climate.

Dr. Middleton misdoubted the future as well as the past of the man who did not, in becoming gravity, exult to dine. That man he deemed unfit for this world and the next.

George Meredith

Painted for the April 1939 COUNTRY GENTLEMAN

Freezing Vegetables

It is necessary to "blanch" most vegetables before freezing. This is done to destroy the enzymes which were there to perform the ripening process. The same enzymes that lead to ripening go on to produce spoiling and without blanching, this process will go on slowly even after freezing.

You needn't be concerned that the blanching will destroy the vegetables' natural vitamin content. The process of blanching is done so quickly that the loss of vitamins is held to a minimum.

After you've prepared the vegetables, plunge them quickly into boiling water for blanching and then into ice water or shake in a colander under cold running water.

The time for blanching different vegetables varies. Use a large pot of at least one gallon capacity with an open wire basket fitted inside. The prepared vegetables are placed in the basket, then lowered into the boiling water for the allotted time as given in the recipe. Move the basket rapidly up and down so that the water reaches all parts of the vegetables.

Pack blanched and cooled vegetables into plastic containers with snap-on lids, glass freezing jars with screw tops, or plastic bags with or without cardboard cartons to hold and protect them. A funnel will help to keep the sealing edges clean, and a stand or rack to hold bags while filling them will be useful. Plastic bags may be heat-sealed or fastened with wire twistees (twist the top of the bag, then turn the twisted end down to form a gooseneck closure before putting on the wire).

Because foods expand slightly as they freeze, it is necessary to leave a little empty space at the top of the container—the head space—except in the case of large, bulky vegetables which will not pack close together.

The containers and utensils used in freezing need to be clean, but they do not need the special treatment required when canning, as freezing will prevent the development of bacteria during storage.

Asparagus

Select young, tender stalks with compact tips. Sort according to thickness of stalk.

Wash asparagus thoroughly and cut or break off and discard tough parts of stalks. Leave spears in lengths to fit the package or cut in 2-inch lengths.

Heat stalks in boiling water according to thickness of stalk:

Small stalks .... 2 minutes
Medium stalks .... 3 minutes
Large stalks .... 4 minutes

Cool promptly in cold water and drain.

Pack into containers, leaving no head space. When packing spears, alternate tips and stem ends. In containers that are wider at the top than bottom, pack asparagus with tips down. Seal and freeze.

Snap Beans
(Green or Wax)

Select young, tender, stringless beans that snap when broken. Allow two-thirds to one pound of fresh beans for one pint frozen. Wash thoroughly. Cut beans into one- or two-inch pieces or slice them lengthwise. Put beans in blanching basket, lower basket into boiling water, and cover. Heat for three minutes. Keep heat high under the water. Plunge basket of heated beans into cold water to stop the cooking. It takes about as long to cool vegetables as to heat them. When beans are cool, remove them from water and drain.

Pack the beans into bags or other containers, leaving ½-inch head space. Seal and freeze. Store at 0 degrees F or below.

Broccoli

Broccoli, like all vegetables, is best frozen as soon as possible after it is picked. Allow about 1 pound fresh broccoli for each pint frozen. Because broccoli packs loosely, no head space need be allowed.

Select tight, compact, dark green heads with tender stalks free from woodiness. Trim off large leaves and tough parts of stems and wash thoroughly.

If necessary, soak stalks for ½ hour in salt water (made of 4 teaspoons salt to each gallon of water) to remove insects. Cut broccoli lengthwise into uniform pieces, leaving heads about 1½ inches across—to insure uniform heating and make attractive pieces for serving. Steam pieces by placing them in blanching basket over rapidly boiling water. Cover kettle, keep heat high, and steam for 5 minutes. Or heat pieces in boiling water 3 minutes, as for snap beans. Remove basket from boiling water. Cool broccoli by plunging basket into cold water. Lift basket from cold water as soon as broccoli is cool and let drain a few minutes.

Pack broccoli so some heads are at each end of the container to get more broccoli in the package. No head space is needed. Seal and freeze.

Lima Beans

Select well-filled pods. Beans should be green but not starchy or mealy. Shell and sort according to size, or leave beans in pods to be shelled after heating and cooling. Heat in boiling water:

Small beans or pods	2 minutes
Medium beans or pods	3 minutes
Large beans or pods	4 minutes

Cool promptly in cold water and drain. Pack into containers, leaving ½-inch head space. Seal and freeze.

Shelled Green Beans

Select pods that are plump, not dry or wrinkled. Shell the beans. Heat in boiling water 1 minute. Cool promptly in cold water and drain.

Pack into containers, leaving ½-inch head space. Seal and freeze.

Beets

Select young or mature beets not more than 3 inches across.

Wash and sort according to size. Trim tops, leaving ½ inch of stems.

Cook in boiling water until tender—for small beets, 25 to 30 minutes; for medium-size beets, 45 to 50 minutes.

Cool promptly in cold water. Peel and cut into slices or cubes.

Pack beets into containers, leaving ½-inch head space. Seal and freeze.

Brussels Sprouts

Select green, firm, and compact heads. Examine heads carefully to make sure they are free from insects. Trim, removing coarse outer leaves. Wash thoroughly. Sort into small, medium, and large sizes. Heat in boiling water:

Small heads	3 minutes
Medium heads	4 minutes
Large heads	5 minutes

Cool promptly in cold water and drain.

Pack Brussels sprouts into containers, leaving no head space. Seal and freeze.

Cabbage or Chinese Cabbage

Frozen cabbage or Chinese cabbage is suitable for use only as a cooked vegetable as it will not retain the crispness desirable in a salad.

Select freshly picked, solid heads. Trim coarse outer leaves from head. Cut into medium-to-coarse shreds or thin wedges, or separate head into leaves. Heat in boiling water 1½ minutes.

Cool promptly in cold water and drain.

Pack cabbage into containers, leaving ½-inch head space. Seal and freeze.

Cauliflower

Choose firm, tender, snow-white heads. Break or cut into pieces about 1 inch across. Wash well. If necessary to remove insects, soak about 30 minutes in a solution of salt and water (4 teaspoons salt to each gallon of water). Drain.

Heat in boiling water containing 4 teaspoons salt to a gallon for 3 minutes. Cool promptly in cold water and drain.

Pack cauliflower into containers, leaving no head space. Seal and freeze.

Greens
(Beet Greens, Chard, Collard, Kale, Mustard Greens, Spinach, Turnip Greens)

Select young, tender leaves. Wash well. Remove tough stems and imperfect leaves. Cut leaves of chard into pieces as desired.
Heat in boiling water for the following periods:

Beet greens, kale, chard, mustard greens, turnip
greens .... 2 minutes
Collard .... 3 minutes
Spinach and New Zealand spinach
Large leaves .... 2 minutes
Very tender leaves .... 1½ minutes
Cool promptly in cold water and drain.

Pack greens into containers, leaving ½-inch head space. Seal and freeze.

Okra

Select young, tender, green pods. Wash thoroughly. Cut off stems in such a way as not to cut open seed cells.
Heat in boiling water:

Small pods .... 3 minutes
Large pods .... 4 minutes
Cool promptly in cold water and drain.

Leave whole or slice crosswise.

Pack into containers, leaving ½-inch head space. Seal and freeze.

Parsnips

Choose small to medium-size parsnips that are tender and free from woodiness. Remove tops, wash, peel, and cut in ½-inch cubes or slices.

Heat in boiling water 2 minutes.

Cool promptly in cold water; drain.

Pack into containers, leaving ½-inch head space. Seal and freeze.

Field Peas
(Black-eyed)

Select well-filled flexible pods with tender seeds. Shell peas, discarding those that are hard.

Heat in boiling water for 2 minutes. Cool promptly in cold water and drain.

Pack into containers, leaving ½-inch head space. Seal and freeze.

Green Peas

Choose bright green, plump, firm pods with sweet, tender peas. Do not use immature or tough peas.

Shell peas. Heat in boiling water 1½ minutes. Cool promptly in cold water and drain.

Pack peas into containers, leaving ½-inch head space. Seal and freeze.

Sweet Peppers

Peppers frozen without heating are best for use in uncooked foods. Heated peppers are easier to pack and good for use in cooking.

Select firm, crisp, thick-walled peppers. Wash, cut out stems, cut in half, and remove seeds. If desired, cut into ½-inch strips or rings.
Heat in boiling water if desired:

Halves .... 3 minutes
Slices .... 2 minutes
Cool promptly in cold water and drain.

If peppers have not been heated, pack into containers, leaving no head space. Seal and freeze. If peppers have been heated, leave ½-inch head space.

Squash
(Summer or Winter)

Summer. Select young squash with small seeds and tender rind. Wash, cut in ½-inch slices. Heat in boiling water for 3 minutes. Cool squash promptly in cold water and drain.

Pack into containers, leaving ½-inch head space. Seal and freeze.

Winter. Select firm, mature squash. Wash, cut into pieces, and remove seeds. Cook pieces until soft in boiling water, in steam, in a pressure cooker, or in the oven. Remove pulp from rind and mash or press through a sieve.

To cool, place pan containing squash in cold water and stir squash occasionally.

Pack into containers, leaving ½-inch head space. Seal and freeze.

Sweet Potatoes

Sweet potatoes may be packed whole, sliced, or mashed.

Choose medium to large mature sweet potatoes that have been cured. Sort according to size, and wash.

Cook until almost tender in water, in steam, in a pressure cooker, or in the oven. Let stand at room temperature until cool. Peel sweet potatoes; cut in halves, slice, or mash.

To prevent darkening, dip whole sweet potatoes or slices for 5 seconds in a solution of ½ cup lemon juice to 1 quart water, or a solution of 1½ teaspoons vitamin C in 2 cups of water.

To keep mashed sweet potatoes from darkening, mix 1 tablespoon orange or lemon juice and 1 teaspoon of vitamin C with each quart of mashed sweet potatoes.

Pack into containers, leaving ½-inch head space. Seal and freeze.

Pumpkin

Select full-colored, mature pumpkin with texture that is fine rather than coarse and stringy.

Wash, cut into quarters or smaller pieces, and remove seeds. Cook pumpkin pieces until soft in boiling water, in steam, in a pressure cooker, or in the oven.

Remove pulp from rind and mash it or press it through a sieve.

To cool, place pan containing pumpkin in cold water. Stir pumpkin occasionally.

Pack into containers, leaving ½-inch head space. Seal and freeze.

Tomatoes

Juice. Wash, sort, and trim firm, vine-ripened tomatoes. Cut in quarters or eighths. Simmer 5 to 10 minutes. Press through a sieve. If desired, season with 1 teaspoon salt to each quart of juice. Pour into containers, leaving head space. Seal and freeze.
Stewed. Remove stem ends, peel, and quarter ripe tomatoes. Cover and cook until tender (10 to 20 minutes). Place pan containing tomatoes in cold water to cool. Pack into containers, leaving head space. Seal and freeze.

Turnips

Select small to medium firm turnips that are tender and have a mild flavor. Wash, peel, and cut into ½-inch cubes. Heat in boiling water for 2 minutes. Cool promptly in cold water and drain.

Pack into containers, leaving ½-inch head space. Seal and freeze.

Using Frozen Vegetables

The following timetable shows about how long it takes to cook tender one pint of various frozen vegetables—and how much water to use. Use the table only as a general guide. Cooking times vary among varieties and with the maturity of the vegetable when it is frozen.

The time required for cooking vegetables at high altitudes is slightly longer than at low altitudes because the temperature of boiling water decreases about 2 degrees with each 1,000 feet above sea level.

Timetable for Cooking Frozen Vegetables in a Small Amount of Water [1]

VEGETABLE	Minutes to allow after water returns to boil [2]
Asparagus	5-10
Beans, lima:	
Large type	15-20
Baby type	6-10
Beans, snap, green, or wax:	
1-inch pieces	12-18
Julienne	5-10
Beet greens	6-12
Broccoli	5-8
Brussels sprouts	4-9
Cauliflower	5-8
Mustard greens	8-15
Peas, green	5-10
Spinach	4-6
Squash, summer	10-12
Turnip greens	15-20
Turnips	8-12

[1] Use ½ cup of lightly salted water for each pint of vegetables with this exception: Lima beans, 1 cup.
[2] Time required at sea level.

The secret of cooking frozen vegetables successfully is to cook the vegetable until just tender. That way you save vitamins, bright color, and fresh flavor. Frozen vegetables may be cooked in a small amount of water or in a pressure saucepan, or by baking or pan-frying.

Cook in a small amount of water: You should cook most frozen vegetables without thawing them first. Leafy vegetables, such as spinach, cook more evenly if thawed just enough to separate the leaves before cooking. Corn on the cob should be partially thawed before cooking, so that the cob will be heated through by the time the corn is cooked. Holding corn after thawing or cooking causes sogginess.

Bring water to a boil in a covered saucepan. The amount of water to use depends on the vegetable and the size of the package. For most vegetables one-half cup of water is enough for a pint package. The frost in the packages furnishes some additional moisture.

Put the frozen vegetable in the boiling water, cover the pan, and bring the water quickly to a boil. To insure uniform cooking, it may be necessary to separate pieces carefully with a fork. When the water is boiling throughout the pan, reduce the heat and start counting time. Be sure pan is covered to keep in the steam, which aids in cooking. Cook gently until vegetables are just tender.

Add seasonings as desired and serve immediately.

Cooking in a pressure saucepan: Follow directions and cooling times specified by the manufacturer of your saucepan.

Baking: Many frozen vegetables may be baked in a covered casserole. Partially defrost vegetable to separate pieces. Put vegetable in a greased casserole: add seasonings as desired. Cover and bake until just tender.

The time it takes to bake a vegetable varies with the size of pieces and how much you thaw them before baking. Approximate time for baking most thawed vegetables is 45 minutes at 350 degrees F (moderate oven). Slightly more time may be required if other foods are being baked at the same time.

Pan-frying: Use a heavy fry pan with cover. Place about 1 tablespoon fat in pan. Add 1 pint frozen vegetable, which has been thawed enough to separate pieces. Cook covered over moderate heat. Stir occasionally. Cook until just tender. Season to taste.

Peas, asparagus, and broccoli will cook tender in a fry pan in about 10 minutes. Mushrooms will be done in 10 to 15 minutes and snap beans in 15 to 20 minutes.

Other ways to prepare frozen vegetables: Vegetables that are cooked until tender before freezing need only to be seasoned and heated before serving. Cooked frozen vegetables can be used in many dishes in the same ways as cooked fresh vegetables. They may be creamed or scalloped, served au gratin, or added to soufflés, cream soups, or salads.

Pumpkin, winter squash, and sweet potatoes may be thawed and used as the main ingredient in pie fillings.

Freezing Fruits

There are several different methods of freezing fruit—in sugar, in syrup, in water and dry. Which to use depends on the kind and condition of the fruit, and the use for which it is intended. All the methods are easy, because only a very few fruits require precooking or blanching.

The only special problem is the tendency of light-colored fruits to darken when cut surfaces are exposed to the air. Here, vitamin C (ascorbic acid) works like magic. Sprinkled directly on the fruit, mixed with sugar or stirred into syrup, it retards darkening, while actually improving the flavor of fruit and adding important nutrition. Add vitamin C only to cold fruit or to syrup after it cools, as it is destroyed by heat.

Pack fruit in rigid containers (glass or plastic) or in plastic bags with or without cardboard cartons. While processing the fruit, use containers and utensils that are made of aluminum, glass, plastic, enamelware or stainless steel. Don't use other metals, as fruit can absorb an unpleasant taste from tin, iron or copper. A colander or wire basket is handy for washing and draining fruit. A few general rules hold good for all the methods suggested here:

(1) Freeze only fruit that is fresh and fully ripened. Some varieties freeze better than others; consult your county home economist if you are in doubt about the varieties available locally.

(2) Process a small quantity of fruit at a time. Wash, peel and slice only 1 or 2 quarts of fruit at a time. Pack that much and put it in the freezer before you process more. If you are buying fruit, buy only what you can process that day; if you are picking from your own trees, pick only what you can process immediately.

(3) Keep it cool! Use cold running water or ice water for washing the fruit. Chilling the fruit will make it firmer and easier to handle, but don't let it stand in water and become soggy.

Thaseolus vulgaris

Painted for a Stokely-VanCamp, Inc., promotion that appeared in 1967.

Water Pack

If there is a diabetic in the family, or someone on a special low-calorie diet, you may want to freeze some fruit without sugar or syrup. Use plain cold water with powdered vitamin C stirred into it to cover the fruit, just as you would use syrup. As a rule, the flavor and texture of the fruit will be less satisfactory than that of fruit packed with sugar or syrup.

Dry Pack

Dry packing is the easiest method of all, but it is used only for berries, grapes and a few other kinds of fruit. Just spread the berries on a cookie tin and place it in the freezer for an hour or so, then pour frozen berries into containers for storage.

Purees

Fruit that is slightly overripe and soft should be cooked and frozen as a puree; it can be served later as a sauce on ice cream or other desserts. Just cook the fruit 2 to 5 minutes in a small amount of water, cool, press through a sieve and sweeten to taste. Pack in rigid glass or plastic containers, leaving 1-inch head space.

Sugar Pack

Mix powdered vitamin C with the sugar you will use. Wash, peel and slice fruit into a measuring cup and then spread in a nonmetal container (a glass baking dish is ideal for this purpose). Sprinkle sugar over the fruit, then mix very gently, using a plastic or wooden spoon or pancake turner, until the sugar dissolves in juice from the fruit. Pack, seal and freeze.

Syrup Pack

Syrup serves to completely surround the fruit and protect it from contact with air, so it is particularly good for freezing the light-colored fruits that tend to discolor. Make the syrup by dissolving the sugar or honey in hot water. Chill it in the refrigerator for several hours or overnight; it should be very cold when it touches the fruit. Sugar is generally less expensive than honey and it is preferred for mild flavored fruits; honey has a rather strong flavor of its own that may not combine well with some fruit flavors. Also, honey may crystallize if your freezer temperature goes higher than 0 degrees F. Add vitamin C only after the syrup is chilled and stir well.

SYRUPS FOR FREEZING AND CANNING FRUITS			
Type of Syrup	Sugar or honey Cups	Water Cups	Yield of Syrup Cups
30-percent syrup (light)	2	4	5
35-percent syrup	2½	4	5 1/3
40-percent syrup (medium)	3	4	5½
50-percent syrup (heavy)	4¾	4	6½
60-percent syrup	7	4	7¾
65-percent syrup (very heavy)	8¾	4	8 2/3

When using syrup, make sure it completely covers the fruit, to protect it from the air. You may use a small piece of parchment or plastic wrap crumpled and pushed into the syrup to hold the fruit down.

Apples

Choose apples that are crisp and firm-textured rather than mealy. Wash, peel, remove cores and cut into 12 or more slices.

Syrup pack: Use medium syrup, adding 1 teaspoon powdered vitamin C per quart. Use glass or rigid plastic containers. Pour ½ cup syrup into a container and slice the apples directly into it till it is nearly full (leave ½-inch head space). Add more syrup if needed to cover fruit, seal, and place that container in the freezer before filling the next.

Sugar pack: To prevent discoloring of apples during preparation, slice them into a solution of 2 tablespoons salt to a gallon of water. Hold in this solution no longer than 20 minutes. Drain and spread in a shallow nonmetal container. For 4 cups of apple slices, use ½ cup sugar mixed with ¾ teaspoon powdered vitamin C. Stir gently till sugar dissolves, pack in rigid containers or plastic bags, seal and freeze.

Applesauce

Prepare as for immediate serving. Pack in rigid glass or plastic containers, leaving ½-inch head space. Seal and freeze.

Apricots

Wash fruit, remove pits and cut into halves or slices. Peel if desired, or heat apricots in boiling water for ½ minute to make the skins tender and then cool in cold water.

Syrup pack: Stir ¾ teaspoon powdered vitamin C into each quart. Slice fruit directly into containers holding ½ cup syrup. Add more syrup to cover, leaving ½-inch head space, seal and freeze.

Sugar pack: Mix ½ cup sugar to which ¾ teaspoon powdered vitamin C has been added with 4 cups of fruit. Stir gently till juice is drawn from fruit and sugar is dissolved, then pack, seal and freeze.

Crushed or puree: Select fully ripened fruit. For crushed apricots, heat in boiling water ½ minute and then cool in cold water. Peel, remove pits and crush slightly, using a wire potato masher or food grinder on coarse setting. For puree, heat to boiling in a small amount of water and then press through a sieve. Mix with 4 cups of prepared fruit ¾ cup of sugar to which ¾ teaspoon of powdered vitamin C has been added. Pack in rigid glass or plastic containers, leaving ¾-inch head space, seal and freeze.

Berries
(Other Than Strawberries)

Berries that are to be served uncooked as dessert fruit should be packed in sugar or syrup, so that their skins will be tender. If the berries are to be used in pies, cobblers or other baked or cooked dishes, dry pack will serve just as well. Follow these directions for raspberries, blackberries, boysenberries, dewberries, loganberries, youngberries, blueberries, elderberries, gooseberries or cranberries.

Choose full-flavored, fully ripe berries that are all about the same size. Pick over carefully to remove stems and leaves, wash and drain.

Dry pack: Spread berries in a single layer on a cookie tin or tray, and place on a shelf in the freezer for an hour or so. Remove tray from freezer and pour frozen berries into plastic bags for storage.

Syrup pack: Use medium or heavy syrup, depending on the sweetness of the fruit. Add ¾ teaspoon powdered vitamin C to each quart of syrup. Pack berries into rigid glass or plastic containers, add syrup to cover (leaving head space of ½ inch or slightly more), seal and freeze.

Sugar pack: Spread berries in a shallow nonmetal container. To 4 cups of berries add ¾ to 1 cup sugar mixed with ¾ teaspoon powdered vitamin C. Stir gently until juice is drawn from the berries to dissolve the sugar. Pack in rigid containers or plastic bags, leaving ½-inch head space, seal and freeze.

Sour Cherries

Select bright red, tree-ripened cherries. Pick over carefully to remove stems and discolored fruit, then wash, drain, and remove seeds. Dry pack is not recommended because the skins are likely to be tough.

Syrup pack: Use heavy syrup, adding 1 teaspoon powdered vitamin C per quart. Pack cherries in rigid containers, add syrup to cover, leaving head space of at least ½ inch, seal and freeze.

Sugar pack: To 4 cups of cherries add ¾ to 1 cup sugar mixed with ¾ teaspoon powdered vitamin C. Crush cherries slightly, to produce juice, as you stir in the sugar. Pack in rigid containers, seal and freeze. Do not freeze cherries in plastic bags, as the juice may remain partially liquid and leak.

Sweet Cherries

Process sweet cherries very quickly, to avoid deterioration of color and flavor. The red varieties usually freeze best. Wash and drain a small quantity of cherries at a time. As you remove the seeds, drop the cherries into a container of light syrup to which powdered vitamin C has been added (¾ teaspoon to one quart of syrup).

Syrup pack: Dip cherries from syrup with a slotted spoon, or pour off syrup into another container. Pack cherries in rigid glass or plastic containers, add enough of the syrup to cover, leaving ½-inch head space, seal and freeze.

Sugar pack: Remove cherries from syrup, as above. Add to 4 cups of cherries 1 to 1½ cups sugar mixed with ¾ teaspoon powdered vitamin C. Crush cherries slightly to bring out the juice. Pack in rigid glass or plastic containers, leaving ½-inch head space, seal and freeze. (Do not use plastic bags.)

Grapefruit
(see Citrus Fruits)

Grapes

Grapes suitable for freezing (check with county home economist for local varieties) may be washed, drained, and spread on a cookie tray in the freezer. Later, pour into plastic bags for storage.

Melons

Cantaloupe, honeydew, watermelon and other kinds of melon can be frozen in syrup. Remove rind and seeds, and cut the choice part of the melon into small cubes or balls. Pack in rigid plastic or glass containers, cover with light syrup (add ½ teaspoon powdered vitamin C per quart), seal and freeze.

Fruit Cocktail

Prepare any combination of fruits as for serving—sliced or diced peaches, melon balls, orange sections, whole seedless grapes and pineapple wedges as desired. (Do not use bananas or raw pears, as neither freezes well.) To prevent discoloration of fruit, slice into a container of light syrup to which powdered vitamin C has been added (½ teaspoon per quart). Dip fruit from syrup with a slotted spoon, pack into rigid containers and add enough of the syrup to cover the fruit. Leave ½-inch head space, seal and freeze.

Oranges
(see Citrus Fruits)

"The Olympian Gods Never Munched Anything Half So Good!"

**Bitter Root Valley
Sweet Cherries**

Peaches

Syrup pack is preferred for peaches since it best protects the soft flesh and light color of the fruit.

Select fully ripe but firm fruit, discarding any peaches with green coloring. Work with small quantities at a time. Wash in cold water, drain, peel and remove pits. Pack as halves or slices, depending on the condition of the fruit and the use for which it is intended.

Syrup pack: Use medium syrup, stirring ½ teaspoon powdered vitamin C into each quart. Pour ½ cup syrup into a rigid glass or plastic container. Slice peaches directly into this container. Add more syrup as needed to cover fruit, leaving ½-inch head space. If fruit tends to float on the surface, use a small crumpled piece of parchment or plastic film to push it down into the syrup. Seal one container and place it in the freezer before peeling and slicing more fruit.

Sugar pack: Slice fruit into a bowl containing light syrup to which powdered vitamin C has been added. When the bowl is full, or when all the fruit has been processed, use a slotted spoon to dip the fruit into a measuring cup and then transfer it to a shallow non-metal container. To four cups of sliced or halved peaches add 2/3 cup sugar mixed with ½ teaspoon powdered vitamin C. Stir gently till sugar dissolves, then pack, seal and freeze.

Pears

Many people feel that canned pears are more satisfactory than frozen ones, but you can try freezing a few and decide for yourself. The following method may give good results:

Drop peeled, sliced pears into boiling medium syrup. Cook 2 minutes. Allow to cool. Drain off and discard the syrup used for cooking. Pack pear slices in rigid plastic or glass containers. Cover with cold medium syrup to which powdered vitamin C has been added (½ teaspoon to a quart). Seal and freeze.

Persimmons

Freeze persimmons as puree and they will be ready to use in making persimmon pudding. The puree need not be cooked. Wash and peel soft-ripe persimmons and put them through a sieve, food mill or blender. Mix with sugar to which powdered vitamin C has been added (½ teaspoon to ¾ cup sugar). Pack into rigid plastic or glass containers, leaving ½-inch head space, seal and freeze. Mark containers with the amount of sugar you have added per cup of persimmon pulp, so you will know how much more sugar to add when you use the fruit.

Pineapple

Select fully ripe fruit. Peel, remove core and eyes and slice as desired, working over a bowl to catch juice. Prepare medium syrup, using juice to replace part of the water and adding ½ teaspoon powdered vitamin C per quart. Pack pineapple spears or slices in rigid plastic or glass containers, covered with syrup (leaving ½-inch head space), seal and freeze.

Plums

Wash plums, cut in halves and remove pits but do not peel.

Dry pack: Place plum halves in plastic bags, seal and freeze. To prepare for serving uncooked, dip frozen plums in cold water and hold them there for 10 seconds or so, to loosen skins. Peel and drop into cold syrup where they will thaw slowly.

Syrup pack: Use medium or heavy syrup, depending on natural sweetness of the fruit. Add ½ teaspoon powdered vitamin C to each quart of syrup. Pack fruit in rigid plastic or glass containers. Add syrup, covering fruit but leaving ½-inch head space, seal and freeze.

Rhubarb

For best results, blanch rhubarb stalks before freezing. Select firm but tender stalks that have a deep pink or red color. Wash, drain and cut into 1- or 2-inch pieces, or cut to the length of the container you plan to use. Bring a large kettle of water to a boil. Place rhubarb pieces in a wire basket or colander and immerse it in the boiling water for 1 minute (start counting the time when the water returns to a boil). Immerse in cold water to cool quickly, then drain and pack.

Syrup pack: Pack rhubarb into rigid plastic or glass containers. Add light syrup to cover, leaving ½-inch head space. Seal and freeze.

Unsweetened: Pack blanched rhubarb into plastic bags or other containers, leave ½-inch head space, seal and freeze.

Sugar pack: Mix rhubarb pieces with ½ cup or more sugar, as desired. Pack in plastic bags, leaving ½-inch head space, seal and freeze.

Strawberries

Because they are soft and juicy, strawberries do not lend themselves to the dry pack method. Most people prefer strawberries sliced and packed with sugar in their own juice, but the syrup pack method may also be used.

Select firm but fully ripe berries. Sort over carefully, wash in cold water, drain and remove hulls. Slice or crush very large berries. Work with a small quantity at a time, keeping the others dry and in a cool place.

Sugar pack: Add ¾ cup sugar mixed with ½ teaspoon powdered vitamin C to 4 cups of berries in a shallow baking dish or similar nonmetal container. Mix gently till sugar is dissolved in juice drawn from the berries. Pack in rigid plastic or glass containers or plastic bags, leaving ½-inch head space, seal and freeze.

Syrup pack: Place sliced or whole berries in rigid plastic or glass containers. Add heavy syrup (stir ½ teaspoon powdered vitamin C into each quart of syrup) to cover berries. Leave ½-inch head space, seal and freeze.

How to Use Frozen Fruits

Serving uncooked: Frozen fruits need only to be thawed, if they are to be served raw.

For best color and flavor, leave fruit in the sealed container to thaw. Serve as soon as thawed; a few ice crystals in the fruit improve the texture for eating raw.

Frozen fruit in the package may be thawed in the refrigerator, at room temperature, or in a pan of cool water. Turn package several times for more even thawing.

Allow 6 to 8 hours on a refrigerator shelf for thawing a 1-pound package of fruit packed in syrup. Allow 2 to 4 hours for thawing a package of the same size at room temperature—½ to 1 hour for thawing in a pan of cool water.

Fruit packed with dry sugar thaws slightly faster than that packed in syrup. Both sugar and syrup packs thaw faster than unsweetened packs.

Thaw only as much as you need at one time. If you have leftover thawed fruit it will keep better if you cook it. Cooked fruit will keep in the refrigerator for a few days.

Cooking: First thaw fruits until pieces can be loosened. Then cook as you would cook fresh fruit. If there is not enough juice to prevent scorching, add water as needed. If the recipe calls for sugar, allow for any sweetening that was added before freezing.

Frozen fruits often have more juice than called for in recipes for baked products using fresh fruits. In that case use only part of the juice or add more thickening for the extra juice.

Using crushed fruit and purees: Serve crushed fruit as raw fruit after it is partially or completely thawed. Or use it after thawing as a topping for ice cream or cakes, as a filling for sweet rolls, or for jam.

Use thawed purees in puddings, ice cream, sherbets, jams, pies, ripple cakes, fruit-filled coffee cake, and rolls.

Serving juice: Serve frozen fruit juice as a beverage—after it is thawed but while it is still cold. Some juices, such as sour cherry, plum, grape, and berry juices, may be diluted 1/3 to 1/2 with water or a bland juice.

Freezing Meat

Economy and convenience are the twin benefits of using the home freezer to store meats, poultry and fish. You can save money by buying these foods in quantity, and it is a joy to have them on hand when they are needed. Freezing is the only easy but safe way to store these foods in the home for use over a period of several months.

Meat, poultry and fish do not need the special preparation that most fruits and vegetables need before they go into the freezer, but they do need very careful wrapping. Also, safe storage for the different kinds of meat and poultry vary quite a lot, so it is important to keep a record of what goes into the freezer when, so all can be used before the quality deteriorates.

Wrapping is very important because these foods need special protection from contact with the air in the freezer. Cold air is dry, and it draws moisture out of anything it touches. If the cold, dry air in the freezer touches the surface of meat it draws the natural juices out. When meat is not properly wrapped and protected from the air it quickly becomes dry and tasteless. At the same time, oxygen from the air penetrates the meat and it may break down fatty cells so as to give the meat a rancid taste.

Meat, poultry and fish need to be wrapped in something that is not just waterproof but also vaporproof. The wrapping material must fit very closely around the meat so that no air can be trapped inside, and it must be tough enough so that it doesn't puncture easily.

The thin plastic film used to wrap meat and poultry for display in stores is not adequate for foods that are to be stored in the freezer more than a day or two.

Special freezer-wrap paper that is laminated to a plastic film is probably the best material for wrapping these foods, but it is expensive. Foil is easy to use, because it can be molded to closely fit around odd-shaped items, but it may be punctured in the freezer unless it has an outer protective wrap of tough paper. Some plastic bags are vaporproof but many are not, so read carefully the label on any plastic bags you plan to use for storing meat, poultry or fish.

Freezing will not improve the quality of meat—a cut that is tough when it goes into the freezer will be tough when it comes out.

See that the meat freezes as quickly as possible. In a chest-type freezer, place your packages of wrapped meat flat against the side walls for at least 24 hours before moving them to bins in the center of the freezer for storage. In an upright freezer, place the packages on the shelves indicated for quick-freezing, leaving at least an inch of space between packages for cold air to circulate. If you are putting a lot of meat into the freezer at the same time, turn the setting to the coldest temperature, so all the meat will freeze as quickly as possible.

When meat freezes quickly, the ice crystals that form inside it are small. Slower freezing produces larger crystals which may break down cell walls within the meat, causing loss of natural juices and flavor.

Don't add salt to meat that is uncooked, as salt speeds up enzyme action and may destroy flavor. Don't add herbs, as they may flavor the meat too highly during storage.

A word about cleanliness: Before starting to work with meat, wash very carefully all surfaces and utensils that will come in contact with the meat. Wash your hands often, using soap and paying careful attention to the nails. This is because freezing does not kill all bacteria, as cooking at high temperatures does.

For quick thawing, freeze individual portions like steaks, hamburger patties or pork chops separately. One way is to stack them, with pieces of freezer paper or plastic film between, and then wrap. When you take them out of the freezer you can pull them apart and lay them out on a tray or broiler pan to thaw.

Maximum Storage Time for Meats

Meats kept longer than the recommended time in the freezer will not make you sick—as meats kept too long in the refrigerator or at room temperature might—but they will not taste as good as they should.

Beef roasts or steaks .... 8 to 12 months
Ground beef or stew meat .... 2 to 3 months
Liver .... 3 to 4 months
Lamb chops .... 3 to 4 months
Veal roast .... 4 to 6 months
Veal chops .... 3 to 4 months
Ground veal .... 2 to 3 months
Fresh pork sausage
   (Unseasoned) .... 1 to 3 months
Pork roast or chops .... 6 to 8 months
Smoked ham .... 1 to 2 months
Variety meats
   (kidney, tongue, etc.) .... 3 to 4 months

Note: The freezing of sliced bacon, wieners, bologna and other delicatessen meats is not recommended.

Cooking Meat After Freezing

Most meats can go directly from freezer to stove, but this may not be the best way to prepare them for serving. The advantage is that meats that begin cooking while still frozen retain more of their natural juices than meats that are thawed before cooking. The disadvantage is that solidly frozen meats need longer cooking times, and the outside of a thick cut of meat may be overcooked while the inside is still partially frozen.

For safety, thaw meat in its wrapper in the storage section of your refrigerator. Allow 12 to 24 hours for this thawing. In an emergency, you can thaw meat more quickly by running cold water over the wrapped package, or turning an electric fan on it.

Meat that is to be dredged in flour must be thawed ahead of time, as no coating will stick to frozen meat. Meat that is to be broiled or pan-fried without breading can go directly from freezer to stove.

Freezing Poultry

Prepare poultry for freezing just as you would prepare it for immediate cooking. Inspect it carefully, rinse it in cool water and dry it with paper toweling. Remove any feathers that cling to the skin, and any lung tissue inside the body cavity. Then wrap vapor-tight and place in the freezer.

Poultry that is to be roasted is frozen whole, although whole birds take up a lot of space in the freezer. Young birds that are to be broiled or fried are usually cut into quarters or individual pieces so they will store more compactly.

If birds frozen whole for roasting are to be stored in the freezer for 3 months or longer it is best to remove the giblets and freeze them separately, as they won't keep as long as the whole birds.

It makes sense to buy and process a number of chickens at a time, when they are available at a good price. When packaging cut-up chicken parts you can make the packages fit the size and preferences of your family—packing breasts separately, or including extra drumsticks for the children. Just be sure to mark on the outside of each package what it contains.

Unless you have a lot of extra space in your freezer you may not wish to freeze the bony parts of the chicken—the back, neck and wing tips—as they take up a lot of space without providing much meat. You may wish to cook these parts to make broth, and then freeze the broth. Just simmer the pieces of chicken in several quarts of water with a few celery leaves, a slice of onion and a bay leaf, if desired, until the meat is falling off the bones. Then strain, cool, and pack the broth in rigid plastic or glass containers, leaving head space of ½-inch. (The scraps of meat and chicken skin will be relished by the family cat.)

Maximum Storage Time for Poultry

Whole chicken or turkey .... 8 to 12 months
Quail, pheasant,
   or other wild fowl .... 8 to 10 months
Cut-up chicken or turkey .... 6 to 8 months
Duck or goose .... 4 to 6 months
Livers or giblets .... 1 to 3 months
Cooked chicken or turkey .... 1 to 3 months

Freezing Fish

Speed is of the utmost importance when fresh fish are to be frozen. This is because fish deteriorates very rapidly, due to a special kind of fatty cells in the flesh, and deterioration begins the minute the fish is caught. A fresh-caught fish is nearly odorless; the "fishy" smell becomes stronger, hour after hour, while the fish is waiting to be cooked or frozen.

If fish must be transported before it is frozen, scale and clean it, wrap it in waxed paper or plastic and put it on ice.

Large fish may be frozen whole for baking, or cut into steaks or fillets suitable for broiling or frying. Small fish may be frozen whole or filleted for frying.

Shellfish are also highly perishable. Crab and lobster may be cooked before freezing. Drop them in boiling water and simmer for 10 to 20 minutes, then drain and cool. Remove meat from the shells and pack it in rigid plastic or glass containers, leaving ½-inch head space. Shrimp may be frozen raw or cooked, with or without the shells.

Maximum Storage Time for Seafood

All fish .... 4 to 6 months
Uncooked shellfish .... 4 to 6 months
Cooked shellfish .... 2 months

Oh ! Jennie, some of the girls came over and they say four boys will be here in a few moments, have we anything in the house for a supper ?

Yes, Miss Grace, the Libby goods were delivered yesterday. The Wafer Sliced Smoked Beef, Pork and Beans, Veal Loaf, Potted Chicken and lots of good things that can be made ready in a few moments.

What Luck ! We'll have Frizzled beef in the chafing dish, and some of those good beans ; you can make sandwiches with the Potted chicken and serve the Veal Loaf cold. That will make a fine supper, won't it ?

Home Canning

Fresh fruits, tomatoes and some pickled vegetables may all be canned by the hot water bath method which is easy and requires little special equipment. This is due to the fact that the natural acidity of these foods inhibits the growth of bacteria and molds that cause foods to spoil.

Other foods—the low acid vegetables like corn, green beans and carrots and also meats, poultry and fish—can be safely canned only by the steam pressure method. These foods may harbor the botulism bacteria which can survive the heat of boiling water (212 degrees F) and live without air inside the sealed jars, creating a poison that may contaminate the food without changing its odor, taste or appearance.

Steam pressure canning procedures hold the food at a higher temperature (240 degrees F) for a longer period of time. For an extra measure of safety it is usually recommended that home-canned vegetables, meats, poultry and fish be brought to a boil and simmered at least 15 minutes just before they are served.

Since freezing is an easy and safe method of preserving these foods—and a method that better retains their natural texture and flavor—it makes sense to use what freezer space you have to store them, and can the fruits and tomatoes that won't fit in the freezer.

If you do plan to can low-acid vegetables, meat, poultry or fish, follow the directions that come with your pressure canner or the directions in the *Home and Garden Bulletin No. 106* available from the United States Department of Agriculture.

Open kettle and oven canning methods described in some older publications are no longer recommended, and it is not satisfactory to use an ordinary pressure cooker (saucepan) for canning.

Hot Water Bath Canning

The most important piece of equipment is a large kettle with rack and lid, deep enough to hold the jars you plan to use with boiling water at least 1 inch over their tops. If you plan to do much canning you will probably want to purchase a hot water bath canner designed for this use.

A colander or wire basket will be helpful for washing and draining fruit, and you will need large sauce-pans or kettles for heating water and syrup. A wide-mouth funnel will make it easy to fill the jars without spilling, and a jar lifter that looks like a large set of tongs will be useful for handling the jars when they are very hot. You will also need a timer that can be set to ring when the processing time is over.

Buy jars and lids manufactured for home canning. The jars you buy food in—like mayonnaise jars—are not made of tempered glass and they are likely to break when heated.

Recommended are wide-mouth pint or quart jars with two-piece lids. The flat lid has a special sealing compound around the edge; it is used just once and discarded. The jars and the screw-on ring bands may be used over and over, year after year.

There are two methods of filling the jars, called raw pack and hot pack.

In raw pack canning you put the washed, peeled fruit directly into the jar, then pour in hot syrup to cover the fruit, cap and process. In hot pack canning you cook the fruit briefly in hot syrup, then dip the fruit out and pack it in the jars and add as much of the hot syrup as is needed to cover the fruit, cap and process. Hot pack is generally preferred for large fruit pieces like peach halves or whole tomatoes, as they fit into the jars more compactly after they are partially cooked and soft.

Fruit may be packed in water or unsweetened juice, but most people think that fruit canned in syrup has better flavor and color. Prepare the syrup as for freezing fruit (see page 295), and heat to boiling.

Have jars clean and hot. You can use your dishwasher both to clean them and keep them hot ready for use, or you can fill the washed jars with hot water. Scald the lids and hold them in very hot water ready for use. The screw-on rings need only to be washed in hot soapy water and rinsed.

Place the rack inside the canner and half-fill it with hot water. Boil more water, in a teakettle or large kettle, to add later.

Prepare fruit as desired. Pack raw and add hot syrup, or boil in syrup and then pack. In either case, leave ½-inch head space to allow for expansion during processing. Wipe the rim of the jar with a clean damp cloth or paper towel—if there is fruit or syrup on this

Cherries

Wash cherries, drain and remove pits and any stems. For raw pack, fill hot, clean jars and shake, to make cherries fit together compactly. Add boiling syrup to cover, using light syrup for sour pie cherries and medium or heavy syrup for sweet cherries. For a better quality product, add ¾ teaspoon of powdered vitamin C per quart of syrup. To hot pack cherries, place fruit in kettle or saucepan and add ½ cup sugar per quart of fruit. Bring to a boil, stirring frequently to prevent sticking, then fill jars. Using either method, allow ½-inch head space for expansion during processing. Adjust lids and ring bands, place in canner and process 20 minutes for pints, 25 minutes for quarts if packed raw; or 10 minutes for pints and 15 minutes for quarts if packed hot.

Grapefruit

Thoroughly ripe grapefruit may be canned using the raw pack method. Canning is not recommended for the other citrus fruits.

Peel grapefruit and separate into sections, removing seeds, when this is possible, along with most of the white membrane. Pack sections into jars, pressing lightly with a spoon to fill the jar compactly. Cover with hot medium syrup to which vitamin C has been added (½ teaspoon per quart of syrup). Leave ½-inch head space. Adjust lids and ring bands, transfer to canner and process 30 minutes for pints, 35 minutes for quarts.

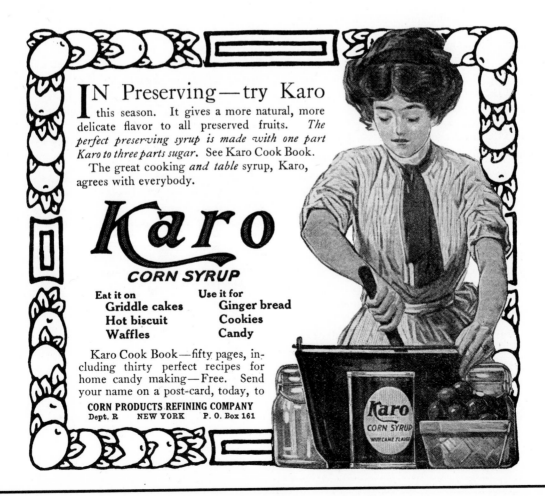

surface the lid will not seal properly. Using a funnel when filling the jars helps to keep this rim clean. Lift a lid from hot water and place it on the jar (use tongs) and screw the band in place as tightly as you can, by hand. Place that jar in the canner, in the hot but not boiling water, before packing the next.

When all the jars are filled and in the canner, add more boiling water as needed to come up at least 1 inch over the tops of the jars. Cover the canner and turn up the heat. When the water comes to a full simmer, remove cover and set timer for processing. Maintain a good simmer or gentle boiling; hard boiling is not necessary and will evaporate the water too fast.

When time is up, lift jars from the canner (use special jar lifter or large tongs). Set them on a folded cloth or rack to cool.

To test for good sealing, press the center of the jar lid down with your finger. If it stays down, the jar is sealed. If you wish, you can remove the ring bands at this time. Label the jars with the date canned, and store in a cool, dry place.

Apples

The hot pack method is recommended for apples.

Core and peel the fruit. To prevent discoloration, slice the apples into a vitamin C solution (stir 1 teaspoon powdered vitamin C into 1 cup of water or follow directions on package). Prepare thin syrup and bring it to a boil in a saucepan. Using a slotted spoon, dip apple slices from the vitamin C solution into the boiling syrup. (Save the vitamin C solution for reuse.) Cook the apple slices 5 minutes.

Using the slotted spoon again, transfer apple slices to clean, hot jars. Add enough of the hot syrup to cover the fruit, leaving ½-inch head space. Adjust lids and ring bands, transfer to canner and process 15 minutes for pint jars, 20 minutes for quarts.

Applesauce

Prepare applesauce as for immediate serving. Sweeten with sugar or mild-flavored honey, as desired. Heat to simmering, stirring applesauce to prevent sticking. For improved quality, stir in ½ teaspoon powdered vitamin C per quart. Pack hot applesauce into clean, hot jars, leaving ¼-inch head space. Adjust lids and ring bands, transfer to hot water bath canner and process for 10 minutes for either pints or quarts.

Apricots

Apricots may be peeled or not, as you prefer. Wash well, cut in half and remove pits. To prevent discoloration, hold fruit in vitamin-C solution (see Apples) during preparation. Pack and process as for peaches.

Berries

Soft juicy berries (other than strawberries) may be packed raw; firm-skinned berries will be improved by precooking.

Wash the berries, pick them over to remove sticks or leaves, and let them drain in a wire basket or colander. For raw pack, spoon or pour the berries into clean, hot jars, shaking the jars to get a full pack. Add boiling syrup, allowing ½-inch head space for expansion. For hot pack, put berries in a saucepan with ½ cup sugar to each quart of fruit. Cover and bring to a boil, shaking pan frequently to prevent sticking. Pack hot berries in their own juice, in clean, hot jars, leaving ½-inch head space. Adjust lids and ring bands and transfer to canner. Process 10 minutes for pints, 15 minutes for quarts.

Cover painting, THE SATURDAY EVENING POST, *September 25, 1943*

Nectarines

Nectarines are usually peeled, and may be canned by either raw pack or hot pack methods. Remove pits, cutting along the seam and then pulling the two halves apart. Pack and process as for peaches.

Peaches

Wash peaches and peel. To remove skins easily, dip the fruit in boiling water, then quickly in cold water. Cut peaches in half, remove pits and slice if desired. To prevent fruit from darkening, hold slices in vitamin C solution (see Apples) during preparation. Drain just before packing.

For raw pack, place fruit in clean, hot jar and cover with boiling syrup (medium). For hot pack, heat fruit in boiling medium syrup before packing. When packing halves, place them so that the cavity is not against the glass, as this may trap air inside the jar. Also, it is a good idea to run a table knife or narrow spatula around the jar, after it is filled, to release any air bubbles trapped between the peach halves. For a better quality product, add ½ teaspoon powdered vitamin C per quart of syrup. Leave ½-inch head space at the top of the jar to allow for expansion during processing. Adjust lids and ring bands, transfer to canner, and process 25 minutes for pints, 30 minutes for quarts if packed raw; or 20 minutes for pints and 25 minutes for quarts if packed hot.

Pears

Bartlett pears are preferred for canning. Wash fruit, peel, cut in half and remove cores, holding cut and peeled fruit in vitamin C solution (see Apples) during preparation. Fruit that is less than perfect can be sliced; the sliced fruit will fit more compactly into the jars. Pack raw or hot, as recommended for peaches. Process raw packed pears 20 minutes for pints, 25 minutes for quarts. Process hot packed pears 15 minutes for pints, 20 minutes for quarts.

Persimmons

Can persimmon pulp as puree, using the hot pack method. Wash ripe wild persimmons and steam them or simmer in a small amount of water until soft. Put through a food mill or colander and sweeten as desired. Reheat to boiling point and pack into clean hot jars, allowing ½-inch head space. Adjust lids and ring bands, transfer to canner and process 20 minutes (either pints or quarts).

Plums

Select plums that are not overripe; they should be meaty rather than juicy. To can whole, prick the skins with a fork; otherwise cut plums in half and remove pits. For raw pack, fill clean hot jars with raw fruit, then add boiling medium syrup to cover. For hot pack, heat to the boiling point in medium syrup, a little water, or, if the plums are very juicy, ½ cup sugar to a quart of fruit. Pack hot fruit in jars, adding enough boiling syrup or juice to cover. Leave ½-inch head space. Put on lid, tighten ring band and transfer to canner. Process 20 minutes for pints, 25 minutes for quarts.

Rhubarb

Eat only the red stems; the green leaves contain oxalic acid, which is poisonous in large amounts. Young tender stems need not be peeled. Cut into short lengths and place in an enamelware or heatproof glass saucepan. Stir in ½ cup sugar per quart of fruit and allow to stand, uncovered, at room temperature for about 4 hours to draw out the juice. When ready to can, bring to a boil and allow to simmer 1 minute. For a better quality product, stir in ½ teaspoon powdered vitamin C per quart of fruit. Spoon into clean, hot jar. Adjust lid and ring band, transfer to canner, and process 10 minutes for either pints or quarts.

Tomatoes

Though they are usually served as vegetables, tomatoes are technically fruit. Because of their high acidity, they are among the easiest of foods to can successfully. The tomatoes should be fully ripe but firm. For easy peeling, dip tomatoes into boiling water for about 30 seconds, then transfer to cold water. The skin should be loosened so it will slip off easily. (Dip several tomatoes at a time, using a wire basket or colander.)

Raw pack or hot pack methods may be used. Do not add water, as tomatoes will make their own juice when heated. You may wish to add ½ teaspoon salt to each pint of tomatoes, or 1 teaspoon to each quart. You may also add ½ teaspoon powdered vitamin C per quart.

For raw pack, spoon whole or quartered tomatoes into clean, hot jars and press down lightly with a spoon. For hot pack, place quartered tomatoes in a saucepan and bring to a boil, stirring frequently to prevent sticking or burning, and pack hot tomatoes in their own juice. Allow ½-inch head space, adjust lids and ring bands, and transfer to canner. Process raw pack tomatoes 35 minutes for pints and 45 minutes for quarts; process hot pack tomatoes 10 minutes for either pints or quarts.

Tomato Juice

Use fully ripe juicy tomatoes for making tomato juice. Wash, remove stem ends, and cut into pieces (do not peel). Heat and simmer until softened, then put through a strainer. Reheat juice to the boiling point.

Pour boiling juice into clean hot jars, leaving ½-inch head space. Adjust lids and ring bands, transfer to canner and process 10 minutes for either pints or quarts.

EASY TO SEAL EASY TO OPEN

Note the advantage of the wide mouth in putting up whole fruit.

The Schram Jar makes of fruit canning a delight.

USEFUL INFORMATION

Equivalents

1 tablespoon = 3 teaspoons or ½ ounce

2 tablespoons = 1/8 cup or 1 ounce

4 tablespoons = ¼ cup or 2 ounces

5 1/3 tablespoons = 1/3 cup

8 tablespoons = ½ cup or 4 ounces

12 tablespoons = ¾ cup or 6 ounces

16 tablespoons = 1 cup or 8 ounces

2 cups = 1 pint or 16 ounces

4 cups = 1 quart or 32 ounces

2 pints = 1 quart

4 quarts = 1 gallon

8 quarts = 1 peck

4 pecks = 1 bushel

16 ounces = 1 pound

½ cup butter = ¼ pound or 1 stick

6 to 8 cups unsifted all-purpose flour = 2 pounds

3 to 4 cups sifted confectioners' sugar = 1 pound

2¼ to 2 1/3 cups granulated sugar = 1 pound

Substitutions

For 1 teaspoon **baking powder**, substitute ¼ teaspoon baking soda plus 5/8 teaspoon cream of tartar.

For 1 ounce **unsweetened chocolate**, substitute 3 tablespoons cocoa plus 1 tablespoon shortening.

For 1 cup **heavy cream**, substitute ¾ cup milk plus 1/3 cup butter or margarine.

For 1 tablespoon **flour**, as a thickener, substitute 1½ teaspoons cornstarch.

For 1 clove **garlic**, substitute 1/8 teaspoon garlic powder.

For 1 tablespoon **fresh herbs**, substitute ½ teaspoon powdered dry.

For 1 cup **honey**, substitute 1¼ cups sugar plus ¼ cup water.

For 1 cup **sour milk** substitute 1 scant cup whole or skimmed milk plus 1 tablespoon vinegar or lemon juice.

For 1 teaspoon **dry mustard** substitute 1 tablespoon prepared mustard.

For 1 teaspoon **sugar** substitute ¼ grain saccharin or liquid noncaloric sweetener.

For 1 cup **sugar**, substitute 1¾ cups confectioners' sugar or 2 cups light corn syrup.

For 1 tablespoon **tapioca**, as a thickener in pies, substitute 1 tablespoon flour.

Definitions

Baste: to moisten food while cooking, usually by dipping pan juices over meat that is being roasted, uncovered, in the oven.

Bisque: a thick soup.

Blanch: to cook partially, or precook. Usually the food to be blanched is plunged into rapidly boiling water for just a few minutes, then removed, drained and cooled.

Bombe: a dessert of molded ice cream or sherbet.

Bouquet garni: a combination of herbs, usually including parsley, thyme and bay leaf, which is tied in a bundle or cloth bag so it can be removed before the dish is served.

Braise: to cook slowly in a covered pan. Meat is usually browned first in a small amount of fat, then covered and allowed to simmer in its own juices till tender.

Bread: to coat food with bread crumbs or a combination of bread crumbs, milk and egg.

Broil: to cook by direct heat, under or over a gas flame, electric broiler or glowing charcoal.

Caramel: sugar that has been melted and allowed to brown without water, sometimes used to color gravies and sauces.

Casserole: an earthenware container with a snug-fitting lid in which food is cooked slowly, in the oven.

Coddle: to cook briefly, until "set" but not hard, in boiling water.

Compote: a dessert made of fruit cooked in syrup and served cold.

Court bouillon: a seasoned liquid in which fish or other foods are to be cooked.

Deep-frying: to cook foods by immersing them in boiling fat or oil, usually at 365 degrees F.

Escallop (or Scallop): to bake food with a sauce or other liquid, usually with crumbs on top.

Fricassee: to cook cut-up poultry or meat by first browning it and then allowing it to cook slowly in broth or gravy.

Glaze: a thin sugar syrup usually cooked till it is partially thickened, used as a coating.

Julienne: vegetables cut into thin strips.

Marinade: a seasoned mixture, usually including oil and vinegar or lemon, in which meat is allowed to stand before cooking.

Pan-broil: to cook on an ungreased hot surface.

Pan-fry: to cook in a small amount of fat or oil.

Poach: to cook in simmering water.

Puree: food that has been liquefied by being forced through a strainer or by use of a food mill or blender.

Ramekin: a small baking-serving dish, used for just one portion.

Roast: to cook by dry heat, usually in the oven.

Sauté: to fry lightly, in a small amount of fat, stirring constantly.

Simmer: to cook in water just below the boiling point (between 180 degrees and 212 degrees F).

Steam: to cook over but not in boiling water. Usually the food is placed in a wire basket or perforated metal device which is placed in a covered saucepan containing a small amount of boiling water.

Steep: to allow food to stand in broth or a seasoned liquid that is hot but not boiling.

Terrine: an earthenware dish in which meat or fish is baked.

RECIPE INDEX

Index

Index